# Embroidering Her Truth

*Also by Clare Hunter*

Threads of Life:
A History of the World Through the Eye of a Needle

# EMBROIDERING HER TRUTH

Mary, Queen of Scots
and the Language of Power

## CLARE HUNTER

SCEPTRE

First published in Great Britain in 2022 by Sceptre
An imprint of Hodder & Stoughton
An Hachette UK company

1

Copyright © Clare Hunter 2022

The right of Clare Hunter to be identified as the Author of the Work has been asserted by her in accordance with the Copyright, Designs and Patents Act 1988.

All rights reserved. No part of this publication may be reproduced, stored in a retrieval system, or transmitted, in any form or by any means without the prior written permission of the publisher, nor be otherwise circulated in any form of binding or cover other than that in which it is published and without a similar condition being imposed on the subsequent purchaser.

A CIP catalogue record for this title is available from the British Library

Hardback ISBN 9781529346244
Trade Paperback ISBN 9781529346251
eBook ISBN 9781529346268

Typeset in Sabon MT by
Palimpsest Book Production Ltd, Falkirk, Stirlingshire

Printed and bound in Great Britain by
Clays Ltd, Elcograf S.p.A.

Hodder & Stoughton policy is to use papers that are natural, renewable and recyclable products and made from wood grown in sustainable forests. The logging and manufacturing processes are expected to conform to the environmental regulations of the country of origin.

Hodder & Stoughton Ltd
Carmelite House
50 Victoria Embankment
London EC4Y 0DZ

www.sceptrebooks.co.uk

*To Nicola Sturgeon*
*First Minister of Scotland*

'We princes are set as it were upon stages, in the sight and view of all the world. The least spot is soon spied in our garments, a blemish quickly noted in our doings.'
Elizabeth I, Queen of England, to Parliament, 1586

# Contents

| | |
|---|---:|
| *List of Illustrations* | ix |
| *A Note on the Use of Terms* | xii |
| *Cast of Characters* | xiii |
| | |
| Introduction | 1 |
| 1. Birds, Flowers, Fruit and Other Embroidered Motifs | 17 |
| 2. The Fetternear Banner | 48 |
| 3. Two Dolls' Dresses Made of Grey Damask Threaded in Gold | 76 |
| 4. A Great Mourning Gown of Black | 109 |
| 5. A Suit of Savage Attire | 148 |
| 6. Three of the Fairest | 176 |
| 7. A Dozen and a Half Little Flowers Painted on Canvas | 206 |
| 8. A Catte | 243 |
| 9. Red Petticoat and Sleeves | 286 |
| 10. A Black Dress and White Veil | 321 |
| | |
| *Endnotes* | 351 |
| *Acknowledgements* | 367 |
| *Bibliography* | 369 |
| *Index* | 391 |

## Illustrations

Portrait of Mary, Queen of Scots. François Clouet, c.1557. © VCG Wilson/Corbis via Getty Images.

A pamphlet from 1558 describing Mary, Queen of Scots' marriage to François II. © British Library Board. All Rights Reserved/Bridgeman Images.

Miniature of François II and Mary, Queen of Scots from Catherine de' Medici's *Book of Hours*. © Bibliothèque Nationale de France.

The coat of arms Mary, Queen of Scots adopted after her marriage to François II. © British Library Board. All Rights Reserved/Bridgeman Images.

An example of sixteenth-century French silk embroidery. Unknown artist, c.1560. © Victoria and Albert Museum, London.

The Scottish Fetternear Banner, c.1520. © National Museums Scotland/Bridgeman Images.

A detail of the banner's central image of Christ as the Man of Sorrows. © National Museums Scotland/Bridgeman Images.

Mary, Queen of Scots' Prayer Book. © Christie's Images/Bridgeman Images.

Portrait of John Knox. After Adrian Vanson, c.1580. © The Reading Room/Alamy Stock Photo.

The title page of John Knox's *The First Blast of the Trumpet against the Monstrous Regiment of Women* (1766 edition). Public Domain, courtesy of Wikimedia Commons.

Portrait of Isabella d'Este. Titian, 1534–36. © Ali Meyer/Bridgeman Images.

Portrait of Mary Tudor. After Hans Eworth, c.1553. © Fitzwilliam Museum/Bridgeman Images.

*List of Illustrations*

Portrait of Catherine of Aragon. Unknown artist, c.1520. © Stefano Baldini/Bridgeman Images.

Portrait of Catherine de' Medici. François Clouet c.1560. © Bridgeman Images.

A doll made by Clare Hunter in 1962. © Clare Hunter.

Fashion doll. Unknown artist, c.1600. Photo: Helena Bonnevier, Livrustkammaren/SHM (CC BY-SA 3.0).

Portrait of Arbella Stuart aged twenty-three months with her doll. Unknown artist, 1577. © National Trust Photographic Library/Bridgeman Images.

Portrait of Catharina van Warmondt with her doll. Isaac Claesz Van Swanenburg, 1596. © Art Collection/Alamy Stock Photo.

Detail of a sixteenth-century gown from a portrait of Queen Elizabeth I. Unknown artist, c.1575. © Tate.

Detail of a sixteenth-century men's outfit from a portrait of Archduke Ferdinand of Tirol. Jakob Seisenegger, 1548. © Fine Art Images/Bridgeman Images.

Portrait of James V and Marie de Guise. Unknown artist, c.1550. © National Trust Photographic Library/Bridgeman Images.

Portrait of Lord Darnley and Mary, Queen of Scots. Unknown artist, c.1565. © The Devonshire Collection/National Trust Photographic Library/Bridgeman Images.

A portrait thought to be of David Rizzio. Unknown artist, 1620. © Royal Collection/Royal Collection Trust © Her Majesty Queen Elizabeth II, 2021/Bridgeman Images.

A photo of David Rizzio's bloodstain at the Palace of Holyroodhouse, Edinburgh. © Royal Collection Trust / © Her Majesty Queen Elizabeth II 2022. Photographer: Peter Smith.

A sketched montage of the scene of Lord Darnley's murder in Kirk o' Field. Unknown artist, 1567. The National Archives, ref. MPF1/366 (1).

Placard of the Mermaid and the Hare. Unknown artist, c.1567. The National Archives, ref. SP52/13 no.60.

## List of Illustrations

*The Memorial of Lord Darnley.* Livinus de Vogelaare, 1567. © Royal Collection/Royal Collection Trust © Her Majesty Queen Elizabeth II, 2021/Bridgeman Images.

Mary, Queen of Scots' embroidery of a 'Byrd of America'. © Victoria and Albert Museum, London.

Mary, Queen of Scots' embroidery of a tortoise. © Victoria and Albert Museum, London.

Bess of Hardwick's monogram. © Victoria and Albert Museum, London.

An example of Bess of Hardwick's embroidery. © National Trust Images/John Hammond/Bridgeman Images.

The cushion Mary, Queen of Scots embroidered for the Duke of Norfolk *c.*1571. © Victoria and Albert Museum, London.

*A Catte.* Embroidery by Mary, Queen of Scots. © Royal Collection/Royal Collection Trust © Her Majesty Queen Elizabeth II, 2021/Bridgeman Images.

*The Execution of Mary, Queen of Scots, 1542–1587.* Unknown artist, *c.*1613. © National Galleries of Scotland/Bridgeman Images.

The warrant signed by Elizabeth I for Mary, Queen of Scots' execution. © Lambeth Palace Library/Bridgeman Images.

The last letter Mary, Queen of Scots wrote before her death, to her brother-in-law, Henry III, King of France. © National Library of Scotland (Adv.MS.54.1.1).

*Blairs Memorial Portrait of Mary, Queen of Scots.* Flemish School, *c.*1600. The Mary Queen of Scots Memorial Portrait: Reproduced by permission of the Scottish Catholic Heritage Collections Trust T9103BLRBM.

*Rainbow Portrait* of Elizabeth I. Marcus Gheeraerts the Younger, *c.*1601. © The Pictures Now Image Collection/Mary Evans Picture Library.

*Scotland as a Queen II*, limited edition print. Ashley Cook, 2020. © Ashley Cook.

# A Note on the Use of Terms

1. **Names**: To avoid the complication of the many Marys who appear all Marys, apart from Mary, Queen of Scots, are referred to with both their first names and surnames. French characters are given the French spelling of their names. James Stewart and Robert Dudley are referred to as Moray and Leicester respectively after they became earls.

2. **Stewart or Stuart**: The French spelling of 'Stuart' was adopted by Mary in the sixteenth century and was retained by the royal Stuarts thereafter.

3. **Yardage**: In the sixteenth century, the length of fabric was measured in ells. The lengths differed from country to country. A Scottish ell was 37", an English ell 45", a French ell 54" and a Flemish ell 27". In England, the term 'yard' was also used.

4. **Translations**: I have taken the liberty of modernising many of the quotes and loosely translating others. Punctuation has also sometimes been emended to make better sense for today's reader.

5. **Calendar**: The Gregorian Calendar was introduced into Britain in 1750. Until then, the year start was 25 March. For reasons of clarity, I have followed our contemporary calendar when assigning years.

6. **Money:** 5 Scots pounds was equivalent to one English pound in the mid-sixteenth century. Any conversion of expenditure offers an indication of their worth today rather than an exact equivalent.

# Cast of Characters

## Scotland

Mary, Queen of Scots (1542–1587)
James IV (1473–1513), King of Scotland, Mary's grandfather
James V (1512–1542), King of Scotland, Mary's father
Marie de Guise (1515–1560), Queen of Scotland, Mary's mother
Mary Beaton (1543–1598, Mary's Lady-in-Waiting
Mary Seton (1542–1615), Mary's Lady-in-Waiting
Mary Fleming (1542–1581), Mary's Lady-in-Waiting
Mary Livingston (1541–1579), Mary's Lady-in-Waiting
Thomas Randolph (1523–1590), Elizabeth I's English ambassador in Scotland
James Stewart, 1st Earl of Moray (c.1531–1570), Mary's half-brother by her father, James V, and his mistress, Margaret Erskine
Margaret Erskine (1515–1572), Moray's mother and mistress of Mary's father, James V
Henry Stewart, Lord Darnley (1545–1567), Mary's second husband
Mathew Stuart, 4th Earl of Lennox (1516–1571), Darnley's father
David Rizzio (c.1553–1566), Mary's private secretary in Scotland
George Buchanan (1506–1582), Scottish Latin and humanist scholar
Lord Bothwell (c.1534–1578), Scotland's Lord High Admiral and Mary's third husband
John Knox (1514–1572), spiritual leader of the Scottish Reformation
Sir James Melville of Halhill (1535–1617), Scottish diplomat and memoir writer

*Cast of Characters*

Jean Stewart (1530–1588), Mary's half-sister by her father, James V, and Elizabeth Bethune

Agnes Keith (c.1540–1603), Scottish noblewoman, wife of James Stewart, 1st Earl of Moray

## England

Henry VII (1457–1509), King of England

Henry VIII (1491–1547), King of England

Catherine of Aragon (1485–1563), first wife of Henry VIII

Mary Tudor (1516–1558), Queen of England, daughter of Henry VIII and his first wife Catherine of Aragon and third wife of Phillip II of Spain

Edward VI (1537–1553), son of Henry VIII and his third wife, Jane Seymour

Margaret Tudor (1489–1541), Henry VIII's sister, queen consort of Scotland by marriage to Mary's grandfather, James IV

Anne Boleyn (c.1501–1536), second wife of Henry VIII and mother of Elizabeth I

Elizabeth I (1533–1603), Queen of England, daughter of Henry VIII and his second wife, Anne Boleyn

Robert Dudley, 1st Earl of Leicester (1532–1588), English statesman, Elizabeth I's favourite

Margaret Douglas, Countess of Lennox (1515–1578), daughter of Margaret Tudor by her second marriage and mother of Lord Darnley

Sir William Cecil (1520–1598), Chief Advisor to Elizabeth I

Nicholas Throckmorton (1515–1571), English diplomat and politician

Sir Francis Knollys (c.1511–1596), English statesman, Mary's first custodian in England during her captivity

Thomas Howard, 4th Duke of Norfolk (1536–1572), English nobleman and politician, one of Mary's suitors in England

## Cast of Characters

Sir William Drury (1527–1579), English statesman and one of Mary's later custodians in England

George Talbot, 6th Earl of Shrewsbury (c.1522–1590), English magnate and Mary's custodian in England for 15 years

Bess of Hardwick (c.1527–1608), Countess of Shrewsbury, the Earl of Shrewsbury's second wife

Arbella Stuart (1575–1615), granddaughter of Bess of Hardwick

Francis Walsingham (c.1532–1590), Secretary of State of England, known as Elizabeth I's spymaster

Anthony Babington (1561–1586), English gentleman involved in a plot to overthrow Elizabeth I and rescue Mary

Amias Paulet (1532–1588), English diplomat and Mary's last custodian in England

Gilbert Clifford (1560–1590), English Catholic spy employed by Francis Walsingham

John Leslie, Bishop of Ross (1527–1596), Mary's Scottish ambassador in England at the end of her reign

James VI of Scotland and James I of England (1566–1625), and the son of Mary, Queen of Scots and Lord Darnley


### France

François I (1494–1547), King of France

Henri II (1519–1559), King of France

Catherine de' Medici (1519–1589), wife of Henri II and Queen Consort, then Regent, of France

François II (1544–1560), son of Henri II and Catherine de' Medici, Dauphin, then King of France, Mary's first husband

Diane de Poitiers (1500–1566), Henri II's mistress

Elisabeth de Valois (1545–1568), daughter of Henri II and Catherine de' Medici, second wife of Philip II of Spain

Anne of Brittany (1461–1522), Duchess of Brittany, queen consort of France to Louis XI and Charles VIII

*Cast of Characters*

## Spain

Charles V (1500–1558), Holy Roman Emperor and Archduke of Austria
Philip II (1527–1598), King of Spain, King of Portugal, King of Naples and Sicily

## Courtiers and other prominent cultural figures

Pierre de Ronsard (1524–1585), French poet
François Clouet (1510–1572), miniaturist and painter
Conrad Gesner (1516–1565), Swiss physician, naturalist, bibliographer and philologist
Isabella d'Este (1474–1539), Marchioness of Mantua
Christine de Pizan (1364–?), Italian poet and author at the French court
Nicholas Hilliard (1547–1619), goldsmith and portrait miniaturist
Agnes Strickland (1796–1874), English historical writer and poet
Sir Walter Scott (1771–1832), Scottish historical novelist, poet, playwright and historian

# Introduction

## 'One of the most perfect creatures'

The Lake of Menteith, which lies near Stirling in Scotland, is romantically – if erroneously – claimed to be the only lake in Scotland. I always approach it with a small frisson of discovery because it is ever changing. An alteration of light or seasonal difference can vary its mood dramatically, shifting it from benign to ominous, beguiling to cautionary. From spring through to late autumn, fishermen are out on the glossy water, spooling in trout from their long, dark boats like puppets silhouetted in a shadow play.

The lake hugs history within its depths. On its far horizon lies the tree-fringed island of Inchmahome, where Augustine monks built a sanctuary nine centuries ago. Eight times a day for hundreds of years, the monks prayed for the salvation of our souls, and something of their devotion has seeped into the ruined stone of their prayer places – the chapel, chapter house and cloisters – and settled in the soil. Inchmahome has a pervasive tranquillity that lingers in the air like a blessing. Within its gloom lies the thirteenth century tombstone of Walter Stewart and his wife, ancestors of Mary, Queen of Scots. They lie forever entwined in a stone embrace as a rare memorial to medieval love.

I went to the island once with my eight-year-old son Jamie. We trailed our fingers over the rough bark of age-old Spanish chestnut trees, one with a trunk so immense that my son could curl up in its hollow like a tree sprite. The bluebells were out in azure drifts, spread over the sacred ground like prayer mats. As Jamie went in search of red squirrels, I sat with our sandwiches near the boxwood bower that Mary, Queen of Scots is said to have planted as a child, trying to catch a whisper of the young queen.

I was at primary school when I first heard of Mary, Queen of Scots. Each spring, when the dandelions appeared, we would hunt them out in the playground and take turns to snap their flowers from their stems. Whoever had possession of the dandelion held it tight below its yellow bloom and administered a forceful flick in the direction of its petals to dislodge and scatter them. As spring turned to summer, those dandelions that had escaped our first wave of destruction now had their gossamer seed heads similarly despatched with a lungful of breath. The child who achieved total decapitation was the champion. This wanton disregard for floral survival was accompanied by the collective shouting of the game's battle cry: *Mary, Queen of Scots had her head chopped off, her head chopped off, Mary, Queen of Scots had her head chopped off on a cold and frosty morning.* We had no idea who Mary, Queen of Scots was. She was accepted into our litany of imaginary characters who peopled our childhood as readily as Wee Willie Winkie and Skinny Malinky Long Legs. We did not know that she really had existed, or that she once had been our queen.

In those days, at the end of the 1950s, Scotland's history was barely taught in its schools. It was an aside, subsumed into a British narrative in which the glory of the Empire and the nature of the Commonwealth were the dominant themes. Scottish children gleaned what fragments of their heritage they could from poetry and songs, from an occasional illustration in an encyclopaedia, or a painting in a museum. Most of what we knew were just names – William Wallace, Robert the Bruce, Bonnie Prince Charlie, David Livingstone – but rarely a story, hardly a history. And it was a past that seemed peopled solely by men. All we knew of Mary was that she had had her head chopped off.

## 'One of the most perfect creatures'

When I was ten years old, however, this gap in our knowledge was unexpectedly filled. Our tweed-skirted teacher was suddenly taken ill, and into her shoes stepped a temporary trainee in a toss of curls and pretty frocks. For two weeks we experienced a joyous reprieve from the surly sarcasm that was usually meted out. The trainee announced that we were to abandon rote learning in favour of a creative project that would involve research and design. We were to make a wall collage of the history of Scotland. Most thrillingly for me, the collage was to be made out of fabric. Already schooled by my mother in basic sewing and rudimentary embroidery, the idea of crafting a large sewn artwork was exhilarating. We were each allotted a person, place, or event from Scotland's past centuries to study and illustrate in cloth. I was given Mary.

The main source of historical study in the school library was Ladybird Books' *Adventure from History* series. Disappointingly, there was no volume dedicated to Mary, but I found her in one devoted to Queen Elizabeth I of England. Being ten, to me Mary's story read like a fairy tale without a happy ever after: a young and beautiful queen who loses not just one but three husbands, and is left defenceless and alone. When I learned of her escape from the clutches of her disloyal nobles, I cheered her on. When I discovered she had been abandoned by the English queen, Elizabeth, I was dismayed. Her end in imprisonment and execution was distressing. The illustrations of a gracious Mary in a sumptuous gown of black and gold greeting her nobility, of a feisty Mary galloping over moorland on a black stallion, and of Mary – still gorgeous in green – surrounded by armed guards, served only to kindle my captivation.

I folded black velvet over a cardboard silhouette of my queen with care and stitched a narrow band of gold tinsel around her hem. I pleated a paper doily into a ruff of pretend lace and made folds of white net to fashion a veil. My mother unearthed some tiny golden beads to adorn Mary's headdress and sacrificed a gold chain to serve as a necklace. When everything was sewn in place Mary, Queen of Scots was stuck down with a liberal dollop of PVA glue, between the heap of dead soldiers slain at the Battle of Flodden in 1513, and a posy of roses and thistles that symbolised the 1603 Union of the Crowns when Scotland and England began to share the same sovereign. The finished collage stretched along one whole wall of our classroom. When our usual teacher made her uncelebrated return and reclaimed her draconian rule, we resumed our droned recitations of catechism and multiplication tables. But the collage remained, bearing witness to our creative efforts to reimagine Scotland's past. It encouraged my interest in Scottish history, and in Mary. She remained, somehow, in my care.

In the histories and biographies of Mary, written during her lifetime and in the centuries following her death, she is generally cast as just one of many characters in the historical pageant. It is other personalities who drive her narrative. Mary appears as neither a catalyst nor a heroine, but a victim of circumstances and her own poor judgement. Her drama lies in loss: of the queen she once was, of the monarch she might have been. Her elusiveness owes much to the bias of her contemporary biographers and historians – exclusively men – who documented and assessed the events of her reign and captivity through a masculine prism, one largely filtered through an oppositional Protestant perspective. At best, they deemed Mary a naïve, hapless ruler who nourished her own downfall through inexperience, royal conceit and female frailty. But to accept this as the truth is simplistic.

Mary lived in exciting times and reigned in a period of accelerating social, political, cultural and religious change. She was shaped by the sophisticated culture of the late Renaissance and influenced by those other women rulers – a surprising number of them in the sixteenth century – who exercised power and fostered credibility for female authority. In a world dominated by male ambition, they were at the vanguard of a new assertion of female capability. And they expressed their confidence and agency through alternative media. These were women who registered their intelligence, knowledge, values and importance through material culture as designers, collectors, consumers and creators. While staying within the confines of acceptable female culture – fashion, hospitality, diplomacy, needlework and motherhood – they amplified their influence and repositioned themselves, if not centre stage, then at least as key players in political stagecraft.

Mary, like her English counterpart, Queen Elizabeth I of England, was young, vigorous and ambitious, not only for herself as a monarch and the kingdom she ruled over, but also for the dynasty that formed her. She was also, at times, reckless, manipulative and headstrong. While her decisions were purposeful, they could also be misguided, their effectiveness further blighted by betrayal. That she pursued her own style of governance is undeniable, and she harnessed the potency of textiles to emphasise her female presence and nurture her network of support. When captivity muted her voice, Mary ensured that her unedited testimony prevailed, preserving it in her embroidery.

Exploring Mary through the fabric of her life – the textiles she inherited, displayed, gifted, and embroidered – is revelatory. Nuanced and propagandist, the material world of Mary, Queen of Scots has been largely disregarded as a source of archival evidence by historians. But within it lies a tangible and intimate insight into the experiences and emotions of the Scottish Queen.

Mary became Queen of Scotland in December 1542, when she was just six days old. Her father, James V, had died a week after her birth and three weeks after the English victory over the Scots at the Battle of Solway Moss. It had been less than

30 years since the tragic Battle of Flodden in 1513, when Scotland had been ignominiously trounced by England. That battle's grievous death toll had claimed over 10,000 Scots and saw the flower of Scottish nobility and its king slain. Solway Moss was meant to be the site of Scotland's triumph: a shrugging off of English aggression and a defiant deflection of the pressure from the English king, Henry VIII, to turn Catholic Scotland Protestant and force it to relinquish its long alliance with France. The Scots had hoped that the Battle of Solway Moss would secure their country's independence from England once and for all. But, once again, Scotland was defeated.

Illness had prevented James V from leading his troops. When told of the outcome, he had despaired. Although the death toll was low and the casualties few, over 1,000 Scots were taken prisoner. There were tales of dishonour and desertion. The news of a new-born daughter brought James little comfort. He was still mourning the loss of his two young sons, who had died within hours of each other the previous year. Mary's birth foreshadowed the end of the Stewart line. With no sons to continue his name, the survival of the Stewart dynasty and its 200 years of sovereignty was in jeopardy. It is said that it was in political sorrow that James V turned his face to the wall and gave up the will to live.

Born when the realm was grieving for the loss of its king and robbed of its hoped-for victory over the English, Mary was crowned on the anniversary of the Battle of Flodden. Her early years were fraught with danger. Henry VIII continued his bully-boy tactics to make Scotland bend to his will, and now the Scottish child-queen was a new pawn in his political schemes. The English king became fixated on forcing a marriage between Mary and his son and heir, Edward. Initially Scotland appeared to bend to Henry's will and, in July 1543, signed a treaty agreeing to the marriage. It was a strategic capitulation, designed to placate Henry, ward off further English aggression, and play for time. When, later that year, the treaty was revoked by the Scottish Parliament, Henry grew impatient. A period that became known as the 'Rough Wooing' ensued: a strategy of sustained English aggression that ultimately proved overwhelming. In April 1544, Henry issued the command that his troops were to:

Put all to fire and sword, burn Edinburgh town, so razed and defaced when you have sacked and gotten what you can of it, as there may remain forever a perpetual memory of the vengeance of God lighted upon them for their falsehood and disloyalty ... burn and subvert it and all the rest, putting man, woman and child to fire and sword, without exception ... and extend like extremities and destructions to all towns and villages ... sparing no creature alive within the same.[1]

Henry died in 1547, but England still pursued the marriage. On 10 September of that year, the Scottish and English armies faced each other once more. The brutality of the Battle of Pinkie Cleugh was designed to coerce Scotland into submission. Chroniclers penned reports of the earth scarred with the fallen, of limbless bodies and cloven heads, of the injured lying half dead in fields, bereft of survivors to give them succour. Thousands of Scots died. Another thousand, some said two, were taken prisoner. Civilians, too, were butchered or abused as a triumphant English army took vengeance on the villages and towns it marched through, plundering, looting and leaving homes to burn. But still the Scots refused to accede.

With England threatening Mary's abduction, there was no choice but to rush the young queen to safety, and it was at Inchmahome that refuge was sought. The four-year-old Mary was ferried across its lake with her small entourage hushed in fear. Scotland lay behind them in a daze of ruination and death. At Inchmahome, Mary found respite, a retreat from terror. And maybe that is what I catch each time I pass the lake, not the murmur of this fickle physical place, but something much more elusive, the undertow of Mary, the child-queen.

As English insurgence continued, Mary was moved to the stronghold of Stirling Castle and then, when English forces advanced too close for comfort, she was taken to the fortress at Dumbarton. There her fate was debated. In July 1548, the decision was taken to sign a treaty with the French and, in return for military assistance, send Mary to France as the prospective bride of its Dauphin, the three-year-old François, the eldest son of Henri II and his Italian wife Catherine de' Medici. The new treaty reinforced the age-old alliance between the two kingdoms, one that had persisted since the thirteenth century. For Henri, the treaty held political allure. He had ambitions to rule over England and secure an empire equal to that of his rival, Charles V, the Holy Roman Emperor. And Mary, through her grandmother Margaret Tudor, held a legitimate claim to the English throne. To some in Scotland, however, it seemed that this new treaty with France supplanted the danger of English rule with the reality of French control.

In August 1548, the five-year-old Mary left her mother, Marie de Guise, and Scotland for France. She was accompanied by a quartet of childhood friends, the four Marys: Mary Beaton, Mary Fleming, Mary Livingston and Mary Seton. Of similar age to Mary, these little girls carried their own stories of loss. The grandfathers of Mary Seton and Mary Livingston had died at Flodden. Mary Livingston's father was one of those taken prisoner at the Battle of Solway Moss. The Battle of Pinkie Cleugh had claimed Mary Livingston's brother, Mary Fleming's father and two of her brothers-in-law. Theirs was a bond that went deeper than that forged in childhood play: the children shared the sorrow of family tragedy. They understood vulnerability. While sad to leave their homeland and families, they must have felt a small thrill in the excitement of escape.

Their voyage was perilous. The small fleet of galleys sent by

## 'One of the most perfect creatures'

Henri II to ensure Mary's safety had to navigate a circuitous route to thwart England's boast of interception. Forced into stormier waters, Mary's entourage cowered below deck, nauseous with sea sickness, but it seems that Mary savoured the adventure. She was to be found cheerfully surveying the swell of the sea and eagerly scanning the horizon of her future. She arrived to a France at the height of its Renaissance glory. A French courtier, writing to Marie de Guise about Mary at the time, says that she was 'One of the most perfect creatures that was ever seen, and such that from that young age, and wonderful and praiseworthy beginnings, she has given so great an expectation of her that it is not possible to hope for more from any princess on earth'.[2]

Mary had left a Scotland scarred and demoralised by war. To keep her safe, her early childhood had been experienced behind the grim walls of fortressed castles. In France she was to find a court which delighted in conviviality and trumpeted its prosperity through material extravagance – a court which epitomised Renaissance ambition. The Renaissance (literally meaning 'rebirth'), that metamorphosis from medieval to early modern society, began in the fourteenth century and was to continue over the next three hundred years. It was not a sudden flowering of cultural innovation, but a slow and measured evolution which, over time, spawned widespread social, political, and economic change. Cities were established, trade routes expanded, new and exotic territories explored and claimed. These developments, coupled with vigorous artistic and scientific advancement, encouraged a different perspective of peoples' place in their widening world. There was a growing fascination with how this burgeoning curiosity and vitality could be expressed, captured and immortalised for generations to come. Those who could afford it became avid collectors of classical antiques, of exotic and exquisite artefacts, in an eager embrace of the potential of cultural heritage. Patronage of the arts and artisans increased, and the elite invested more heavily in material wealth. Architecture and portraits, personalised artefacts and textiles became more consciously embedded with individual and national narratives, valued not just as expressions of present selves but also as material biographies for future appraisal.

People were on the move: preachers, musicians, merchants and mercenaries were all seeking out opportunistic adventure. Increased mobility generated a heady intermingling of ideas and nationalities that coalesced across borders and nurtured invigorating cross-cultural exchanges and connections. And mobility was not simply geographical. A wealthier and upwardly mobile middle class – merchants, lawyers, bankers – was snapping at the heels of a hitherto unassailable elite, competing with it for court positions, privileges and power. More ominously, the sixteenth century was when the spark of religious disaffection began to flame with the rise of fervent Protestantism. Its acceleration threatened the overthrow of the old order of papal and royal control. With the advent of print and advances in literacy, opinions and debate that diverged from crown and state were circulated more widely. Traditional social boundaries were in danger of becoming blurred, settled hierarchies unmoored. The social and cultural shifts engendered by the Renaissance heralded a heightened preoccupation with appearance: the outward show. They led to a more considered and expansive display of self, along with a deeper sensitivity to, and a greater awareness of, otherness. The objects the elite – and those aspiring to it – possessed, the environment they inhabited, the people they surrounded themselves with and the clothes they wore became declarations of not just who they were but who they wanted to be and how they wished to be regarded. A new humanist sensibility saw a greater emphasis placed on eloquence as a marker of civilised expression, in things as well as people. It encouraged finesse. As the Renaissance ripened, the chivalric traditions of medieval times fused with humanist principles to foster an elaboration of ritual, ceremony and etiquette. The qualities of the mind, body and soul were seen as reflections of each other and their visual harmony became desirable as evidence of personal and cultural progress. The appearance of conduct manuals – Baldassare Castiglione's *Il Cortegiano* (The Courtier) in 1528, Sir Thomas Elyot's *The Boke Named the Governor* in 1531, and *Il Galateo, Overo de' Costumi* (Galateo: Rules of Polite Behaviour) by Giovanni della Casa in 1558 – coupled with the 1530 publication of the humanist proselytiser Desiderius Erasmus's *De Civiliatae Morum Puerilium* (On Civility in Children), a treatise on children's moral and social education, shaped increased refinement of behaviour and thought within European courts.

Expanding trade and interaction with other cultures increased consumption of a greater volume and wider range of luxury goods. This led to a deeper appreciation of artisanal skill. Material culture was perceived as the medium through which people could most clearly articulate their inner selves and outer status. European monarchies appropriated its potency with zeal. It was no idle impetus that led Charles VIII of France, in the late fifteenth century, to bring back from his Italian campaign a goldsmith, alabaster worker, marquetry specialist, tailor and embroiderer.[3] He recognised in them a new sophistication of material design. These were craftsmen who could project majesty. They could transmit emotions and thought through a visual rhetoric, evoke sensuality and desire, and manifest learning, lineage and ambition through intricate imagery, symbolic meaning and material texture. Until recent decades, predominantly male historians have concentrated on the transformative impact of the Renaissance on art and architecture. But it was as readily realised through its crafts, and key among them were textiles. Textiles not only played a significant role in economic expansion but also translated exploration, colonisation and innovation into a visible manifestation of progress. In sixteenth-century Europe, textiles had commercial, cultural and political currency. It was textiles that most potently harboured the spirit of the age.

Cloth was a currency in its own right. Deposit banks, as we know them today, did not exist until the second half of the seventeenth century. Instead, the rich safeguarded their wealth in other ways. The value of luxury textiles and their embellishments made them a viable alternative to coinage. They could be sold, exchanged, pawned or act as surety against loans. Henry VIII spent nearly as much on cloth as he did on his artillery: it was a guaranteed source of material affluence and monetary defence.[4] In a century assailed by economic volatility and sudden fluctuations in the supply of imported goods, fabric could lie undisturbed by political, financial or social turbulence. It retained its value. Fabric was also an appreciable payment-in-kind. Servants and officials were remunerated not only in money, but in cloth and clothing, the monetary worth of both often exceeding what household members received in wages. Livery's distinctive colours and design branded its wearer with the mark of royal protection and privilege. Gifts of other clothing and textiles indicated a monarch's favour and demonstrated their largesse. Given the volume of textiles that circulated within a court and the expenditure such transactions incurred, courts maintained their own workshops and permanent teams of wardrobe staff.

As people's appetite for luxury, variety and novelty grew, and with it a greater demand for accessories and adornments, the commercial trade in textiles flourished. Merchant adventurers grew rich by monopolising the latest dyestuffs and supplying the newest fabrics. An extravagance of cloth migrated across borders. Silk cloth and cotton came to Europe from China and India, silk thread from Spain, embroidered carpets from Turkey, tapestries from Flanders. From Italy came the finest textiles: gold brocade from Florence, silk velvet from Venice, damasks

'One of the most perfect creatures'

from Genoa. And skilled textile artisans sought lucrative opportunities in other countries. When they relocated, they brought their knowledge with them, enabling more innovative techniques of textile production to be replicated elsewhere.

Sixteenth-century Scotland, however, had neither the climate, the terrain nor the infrastructure to enjoy the profitable expansion of those textile trades experienced elsewhere in Europe. It was hampered by hazardous topography, a scattered population and poor transport links. Largely agricultural, with four-fifths of its people toiling on a reluctant land, Scotland could only produce the most basic of products. Poor harvests were frequent. Famine was common. With its long, dark winters curtailing the number of productive hours available for manufacture, most crafted goods were functional rather than decorative. Innovative native artisanal skill was rare. With the increasing demand for luxury goods unsatisfied by the domestic market, such goods had to be imported. What Scotland could export – rough wool, hides, salted fish, coal – was of low value. Its most profitable export was its fighting men.

Moreover, Scotland's population was small compared to that of other European countries – by the sixteenth century a mere 700,000, compared to France's 4 million and more.[5] It had, nevertheless, managed to maintain a politically strategic position on the European stage. Its geographic proximity to England made it a useful ally to foreign powers contemplating an invasion of England, and the Stewart monarchy's potential to inherit the English throne increased its political appeal. But its reputation was that of a remote, insular and barbaric kingdom. In 1529, the Papal nuncio described Scotland as 'the arse end of the world'.[6] Even thirty years later, when Mary had returned to Scotland, remoteness was still an issue. In 1561, the Scottish politician William Maitland of Lethington sent a plaintive letter to Sir William Cecil, Elizabeth I's chief advisor, lamenting: 'We are here in a corner of the world, separated from the society of men, and so do not know what others are doing abroad'.⁷

Socially, Scotland had evolved as a partisan culture characterised by division of clans, customs and language. What nobility there was tended to stay close to home, only visiting the court for essential business. Although they would adopt the sartorial finery and manners expected of their status for such visits, it was a finesse discarded when they left the city walls. Homes were built to withstand harsh winds and persistent rain. Even the grandest houses and castles were designed as robust defences braced for attack. Nevertheless, sixteenth-century Scotland cherished cultural aspirations. The Renaissance ambitions of Mary's grandfather and father, James IV, and V, were inspired by Scotland's close relationship with France. Exposure to its cosmopolitan court and its material grandeur led to emulation. Both Scottish kings embarked on expansive projects to make of their palaces and castles Renaissance dreamscapes of glory. The castle at Stirling was extended to accommodate spacious royal apartments and a great hall of a scale to rival any of those found in Europe. A lion roared in its menagerie and swans swam in the surrounding waters. Other palaces were also enlarged and provided with the charm of gilded carvings, elaborate fountains and painted glass windows.

These Scottish kings were bent on cultural progress. In their courts, African drummers and French astrologers mingled with German musicians and Italian singers. In 1505 James IV granted a charter to establish a Royal College of Surgeons, the first in Britain. Two years later, he authorised the creation of Scotland's first printing press. He and his son, James V, were spurred on by the desire to realise political cohesion in Scotland. Both were intent on fostering a more emphatic expression of national identity: one that respected tradition but embraced innovation. They introduced chivalric and humanist ideals to the culture of the Scottish court mounting tournaments, commissioning

## 'One of the most perfect creatures'

poetry and plays and dressing their palace interiors in tapestries and luxurious textiles. They also exploited Scotland's natural resources as best they could, excavating coal, gold and pearls. Progress, however, was hindered by the volatility of international politics. The relationship with England remained uneasy and at times became adversarial. The alliance with France was at best mercurial. Throughout the sixteenth century, Scotland remained politically vulnerable.

Scottish independence had been fiercely guarded through the centuries. The Wars of Scottish Independence (1296–1328 and 1332–1357) had inculcated a Scottish sensibility, some might say an over-sensitivity, to Scotland's right to maintain its separate cultural and political identity and not see it dominated by England, or other European realms. Through subsequent centuries, independence became ingrained in the Scottish psyche, enshrined in a letter, now known as the Declaration of Arbroath, which in 1320 was sent to the Pope by fifty Scottish nobles on behalf of the Scottish people:

for as long as a hundred of us remain alive, never will we under any condition be subjected to the lordship of England. It is in truth not for glory, nor riches, nor honours that we are fighting, but for freedom alone, which no honest man gives up but with life itself.[8]

It was the Stewart monarchy that inherited the rallying cry. While James IV and James V had managed to stall England's predatory ambition, it was a danger that persisted, despite James IV's marriage to Margaret Tudor, the sister of Henry VIII. These Stewart kings were vested in the values of their ancestors: a belief in Scotland's worth and distinctiveness, a determination that the kingdom would neither be absorbed nor overlooked by others. Mary inherited the challenge of protecting Scotland's place on the European stage as an independent country. She became fixated on the idea of Queen Elizabeth I of England naming her – Mary – as her successor: a crown passed from female monarch to female sovereign and a kingdom protected by its queen from insurgence or domination.

In 1603, England and Scotland came under the joint sovereignty of James I and VI of England and Scotland, although they remained separate states. In 1707, with the Acts of Union, Scotland came under the governance of the United Kingdom Parliament dominated by English interests. Over subsequent centuries, Scotland has chafed at its subservience and the loss of its independence. Attempts have been made to break away from the union with three referendums on Scottish devolution and independence that took place in 1979, 1997 and 2014 respectively. While the 1997 referendum secured Scotland's devolution and the restoration of its parliament – after a 300-year slumber – it did not realise full independence. The 2014 referendum was the closest the nation has come to that. But the ambition remained elusive when those who voted in favour of independence lost by a narrow margin. What they were recoiling against was disregard, an English government's lack of empathy for, understanding of or interest in Scotland's difference. The experiences and emotions of the past linger to influence the present day; the distrust and unease fuelled by the experiences of earlier centuries persist. It is political vulnerability that lies at the heart of Scotland's history. The spirit of independence has never been extinguished. Its flame continues to be carried.

# I
## Birds, Flowers, Fruit and Other Embroidered Motifs

I have become strangely obsessed with the Accounts of the Lord High Treasurer of Scotland, 1463–1580. Its thirteen lookalike volumes are kept on a low shelf at the National Records Office of Scotland in Edinburgh. The library is a silent haven for serious researchers who sit hunched over thick tomes, scanning maps, peering at the small print of old newspapers and carefully turning the pages of large leather-bound books, searching for long-neglected clues into other peoples' lives. In my quest for insight into Mary's material world, it is the Treasurer's accounts that give me hope. Luckily for me, learned antiquarians of the late nineteenth and early twentieth centuries were similarly captivated. They took the trouble of transcribing the accounts from their original crammed flourish of cursive handwriting and seeing them through to publication. Despite having taken a course in palaeography (the study of old handwriting) and the turgid hours spent, magnifying glass in hand, trying to decipher idiosyncratic penning, the little knowledge I gained would have been lamentably inadequate to follow the minutiae of the expenditure of the Stewart monarchy. It is not only the handwriting that has to be conquered but the language, or rather languages, in which the accounts are recorded. There is Latin, Older Scots and, at times, a smattering of Old French. Spelling is erratic, and abbreviations self-styled to suit personal taste and strictures of time. So I have these nineteenth-century pedants to thank for saving me the torment.

The accounts are a version of today's online purchase history.

They track the day-to-day spending of Scotland's monarchs and regents from the mid fifteenth century onwards. While there are gaps, both within the volumes themselves and in their transcription to print (stopping at 1580), the extant records contain a wealth of information, not only of expenditure, but also of royal proclamations and hurrying messengers. In them we can learn whose lands are in danger of being forfeited and who risks being outlawed unless they comply with whatever command they are trying to avoid. We can track court employees through their wages and receipt of livery, and gauge the intimacy of sovereign relationships through the gifts they bestowed on others. We can follow royal progresses through the realm in the travel expenses incurred. The entries relating to textiles are, at times, rewardingly detailed and, at others, frustratingly terse. Where fabric is involved, its colour is generally noted: 'tawny [orange-brown], incarnate, violet' as is its cost per ell, the number of ells ordered and the total amount spent. The place of origin, Paris black, Genoese silk, English blue, is sometimes identified and the specifics of the fabric purchased 'camlet, serge, velvet, canvas' are almost always documented.

During the coronavirus lockdown in 2021, when I no longer have access to the bound volumes in the Records Office, I order facsimile copies from India, and sit up in bed at night scanning the 600-plus pages that comprise each volume until the information they contain begins to invade my dreams. My husband suggests I return to lighter bedtime reading, a magazine perhaps, and I concede. But as I flick through glossy pages filled with celebrity glamour the accounts still haunt me. They have become my treasure maps.

The accounts for the months leading up to Mary's departure for France in 1548, are informative. We can glean from them the turmoil and fear that beset Scotland in the years following the Battle of Pinkie Cleugh and Mary's birth. Artillery is moved hither and thither as English troops gain a firmer foothold on

Scottish soil. Gunpowder, pikes, spears and fighting men are commandeered and relocated. Of Mary, there is little evidence: no purchases of luxury cloth to furnish her wardrobe, no fees to a tailor to replenish it. With the Earl of Arran as Regent, it is his family that the treasury decks out in silks and velvets, his son and daughter who are dressed in sartorial finery to accompany the child-queen to France. There is, however, an entry for 2,000 Scots pounds to be sent as payment and reimbursement to the nobles safeguarding Mary at Dumbarton and, on 18 July 1548, another entry records that a herald was sent to Fife to call up mariners to serve in the galleys that 'pass to France with the Queen's Grace.'[1]

Mary arrived at the French court when it was at the height of its Renaissance brilliance. This was a court honed on chivalric and humanist ideals, inspired by Italian classical grandeur, its political ambitions manifested in monumental architecture, conspicuous material consumption and magnificent ceremonies. Mary encountered châteaux draped in cloth. Since interiors at that time were sparsely furnished, every surface was a potential site for textile propaganda. In the European courts of the sixteenth century, it was textiles that articulated power.

Investment in the material show of monarchical rivalry and prestige became more urgent and pronounced as the century unfolded. Nowhere were textile declarations of power more keenly expressed than in the French court of 1548, where Henri II had been newly crowned the previous year. This was a king who had spent his early years incarcerated as a captive of Charles V of Spain, sacrificed along with his brother as ransom for their father. For four years the brothers languished in a land of enmity, humiliated and malnourished. When the French envoy came to claim them, it is said he cried at these scarecrows of boys whose childhood had been robbed of emotional and material comfort. Little wonder, then, that on becoming king Henri surrounded himself with luxury. His armoury of fabricated majesty was a rejoinder to the author of his captivity and ignominy: his rival, Charles V.

Sumptuous clothing was a glory for which monarchs and the elite sought protection and exclusivity in law. Sumptuary laws, originally designed to regulate trade, increasingly legislated on matters of dress to safeguard the stability of a hierarchical society. Such laws ensured that social supremacy was visibly reiterated through sartorial control. Access to luxury cloth, fine furs, embroidery, feathers and lace was prohibited to all but the highest echelons. In 1429 the Scottish Parliament commanded that:

No man shall wear clothes of silk, nor furs of pine martens ... nor any other rich fur, except only knights and lords of 200 merks at least of yearly rent ... And that no other person to wear embroidery nor pearl nor bullion.[2]

In 1516, in England, only sons of Knights of the Garter and those ranked above them were entitled to wear embroidered garments. And, ever conscious of his image and the need to project a unique and unassailable sovereignty, Henry VIII, in an Act of Parliament in 1533, prioritised his and his family's prerogative to wear the colour purple or cloth of gold, decreeing that 'no person or persons of whatever estate, dignity, degree or condition whatsoever they be ... can use or wear in any manner their apparel or upon their horse, mule or other beast any silk of the colour purple, nor any cloth of gold tissue but only the King, the Queen, the King's Mother, the King's children, the King's brethren and sisters and the King's uncles and aunts'.[3]

Not content with the privileges that sumptuary laws protected, Henry offered a Florentine merchant-venturer bribes to guarantee the English king first choice of the latest fabrics the merchant imported.[4] This was more than a lust for opulence. Henry desired to be viewed as a monarch not just of the present but of the future and, by association, England as a kingdom which was not just modern but progressive. Rich textiles signalled status, wealth, and prosperity, but innovative fabrics demonstrated vision. Through the sixteenth century, advances in weaving technology, textile design and the manipulation of cloth accelerated. It was an age of artisanal ingenuity, when a fascination with texture was both appreciated and exploited by those who had the need – and the means – to appropriate it as an expression of personal and political charisma. In his later years, when the seemingly indestructible Henry VIII grew old, obese, and plagued with infirmity, he resorted to increasingly gaudier splendour. Through it he hoped to sustain his sovereign appeal. In an era fraught with the uncertainty of monarchical and dynastic survival, what rulers had to perform was bravado. For European sovereigns – often ruling over cash-strapped courts, impoverished by war and monetary devaluation – the flaunting of luxurious textiles masked personal and political vulnerability. Textiles became more intensely propagandist. More pronounced use was made of heraldic and emblematic imagery. The fleur-de-lis of France, the Tudor rose of England, the thistle of Scotland were increasingly used as a chorused insistence of dynastic supremacy and national power.

A public show of wealth was required of a monarch. It served to reassure subjects of their country's solvency – however fictional that was – and inform competitive kingdoms of a rival's prosperity. The quality of accumulated textiles was recorded as meticulously as jewels in royal treasury accounts. It was the precise hue of a fabric and the place of its manufacture which signalled its financial worth. By the end of his reign Henry had accumulated over 50,000 lengths of precious cloth.[5]

For the coronation of Henry's son, Edward VI, in 1547, over 6,000 yards of red fabric were distributed to his household staff and courtiers to fashion clothes for the celebration. A record was kept of their dispersal, charting the specifics of the quantity, quality and 'redness' of the cloth handed out to more than

1,000 recipients: to William St John, the Lord great master, thirty-eight ells of Italian crimson velvet; to Mr Haynes, Secretary, ten ells of crimson satin; to the apothecary, Mr Carleton, five ells of scarlet. The wood bearer, unnamed, received just three ells of red cloth. Crimson, scarlet and red were distinct not just in colour but as signifiers of social position. While kermes – a Mediterranean insect whose crushed body yielded the main ingredient of the colour scarlet – had been popular since the Middle Ages, in the sixteenth century it was supplanted by a dye harvested from cochineal insects of North and Central America. Spain's conquest of the Aztec region in the first decades of that century had fostered the export of the cochineal dye to Europe. It produced a superior red, both in density and colour-fastness, becoming a staple of Italian luxury cloth production. Given that thousands of cochineal insects were required to yield just a few ounces of dye, merchants could justify its expense. Other reds were realised from more mundane sources – from the common perennial plant, madder, and from red onion skins – but they were duller in tone and quicker to fade. Such variance in colour carried a social code. It delineated status.[6]

Cloth in sixteenth-century Europe was also persuasive. After the disaster of Flodden, when Mary's father, James V, had sought to strengthen Scotland's alliance with France and better protect his realm from English trespass, he determined on a marriage with Madeleine, the eldest daughter of the French king. When François I demurred, citing his daughter's frailty as the reason for his prevarication, James – with the approval of his government – embarked on a material offensive. He and a band of Scottish nobles descended on France with 19,000 Scots pounds in their pockets. The Scottish king set out on a spending spree that thrilled the chroniclers of the day, one gleefully reporting that James:

hath beggared all Scotland, as they say, ere he came out of it ... Now being here ordering himself so foolishly, running up and down the streets of Paris with only a servant or two buying every trifle himself, believing that no man knows him, whereas every carter points to him with their finger, saying 'La voila le Roy d' Ecosse.'[7]

James's spending was not indiscriminate, however. He wanted his excessive consumption of the finest and most expensive goods to be noticed. Unable to afford the 2,000 tapestries Henry VIII was said to possess, the Scottish king trumped him with quality, using his discernment and the advice of his scouts to purchase the most fashionable and arresting of what contemporary design could offer. He not only bought tapestries, but also expensively embroidered cloths of state (the canopy and back cloth above and behind a throne), Persian carpets, velvet-covered chairs and 200 skins of costly fur. He purchased sixty lengths of cloth of gold, enough to drape an entire room in luminous majesty. In Paris, he invested in over 130 ells of Genoese velvet, Florentine silk damask and taffeta to furnish a travelling bed of state. It was this bed that was to be the backdrop to the nuptial negotiations James pursued during his three-week sojourn through the Loire valley with François I.[8]

James also summoned his tailor, Thomas Arthur, from Scotland to transform the Scottish king into a cosmopolitan monarch. A doublet and gown of crimson satin was fashioned with a riding cloak of Parisian velvet ablaze with one hundred 22-carat gold and lapis lazuli buttons. Another gown of cloth of gold was lined with crimson satin and embellished with 49,500 pearls. James's investment in material flamboyance proved seductive: François I agreed to the Scottish king's marriage with Madeleine.[9]

James recouped far more than he had spent in his marriage settlement. Madeleine's generous dowry yielded a substantial cash dividend. Her movables, including textiles, represented a further assured store of wealth. Ships, artillery and other valuable gifts were bestowed on the Scottish king. Even more precious was the accolade James was afforded by François: a ceremonial entrée into Paris, a privilege usually only accorded to the Dauphin. While defeat at Flodden had brought demoralisation, James's show of magnificence and the visibility of his appetite for material consumption had reassured the French king of Scotland's ambition, and his support of James restored Scotland's standing on the international stage.

François I had been right, however, to be concerned for his daughter's wellbeing. Madeleine died just two months after she arrived in Scotland. James was genuinely grieved at her death, but he was equally devasted by the loss of what she personified: Scotland's alliance with France. Her funeral was orchestrated to demonstrate not just James's personal sorrow but Scotland's tragedy. Mourners were summoned from throughout the kingdom and commanded to attend the funeral dressed in black: the first show of national mourning ever seen in the nation. However, as Madeleine's black-shrouded funeral cortège wound its way through the Edinburgh streets, a messenger was already sailing fast to France to tell François of her death and to request another French bride. The young widow Marie de Guise was chosen, a member of one of the most powerful families in France. Married by proxy, just ten months after Madeleine's death, Marie de Guise not only safeguarded the Franco-Scottish special relationship but – much to James's satisfaction – brought with her yet another generous dowry. With his new riches, James further embellished his Scottish court with Renaissance grandeur. The advance of Stewart power was encapsulated in its manifestation of its new-found material wealth.

The textile materiality of sixteenth-century Europe went beyond an appreciation of the qualities inherent in any specific cloth. It was the cumulative effect that was telling. Textiles were not only to be seen, but also to be interpreted and experienced.

Their audience was invited to decipher the meaning behind their arrangement as much as their patterns, symbols, and colours. In châteaux arrayed in embroidered cloth, textiles were a form of conversation.

In 2019, I went to France to visit the châteaux of Mary's youth. And it was at the Château de Fontainebleau that I realised what visual joy French royal interiors must have fostered in her. In its ballroom, I felt that Mary was there, pulling at my sleeve, willing me to appreciate its artistry, wanting me to understand the dazzle of the material world that shaped her. The ballroom is radiant in texture and colour, autographed by Henri II and Catherine de' Medici with their intertwined initials on its walls and ceiling. There is a panorama of exuberant frescoes that glint gold in the afternoon sun. They trap pleasure and desire, the thrill of the chase and the lust of the dance in a painted display of sensual energy. Mary was at the French court when its artists and artisans locked away their precious pigments and slid chisels back into their pouches. She and the Dauphin, soft soled in velvet slippers, would have baptised this floor with their dancing, turning to take each other's hands as the melody of viols and tambours drifted from the minstrel gallery. In this room, Mary would have been an enchanted queen, twirling in the folds of her gown of gold, a gown which reflected the colours that played around her in the flickering candlelight.

There were few textiles left at Fontainebleau when I visited it. The drapes around its state beds offered little more than a dull brocade. Here and there, an isolated tapestry hung in an apology to grandeur. In the sixteenth century, this château and others would have flaunted a swathe of narrative tapestries: the stories of classical, biblical and allegorical heroes and heroines and their moral and martial victories, of Hercules and Samson, Esther and Diana. Floors were strewn with embroidered carpets, bed hangings stitched with intimate motifs that referenced dynastic history and personal sentiment. Among them would have been scattered other textiles as a tactile subtext: velvet cushions for benches, silk screens for commodes, damask tablecloths, book covers adorned with sewn monograms and emblems: motifs repeated on the chapel's altar cloths and household linen.

It is impossible for us now to experience the visual intensity, the physical sensation, of Fontainebleau and other royal residencies of sixteenth-century France. Neither the exact hues, the quality and allure of the cloth, or its appearance under candlelight can be replicated.

These courtiers regarded the fabric of their world with keen discernment. They could absorb its multi-layered meanings instantly: reading colour, texture and content as we might read words on a page, with a practised eye. They understood the intention behind a classical or biblical allusion and could quickly appreciate the purpose encoded in sewn symbols. A woven Labours of Hercules, the mythical Greek hero and god, signified a monarch's martial and moral strength. It also acted as a talisman. With Hercules associated with fertility, his woven presence was conducive to the begetting of heirs. Embroidered animals and plants appropriated nature's power and the attributes of specific species: the industry of a bee, the courage of a lion, the defence of a thistle. The inclusion of an embroidery of a mirror would summon up the proverb 'Know thyself' and stitched scales would evoke the Roman proverb 'Avoid injustice'. In anticipation of the presence of instructive textiles, visitors would accord them much more than a casual glance. Their close perusal could yield insight. Through them, a visitor might better gauge the personality, aspiration, even the mood of a monarch.

Henry VIII chose his tapestries with an agenda in mind. In the late 1520s when the English king was attempting to divorce his first wife, Catherine of Aragon – on the grounds that, as she had been his brother's wife, his marriage to her was a transgression of God's law – he commissioned a vast set of tapestries depicting the story of David. This biblical tale sees the adulterous David encountering God's wrath. Henry's display of it offered a visual argument to validate his pursuit of the divorce. In 1532, for a meeting with the French king Francois I, Henry draped his walls with tapestries which illustrated The Triumph of Scipio, an unvanquished Roman general and counsel. The backdrop was intended to identify Henry with Scipio: a leader of intellect and courage, of martial prowess and culture.[10] Such textiles were arranged to mirror the purposeful interior architecture of palaces themselves. As visitors ventured further into the court's interior and came closer to the royal apartments, the quality and content of the surrounding textiles changed. The finest and most intimate textiles were reserved for a monarch's inner sanctum, to which only a privileged few had access.

In the heightened theatrics of Renaissance court life, light was a quintessential quality. Until the seventeenth century, glass windows were a novelty, a luxury only afforded by the very rich and then only installed in the finest of buildings. To produce glass of even translucency and thickness was challenging. Only those fragments which reached the required quality were selected from what was produced. They would be excised, paned in small sections and joined with narrow lead strips. Others might disguise their flaws with painted designs. In the French châteaux of Henri II, glass signalled innovation and wealth and, as a boast of extravagance, larger glass windows were installed. It must have been a revelation to have interiors bathed in daylight, to be able to scan panoramic vistas through clear, uninterrupted glass. If the glass was stained or painted, colours could glow across palace chambers. In the French court, light became, like thread and cloth, a medium of display.

The lustre of fabrics themselves – the figured velvets, shot silks and sheened damasks – was heightened by the gold and silver of their embroidery. The glimmer of these among denser hues was sometimes deliberately intensified: the cloth scratched or razed to release a frayed quiver of luminosity. Spangles, called 'trambulants', were sewn on intentionally loose to ensure that they caught the light during movement. Silk embroidered cloths were laid beneath silver plate or Venetian glass on banquet tables and cupboard shelves to create spilled refractions of colour. It was light that animated cloth. Slivers of light bounced from textile surface to textile surface to create a moving energy that contrasted with their solid surroundings of wood and stone. And textiles were deliberately positioned to effect a change of atmosphere and mood, to maximise the impact of their sheen and the glint of their embellishments in different kinds of light – daylight, moonlight, candlelight and the reflected light of mirrors. The changing appearance of textiles was exploited in fabric production. Velvets were voided to create different surface levels that picked up light in different ways, or they were woven with underlying gold or silver threads to ensure they glistened under candlelight. Taffeta was often woven in two or more colours, its hue shifting from one to another when light changed direction. At the court of Henry VIII, in his Westminster Palace in London, five glass mirrors were framed in crimson velvet which was encrusted with embroidery wrought in variants of gold thread from Venice and Damascus. The frames were studded with garnets. Their glittering presence would have been magnified in the reflection of each mirror, one to the other.[11]

Textiles had the advantage of portability as well as versatility. While some trappings of power remained in situ to mark royal authority even when a monarch was absent, others were used to carry information from place to place, person to person, room to room, even country to country. Silken pavilions accommodated hopeful victors at times of war; tapestries decorated transient courts and relocated stories of sovereign virility and virtue from palace walls to city streets at times of celebration.

## Birds, Flowers, Fruit and Other Embroidered Motifs

The textile paraphernalia of monarchy – bed furnishings, throne canopies, livery and banners – accompanied monarchs wherever they went. Textiles could rapidly change an environment and provide more pertinent backdrops to diplomacy, or be replaced to better suit the message that a sovereign or high-ranking official wished to convey. It was said that Cardinal Wolsey, Henry VIII's Lord Chancellor, changed his tapestries on a weekly basis. Since he owned more than 600, it was a transformation the prelate could well afford. At Hampton Court, Wolsey also had 230 sets of embroidered bed furnishings at his disposal, a store which enabled him the luxury of choosing which to display according to the season and the status of his guests.[12]

Throughout the Renaissance, courts moved regularly from one royal residency to another. It was a necessary relocation. Local produce was inadequate to supply a court's needs over a long period. Provisions ran out and the build-up of sewage became unsustainable. The French court moved regularly from château to château in a vast cavalcade which could encompass as many as 18,000 people, 12,000 of them on horseback. For Mary, the scale and pageantry of a royal French progress must have seemed like a moving festival with courtiers and their liveried servants filling country lanes and journeying through city streets in a glorious spectacle of material plenitude. To the peasant poor, this passing river of visible sumptuousness reiterated the gulf between masters and servants, between power and dependency.[13]

For civic processional spectacles, the participating nobility, dignitaries, clergy, costumed revellers, musicians, members of the merchant and craft guilds all vied for sartorial splendour. They processed in groups, their collective rank distinguished by distinct motifs, colours and fabrics. Processions in the sixteenth century were also political. In 1504, the fourteen-year-old Margaret Tudor, sister of Henry VIII, processed from England to Scotland as the chosen bride of Mary's grandfather, James

IV. The marriage was designed to cement and protect the new accord between the two kingdoms, with Margaret as the embodiment of their amity. She and her extensive entourage of hundreds signalled English power. The procession was an emphatic show of grandeur and strength. The Tudor colours of green and white were dominant, the Tudor emblems of roses and portcullis proliferated. Among them, Margaret was a shimmering presence in cloth of gold. When representatives of the two nations converged at the Anglo-Scottish border, Margaret's retinue swelled to thousands, augmented by the large deputation of Scottish nobility sent to greet her and escort her into Scotland. The skyscape of their banners as they progressed across the border, the intermingling of Scottish and English heraldry, must have been an extraordinary sight to those who witnessed it: the Stewart and Tudor dynasties visually merged to declare the reconciliation of kings and proclaim peace.

In 2017, I attended a study day at the University of Glasgow entitled *Dress and Décor in Medieval and Renaissance Scotland*. It might not be everybody's idea of a good day out but, starved as I was of fellow enthusiasts of sixteenth-century material culture, it had kindred appeal. The celebrities of the world of Renaissance historical research were there, among them Professor Maria Hayward, the expert on dress at the court of Henry VIII; Dr Alison Rosie, the archival guardian at the National Records of Scotland; and Dr Sarah Carpenter, who includes chivalric games and masques (the dramatic entertainments performed at Renaissance courts) among her research specialisms. Late on in the afternoon, Dr Giovanna Guidicini from Glasgow School of Art, took to the podium to present her paper: 'Textiles, Spectacle and the Creation of Imaginary Worlds during Edinburgh Triumphal Entries'.[14] She expounded on the malleability of Renaissance textiles as a medium not only to establish the atmosphere of interior spaces, but also to alter the outdoor experience of monarchy. Using Elizabeth I's coronation on 15

## Birds, Flowers, Fruit and Other Embroidered Motifs

January 1559 as an example, she described how Elizabeth's processional route from the Tower of London to Westminster Abbey was purposefully walled in textiles, their blaze of embroidered and painted cloths intensified against that winter's snow. Later I found a contemporary report of the celebration, describing 'rails hung with cloth ... rich hangings, as well as tapestry, arras, cloths of gold, silver, velvet, damask, satin, and other silks, plentifully hung all the way as the Queen's Highness passed from the Tower through the City'.

This material decoration of London's city streets was, Dr Giovanna Guidicini explained, a deliberate ploy to create an enclosed, intimate world. Elizabeth's coronation was a public event of international significance set-dressed as a private and patriotic celebration. With her right to the succession disputed, Elizabeth had more reason than most to launch her sovereignty with a material offensive that asserted her claim to the English crown. It was vital that she was seen to belong to her people and this closing off of the city with banners and hangings intensified her subjects' experience of sharing a separate privileged space with their queen. Acutely aware that the event would be documented, sketched, discussed, disseminated and remembered, it was designed as a spectacle of propagandist material glory – a visual metaphor for civic welcome and protection.

The sixteenth century witnessed a resurgence in the appeal of embroidery. It was seized upon not merely as a decorative addition, but as another medium for the playful and intellectual challenges that delighted and diverted its educated elite. As with poetry, the composition of embroidered images and their accompanying mottos was a show of mental dexterity through which identity, wit, erudition and emotion – coded in symbolism and allegory – could be offered up for interpretation. Through juxtaposing symbols – which themselves offered a variety of meanings – with sewn anagrams or mottos, cryptic visual clues could be presented as a cohesive image. Their full meaning could only be fully unpicked by those educated few who had a thorough knowledge of the classics, the bible, heraldry and the gamut of symbolism. Only they could trace an abbreviated Latin motto to its original source or read beyond the simplicity of a rose to recognise the difference between a five-petalled Tudor rose and its political implication and the more naturalistic rose that spoke of emotional love or spiritual regeneration. Moreover, among the babel of increasingly international courts, where foreign spouses and their entourages sought acceptance, and where ambassadors, diplomats, spies and visiting nobility intermingled, the visual rhetoric of embroidered textiles provided a common language.

Embroidery was an essential component of French court culture. Henri II employed more than a dozen professional embroiderers in his royal workshops. Catherine had her own dedicated embroidery designer, the Florentine Frederic Vinciolo who, in time, would dedicate one of the earliest books of stitched patterns to her.[15] Catherine herself was a practised and enthusiastic embroiderer. She wrought small pieces of lacis work which, once completed, were applied to larger lengths of cloth. This was a form of open net-work in which patterns and images were created through stitches. The French chronicler Pierre de Brantôme described how Catherine was to be found absorbed in her embroidery each day after dinner, an art she had learned at the Convent of the Murate in Italy, which was renowned for its exquisite needlework.[16] In 1527, when the rule of the Medici dynasty in Florence was overthrown, Catherine had been taken hostage and sequestered in a series of convents, among them the Convent of the Murate. Two years later when Florence came under siege, the twelve-year-old Catherine had faced threats of abduction and incarceration in a soldiers' brothel. In time, she had escaped disguised as a nun. It is easy to imagine that, safely installed as France's queen, she might have found respite from past nightmares in her needlework.

## Birds, Flowers, Fruit and Other Embroidered Motifs

A bride to Henri II when she was fourteen years old Catherine not only had to assert her place as Henri's queen in a foreign court, but also to accept being eclipsed – sexually, socially and politically – by Henri's mistress, Diane de Poitiers. Diane was a woman of practised power and celebrated beauty: sophisticated and intelligent. Much older than Henri, she had established her authority at the court before Catherine's arrival, a supremacy which continued unabated. When Catherine had difficulty conceiving – a setback which clouded the first ten years of her marriage – it was Diane who insisted that Henri continue to fulfil his conjugal duties to secure an heir to the Valois dynasty. When Catherine finally conceived she tolerated Diane's assumption of maternal duties over her own children. It was Diane who appointed the royal children's household, she who oversaw their education and care, amused and comforted them. Catherine, forced to accommodate a *ménage à trois*, used sewing as her emotional retreat and salve. Her embroidery became an obsession. When she died, in 1589, there were nearly a thousand pieces found among her belongings, many unfinished.[17] The intricacy of Catherine's chosen technique, the concentration it required and the volume of her output, all indicate that, for Catherine, sewing was a prop, a way of coping with her displacement at court. Through it, she could appear to maintain a serenity which must have been elusive at times. She could register her survival and stoicism stitch by stitch. Needlework, it seems, was her consolation.

Henri conferred titles on Diane that elevated her to near-royal status. He gifted her the châteaux of Anet and Chenonceau, to which Mary, with the French royal children, was a frequent visitor. It was there that the young Scottish queen developed her passion for falconry, and it was through Diane's literary salons that Mary's love of poetry was nurtured. Diane became Mary's mentor and role model. Here was a woman untethered by male authority, an arts patron in her own right and at her own expense. Diane was a mistress, confident in her expressions of female sensuality and sexuality who invested – practically and intellectually – in female culture. In an age when the wearing of colours signalled allegiance, Mary chose to wear Diane's colours of black and white. They were worn to honour her and to publicly declare her attachment to Henri's mistress. And theirs was a mutual affection. In 1555 Mary wrote to her mother about Diane, saying that she was 'indebted for the love and more love she shows me'.[18]

Under Diane's direction, the châteaux Henri gifted her were transformed into innovative exemplars of a new and more emphatically female expression of sensory delight. Interiors were designed for intimacy and domestic diversion. Opportunities for tactile exploration and discovery were key. Views glimpsed from windows offered meditative vistas, grounds were laid out with the pleasure of promenading in mind. Diane commissioned extravagant gardens that displayed native and exotic plants, were suffused in the perfume of lilies and musk roses and offered the novelty of artichokes and banana trees. At the Château de Chenonceau, 13,000 hawthorn and hazel bushes were planted, bordered by 9,000 wild strawberries and fragrant violets.[19]

As gardens began to flourish beyond the boundaries of monastic orders, so too, embroidery moved into secular hands, no longer the preserve of nuns seeking salvation through their stitching to honour God. A synergy emerged between garden design and embroidery. They became viewed as intertwined disciplines, both exemplars of elite creativity. The arrangement of both favoured compartments, whether by planting borders of low-growing box or by stitching down narrow strips of ribbon or braid. Compartments allowed the specifics of a single flower or motif to be more pronounced through isolation. Strapwork (the stylised flourish of ribbon-like forms) featured in both disciplines. Knot gardens and mazes, stitched knot designs and scrolls both shared the Renaissance appeal of symbols and puzzles, with knots signifying bonds that could not be undone and mazes or scrolls offering visual challenges. Emblems long adopted in embroidery began to feature in outdoor topiary and floral design. And elements of the vocabulary used by gardeners and embroiderers became interchangeable. 'Parterre' (a formal garden laid out with interconnecting paths) was also called in France 'broderie', the word for embroidery. Slips, cuttings and trellis were other terms used by both disciplines. Embroiderers called the cloth they worked on 'the ground', gardeners created 'tapestries of flowers'. Both gardeners and embroiderers scoured the same recently published books of botanical drawings for inspiration.

Designs were not simply chosen for their visual impact. Gardens and embroideries were planned to evoke sensual pleasure. The olfactory experience of lavender and roses, aromatic herbs and exotic spices was paramount to both. In a world where the stench of insanitary conditions was unavoidable, any opportunity to counteract it was welcome. Sweet smelling herbs and the petals of perfumed flowers were strewn on straw floors and layered among folded clothing. It was not only the scent of such plants that was coveted, but their protective medicinal properties. In London, Cardinal Wolsey added saffron to his rush floors as a safeguard against the plague.[20] Dried blossom was encased in pomanders, secreted in jewellery and carried in small embroidered bags as a deterrent to infection. While gardeners tended scented flowers, embroiderers illustrated them to vicariously evoke their perfume and medicinal shield.

In the sixteenth century, even aristocratic women had limited access to the outside world. They rarely travelled. But gardens gave them a domestic setting that offered exploration. They could transpose the external world to their interiors with the skill of a needle. Moreover, nature's seasonality could be disregarded in needlework, its bounty made forever present. Through sewing, women could capture and fix a world beyond their physical reach.

Among the possessions of Catherine de' Medici listed in the 1589 inventory made after her death were:

Bed furnishings of crimson red velvet enriched with diverse octagons worked in petit point, their designs representing birds, flowers and fruit and other embroidered motifs worked in gold, silver and silk thread, with representations of the salamander, and the rest filled with compartments pieced from cloth of gold and embellished with leaves made from scraps of gold cloth.[21]

The embroideries of flowers and fruit might appear to be mere decorative flourishes, but they held multi-layered meanings. The embroidered birds were inspired by illustrations in recently printed books on natural history. Such books allowed women access to global scientific study and the wider realm of discovery. Their inclusion represented Catherine's scientific curiosity and geographic erudition which she nurtured through her extensive library of books and maps. The flowers and fruit recorded her botanical and medicinal knowledge. They were an encyclopaedic aide. Furthermore, they had symbolic value, referencing personal attributes and aspirations: a lily for virtue, pomegranates for fertility. Their form and arrangement would have reinforced Catherine's ordering of her world, her control of nature itself.

The salamander – representing passion and the ability to face challenges – had both emotional and political significance. It was the emblem of Catherine's father-in-law, François I, who, through agreeing to her marriage with his son, had rescued Catherine from threatened ignominy, even assassination. Its inclusion was both an homage and a proclamation of her power through her Valois alliance. More than a garnering of a visual miscellany, Catherine's bed furnishings were a stitched version of a cabinet of curiosities: a library of knowledge, a collection of personal memorabilia and intimate confidences. At a time when women's writings were rarely conserved, these embroideries bore testimony to not just who she was but what mattered to her.[22]

In 1551, the French treasury accounts detailed payments to Pierre Danjou, one of Henri's embroiderers, for his ornamentation of Mary's garments. He was tasked with embroidering her a crimson red velvet petticoat front and matching sleeves and embellishing a gown of fine black velvet with silver stitchery. Another gown was to be stitched with intricate gold foliage and flowers. It was Pierre Danjou who was responsible for the ciphers and devices of Mary and the Dauphin, François, that were embroidered on the favour, the gift of a love token, which Mary would later present to François.

The accounts illuminate the amount of money that Henri II was prepared to spend to clothe the young queen, and the range of artisans involved in creating her image. The inventory which lists the fabric, clothing and other items bought for Mary in 1551, records payments to cloth merchants, shoemakers, furriers, haberdashers, lingerie seamstresses, glove makers and numerous payments to Mary's own tailor, Nicolas du Moncel. In just that year alone, over 100 ells of fabric were needed for the nine-year-old's wardrobe. The cloth purchased was expensive: violet and crimson velvet, Venetian satin, yellow and incarnate shot taffeta, cloth of silver, gold damask. Its value was increased by its surface embroidery, borders of velvet, hand-wrought braids of silver and gold and the addition of pearls and precious stones. One of Mary's bodices boasted 120 diamonds and rubies, while a masque costume – worn for just one night – was sprinkled with 2,000 large gold and silver spangles, each one stitched on by hand. The nine ells of lustrous black velvet for a gown, which Danjou was instructed to encrust with bands of silver embroidery three fingers deep, cost nearly twice what he was paid for his intricate embroidery.

That same year, when Mary's tailor, du Moncel, made thirteen gowns, six pairs of sleeves and five petticoat fronts, plus assorted collars, coifs (women's close-fitting caps), bodies and manteaux for the young queen, he received less than Danjou had been paid for his embroidering of Mary's black velvet gown. His fee for his labour was less than the cost of the fabric for one of Mary's gowns of violet and crimson velvet. It must have been unnerving for du Moncel to smooth out on his table a length of velvet whose value equated to more than his weeks of toil, to cut into cloth that cost more than months of his skill: all this for a small girl's gown that she would outgrow before the year was out.[23] But Mary was not simply a child, but a queen. Her wardrobe had to reflect her status and her political importance. When power was calculated through the richness of apparel, the evidence of the quality of Mary's attire lay both in the discernible costliness of its fabric and in the skilled labour involved in its fashioning. These and its elaborate additions heightened her value and marked her out as a prize worth having.

The following year, in 1552, the treasury paid for wools for Mary to 'apprendre a faire ouvrage' (to learn to make works) – that is, to be taught needlework.[24] All girls in the sixteenth century learned basic sewing, even queens. But embroidery was an elite art. Only the wealthy could afford costly silk thread and fine needles, and had access to professional embroiderers to draw out designs for their needlework. Sewing, however, was just one of the many accomplishments Mary was taught. She was schooled in dance, horse-riding and hunting. She was expected to master musical instruments and the art of poetry. She also learned archery, how to play chess, train a falcon, and play tennis. Such talents were vital components of queenship. Not only did they ensure a queen could partner her husband in his pastimes, but they also endowed her with a repertoire with which to participate in more informal diplomatic encounters. Her skill in these, and the confidence with which she performed the ceremonial rituals demanded of her, were barometers of her capacity and finesse. Witnessed by her subjects, reported on by ambassadors and discussed among rivals, they were tools of sovereign prestige.

Furthermore, an academic curriculum was obligatory as a preparation for monarchy. Mary was tutored in Spanish and Italian as well as French in order to acquire the diplomatic fluency necessary for effective international negotiation. She learned Greek and Latin alongside the Dauphin. At the age of eleven she was tested on her progress, required to present a Latin oration in defence of the value of women's education in the Great Hall of the Louvre before the whole court. She did not disappoint. It was reported that she handled the ordeal with graceful aplomb.

Most importantly, Mary was groomed as François's consort and inducted into her role as joint monarch. This required her to be immersed in the culture of France and its court. On her arrival in France, her four Marys were summarily despatched to a convent. While the services of her Scottish governess, Mary Fleming, were retained, most of the other Scottish courtiers who had accompanied the young queen to France returned home. Mary was deliberately severed from her native culture and encouraged to form new attachments untrammelled by familiarity. Of primary concern was her attachment to the Dauphin. They were brought up as one unit. As François was frail and sickly, it was even more vital that his chosen wife would not just compensate for, but mask, his deficiencies.

Although she was separated from her mother and her four Marys, in France Mary discovered the stability and embrace of family. Her Guise grandparents, cousins, uncles and aunts, and her extensive adopted Valois family, gave her an intimate world of guidance and company. At the heart of her affections, however, was always François, her petulant boy-husband to be.

Their delight in each other caused one observer to remark of their proposed union that 'the Dauphin cares for her and loves her like his sweetheart and his wife and that it is easy to judge that God caused them to be born for each other'.[25]

Mary's intensive curriculum and her introduction to the charm and craft of monarchy was alleviated by play. Eight of Catherine's ten children were born while Mary was in France. Mary, Elisabeth de Valois (Henri and Catherine's eldest daughter) and François had an expanding troupe of younger children to direct in their frolics. With the addition of the children belonging to members of the royal household, Mary had more than thirty-five playmates to keep her amused, along with twenty dogs, the lions and bears in the court's menagerie and the exotic birds in its aviaries. The foolery of clowns and the skill of jugglers added to her entertainment. In their royal apartment, Elisabeth and Mary established their own play-kitchen where they concocted jams and other delicacies. This culinary activity bred the myth that it was Mary who invented marmalade while recuperating from an illness, a mischief of word play on *Mary malade* (French for 'ill') and 'marmalade'. That Mary did make jam is indisputable, evidenced by treasury payments to an apothecary for ingredients. But it was quinces that were ordered for the girls, not citrus fruit. Like so much written about Mary, Queen of Scots, this story is only partly true.[26]

As Mary and François grew up, their lives became more separate. In March 1553, at the age of ten, François was given his own household. Mary's household was not established until the following January when she reached her majority: the age at which she became Queen of Scots in her own right. But a wrangle ensued over who was to meet Mary's household bills. Henri now looked to Scotland to cover the Scottish queen's expenditure. Discussions became protracted and, as financial negotiations wore on, Mary's material comforts became sparser. Her governess, Madame de Parois, was forced to write to Mary's mother, Marie de Guise, to voice her concern about Mary's situation: her poor credit; the arrears of staff wages; a wardrobe in dire need of replenishment; the exclusion of Mary from royal progresses as she lacked the necessary funds to afford to travel with the court. Meanwhile, the adolescent Mary was rebelling against the strictures of Parois's control and beseeching her mother for more fashionable clothes: for a dress of cloth of gold to wear at a wedding, for her cipher to be embroidered on her gowns, for two new outfits 'for reasons of prestige', as well as money to pay her servants.[27] The situation was eventually resolved, but it required Marie de Guise, already financially stretched, to relinquish much of her pension and dowry from her estates in France. These, with a hefty contribution from the Scottish treasury, ensured that Mary – generous and self-indulgent – could maintain not just her monarchical dignity but a lifestyle of continuing opulence and largesse.

The wedding between the fourteen-year-old François and the fifteen-year-old Mary took place on Sunday 24 April 1558 at the Cathedral of Nôtre-Dame in Paris. It was designed with fitting pomp. François wore a robe of rich red velvet, lined and embellished in gold. Mary, her long auburn hair flowing free, wore a white gown with a train six ells long and a purple velvet overmantle embroidered in gold with the arms of Scotland. Her bodice was covered in dazzling jewels, and on her head she wore a crown ablaze with diamonds, emeralds, sapphires and pearls. The teenage François and Mary made their vows under rippling blue silk decorated in gold repeats of the fleur-de-lis. As a shower of coins was thrown to the watching crowds, a swell of fifes, tambors, viols and trumpets sounded hallelujahs. Mary wrote to her mother that morning to say she was 'the happiest woman in the world'.

For the festivities that followed, the Great Hall of the Louvre Palace was transformed. Under the light trails of thousands of candles, the legend of Jason and his quest for the golden fleece was re-enacted. The story was a metaphor for French power, the quest itself representing France's ultimate victory over unworthy usurpers. With religious unrest already stirring in France, the message was aimed as much at French Protestants as at predatory European monarchs. Following this and a choral jubilation, the vast polished floor became a sea of undulating blue, with fabric eddying in an artificial breeze. Controlled by mechanisms unfathomable to onlookers, the waves lapped around a flotilla of six ships decked out in red and yellow satin, the heraldic colours of Scotland, which glided through the textile waters with sails that shimmered in luminous silver. Each ship (the Catholic symbol of safety in time of persecution) was captained by a member of the royal family – Henri II, the Dauphin, the King of Navarre, the Duke of Lorraine and others – each claiming in turn a queen or a princess. And in that hall, suffused with the scent of flowers and mesmerised by music, the ships gracefully danced a *passamezzo,* a sixteenth-century Italian folk dance, as if by their own volition. It was a spectacular celebration of French sovereign power, present and future: ambition played out in sensual and material majesty to trumpet the ascendency and tripartite strength, of a new Valois, Guise and Stewart alliance.[28]

Celebrations of the marriage were also organised in Scotland. Marie de Guise ordered velvet, satin and taffeta for 'the solemnisation of the wedding of our sovereign lady to be "counterfeited" in Edinburgh on 3 July'. Processions were arranged and bonfires lit throughout the country.[29] The Scottish Latin scholar George Buchanan penned an epithalamium (a classically inspired set of verses) to commemorate the event. His verses were a reminder to Mary that it was not just her woman's body that she would yield to her husband, but her body politic as Scotland's queen. At a time when the issue of a woman's right to rule was fuelling political, literary and intellectual debate, Buchanan's congratulatory verses were a thinly veiled commentary on women's inferiority. His advice was condescending, advising Mary to 'learn to be subject to your husband's direction' and reminding her of her duty to produce an heir.[30]

The marriage, however, brought succour for Marie de Guise. The French alliance was secure. Unbeknownst to her nobility, however, it came at a political price. Just days before her wedding, Mary had signed secret documents. They included the agreement that François was to be granted the Crown Matrimonial, making him king of Scotland and joint sovereign with Mary. Should Mary die or prove infertile, it was François and his future progeny who would inherit the Scottish crown. Whether through Mary's infertility or death, the treaty gambled on France being able to procure the Scottish throne for itself. With François's delayed puberty known about in court circles, and Mary's uncertain health having already caused anxiety, it was an invidious political strategy. When the pact came to light, the Scottish nobles delayed its ratification and refused to accede to Henri's demands to send the Scottish royal regalia to France.

In the months that followed her marriage, tensions grew between the ever-volatile countries of Europe. The English queen, the Catholic Mary Tudor, died in November 1558, to be replaced by her half-sister, the Protestant Elizabeth: her sovereignty unrecognised by Catholic Europe. In France, Mary's Guise uncles took advantage of their growing political power now that their niece was the Dauphine, and the questionable legitimacy of Elizabeth's sovereignty, to assert Mary's rights to the English throne. They ordered that her coat of arms, which on her marriage had been halved with those of France, was now to be quartered with those of England. The new heraldry, audaciously appropriated, was displayed at the wedding festivities of Princess Claude de Valois to the Duke of Lorraine in March 1559, an event attended by a host of international nobility. By summer, the French heralds were proclaiming at Mary's entrance 'Make way for the Queen of England'. When the English ambassador to France, Nicholas Throckmorton, was served his supper on plate engraved with Mary's new coat of arms, he sent William Cecil, Elizabeth's chief advisor, a sketch of the outrage. Elizabeth was not amused. Mary's precocious adoption of the English coat of arms was a predatory act that was neither easily forgiven nor forgotten.

By 1559, loss and threat surrounded Mary like a shroud. Scotland was assailed by religious division. The strengthening power of its Protestant reformers increasingly threatened the overthrow of Marie de Guise's regency. Civil war broke out. On 11 July, Henri II was fatally wounded in a tournament. Diane de Poitiers was immediately banished from court and Catherine de' Medici claimed Diane's château at Chenonceau for her own use. Moreover, Mary's childhood companion, Elisabeth de Valois, was married by proxy to King Philip of Spain and left France later that autumn.

François's coronation, in September 1559, was a sombre affair. The wearing of gold work or embroidery was forbidden. Catherine and her daughters dressed in black, while Mary wore white as she had on her wedding day, appearing, one onlooker observed, like 'a dove amongst crows'. The 700 goldfinches and other songbirds released to celebrate the coronation were of small comfort in a land in the throes of Protestant unrest and increasing financial debt and reigned over by a fragile boy. The following March, the Valois pleasure palace of Amboise was stormed by Protestant Huguenots determined to overthrow the fledgling monarchy and eliminate the power of the Catholic Guise. Retribution was swift and savage, with Mary's uncle, the Cardinal of Lorraine, ordering the mass hanging of hundreds of rebels, their bodies hung around the castle walls as a gruesome deterrent. François was reported to have declared that 'I desire nothing more than to exterminate them entirely and cut down their root so well there should be no future growth'.[31] Such vengeful acts and words attracted the condemnation of Protestant England and the pro-English Protestant lobby in Scotland. Mary's popularity waned, tainted by her Guise association.

The year 1560 brought more deaths and conflicts. In June, Marie de Guise died in Edinburgh. And, in July of that year, Mary and François refused to ratify the Treaty of Edinburgh, an agreement made between Elizabeth and the Scottish Reformist nobles that established a new Anglo-Scottish accord. Through it, both English and French troops were to leave Scotland and Mary was to abandon her use of the English coat of arms. Mary's refusal to sign it bred further distrust and ill-feeling towards the Scottish queen. When Mary fell ill later that autumn, Sir James Mason, an English courtier, wrote to Cecil: 'The Queen of Scotland is very sick and these men fear she will not long continue. God take her to Him so soon as may please Him.'[32]

In November 1560, eight days before the French Estates General, the legislative and consultative assembly of different classes of French subjects, was due to be convened in a conciliatory effort to prevent civil war, François became ill. His sickness quickly escalated. What began as an ear infection developed into fever. He became delirious and on 5 December he died, just a month before his seventeenth birthday and a week before Mary became eighteen. François had been Mary's close companion for more than thirteen years; they had been raised together as an inseparable unit in preparation for their joint monarchy. Mary's power had been subsumed into his. On 5 December, Catherine de' Medici signed a receipt for the reclamation of the royal jewels in Mary's possession. Mary's glory days in France were over.

An orphan, and now a widow, the eighteen-year-old Mary secluded herself in a black-shrouded room as decreed by tradition. There she stayed for the next forty days, enveloped in white cloth, the *deuil blanc* of French mourning. The artist François Clouet made a small portrait of her at this time. Mary is wearing her widow's weeds, her face ethereal against the gossamer of her veil. A contemporary chronicler described her distress:

> she is dispossessed of the Crown of France, with little hope of recovery of that of Scotland, which is her sole patrimony and dower. [It] so afflicts her that she will not receive any consolation, but, brooding over her disaster with constant tears and passionate and doleful lamentations, she universally inspires great pity.[33]

Catherine vetoed the proposal that Mary should marry François's brother Charles, a marriage which would have continued Mary's tenure as queen of France. At eleven years old, Charles was still in his minority, and Catherine was determined to assume the role of regent, governing France and Charles herself. She also blocked the idea of Mary marrying Don Carlos, the son of the King of Spain, as Catherine did not want Spain to forge an alliance with Scotland. She was also hoping that Don Carlos might marry her own daughter, Marguerite de Valois. For Mary, with few other prospects appropriate to her rank, what was left to her was Scotland. It was a country shaped by division rather than joy, a kingdom under Protestant rather than Catholic rule, but Mary was its undisputed queen and she decided to return home.

As I meandered through the châteaux of Mary's girlhood during my visit to France, I wondered what of them she would have remembered. Flying her falcon at Chenonceau, following its flight and swoop, melting sugar in her play kitchen with Elisabeth, or smoothing her hand over her white gown as its train trailed across the blue embroidered carpet at the Cathedral of Nôtre-Dame? Standing in the Louvre Palace in front of the French court defending, in Latin, the right of women to a proper education, or dancing with François under the gilded frescoes in the ballroom at Fontainebleau? Would the heady scent of flowers in Diane de Poitiers' exuberant gardens linger, the faint strains of French court music still play in her head? Would she recall sitting huddled with François in the Château d'Amboise as the sound of dying echoed through its thick walls, or sitting beside his bedside as he reached death slowly? I found little trace of Mary when I went to France. She was rarely mentioned in the information panels in the châteaux I visited, rarely featured in the postcards of past French monarchs in the châteaux's gift shops. Yet France scripted Mary; it formed her faith and her sensuality. Ahead of her lay Scotland, and within it lay her fate.

## 2

## *The Fetternear Banner*

It was the allure of Catholic textiles, their material appeal, that first ensnared me into a love of embroidery. At the age of six, it was the improbable gorgeousness of my first communion dress – its glistening white satin and lace edged cuffs, and the delicacy of the translucent veil fixed to my bobbed hair with a crescent of silk flowers – that was seductive. But weekly mass was the real enchantment, with each liturgical season marked out in sewn differences. On Easter Sunday, our parish priest rustled to the altar in cream brocade appliquéd with an ivory dove winged in gold. There was pristine white for Christmas and black doom for All Souls' Day. The moods and mysteries of faith were played out in a material chronology of Christ's life with symbolic colours and motifs. For Good Friday, the priest would don a cope of purple emblazoned with a silver cross that glinted in the late afternoon light. As he genuflected at each of the fourteen stations of the cross, we swooned at the heady vapour of myrrh escaping from the swaying orb and watched as he, elderly and stiff, was helped by two altar boys each time he knelt and rose, literally bowed down by the burden of his office, the embroidered and encrusted weight of his spiritual authority.

Before the Protestant Reformation, Scotland had been a Catholic country for over ten centuries. Its Catholic culture was embedded in its devotional practice. It boasted a strong monastic – and through it scholastic – tradition of international regard, and venerated its own canonised saints. Outside of its royal residences, whatever architectural grace the country could lay claim to was manifested in its ecclesiastical landscape: its cathedrals, collegiate churches, abbeys and friaries. These housed not only places of worship, but also schools and hospitals, sanctuaries and physic gardens. It was through the artistry of monks that the miniature glories of holy manuscripts were illustrated, through nuns that biblical tales were depicted in exquisite embroidery. The social calendar of urban and rural communities was wrapped around Catholic feast days of Christmas, Candlemas, Corpus Christi, the Epiphany and more, the high days and holidays of religious festivals celebrated in decorative processions and costumed revelries. In 1531, Edinburgh's guild members were instructed by the city's provost and council to appear 'in their best array, to keep and decorate the Procession on Corpus Christi days and Candlemas as honourably as they can, every craft with their own banner, with the arms of their craft thereon'.

The list that followed detailed which saint each guild was to honour in the accompanying pageant. The fleshers (butchers) were, somewhat appropriately, responsible for depicting 'St Sebastian and his Torments'; the tailors, the Coronation of Our Lady; the wrights, masons, slaters, coopers and other trades were allocated the Resurrection, St Steven, St Lawrence, St Martin, St Nicholas, St John and St George.[1]

In a country that lacked the means to manufacture much in the way of commercial beauty, and with the royal court accessible only to a minority, it was the Church that offered wonder to most of the population. Its carved rood screens, painted frescos, stained glass windows, embroidered vestments and wooden statues were sources of visual delight and spiritual inspiration.

This was not a country of idle or complacent faith, but a place of devout pilgrimage. Scotland had hundreds of shrines scattered throughout the country to revere its holy men and women. Along with churches and cathedrals, many of them cherished the relics of saints as their key attraction. A church could boost its standing and revenue through the relics it harboured. In the fifteenth century, Glasgow Cathedral did better than most. It had remnants of wood from the cross of Jesus's crucifixion, the hair of the Virgin Mary, the skin of St Bartholomew and the bones of St Eugene and St Enoch. The cloth of the holy was talismanic, thought to be imbued with the essence of its owner. Scotland's possession of the shirts of its saints – St Cuthbert, St Columba, St Kentigern and St Margaret, among others – made it a country of significant Catholic heritage.[2]

The belief in the efficacy of relics originated in pagan rituals. Pagans believed that objects could transmit emotional power and connect them to the supernatural. As animists, they accorded everything in the world around them with a transferable spirit that could bolster human resilience. The early Christian missionaries subsumed elements of pagan worship into Catholic devotion to ensure that the transition from one to the other was neither socially nor spiritually disruptive. But it was the Crusades, that lasted from the eleventh to the thirteenth century, that fanned the cult of venerating relics. The biblical provenance of the crusaders' trophies endowed them with greater sacred as well as financial worth. Relics made of cloth were believed to be more potent than others, as fabric absorbed the bodily fluids of the divine: their tears, blood and saliva. They made faith tangible, and inherent in them was the physical residue of invisible sanctity. The veil of Veronica, fragments of the Virgin Mary's veil, scraps of Mary Magdalene's garments were all believed to be authentic and were brought back by the Crusaders as investments in the spiritual store of Catholic realms.

If relics were one aspect of sacred appeal, another was ecclesiastical textile treasures. An inventory of the vestments in Glasgow Cathedral compiled in 1422 lists the material opulence the church possessed. Much of what it owned was donated as a barter for salvation. The guilty conscience of James Stewart, Lord of Darnley, in the early fifteenth century was eased by the bestowal of two magnificent copes: one of brown damask interwoven in gold and embroidered with his coat of arms, and another of ruby and green velvet, brocaded in golden flowers and leaves and banded in gold-stitched orphreys. Within the cathedral's coffers lay copes and chasubles of stunning splendour, made of silk, velvet and cloth of gold. Their brilliance was purposefully breathtaking, sewn in silk threads and studded with precious stones. This textured iridescence conjured the light of God and, by association, evoked the spiritual supremacy of his chosen clergy, the transmitters of God's grace. The vestments in Glasgow Cathedral animated the wonders God had created. They were adorned with sun rays and stars, flowers and leaves, birds and beasts, stags and porcupines: here a green silk altar cloth stitched with dolphins, there a sky-blue carpet strewn with golden roses.[3]

Yet such magnificence was subject to criticism. It seemed to many that the Catholic Church wore its spiritual authority too extravagantly. The riches and luxuries accumulated by its chief prelates seemed to disregard the biblical tenets of probity. Chastity was also an issue. There was discomfort in the knowledge that some priests lived openly with their mistresses and sired children in defiance of their vows of celibacy. Attempts at reforms were sporadic and ineffectual and spiritual malpractice continued.

In the years preceding Mary's return, Marie de Guise had done what she could to quell religious disaffection in Scotland. Scottish Protestantism, which followed the teachings of the French reformer John Calvin, was taking hold. He advocated following only the sovereignty of God, and the study of the scriptures as the path to salvation. During Marie de Guise's regency, those bent on Protestant reform gained ground. They became increasingly confrontational, demanding that their faith be acknowledged, that they be allowed the right to practise it freely and publicly, without suppression. Marie de Guise tried to maintain religious equilibrium through adopting a conciliatory policy. But it was challenging. As religious division became more overt, incidents of iconoclastic purging of churches became more widespread. By 1559, the reformers had turned militant. Now styling themselves the Lords of the Congregation, they gathered armed troops. A religious war ensued. The reformers – funded in part by the newly Protestant England – exploited the faltering of Marie de Guise's political and physical strength to advance their power. By October 1559, she had been deposed. By June 1560, she was dead. The reformers seized control of the country and began to forge a Scotland framed by their Protestant perspective and shaped by a Calvinist aesthetic.

Under Protestant rule, Scotland's Catholic culture was doomed to erasure. Instructions were sent out for the material expressions of Catholicism to be removed and openly burnt, and for its altars to be destroyed. In the city of Perth in May 1559, John Knox, the spiritual leader of the Scottish Reformation, preached a sermon against idolatry. His rant incited mob violence and a desecration of churches ensued. In Fife, zealous reformers 'put down the priory of St Andrews in this way: altering the habit, burning of images and mass books and breaking of altars.'[4] Edinburgh Council was forced to hire soldiers to protect its church of St Giles. When Glasgow Cathedral was threatened, members of the city's trade guilds made a human cordon around it, declaring that the first person to throw a stone would be buried under it. The cathedral remained intact.

Fearing the loss or damage of their sacred store of devotional objects, and unsure whether the religious shift was just a temporary hiatus, Scottish Catholics and their clergy began to sequester valuable Catholic artefacts and put them into the safekeeping of secular guardians, or ferry them abroad. The church gear and ornaments of St Machar's cathedral in Aberdeen were lodged with the Catholic Earl of Huntly. An inventory made of his possessions in 1562 lists fifty embroidered copes, chasubles and tunics, some of which would have been for use in his family's private chapel, but most of which would have come from the cathedral. The most precious of these were made from the gold silk pavilion used by Edward II at the Battle of Bannockburn in 1314 and seized by the victorious Scots as a spoil of war. After the battle, its cloth was distributed among Scottish churches, including St Machar's, to be refashioned into vestments and altar frontals as an act of appropriation. In an age when people believed in the protective, magical qualities of cloth, the possession of such a trophy was thought to be talismanic.[5]

For churches lacking the foresight of St Machar's cathedral, the Reformation brought grievous loss, with Catholic treasures prised from their shelter. What began as a series of sporadic assaults on church property became a more systematic, officially sanctioned elimination of 'popish trumpery', which was destroyed, recycled, sold or relocated to secular sites. This destruction ensured a cleansing of Catholic churches to make them fit for Protestant worship.

The veneration of relics, statues and other Catholic imagery was an intrinsic part of Catholic devotion. It was believed to intensify the spiritual experience. Catholicism was a physical as well as a spiritual culture, in which sacred objects did not just personify Christ and his followers, but animated them. Seeing and touching, the sensory acts of devotion, were essential ingredients of ritual worship and divine connection. The feelings such acts evoked allowed for a deeper, more highly charged religious experience which brought petitioners closer to God's presence. And the ritual blessings that formed part of processional devotion, the religious festivals and Catholic rites of passage in which statues and other Catholic symbols would be publicly blessed, recharged the power of the sacred through the collective performance of faith. They reiterated the social cohesion of the community. They were restorative.

In France, Mary was shaped by her Catholic faith. Her life was regulated by the rhythm of daily mass and the liturgical calendar. The royal chapels where she worshipped were designed to honour God with the beauty of their surroundings, in their vaulted ceilings, painted frescoes, patterned mosaic floors. God's magnificence was manifested in the lustred finery of prelates, his glory celebrated in the harmony of hymns and honoured in the drowsy scent of myrrh. Mary's faith would have been experienced through such sensual pleasures. Through Catholicism she participated in the elaborate rituals in which she, as queen, would eventually play a central role. There was the re-enactment each Maundy Thursday (the Thursday before Easter) of Christ washing his disciples' feet when the monarch – in a pristine white apron, towel in hand – bent over the feet of his carefully selected, and usually virginal, subjects as an act of humility. More joyous was the election of the Queen of the Bean at the Feast of the Epiphany, when whoever found the bean in the celebratory cake supplanted the monarch and 'reigned over' the ensuing festivities. With a Guise uncle who was a Cardinal and two Guise aunts who were abbesses of French convents, Mary was steeped in a Catholic culture. The importance of her faith can be tracked in the religious books she possessed in her library in Scotland: the writings of St Augustine and St Ignatius, the life of Christ, books on devotion and penitence, on sacrament and prayer.[6] In France, Mary also donated, as instructed by her mother, her redundant gowns to the Catholic cause, sending them to her aunts' convents. There, the richest of their embroidery and trimmings would have been removed and re-applied to vestments as a gift to God.[7]

\* \* \*

## The Fetternear Banner

The Fetternear banner is named after the barony of Fetternear in Aberdeenshire where it had been conserved by the Catholic Leslie family of Balquhain. They donated it to the local church in 1859. It is a rare survivor of Pre-Reformation Catholic Scotland. Thought to have been made around 1520, it is the only known Scottish ecclesiastical banner to have escaped the Reformation purge. The banner is displayed in the National Museum of Scotland as often as its fragility will allow. Still colour-bright, it is double-faced, enabling its detail to be seen by those sitting behind or in front of it. On a single length of linen cloth, Christ is depicted as the Man of Sorrows. He is wearing a crown of thorns, his humiliation countered by a golden halo. His body is stabbed in multiple wounds stitched in red silk. In his left hand he holds a reed, the mockery of a sceptre forced upon him by Pilate's soldiers. And around Christ's body are intricately embroidered motifs which narrate, in compacted imagery, the story of his last days on earth: the purse of Judas's betrayal, the cockerel of St Peter's denial, the spear thrust into his side, the vinegared sponge offered to tease his thirst and the seamless shroud of his burial.

The banner has three decorative borders. The outer border is a simple repeat of symbols: the columbine for the Holy Ghost, the acorn for immortality and the scallop shell, the pilgrims' emblem. The middle border is more complex, translating the knotted cords of the Franciscan monastic order into an interlaced chorusing of Celtic origin. With no discernible beginning or end, it signifies eternity. The intertwining cords are punctuated by silken sacred hearts set within stars and four heraldic shields. One shield, emblazoned with a dove with outstretched wings, depicts the emblem of St Columba. A coat of arms on another shield references the Graham family and a third is attributed to Gavin Douglas, then the Bishop of Dunkeld. The fourth is incomplete. The inner border represents the rosary in a light-catching row of silk-sewn beads, each decade separated by a red rose.[8]

It is the detailed imagery of the Fetternear banner and its layered symbolism that are so telling; they indicate the complex visual language of Scottish church textiles at the time. Ecclesiastical textiles in the sixteenth century were generally made from richer fabrics, densely embroidered and beaded. It was their encrusted surface that mattered: its weight, ornamentation and crammed imagery which signalled wealth and power. But the Fetternear banner is deliberately simple. Its complexity lies in its symbolism, not in the quantity of its imagery. This is not a declaration of power; it is an expression of faith.

While its provenance is unknown, it is doubtful that it was stitched in Scotland, but it is thought to have been commissioned by Edinburgh's Confraternity of the Holy Blood, a lay religious brotherhood. In 1505 it welcomed James IV as a member and the treasury records payment for '2 ells of crimson satin for the king's hood when he was made [a] brother to the Holy Blood'. That same year, the king made an offering – a donation of money – to the Holy Blood Mass at St Giles Church, and in 1512 made another to its Holy Blood altar where the banner would have hung, an altar whose location is still marked in the present-day cathedral.[9] The confraternity comprised merchants, burghers and guild members who joined together in collective worship at the weekly mass held at their dedicated altar. They publicised their civic prestige and prosperity in processional spectacle, embroidered banners, ceremonial attire and charitable largesse. James's participation in the confraternity strengthened the king's bond with his civic community, but it also confirmed the value Scotland placed on its commercial ties with the Netherlands. It was Bruges that was the cradle of the Holy Blood cult and, through James's membership and participation in Edinburgh's confraternity, the king was reinforcing a spiritual empathy with its Bruges counterparts as a boost to trade.

On a bright summer's morning I meet Helen Wyld, Senior Curator of Historic Textiles at the National Museum of

Scotland, to talk about the Fetternear banner. She is a keen researcher into the sacred significance of pre-Reformation fabrics of faith and she enlightens me on the cultural impact of the religious change experienced after 1560. She bemoans the loss, not just of Catholic artefacts, but of their connection to, and our understanding of, the nature and purpose of Scottish devotion before the Reformation. Helen is acutely aware of how different the Scottish experience was compared to those of its European counterparts. In Scotland, the zeal of its reformers and their strong Calvinist beliefs led to a much greater emotional and sensory dislocation than that of other countries, a cultural disruption which persisted over the centuries which followed.

We talk of the Fetternear banner. To Helen's mind, it was not abandoned because it was incomplete, as I had assumed; on her laptop she shows me the evidence of its wear and tear at the uppermost corners. This was a banner that had been hung up over and over again – privately or covertly, but used nonetheless. While she feels it was unlikely that it ever reached its planned destination in St Giles Church, she is sure it continued to play a role in the exercise of Scottish Catholic faith. We pore over its images, the double-sided stitchery – unique in its time – and she zooms in on her computer to allow me to see more clearly how its silken split stitch was executed so precisely front to back and back to front, to achieve an exact mirroring of the imagery. I am also able to appreciate the deliberate and careful changes of stitching direction to better contour the agony on the face of the dying Christ. This is certainly masterly sewing.

Helen explains that the profusion of Christ's red-threaded wounds were an integral part of the Holy Blood cult. To members of the confraternity, this was not simply a sewn illustration of blood, but a re-materialisation of Christ's suffering. During the veneration of their banner, the confraternity experienced the red silk wounds as the blood of Christ. They brought him into their presence as a living entity. It was – as with the moment of transubstantiation in the Catholic mass when the wine is believed to become the blood of Christ – an act of reincarnation. To pray while meditating on the banner was to be with him and of him, suffering his pain, feeling his agony, accepting both as a sacrifice of faith. She tells me how the use of linen for the Fetternear banner as a background for its embroidery was unusual for the time but how linen cloth had a special significance in Catholic worship. It symbolised purity and was associated with the shroud of Turin, the linen sheet thought to have been wrapped around Christ's body at his burial and believed to be impregnated with his image. It was linen that the Catholic church used for its sacramental and altar cloths. For those who cared for such cloths, who washed and mended them, their care was an act not just of purification but of devotion.

We discuss why Catholic iconography was so anathema to the Protestant reformers. Helen explained that what Protestants found so offensive was the fact that Catholics imbued their devotional images with sacred power, believed them to be mediums of divine connection, or talismans with the power to heal the sick and effect miracles. Churches had to be erased of all that was idolatrous to put an end to people's dependency on physical objects as conduits to forgiveness and salvation.

For the reformers, such sensory triggers were expressions of emotional piety rather than cerebral religious understanding. They had no place in a Calvinist faith based on the written word of God. In 1561, Calvin published his treatise condemning the cult of relics and the worship of sacred objects. His condemnation of them differed from the view promulgated by the other key Protestant leader of the time, Martin Luther, who defended the continued display of Catholic religious imagery, declaring that it was useful 'for the sake of memory and better understanding'. But Calvin's repudiation of it cemented the fate of

Scottish Catholic material culture. The Reformation in Scotland excised the touch, feel and visual celebration of Scottish faith. In their place came an austere aesthetic.

Mary left France on 14 August 1561. As Elizabeth had refused her safe passage through England in retaliation at Mary's refusal to sign the Treaty of Edinburgh, the eighteen-year-old widowed queen had to take an alternative route. Among her possessions was a single holly thorn, a gift from Henri II before his death. The thorn was believed to have been salvaged from Christ's crown at his crucifixion. As such, it was not only sacred, but also a powerfully protective talisman against misfortune. Mary had sore need of such an amulet. Her departure from Calais was marred by calamity. As her fleet was about to set sail, another boat, nearing home, suddenly capsized. She watched in horror as men flailed helplessly in the water, screaming for rescue. All were drowned. Some saw it as an omen, a warning of the dangers that lay ahead, not just in the sea but in Scotland itself. Chroniclers recorded the sorrow of Mary's departure, the young queen in tears as she said her last farewell, her 'Adieu, France' fading in the wind. Her arrival in Scotland five days later was as inauspicious as her departure from France. With fair winds speeding her voyage, Mary reached her kingdom much earlier than anticipated. Her nobles, who had been summoned to greet her at the end of the month, were absent. There was no grand welcome. Instead, messengers had to be sent in haste to announce the queen's return. Mary and her entourage were taken to a nearby merchant's house to wait while the nobility dressed in their finest clothes and had their horses made ready. It was already evening when they came to fetch their sovereign and escort her to the Palace of Holyroodhouse in Edinburgh.

There was another — and for some more troubling — blight that morning. Despite it being summer, an unusually heavy mist hung in the air, that darkened the sky and seemed to turn day into night. John Knox, the spiritual leader of the Scottish Reformation, saw it as a sign from heaven, an ominous portent for her reign:

The very face of heaven at the time of her arrival did manifestly speak what comfort brought into this country with her (to wit) sorrow, dolour, darkness and all impiety; for in the memory of man that day of the year was never seen a more dolorous face of the heaven, than was at her arrival, which two days after did so continue ... That forewarning, God gave unto us; but alas! The most part were blind.[10]

Knox's was a stridently adversarial voice and, even when she was in France, Mary was wary of his presence in her kingdom. Nicholas Throckmorton, the English ambassador in France, had reported to Elizabeth that:

the queen of Scotland is thoroughly persuaded that the most dangerous man in all the realm is Knox and is therefore determined to use all means to banish him hence, or else to assure them that she will never dwell in that country as long as he is there.[11]

Knox, however, was useful to Scottish Protestant nobles as a passionate proselytiser of their faith. And although at times even they recoiled at his invective, they did not insist on his exile. Originally, Knox had planned to settle in England, but when, in 1558, he published his contentious, now infamous, diatribe against female monarchy, *The First Blast of the Trumpet Against the Monstrous Regiment of Women*, aimed at Mary Tudor and Marie de Guise, he lost acceptability. Despite Elizabeth I's Protestantism, she took umbrage at his defamation of female rule and had no desire to risk becoming a target for his vitriol. When his petition for a passport to England was refused, Knox returned to his homeland of Scotland. But his presence filled Mary with foreboding.

## The Fetternear Banner

John Knox had been ordained a Catholic priest before aligning himself with the Protestant reformers. In the aftermath of the murder of Scotland's leading Catholic prelate, Cardinal Beaton, in 1546, Knox had joined the perpetrators of the Cardinal's assassination. When they were eventually captured and taken to France as prisoners, Knox found himself in chains as a galley slave. He endured months of harsh treatment before being freed in 1549. Initially he found refuge in England, becoming chaplain to Edward VI. But when the Catholic Mary Tudor ascended the English throne, Knox was ousted. He moved to Geneva, where he became a disciple of the Protestant theologian John Calvin. In 1559, Knox returned to Scotland in time to participate in the Protestant overthrow of its Catholic faith. He became minister of St Giles Church, only a stone's throw away from Mary's Palace of Holyroodhouse. His stipend was met by the sale of the church's textile wealth, with the burgh's council ordaining that:

The vestments and kirk gear be gathered up and sold with diligence and, of the ready money they fetched, around fifty pounds, to be dispersed and delivered by Master James Watson to John Knox, to refund and repay him again.

The following year, under Knox's ministry, the council of St Giles ordered that 'the idol of Saint Giles be cut out from the town's standard and a thistle put in its place.'[12]

Knox's sermons against idolatry were designed to fuel unease at the power of a Catholic queen as well as a loathing of Catholic iconography. He protested against any show of material vanity using Mary as his quarry. He criticised her dress, denounced her behaviour and regularly railed against her Catholicism.

Mary had returned to a Scotland that was being moulded by a morally censorious reformist agenda. With the Catholic faith proscribed and the alliance with France unravelling, any hold on political and religious stability was fast dissolving. The fourteen months that had elapsed between the death of Marie de Guise and Mary taking up her reign in person was time enough for Protestant allegiance to strengthen and consolidate. The country experienced a period not just of monarchical absence, but collapse. No one knew, however, whether Scotland's embrace of Protestantism would be short-lived. In England, the change of monarchy from Edward VI to Mary Tudor, and from Mary Tudor to Elizabeth, had seen Protestant England returned to Rome and then revert to Protestantism all in just over a decade. Now Scotland was to have a Catholic queen, and with her arrival its religious future seemed uncertain.

Knox's determination to sustain Protestantism in Scotland was threatened not only by Mary's refusal to adopt the Protestant faith, but also by the fact that she represented the hope of Catholic Europe that she would effect a reversal of Protestantism in Scotland and, if she was named Elizabeth's successor, England too. Knox was appalled that James Stewart – Mary's older, Protestant half-brother, the illegitimate son of her father, James V – had promised Mary, before she left France, that she and her French retinue would be allowed to practise their faith unmolested in Scotland and hear mass in the privacy of the royal chapels. The continuance of mass, albeit in the confines of the court, was a privilege to which Knox was vehemently opposed.

At the first mass Mary attended in the palace chapel, a group of reformers gathered, shouting that they had come to murder the officiating priest. Only the intervention of James Stewart prevented violence. Unnerved by the incident, and all too conscious of the fractious and violent escalation of the religious war in France, on the very next day Mary issued a proclamation to allay fears that she might force a religious reversal:

Charging all and sundry [of] our Sovereign Lady's subjects that they contain themselves in quietness, and that none of them take upon hand privately nor quietly to make any alteration in the religion or attempt anything against the form which was publicly and universally standing at the arrival of the Queen's Grace's coming home, under pain of death.[13]

The following week, Mary made the traditional ceremonial entrée into the city of Edinburgh. An entrée, the most public of royal ceremonies, was a ritual welcome accorded by each city to its new sovereign. It comprised a series of dramatic interludes played out in classical and mythological allusion, designed to endorse the temporal and spiritual legitimacy of the new ruler. The Council of Edinburgh was tardy in its preparations. It was not until the week before that it finalised its budget, agreed on the nature of its tableaux, confirmed its dignitaries' attire and settled on its gift to their queen. Its burgh and guild members were summarily kitted out in black. Sixteen officials were chosen for the honour of bearing the queen's processional canopy – the symbol of civic protection – which was to be made of purple velvet and fringed in gold, its bearers costumed in crimson doublets and long black velvet coats and bonnets. Young men of the town were advised to find their own outfits but were requested to wear taffeta or some other silk fabric.

The entrée began in the traditional way with, on the eve of the main procession, the firing of cannons, the lighting of bonfires on surrounding hills and a twelve-hour banquet. For the main public event – the progress through the city – Mary rode flanked by her sixteen crimson-clad officials, accompanied by an escort of fifty local young men dressed as Moors, who had been recruited as her guard of honour.

The procession took the age-old route, beginning at Edinburgh Castle and progressing down the High Street to the Palace of Holyroodhouse. This represented more than a journey between two royal residences. It was a physical manifestation of the territory shared by community and crown. The tableaux that punctuated it were purposefully erected at sites of political, commercial and social significance: the royal palaces, the Mercat Cross, the Butter Tron, the Tolbooth. Entrées were much more than celebratory rituals: they were dramatic interpretations of the relationship between crown and state, translated into a visual conversation.

Edinburgh's Council had been elected the previous October and was largely Protestant. Once in post, its officials had established religious reform with alacrity: proscribing the mass, ordering friaries to be demolished, erasing Catholic iconography. Now it seized the opportunity to subvert Mary's entrée and promote a Protestant agenda. The event seemed to follow the tropes expected of it. There was the tableau of beautifully costumed young women personifying the virtues desirable in a monarch: Prudence, Justice, Temperance and Fortune. A boy dressed as an angel descended from a mechanically operated cloud to hand Mary the keys of the city in an act of symbolic fealty. A fountain spurted wine that was drunk by key participants to signify the shared hope of continuing prosperity. There were the usual decorative triumphal archways.

Other elements, however, were deliberately loaded with Protestant assertions. At the Palace of Holyroodhouse, where Mary's city burghers, or burgesses as they were known in Scotland, presented her with their gift of gold plate, children made speeches against the mass and sang Protestant psalms. One pageant dramatised the Old Testament story of Korah, Dathan and Abiram: rebels who suffered the wrath of God for their idolatry. The boy angel who presented Mary with the keys of the city also gave her a psalter and bible, both written in the vernacular. The verse which accompanied his gift was pointed:

> A gift more precious could we none present
> Nor yet more needful to your Excellence
> Which is God's laws his words and testament
> Truly translated with fruitful diligence

As Knox was pleased to note, 'when the Bible was presented, and the praises thereof declared, she began to frown for shame she could not refuse it'.[14]

Among such barbs there were others that were more confrontational. A dragon was burnt on a scaffold – a seemingly innocuous theatrical diversion inspired by a mythological past. But its selection was deliberately provocative. The dragon was a controversial figure in sixteenth-century theology. It appears in the Book of Revelation, the final book of the New Testament, where it symbolises the evil destroyer of God's people. The narrative is a complex one, concerning a woman crowned with stars who is saved from the dragon's fire but is sent into the wilderness. Her newborn son is taken away from her and put under God's protection and the dragon cast out. Martin Luther, the Protestant leader, had interpreted the passage as the prophetic triumph of the true religion over the papal Antichrist. And the painter and print maker Lucas Cranach the Elder who illustrated Luther's translation of the New Testament depicted the dragon as the Antichrist in a papal tiara, an image which was widely circulated at the time. The burning of the dragon was a blatant warning to Mary of the retribution that would be meted out to her if she revoked her promise to uphold the new religion. (An earlier plan, to burn an effigy of a priest dressed in his vestments in the act of blessing the Holy Eucharist, had been vetoed by the Catholic Earl of Huntly). The threat inherent in the dragon's destruction would have been readily understood by its audience. This was not just bravado, but insolence. To the newly arrived young queen, accustomed to the deference shown to her at the French court, a queen of divine right and appointed by God to rule, such a flagrant lack of respect must have been frightening. It demonstrated the confidence of Edinburgh's Council that it was prepared to so publicly undermine the conciliatory tradition of the monarch's entrée in order to drive home its message.

As a Catholic, Mary was marginalised from the main body of her court and her government. Under the Treaty of Edinburgh of 1560, the French had been removed from any office of authority, and the Reformist revolt had seen Catholic Scottish nobles become a minority. Mary sensed her religious isolation most keenly on the first anniversary of François's death in December 1561. To honour it, she asked her nobility to don mourning clothes and invited them to attend François's memorial service in the chapel of the Palace of Holyroodhouse. They did neither. Mary's personal feeling of abandonment must have been acute; their demonstrative lack of regard and compassion was chastening. In the sixteenth century, politics were personal. There were no organisations to act as brokers between monarchs and their subjects, between the governing council and their queen. Relationships were intensely and simultaneously personal and political. This created a complex web of loyalty and intimacy that was challenging to navigate. Moreover, the narrow social network of kinship established in the Scottish court bred a culture of reciprocal fealty. Whatever ruptures or alliances emerged had personal as well as political repercussions.

Mary was isolated not only as a queen and a Catholic, but also as a woman. Her sex excluded her from the ingrained and traditional male culture of the Scottish court. By the mid-sixteenth century women's right and capacity to rule was a hot topic of debate, so she was subject to closer judgement. One of her most incendiary challengers was Knox. Never one to mince his words, Knox had denounced women's right to monarchy with the arrogance of male certitude:

To promote a woman to bear rule, superiority, dominion or empire above any realm, nation or city is repugnant to nature, contumely [insulting] to God, a thing most contrarious to His revealed will and approved ordinance, and finally it is the subversion of good order, of all equity and justice.[15]

Mary epitomised all that Knox deplored: a female monarch, a Catholic, shaped by what he saw as the dissolute court of France. His opinion of her was damning: 'If there be not in her a proud mind, a crafty wit, and an indurate heart against God and His truth, my judgment faileth me'.[16] Mary and her French household became the focus of Knox's diatribes against corruption in the kingdom. When famine broke out he laid its cause at Mary's door:

And so did God, according to the threatening of his law, punish the idolatry of our wicked Queen, and our ingratitude, that suffered her to defile the land with that abomination again, that God so potently had purged, by the power of his word. For the riotous feasting, and excessive banqueting, used in Court and country, wheresoever that wicked woman repaired provoked God to strike the staff of bread, and to give his malediction upon the fruits of the earth.[17]

Mary met Knox on four occasions, encounters in which she tried to defend her right to practise her personal piety untrammelled by interference. But to no avail: Knox remained her fiercest critic. On one occasion, Mary became so frustrated at his intransigence that she was reduced to tears in his presence.

It seems that Mary had been well aware of the Protestant criticism she might encounter in Scotland even before she left France. Sensitive to the disquiet her continuing Catholicism might provoke, she resolved to be circumspect. In France, Mary had ready access to exquisite Catholic textile opulence. But she brought to Scotland only one set of church textiles. It signalled compliance. Although she could have imported the finest of French ecclesiastical textiles, she contented herself with this sole set:

A chasuble of crimson velvet furnished only with a stole and fanon… a cloth of crimson velvet to hang above the altar and another to hang below wherein there is a crucifix and the Queen's arms and the rest ornamented with gold embroidery ... a rug of the same velvet lined with buckram ... a corporal case of embroidered crimson velvet. [18]

Such a paucity of church textiles messaged to her court that Mary had no intention of encouraging a restitution of Catholic materiality or of flaunting the finery of her own faith; that she was prepared to respect religious change. Even the little she brought remained in storage until 1565. Moreover, in the first years of her personal reign in Scotland, Mary demonstrated her acceptance of the new religion in a variety of ways. She redistributed church revenues that the crown received from its beneficiaries to Protestant coffers to help cover the costs of preachers' salaries. When the Jesuit papal nuncio pressed for a meeting she did her best to discourage him, and although she did eventually agree to see him, she was careful to conduct the audience in English rather than Latin – a language she was well versed in – so others could follow their conversation and witness her reticence. When he requested that Scotland send a representative to the 1563 Council of Trent, where delegates of the Catholic Churches of Europe were to gather to debate the reform of the church, Mary refused. And, while the Scottish queen's household was mainly composed of French Catholics, Mary ensured that the majority of her Privy Councillors were Protestant. She even attended a Protestant baptism. In 1562, spurred on by her half-brother James Stewart, she oversaw the diminution of one of the most powerful Catholic dynasties in Scotland.

George Gordon, the Catholic fourth Earl of Huntly was the son of an illegitimate daughter of James IV and tied by blood to Mary herself. As Lord Lieutenant of the North, he controlled territories from Inverness to Aberdeen and in 1546 had been appointed Chancellor of Scotland. To the reformist lords, he was a dark shadow looming over their ambition to control the country with a pro-English Protestant agenda. Huntly, through an intermediary, had suggested to Mary that, on her return to Scotland, she should disembark at Aberdeen, not Leith, where he would be waiting with an army to lead Mary in Catholic triumph into her realm. Mary had declined the offer, but Huntly remained a dangerous adversary to the Protestant cause. He controlled much of the north of Scotland which, to the reformers' frustration, remained largely Catholic.

In the autumn of 1562, Mary set out on a northern progress. There had been growing hostility between Huntly and James Stewart, and one of the aims of the progress was to subdue the Catholic earl. It was not only Huntly but his son, John Gordon, whose wings needed to be clipped. After a serious altercation with another noble, John Gordon had been imprisoned. But he had escaped to the family seat in the north and refused to comply with the command to give himself up. When he was threatened with being outlawed, he retaliated, raised a thousand followers and stalked Mary on her progress. It was rumoured that he planned to murder James Stewart, abduct the queen, and force a marriage between himself and Mary. Unwillingly embroiled in his son's defiance, Huntly also found himself threatened with exile and the forfeiture of his titles and lands. Undoubtedly prompted by James Stewart, Mary refused Huntly's proffered attempts at conciliation and armed combat became inevitable.

At the Battle of Corrichie on 28 October 1562, Mary's troops, led by James Stewart, were victorious. Huntly died in the field of battle, having collapsed from apoplexy. Two of his sons were slain. John Gordon, said to be 'in the flower of his youth', was captured, imprisoned, tried and executed. The power of the northern Catholic clans was culled. Two shiploads of Huntly's belongings were appropriated by the Crown and shipped from Aberdeen to Leith, where their cargo was divided up between Mary and James Stewart. Among them were the textiles from

St Machar's cathedral that had been given to Huntly for safe-keeping.

At the end of that month and into November, Mary ordered quantities of black velvet, taffeta and other black cloth: nearly 200 ells, all told. More black braid, fringing and trimmings were purchased. Her palace walls were re-draped, new black tablecloths and cushions made; chairs, stools and coffers re-covered in black. With the second anniversary of François's death approaching, it seems that Mary was determined to display her loss in a way that could not be ignored. Huntly and his sons' deaths in such a short space of time perhaps intensified Mary's sorrow by echoing at the deaths of Henri II and his son François. Whatever the motive, Mary spared Huntly's other sons.[19]

It was not the end of Huntly's story, however. His body was embalmed with spices and transported to Edinburgh. Nearly eight months after his death, it was his body that was put on trial:

The coffin was set upright, as if the Earl stood upon his feet, and upon it a piece of good black cloth with his [coat of] arms pinned fast. His accusation being read, his proctor answering for him, as if himself had been alive ... The verdict was given that he was found guilty ... Immediately hereupon the good black cloth that hung over the coffin was taken away, and in its place a worse hanged on, the arms torn in pieces in sight of the people.[20]

The act of destroying cloth that was emblazoned with the heraldic devices of a defeated adversary was a traditional ritual designed as a dramatic deterrent to other potential traitors. But for Mary, this public destruction of Huntly's embroidered emblems had other advantages. It sent a clear message to her court and her people that their queen put the safety of her realm and her person before her own religion. It also, and perhaps even more significantly, signalled to Elizabeth that Mary could and would protect the Protestant religion of the kingdom she ruled over: that she was fit to be Elizabeth's successor. The Huntly humiliation, however, would have been challenging for Mary, a Catholic queen, to sanction. Through her actions, Mary hoped to safeguard the political and religious equilibrium in her realm and demonstrate her trust in her political mentor, James Stewart. What she was opposing was not Huntly's Catholicism but his political arrogance; but in her destruction of his power, she risked losing Catholic support in Scotland and on the continent.

The reformers, despite their ambition and determination, lacked the infrastructure and resources to dismantle Scottish Catholicism overnight and establish widespread change. This was no sudden national spiritual conversion. Pockets of the country, particularly in the north, continued to practise the old religion, albeit in more muted or covert form. Some religious orders were allowed to remain, their buildings becoming dilapidated, their numbers dwindling over the natural course of time. In 1560, Knox and others produced a template for the new Protestant Scotland. *The First Book of Discipline* set out the nature of the organisation and implementation of Scotland's reformed church. It promoted a democratic agenda. There was to be education for all, extensive distribution of poor relief and congregational governance. They encouraged group worship which could be witnessed and shared by all. Despite such laudable aims, the Calvinist culture they imposed was founded on something much more insidious: moral censure. It gave greater licence to defamatory rumour and community judgement. This was a creed that proposed controlling and monitoring private conduct through public shaming, and introduced the practices of public confession, humiliation and punishment. While it would take another fifty years before the recommendations of *The First Book of Discipline* were fully adopted, it heightened scrutiny of personal and public behaviour. The pulpit became the central locus of condemnation, and Knox was foremost in using it for his inflammatory sermonising.

Subsequent centuries have shown that the most savage purge of Catholic materiality was exacted on Scotland's ecclesiastical textiles. Here, little was spared. To destroy a priest's vestments or a monk's habit, not only divested wearers of their visible claim to spiritual authority, but also discharged the cloth itself of any presumed divine agency. The same was true of the destruction of Catholic sacred textiles.

The Scottish Reformation not only destroyed Catholic material and spiritual culture, but also the memory of it. Although England's Reformation and the dissolution of its monasteries had led to a widespread clearance of religious artefacts, it did not lead – as in Scotland – to their widespread disappearance. Many English ecclesiastical textiles remained in circulation. There was money to be had in the spoils of religious disaffection, and England had an entrepreneurial network of merchants and artisans quick to transform the church's material wealth into something serviceable and desirable for a market eager for finery. Tailors and embroiderers bought up what they could to refashion into secular splendour. Church ornaments were altered to suit civic consumers, and vestments were refashioned. Noble families retrieved the ecclesiastical gifts they had bestowed and reinstated them within their own households. Others were purchased or confiscated to augment textiles in grand houses. In England, as was reported at the time, 'many private men's parlours were hung with copes instead of carpets'.[21]

In 1560, the Church of the Holy Trinity in Chester sold its vestments to a theatrical troupe of players, while the warden of the church in Chelmsford rented its sacred robes to visiting actors.[22] Sometimes the vestments themselves were destroyed, but their embellishments saved. Treasury accounts record payments to goldsmiths for the burning of vestments to extricate the gold and silver gilt used in their embroidery.[23] Although the churches themselves were denuded of their finery, many stored their textiles out of sight while inventories were made by the officials sent to calculate the value of what was owned. The most precious items were sent to swell the coffers of the crown. At the English court, Catholic visual splendour continued unabated. Henry VIII and Elizabeth had no qualms about dressing their Protestant faith in the confiscated glory of Catholic ecclesiastical magnificence, and amplified their own chapel furnishings with those stripped from monasteries and cathedrals. England's Reformation engendered more of an alteration of ownership than an elimination of Catholic materiality, and vestiges of its spiritual heritage were salvaged.

Not so in Scotland. Scotland suffered long-term cultural damage. The Reformation ruptured the history of its arts and crafts and the continuity of its craft practice: its skills, designs, traditions and techniques. Much of its artistic heritage was lost, and with it a uniquely Scottish visual and symbolic vocabulary. The material expressions of sensuality, emotion, imagination and creative delight were all but eliminated and, in time, forgotten. Not only was Scotland's creative legacy erased, but also the patronage of religious arts and crafts. It left limited, and solely secular, opportunities for Scottish artists and artisans. Its artists were no longer asked to paint the vision of heaven on frescoed walls or evoke the colours of paradise in stained glass; embroiderers were no longer tasked with conjuring the ecstasy of saints or the suffering of Christ in meditative stitches.

Blairs Museum in Aberdeenshire, the only Catholic museum in Britain, displays some of the few survivors of Scottish pre-Reformation church textiles in its collection. Its curator, Elinor Vickers, is guardian to three sets of fifteenth- and sixteenth-century vestments, one of them rumoured to be associated with Mary. A red velvet fifteenth-century chasuble is thought to have been used by the church in Corgarff, a hamlet in the Grampian mountains. It depicts a medley of saints whose silk stitched faces are slashed – damaged, it is thought, by an act of Reformist iconoclasm. Another chasuble depicts the life of St Anne, the mother of the Virgin Mary and the patron saint of tailors. It too originated in the north of Scotland. What is astonishing about these vestments is their sharpness of colour, the continuing gloss of their silk thread. Surprising, too, is the expressiveness of their embroidery: saints' faces sewn to capture distinct personalities: the shape of a collar or the decorative pattern of a cope precisely detailed. One set is pieced from different embroideries: this set is thought to be connected to Mary, possibly containing a piece from her era, maybe even an embroidery wrought by the queen herself. But this has never been verified and textile experts are sceptical. With scant knowledge of how these vestments came to be in Scotland and little certainty that they are Scottish in origin, experts feel it is more likely that they were created elsewhere in Europe and brought to Scotland either prior to the Reformation, or in later centuries to replace those that had been lost.

Those rare remnants of Scotland's discarded faith that were salvaged were housed in grand houses, inaccessible to most of the population. Scotland's church interiors became dulled by a severe aesthetic. Domestic decoration focussed on moral tales or personal emblems; portraits of John Knox began to adorn the walls.

As Mary progressed through her realm at the start of her personal reign in Scotland in 1561, the queen must have felt uneasy. This was a country physically and visibly scarred by political and religious adversity. The despoilment of its architecture wrought by English armies and Scotland's own internal battles would have been disheartening: a landscape denuded of its material beauty and sensory identity. In 1563 the Scottish poet and Keeper of the Privy Seal of Scotland, Richard

Maitland of Lethington, mourned the passing of Scotland's Pre-Reformation culture in a lament that would have echoed across the land and sounded in Mary's heart.

> Where is the blitheness that has been,
> Both in town and country seen,
> Among lords and ladies shined,
> Dancing, singing, game, and play?
> But now I know not what they mean:
> All merriment is worn away.[24]

In 1573, the General Assembly of the Scottish Kirk declared:

We think all kinds of embroidery unseemly, all colours of velvet, in gown, hose, or coat and all superfluous and vain cutting out, stitching with silk ... costly sewing on of lace and braids ... light and variant hues in clothing, as red, blue, yellow and such like ... all kinds of gowns, doublets or breeks of velvet, satin, taffeta and such like.[25]

# 3
## Two Dolls' Dresses Made of Grey Damask Threaded in Gold

My mother has lit a bonfire in the garden. She is burning the memorabilia of my childhood: old school jotters, tattered teddies, pop-star posters, the dolls my sisters and I tucked up at night. My father's unexpected death, only a few weeks earlier, has left her virtually penniless. The family home must be sold, and we must downsize. A small flat is all that can be afforded, a flat too small to accommodate everything the family has accumulated over the last twenty years. For my mother, this clearing out is practical but also cathartic; an act of protest against a future she has not chosen. With my father nearing retirement and me, at nineteen, near the finishing-line of care, she had anticipated liberation from the daily grind of motherhood, time at last for her, for them, to travel and talk. Instead, she now needs me at home and faces a continuum of maternal duties. I am dispatched to join my sisters for a while in London and leave her free to 'sort things out'. I had no idea she had a bonfire in mind.

It turned out that my mother's burning of our belongings was random, with only small consideration given for what might be precious. On my return, I discovered a home emptied of its familiar, nostalgic clutter – the fairy stories I had pencilled as a child, the stamp albums redolent with future discovery, the hoard of illicit Beatles bubble gum wrappers – and in their place was absence, a paucity of material memory. Her destruction was not wholesale, however. Some things had escaped the flames, among them a doll I had made as a child. It was dressed in brittle lace, a fabric that had once belonged to a grandmother I had never known. I still have that doll, a touchstone of a time of loss when I was on the cusp between settled family life and a different future.

In a 1578 inventory of Mary's possessions, among her books, clothing, jewellery and accessories was a basket of what were described as 'pippennis'. More were unearthed in a coffer, which contained:

certain replicas of women called *pippennis*, being fourteen in number, large and small. There are fifteen farthingales for them; nineteen outer gowns, kirtles, and skirt fronts; a bundle of shirts, sleeves, stockings and slippers, a bundle with furnishings for a doll's bed, and another bundle of little conceits and trifles made from bits of gauze and other fabric and two dozen and a half masks'.[1]

It was the Scottish research and history consultant, Michael Pearce, who made the lateral leap. He connected these entries with two others in an earlier wardrobe account compiled during Mary's reign. In September 1563, Servais de Conde, Mary's *valet de chambre*, recorded that he had issued: 'Jacques [de Soulis] the tailor with two small pieces of grey damask decorated with gold to make a gown for a *poupine*', and 'three quarters and a half ells of cloth of silver and white silk to make a petticoat, and other things for the *poupines*'.[2]

Historians who have made any mention of these *pippennis* or *poupines* have hitherto translated the word as 'puppets'. Although in the courts of sixteenth-century Europe Italian marionettes were beginning to make an appearance, most puppeteers used glove puppets designed as stock characters, with their costumes and facial features an intrinsic part of their persona and performance. The *pippennis* and *poupines* that Mary had in her care were not only dressed in different outfits, but were also provided with new garments by her court tailor. They were, in fact, dolls.

These inventoried dolls might have been kept by Marie de Guise as mementos of her daughter's childhood, or brought back by Mary from France as nostalgic reminders of her girlhood there. But fourteen or more dolls seems to suggest something more than a sentimental attachment. Their interchangeable wardrobe indicates that these dolls were dressed and re-dressed. Moreover, their new clothes were not fashioned from the redundant scraps in a tailor's rag bag, but from cloth inventoried because of its value. They must have had some purpose in court culture.

It is likely that the dolls' function was to facilitate Mary and her women in the rehearsal of female participation in court festivities and ceremonials. Substantive evidence is frustratingly elusive. This possibility, however, is reinforced by the presence of the thirty masks packed away with the dolls' clothes and accessories. Adult masks and masking costumes are listed in a separate section of the inventory. If the thirty masks were for the dolls, it suggests that they not only had changes of clothes but of costumes; that they were used as miniature replicas of Mary and her entourage. Using dolls, the women could rehearse their roles in court revelries. Their entrances and exits, their spacings and groupings could be choreographed. In a culture where the arrangement of colours and textures was an integral part of the visual message, dolls allowed Mary and her women to experiment with the visual impact of their public performances.

The dolls offer an insight into how women contributed to the cultural life of the court. It is a subject scarcely documented. Contemporary chroniclers had scant interest in women's culture as distinct from men's. Even modern historians of sixteenth-century Scotland are more interested in the complexity of political ambition and dynastic survival, and the dramatic turning points in Mary's life, rather than the details of female social and cultural interaction. There are, thankfully, some notable exceptions. But such insights are thin on the ground.

The existence of Mary's dolls, their clothes and accessories suggests that Mary and her retinue used alternative female tropes to those adopted by men to counteract the dominant male-centric culture of the Scottish court. Playing with dolls, while seeming innocuous – just a pastime of girlish pleasure – was possibly a way for these women to share creative ideas, direct their public appearances and ensure that the parts they played in the political diplomacy of court diversions and ritual ceremonies were effective and impactful.

In sixteenth-century Europe, dolls also showcased fashion. They were the precursors of fashion illustrations and catwalks, tools of sartorial forecasting. When the detail of fashion changed rapidly – the way you tied your sleeves, the shape of your headdress, the size of your ruff – your lack of knowledge of the latest vogues was easily betrayed. But dolls enabled women to keep abreast of recent trends and share their fashion intelligence across borders and cultures. They provided a lifeline for women distanced from the established centres of European style and a way for female visitors or newcomers to a foreign court to prepare appropriate wardrobes. Moreover, the clothes worn by a queen and their emulation by the women around her was strategic. A queen's clothes were agents of political power. As the arbiter of court fashion, a queen could reference not only modernity and sophistication but cultural and political connection. She could signal her influence over court culture through its adoption of her sartorial style.

In a visually curious and observant culture, there needed to be exactitude in replication. The fullness of a skirt, the shape of a sleeve and the placement of trimmings all demanded precision. Only the right material and the talent of experienced tailors could capture the shape and effect of specific garments and exactly register their colour, texture, luminosity and flow.

Given the inordinate expense of luxury fabrics, it was prudent for tailors to make miniature versions of new styles rather than create full-size examples.

The historian Yassana Croizat-Glazer, an arts adviser in New York, took the history of fashion dolls seriously. Her article '"Living Dolls": Francois I Dresses his Women' is an oasis in a research world parched of investigation into the covert culture of Renaissance women.[3] It is her scholarship and that of Michael Pearce that we have to thank for the stories of dolls sent from parents to their children, from grooms to their brides, from one woman to another. They reveal the significance of fashion dolls as mediums for acts of care, empathy and consolation.[4]

In 1396, the French queen, Isabeau of Bavaria, wife of Charles VI, paid her embroiderer 496 livres 16 sols to create dolls with different outfits for her daughter, the six-year-old Isabella de Valois, who had been sent to England as the queen of Richard II. It was an enormous sum, much more than would have been spent on any plaything, but these dolls were not just recreational. Their clothes – which would be translated by tailors into outfits for the young queen – emphasised her provenance. Such clothes were powerful props to aid her acceptance at court. It was essential that Isabella maintained her distinct and separate identity as a valuable political prize. Young as she was, she was not just an ambassador for France, but its personification. The clothes she wore proclaimed her nationality and status; but they also promoted the prosperity, cosmopolitan alliances and sophistication of her nation.

Husbands-to-be were also exercised in the expediency of sartorial exchange, although their motives were generally to ensure that their brides were outfitted in the fashion of the court that they were entering, rather than the one they had left behind. Henry IV of France responded to the request of his fiancée, Marie de' Medici, to send her a doll dressed in

## Two Dolls' Dresses Made of Grey Damask Threaded in Gold

fashionable attire, saying that he sent her a 'doll made by a very good tailor'. Philip II, when he became betrothed to Elisabeth de Valois, sent her dolls dressed in the current style of the Spanish court so that she could prepare her trousseau accordingly.

While the gifting of dolls was common practice among Renaissance male monarchs, not all the dolls they commissioned were as innocent as they seemed. Isabella d'Este, the Marchioness of Mantua in the late-fourteenth and early-fifteenth centuries, was renowned for her fashionable dress and thought to be the most glamorous among the contemporary European female elite; her style was much emulated. In 1515, the French king François I requested her to send him a doll ... dressed in the fashions that suit you of shirts, sleeves, undergarments, outer garments, dresses, headdresses, and hairstyles that you wear'.

The letter explained that the king desired the doll in order to have its clothes copied for the women of his court. But François I was a notorious and flagrant lover of women, a collector of beauties. He purposefully decorated his court with female allure and indulged his own sexual appetite with a raft of mistresses. He had once attempted to meet Isabella d'Este, but had been rebuffed. His need of a doll was, perhaps, a ruse to secure a possession of sorts. Isabella did send him his doll, but her response was terse. She replied that 'his Majesty will not see anything new, for the styles we wear are equally worn in Milan by the Milanese ladies.'[5]

Dolls were also exchanged as sisterly acts, as a support to other women who found themselves having to navigate the delicate path of assimilation into alien courts. And the dolls they gifted sometimes offered empathy as well as support. In 1564, Catherine de' Medici planned to despatch dolls with different costumes as gifts for Elizabeth. She reputedly sent the English queen another doll as a token of sympathy on the death in 1584 of one of Elizabeth's suitors, the French Duke of Anjou and Alençon. It was dressed in a black mourning dress, and the English queen was said to have copied its mourning clothes for her own attire. At the time of her gift, Catherine herself was a widow dressed in black, a colour she cleaved to until her death. When Henri and François died, she had her tailors re-clothe at least two of her dolls in mourning dress. Her inventory of 1589 states that of the fifteen dolls found, two were dressed in mourning garb and another five in black. She kept these small, sorrowful companions for the rest of her days.[6]

Dolls, like those belonging to Mary and Catherine, were often treasured through life and recorded in the inventories of the women who owned them. On the death of Queen Juana of Spain in 1555, two dolls in elaborate dresses and over-gowns lined with fur were found among her possessions. Three dolls, described as 'babies', were discovered amongst the belongings of Jane Seymour, the third of Henry VIII's wives, at her death in 1537, one dressed in a gown of cloth of silver and a green velvet kirtle, and the others in gowns of crimson satin and white velvet.[7]

When their garments became outdated and they were no longer needed for fashion reference, some dolls were handed down to children. There are a few charming sixteenth-century portraits of little girls carrying their inherited dolls. The twenty-three-month-old Arbella Stuart was painted in 1577 clutching a doll clothed in outmoded fashion. Catharina van Warmondt's portrait was made in 1596 when she was two years old. She holds the weight of her doll in the crook of her arm, and its rigid gown heavy with black velvet and gold braid is similar to one Mary might have worn decades earlier. The 1582 portrait of six-year-old Louise Juliana of Orange-Nassau has her and her doll wearing matching gowns of crimson and silver. Marie of Saxony (dates unknown), who died when she was four years old, was painted after her death standing beside her two older sisters. The doll she carries is a miniature version of herself as she might have been, had she lived. It is a memorial for the woman she would never become.

There is only one extant sixteenth-century fashion doll. Its provenance is uncertain but it is thought to have belonged either to Catherine of Sweden or Christina of Holstein-Gottorp, the second wife of the Swedish king, Charles IX. Although its colours have faded, the underside of its garments harbours enough of their original hue to gauge its original vibrancy. The doll's gown is of purple silk, hemmed in blue and braided in gold lace. Her red silk sleeves are couched in gold thread to form a lozenge pattern. Each lozenge is studded with a pearl. Pearls are also incorporated in the doll's tiny gold diadem and her doll hands are tucked into a red muff minutely embroidered with gold and silver fleur-de-lis. Under her gown, the doll wears petticoats: one of pink, the other of gold velvet trimmed with silver lace. Her hair is human, her facial features embroidered in silk. The attentiveness to detail is impressive, alerting us to just how assiduously such dolls were studied as exemplars of fashion. The tailor and embroiderer who crafted her took care to recreate her attire in microscopic precision. Just 16cm tall, this solitary known survivor of sixteenth-century female sartorial culture is now in the collection of *Livrustkammaren* (Royal Armoury) Museum in Stockholm.

Maureen Payne is an American artist and craftsperson who is fascinated by Renaissance culture. Through her blog *Tudorosities* and her YouTube channel of the same name, she shares her interest and curiosity in all things Tudor by exploring and recreating its material culture. In 2013, she decided to take on the challenge of replicating the fashion doll in the Stockholm Museum. The reproduction of the doll's extensive and complicated layering of detachable clothing proved time-consuming and technically complex. Sourcing fabric that best mimicked the quality of the doll's clothes was difficult, particularly given the plethora of materials used: at least thirty, including a variety of fabrics, lace, beads, ribbon and silk thread. She found the intricate frills of lace hardest to reproduce, eventually resorting to wire as it gave her the control and flexibility to imitate their delicate patterning. But the real challenge lay in the small scale: the fiddly pleating, the intricacy of the embroidery. It was a brave experiment. What it revealed was the amount of concentrated work required to create the doll. It was testament to the skill of the doll's original creators, who wrought such a tiny and exact replica of sixteenth-century fashion. Their persistence was an accolade to their craft.[8]

In the Scotland of the 1560s, Mary discovered a court dominated by an ingrained male culture. Women's agency had been diminished. On being widowed, both Margaret Tudor and Marie de Guise had struggled and failed to retain power in a country shaped by men. Moreover, Scotland had evolved its own emphatically male culture based on belligerent confrontation and kinship. Its reputation was for fearless fighters. The battles of Flodden, Solway Moss and Pinkie Cleugh had seen the decimation of Scottish men: 10,000 were slain at Flodden alone, and thousands more at the Battle of Pinkie Cleugh. A generation of male Scottish aristocracy had been wiped out. Those who were left carried the banner of sacrifice not in unity but in factional adversity and partisanship. Scottish male supremacy fed on personal slights, energised by clan feuds and glorified by tales of vengeful reprisals. It was an unusually volatile kingdom where male virility was played out through physical violence. Men's power was vested in the land they owned and lorded over, in the positions they held as chiefs, lairds, earls, beneficiaries of ecclesiastical property or keepers of royal residences. These were jealously guarded and vehemently protected, not just through law but through brutal assault.

Male virility was also expressed through sexual dalliance.

Among the nobility, until Protestantism took hold, male sexual encounters outside of marriage were accepted, even expected in a king. The mistresses and illegitimate children of Scottish monarchs were generally acknowledged and accommodated at court. Mary's father, James V, had enjoyed numerous sexual liaisons from a young age, encouraged, it is said, by nobles hoping to distract him from any interference in political affairs. Of his illegitimate children, those who were raised at court looked to Marie de Guise as their surrogate mother, a role expected of the queen. Illegitimacy was no barrier to advancement, and the Scottish nobility had its fair share of aristocrats who owed their paternity and position to Mary's grandfather or father.

In the rugged landscape of Scotland, men were raised in resilience. These were men proud of their toughness, hardened by Scotland's rough terrain and its harsh and unforgiving climate; they could withstand the freeze of winter and the whip of the wind. They fought, adventured and hunted for the most part in exclusively male company. Scottish male material culture was manifested most emphatically through weaponry. This was clearly demonstrated in the largesse of the Earl of Arran who, upon his elevation to regent on the death of James V, gifted his kin – and those nobles whose loyalty he sought – with the dead king's swords, spears, crossbows, culverins, arrows and rapiers.[9]

But Scottish male identity was shaped by something more intangible than their arsenal of weapons. It encapsulated the idea of kinship, a tribal bond based not on social distinction, but on an honorific code of supportive reciprocity, based partly on blood ties but also rooted in service. This was a code upheld through generations and it brought laird and peasant together in an equal regard for protecting each other's honour. Although Scotland had no standing army, fighting troops could be readily mustered by this tradition of bond, an understanding of loyalty which required no explanation or debate. It was a faithfulness long practised. But it was a culture that Mary, given her gender and her French upbringing, was estranged and excluded from.

Having been under regency rule for nearly twenty years, with Mary's arrival the Scottish court could re-establish its monarchical focus. But this was to be a court different from those of the past. The youth, French upbringing and gender of Mary and her entourage inevitably and abruptly altered the court dynamic. The established balance of gender and age was overturned. The court found itself reinvigorated with youthful energy and sensuality. At its centre was its eighteen-year-old queen, surrounded by high-spirited women who, like Mary, were mere teenagers. They were not only unmarried and untethered to male discipline but, even less conventionally, they were uncowed by their sex. They made their presence felt to the outrage of John Knox, who decried the 'French fillocks, and fiddlers, and others of that band, going about the house alone where there might be seen skipping and dancing with 'joyouestie' not very comely for honest women'.[10]

The arrival of these young women heralded a new frisson at court which fuelled the heady atmosphere of fun. Thomas Randolph, the English ambassador, was exhilarated: 'My pen staggers, my hand fails further to write. I never found myself so happy, nor never so well treated'.[11] At forty-one years old, Randolph was seduced by the charms of the twenty-one-year-old Mary Beaton, who he wooed with alacrity. Other diplomats and nobles became equally besotted with their new-found playmates: John Sempill with Mary Fleming, Sir William Maitland with Mary Livingston. Like Randolph, these were men decades older than the girls they pursued. John Sempill was forty-four when he eventually won his prize, William Maitland eighteen years older than Mary Livingston. For a Scottish court, weighted as it was towards a masculine martial culture, the advent of such an intensely female one was a diversion. Unlike Knox, most did not view the high spirits of these young women as transgressions but as a welcome release.

Hospitality was key to the resurgence of a court newly regrouped around its sovereign. In Scotland, chivalric and cultural entertainments had been fostered by James IV and V as a political strategy to encourage social cohesion among politically disparate nobles. They had cultivated a Scotland re-invented as a kingdom of sophisticated discernment and hospitable largesse. For Mary, court revelries served a similar purpose, but they also allowed her informal opportunities to become acquainted with her nobles and visiting statesmen. Unlike in her council, which was dominated by men, in court entertainments she was indisputably at the centre as hostess and queen. Court diversions afforded her a more equitable arena to exercise her authority in a non-confrontational way.

In the sixteenth century, the political and the personal were intertwined. In a country as small as Scotland, relationships within and between dynastic units were inevitably further compressed. Elite families were tangled together in a dense network of historic alliances and kinship ties – legitimate and otherwise – which were difficult to infiltrate and hard to unravel. In such a climate, trust was a luxury few could afford. Mary had to be wary of appearing to favour one faction over another. Instead, she made her most intimate attachments with those of lower rank than her nobility, where there was less chance of confusing political alliance with personal amity. But it led to disaffection among her nobility, who felt usurped in her attentions by those they deemed inferior.

In his writings about Mary, George Buchanan, the Scottish humanist scholar and historian who practised reading Latin with her, accused the Scottish queen of hosting a 'constant succession of games and festivals' when 'the day was employed in tournaments and the night spent in masquerades'.[12] But through involving her nobility and foreign ambassadors in entertainments and ceremonies, Mary hoped to raise Scotland from its stupor of war weariness and inject greater social and political unity. Contemporary historians and commentators have made much of Mary's penchant for dancing, feasting and play-making, interpreting such diversions as the efforts of a vacuous queen intent on escaping her political duties. But in France Mary had learned that a repertoire of entertainments was not only a political tool, but a way for women to influence political diplomacy. Women were often used as political bait in the sixteenth century. François I had a 'fair band of ladies' to act as his spies and informants, to lure adversaries into traps of ill-considered confidences and, at times, unfortunate liaisons. Catherine de' Medici, on becoming regent of France in 1560, established her *escadron volant*, or Flying Squadron, a hand-picked band of eighty seductive women who were loyal to her and deployed to search out the secrets, frailties and disloyalties of Catherine's court. Mary's involvement of her entourage of women was less devious. She did not manipulate her female companions as agents of her own political advancement. But she did use the mask of informal fun to gather useful intelligence and create alliances that supported her political purpose.

When Margaret Tudor and Marie de Guise had begun their reigns as Scotland's queens, they were consorts of the king, not queens in their own right. They had, however, their own entourages, largely comprising the women and servants who had accompanied them from England and France respectively. When they were widowed and their power dwindled, their households metamorphosed over time to better suit the insecurities of the male regents who wrested power from them. Both experienced a culling of their female support, replaced by greater male surveillance. In the list of Marie de Guise's household compiled at the time of her death in June 1560, out of the ninety-seven named only eight were women.[13] This was not the case for Mary; she was free to determine the nature of her intimate circle. At its heart were the four Marys and their mothers and sisters – relationships sustained since childhood and strengthened by shared experiences. Her household, however, did change when she came to Scotland. We have the historian Rosalind Marshall to thank for her detailed analysis of its composition. In France, Mary had twenty-seven ladies-in-waiting, but only nine in Scotland; she had ten maids-of-honour in France but only seven at the Scottish court. Not only was their number diminished, but in Scotland they were also significantly younger and of lower status than their French counterparts.[14] The nucleus of Mary's household in Scotland continued to be French. While this might have been a comfort to Mary, it served to emphasise her foreignness. Moreover, the majority of her household was Catholic, and as such remained an insular group, largely unconnected to the thrust of Scottish, mostly Protestant, political activity.

Furthermore, in Scotland Mary had no legitimate kin. In France she had been surrounded by an extended family network of Guise and Valois relations, but in Scotland, she had no family to call her own. There were illegitimate relatives, but none of them shared her status. She also lacked the political and female mentors she had relied on in France; guidance sorely needed by an eighteen-year-old queen who found herself in a country which, despite being the place of her birth, was unfamiliar. In France she had Catherine de' Medici and Diane de Poitiers; in Scotland, her closest female associates and confidants were the four Marys, but they were of lowlier birth and were subservient to Mary as her ladies-in-waiting.

By upbringing and inclination, Mary was at heart a European. She had been educated in a cosmopolitan court with access to ideas and people from across Europe and the wider world. The elite women who frequented the Scottish court were, in the main, poorly educated, insular and untravelled and their marital and familial relationships sometimes compromised their loyalty to Mary. She made what female alliances she could with her half-sister Jean Stewart, the illegitimate daughter of her father, James V, and with Agnes Keith, who married James Stewart in 1562 and was herself a descendant of James I. She nurtured friendships with them and other women by eliciting their involvement in entertainments, celebrating their marriages and becoming godmother to some of their children.

It was to her half-brother, James Stewart, that Mary turned for guidance. In 1536 he had come close to becoming heir to the throne when his father, James V, had attempted to marry his mistress, James Stewart's mother, Margaret Erskine. But she already had a husband and the pope refused to grant an annulment. James Stewart, however, was an unreliable adviser. He was pro-English, firmly anchored to the Protestant cause and ambitious to be influential in Scotland's destiny. He was certainly no William Cecil, then Elizabeth's Secretary of State. Cecil saw his role as Elizabeth's mentor, the guardian of her sovereignty and safety. He advised, honoured and protected her. As a politician he was astute, loyal, devious and cultured. This was a man, unlike James Stewart, of sophisticated politics.

Mary found herself marooned and unprotected. In 1561, in a letter to Philip II of Spain, she described herself as 'the most afflicted woman under heaven, God having bereft me of all that I loved and held dear on earth and left me no consolation whatsoever'.[15] By 1563, she had become even more troubled, with Randolph reporting that 'for two months she has been melancholy diverse times, her grief is marvellously secret, and she often weeps when there is little apparent reason.'[16]

What Mary yearned for was a soulmate, and she hoped to find one in Elizabeth. In December 1561, Randolph had reported to Cecil of 'a reciprocal goodwill in my mistress towards yours, that I think for the present she has no friend in whom she puts more confidence, and not many to whom she will more frankly impart any of her affairs of any consequence'.[17] The English queen was Mary's closest blood relation – as cousins, they shared a dynastic lineage. Barring their religious differences, they had much in common. They were both rulers in their own name, independent of parents or husbands, and both were highly educated. These were women who epitomised their age, cultural mirrors of each other, who delighted in dancing, poetry and music. Through their correspondence they nurtured a curiosity in each other and a genuine sense of sisterhood. Mary hoped for and lobbied for a meeting, and was overjoyed when one was arranged for the late summer or early autumn of 1563. She wrote that:

This is the thing I have most desired, ever since I was in hope thereof ... by the time we have spoken together, our heads will be so eased that the greater grief that ever after shall be between us, will be when we shall take leave of each other and let God be my witness, I honour her in my heart, and love her as my dear natural sister.[18]

The postponement of the proposed meeting was a major setback both personally and politically for Mary. While other meetings were mooted, they too were abandoned. Mary's hope of finding female empathy with Elizabeth remained unfulfilled.

Eager to better understand the kind of life Mary experienced at the Scottish court, I arrange a private tour of her apartments with the palace's past and present curators, Deborah Clarke and Emma Thompson.

There have been many alterations to the Palace of Holyroodhouse since the sixteenth century, but the queen's apartments, created by Mary's father for Marie de Guise, remain much as they were. The three of us meander through the king's chambers on the first floor, which, although they retain the structure of their earlier incarnation, no longer house anything directly connected to the Scottish queen. We move swiftly on through and up to the second floor, to Mary's chambers. Here, remarkably little has changed in nearly 500 years. They comprise a cluster of small rooms: an outer chamber which originally contained an alcove as an oratory, a bed chamber, a supper room and Mary's cabinet room, a small chamber which the queen used as an office and a place of retreat. Even though the outer chamber – where she would have received guests and held small soirées – is the largest of the four, it is hardly spacious. The supper room is tiny, her cabinet room scarcely larger. Not much remains by way of original features apart from a handsome panelled ceiling in the outer chamber which is gloriously carved in the gilded emblems of the Stewart, Valois and Guise dynasties. And in Mary's bed chamber and cabinet room, the original stone fireplaces still survive.

I have a sensory leap back in time, to when a fire crackled and flamed in the grate of Mary's bed chamber, to a queen's bed festooned in densely embroidered cloth, its gold thread glimmering in the flare of the fire which catches at the colours of a silk stitched carpet. Add the gold of candle sconces and their flicker of candles, an embroidered counterpane, a velvet covering for a stool or two, the gleam of a polished wood coffer and the fragrance of beeswax and the room is transformed. It becomes a haven.

What strikes me above all – as it does most people who visit Mary's apartments – is their scale. This is a huddle of chambers. The staircase we climb up is spiralled and narrow – tricky to manoeuvre, one would imagine, in farthingales, the hooped petticoats popular at the time. And in Mary's bed chamber, Deborah and Emma pull a curtain aside to show me another, even narrower spiral staircase which connected the queen's apartments to those of the king below, and was strictly for their personal use.

Compared to the vast array of rooms at her disposal in the châteaux of France – the 400 rooms, for instance, that the

Château de Chambord could boast – the Palace of Holyroodhouse feels not just compact, but claustrophobic. In these small rooms Mary played out some of the most dramatic episodes of her reign. Due to the attentiveness of Mary's father and grandfather, the Palace of Holyroodhouse and Mary's other royal residences do not lack charm or Renaissance flourish. But they still betray their origins as fortresses. The thick walls of the Palace of Holyroodhouse seem to close in on themselves rather than spread out to sky-filled horizons. While its footprint includes extensive gardens, recently restored and recultivated, Mary would have viewed them through one of the small panes in the leaded windows. It would have afforded just a glimpse of nature, not the expansive vistas that French châteaux provided.

Deborah, Emma and I talk about what these rooms would have felt like to Mary. Were they claustrophobic, or did their small scale feel protective? Deborah explains that even in the Renaissance's grandest palaces it was normal for a monarch's private chambers to be intimate. And I think back to Diane de Poitiers' bed chamber at Chenonceau, which became Catherine de' Medici's, and yes, they were not much bigger than those Mary found at the Palace of Holyroodhouse, although in France the queen's apartments were more deeply buried within an expanse of outer grander rooms. The apartments of Renaissance kings and queens were designed as sanctuaries, domestic in scale, an escape from the grandiose public arenas of council chambers and ballrooms, from the sprawl of reception rooms and galleries; they were inner sanctums where monarchs could entertain their closest associates. While I understand the rationale, I still could not envisage how it worked in practice. Mary's apartments must have shrunk when inhabited by even a small group of people, the women in their expansive skirts and ruffs, the men in their padded doublets and short capes. Add some servants, a musician or two and it must surely have been a tight squeeze.

The layout of Mary's apartments is curious. Her supper and cabinet rooms are part of her bed chamber, accommodated in its right and left corners. Deborah tells me that David Rizzio, Mary's private secretary, worked alongside the queen in her cabinet room and dealt with her correspondence there, much of it politically sensitive. Such tasks demanded privacy. But, given the location of the room, it is no wonder that his regular attendance in such an intimate space bred suspicion, and rumours of a liaison. In the Renaissance court, so enthusiastic about display and revelation, what was hidden was always suspect. Deborah says that there were reports of Rizzio sometimes sleeping in this room. After an evening of company and conversation, music and gambling, drowsy from the smog of the fire and heavy with wine, it is easy to see how tempting it must have been to slump in the cabinet room rather than navigate the treacherous narrow spiral stairs. But it led to speculation.

Thick with the comings and goings of the court – the household staff, dignitaries, musicians, court administrators, courtiers and others who scurried in and out – the palace must, at times, have seemed crowded with commotion. With such insistent clamour, Mary must have longed for space, for peace. And she must also have yearned, if not for solitude, then at least for privacy. On 3 September 1561, two weeks after she arrived in Scotland, Mary bought nearly sixty ells of green cloth to line the walls of her cabinet room.[19] Her purchase of the cloth was a priority because her cabinet room was to become her refuge: the place where she wrote her letters, where she read and where, as Randolph reported, she went to cry.[20]

In this room Mary installed a cabinet of curiosities. Randolph described it as 'her secret cabinet where she kept those things she esteems either for antiquity, novelty, or that she takes pleasure in'.[21] A cabinet of curiosities was a relatively new phenomenon in the sixteenth century: a series of small cupboards that harboured keepsakes, exotic specimens, small portraits and other items of personal interest. It was a material archive which, unlike those in the museums of later centuries, demanded to be touched. In the sixteenth century, tactile exploration – the sensory discovery of texture, temperature, weight and feel – was thought to be a conduit to deeper thought and emotion: information gathered through the experience, not just the viewing, of objects. The organisation of the items collected was sometimes purposely random, as it was the happenchance of their juxtaposition which provided stimulus. The jostling together of the familiar and the strange provoked surprising associations and connections. This was an appreciation of objects as a form of mental and emotional travel which, for Mary, enabled a vicarious enjoyment of wider horizons than those afforded by the Scottish court. In Scotland, she must have missed the easy access to the continental culture of the French court. In his memoirs, James Melville of Halhill, the Scottish diplomat, noted her sense of cultural isolation, saying 'she had a quick spirit, curious to know and get intelligence of the estates of other countries and would sometimes be sad when she was solitary, and glad of the company of them that travelled to other parts'.[22]

Mary was well acquainted with the fascinating allure of cabinets of curiosities. At the Château de Blois in France, François I had what was called a *studiolo*: an Italian-inspired room lined with gilded panelling in which there were four concealed cabinets that could only be opened by a hidden mechanism. In them he kept *objets d'art* and specimens from adventuring explorers. Catherine de' Medici had a separate room which contained numbered drawers secreted behind its woodwork. In it she assembled a miscellany of discovery: pieces of antiquity, oddities, mementos, cameos, rare examples from the natural world as well as her private papers and other items of personal significance. These cabinets would have been a delight to explore. As a child, Mary would have been invited to finger a piece of coral or smooth her palm over the cool surface of a tiny marble statue; to listen to the rasp of an unfolding leather fan and test the weight of a large mussel shell that had once held a prized pearl. These curios were microcosms of worlds that lay in the past, in the heart and on distant horizons. In time, they were given other names, such as wonder rooms, theatres of memory and summaries of the world. One night, after I had been researching these harbingers of Renaissance discovery, I dreamed of a cabinet of curiosities. It was of dark mahogany, its doors intricately carved, and it was designed in three horizontal sections, each acting independently of each other. When opened, each section revealed a series of display panels that held a separate object of interest which swung out, one after the other, like pages in a book. When I asked the young girl sitting near me what it was called, she answered 'a kleptomaniac'. It seemed, when I woke, that it was as good a name as any for these repositories of memory and exploration.

Mary's dolls would have been housed, as Catherine de' Medici's were, in her cabinet of curiosities. The 1587 inventory of Mary's belongings provides some insight as to what else, apart from her dolls, the Scottish queen treasured: a little green bag with chessmen, a cameo of François II, a painted box filled with beads. There was a beak of an exotic bird, a red velvet quiver for arrows, one white taffeta fingerless mitten.[23] This collection of heart-kept tokens and exotica represented a material encyclopaedia of Mary's past, encompassing knowledge, connections, emotions and experiences. Her cabinet room was not just a retreat but a repository of self, a place of self-affirmation. It was where she could share a fuller sense of who she was with her closest confidantes, telling the stories that lay behind each object, replaying the physical or sentimental journey that had brought them into her care.

## Two Dolls' Dresses Made of Grey Damask Threaded in Gold

Mary not only had to contend with the cultural difference of Scotland, but also cope with its climate. The Scottish winters of the 1560s were especially severe. By the mid-sixteenth century, the world, in particular the northern hemisphere, was experiencing what became known as the Little Ice Age. Temperatures dropped dramatically, signalling a change in the world's climate that since the thirteenth century had experienced more extreme fluctuations. At the start of 1562, as the shiver of winter bit deep, Mary ordered quantities of sheets, curtains, mattresses, bolsters, pillows, bed canopies and blankets for her ladies and chamber children, the young servants who were under her care, to help ameliorate the cold. More followed through subsequent winters.[24] The winter of 1564 was so severe that, as one chronicler recorded: 'The fowls of the air died and might not fly, and the sea stood still neither ebbing nor flowing'.[25] Mary's cosseting of her household was part of her queenly duty of care, the maternal solicitude expected of a queen. But, more than that, in Mary it was also an act of natural kindness. When she heard that Randolph, the English ambassador in Scotland, was absent from court because of ill health, he was surprised and touched when Mary sent her own physician to his bedside to quicken his recovery. When Elizabeth fell ill with smallpox, Mary sent her a letter of genuine concern saying that she was sorry that 'I did not know it sooner, for I would have sent you him whom I consider excellent for this ...'. She lamented that she no longer had access to the recipe for a cream her previous French physician had concocted which helped to prevent scarring. Mary knew that for women the dread of smallpox was disfigurement; she understood Elizabeth's fear and shared her anxiety.[26]

In the early part of her reign in Scotland, the repair and renewal of the interiors of Mary's palaces and castles – at Stirling, Edinburgh, Falkland and Linlithgow – was a priority. Marie de Guise had had few resources and little energy to maintain their splendour in her last years of political conflict.

Her own funds and her treasury's coffers had become depleted by their contribution to Mary's household in France and the cost of defensive warfare at home. It left little to spend on interior decoration.

There was another reason for Mary's focus on renewal and repair. The fading colours and the neglect of the royal interiors signalled a country in decline. Mary was determined to offer visible proof of its renewed spirit under her queenship. Her eligibility for marriage depended on her projecting Scotland as a kingdom of vitality and prosperity. Historians and commentators have criticised Mary's apparent reluctance to progress the architectural schemes started by James IV and V. But for queens, interiors were more relevant as backdrops to power. Women's frontiers were limited, demarcated largely by their domestic surroundings. While Mary led a physically active life, and was skilled in hunting and other sports, it was her palace interiors that were her main political stage. Improving them was as much a demonstration of Stewart and Renaissance ambition as the architectural achievements of her father and grandfather. Her material offensive was as determined as theirs had been, much like that of her father when he went on his spending spree in France to secure a royal bride. Like him, Mary was preparing the way for a prestigious marriage.

When, in September 1561, less than a month after she had returned to Scotland, Mary embarked on her first progress through her realm, she covered over 500 miles on horseback, and nearly 800 on her second. In its hinterland, Scotland was still a wild landscape with few serviceable roads. The severity of its winters and subsequent poor harvests meant that there were scant supplies along the way. But Mary was determined to continue a tradition set by her ancestors, who saw royal progresses as a way to promote sovereign accessibility. There is no doubt that Mary found in them the thrill of adventure, freedom and release. In 1562, Randolph reported that:

I never saw her merrier, nor dismayed, nor never thought a stomach to be in her that I find! She repents but, when the lads and others at Inverness came in the mornings from the watch, that she was not a man to know what life was to lie all night in the fields or walk upon the causeway with a jack and knapscall (helmet) a Glasgow buckler and a broad sword.[27]

For Randolph, bred in gentler English climes, the experience was arduous and dispiriting: 'cumbersome, painful, marvellously dear and (the) corn that is never like to come to ripeness'. He was astonished at Mary's stamina.[28]

Such expeditions allowed Mary to display her physical robustness. At a time when the physical energy of monarchs was correlated with the health and vigour of the realm, Mary regularly participated in many of the sports enjoyed by men. She hunted, played golf, tennis, archery and bowls: displaying both her sovereign fitness and her competitive edge.

A monarch's health was subject to constant surveillance. For a queen of child-bearing age, intense interest was paid to the regularity of her menstrual cycle. Pregnancy and miscarriage made women more vulnerable to extended periods of frailty and illness. Through the sixteenth century, the threat of death from smallpox and plague were ever-present. The plague stalked the kingdoms of Europe like a grim reaper. There were recurrent break outs, some deadlier than others. By the end of August in 1563, as the plague swept through London, over 1,000 people were dying there every week.[29]

Each time the plague visited London, Elizabeth's court was relocated to palaces on the fringes of the city. While her proclaimed virginity left the English queen free of the travails of pregnancy and motherhood, she did not escape the debilitating effects of recurrent sickness. Her illnesses were noted with fretful anxiety. In 1559, state papers recorded: '23 January: Queen indisposed; 27 July: Queen unwell; 10 August: Queen still has a burning fever; 22 Aug: Queen indisposed; 24 August: Queen half in doubt of an ague'.[30]

In France, Mary had been prey to sudden fainting fits and had a propensity to fever which alarmed her physicians. She was diagnosed with chlorosis, a form of anaemia, which was manifested in nervous exhaustion, a condition especially prevalent amongst teenage girls. Her debilitating ailments, however, were never fully diagnosed. In Scotland Mary continued to have episodes of unexplained collapse. Fevers were frequent. They seemed to be triggered by emotional upset, with Randolph observing: 'I hear she is troubled with sudden passions after any great unkindness or grief of mind'.[31] More recently it has been suggested that Mary suffered from porphyria, the so-called 'royal disease' that caused the temporary madness of the eighteenth-century English monarch George III. Whatever the true diagnosis, it is undeniable that Mary experienced periods of physical disempowerment. They caused political concern. Mary was the body politic – she personified Scotland. Any lessening of her physical strength, even fleetingly, represented a decline of Scottish power, unless its cause was pregnancy.

The prime function of women in the sixteenth century was reproductive. For queens, their political and sometimes personal survival was dependent on their ability to secure the royal blood line and safeguard the succession through producing an heir. It is an expectation of royal brides even today that through their progeny they will ensure the continuity of the crown. Queen Elizabeth II had four children; her heir, Prince Charles, two sons. And his eldest son, William, and his wife Kate have created the next, future, generation of Windsor royals: duties still realised; the succession still assured.

In earlier centuries, royal children were political pawns from the moment they were born, their marriages usually arranged at a very young age and formally constituted around the age of twelve. Some, like Mary Tudor, the first daughter of Henry

VIII, were used like shuttlecocks to gain political advantage. From when she was two years of age, Mary Tudor was used to broker and then break marital alliances with Spain, France and Bavaria. It was only when she became queen at the age of thirty-seven in 1553, that she finally was able to arrange her own marriage with Philip II of Spain. Despite fears that she was past child-bearing years, she did become pregnant, only to discover that it was a phantom pregnancy. She died childless.

Sixteenth-century Europe witnessed a criss-crossing of princesses leaving their families and familiar courts to marry elsewhere. Their marriage settlements often meant they had to undertake dangerous journeys into unknown territory to what had hitherto been an enemy state. Some, like Mary's grandmother Margaret Tudor, feared for their lives. At thirteen in 1503, she was married by proxy to the King of Scotland to bolster what was at best a delicate alliance with England's age-old adversary. Margaret of Beaufort and Elizabeth of York, Henry VII's mother and wife respectively, intervened on her behalf to delay her marriage, fearful that 'the King of Scotland would not wait but injure her and endanger her health'.[32] Margaret travelled north the following year, a bartered bride, a peace offering. These young royal brides had not only to negotiate their new status and roles as queens and wives – often of much older men – but also to acclimatise to a foreign country and an alien culture. They had to accommodate illegitimate royal children, some much older than themselves, and mature mistresses determined not to relinquish their power. Many of these girl-brides were also hampered by language difference. The Italian Catherine de' Medici was fourteen when she came to France; her daughter and Mary's companion in France Elisabeth de Valois was the same age as her mother when she was sent to Spain as the wife of the Spanish king. These young women were reliant on the entourage that accompanied them for emotional shelter. It was their retinues who carried the stamp of home, with whom they could continue to share a common culture and history. Many were also forced to separate from their mothers at a young age. Mary was five years old when she left Scotland and her mother Marie de Guise. Elizabeth was just two when her mother, Anne Boleyn, was beheaded. Mary Tudor was an exception. She stayed close to her mother, Catherine of Aragon, until she was fifteen, when Catherine was banished from the court to make way for Anne Boleyn. Mary Tudor was not allowed to see or correspond with her. Contact was only to be allowed when Mary Tudor had endorsed Henry's new marriage. When she refused, Henry severed her relationship with her mother. Even when Catherine was dying, Mary Tudor was not permitted to go to her side.

For women close to the royal succession, unsanctioned liaisons met with severe repercussions. When, in 1537, it was discovered that Margaret Douglas, the daughter of Margaret Tudor, had covertly entered into a marriage contract with Lord Thomas Howard, the youngest son of the Duke of Norfolk, they were both sent to the Tower of London, which had been used as a royal prison since the twelfth century. While Margaret was eventually released, Thomas died in captivity the following year. Over seventy years later, when Margaret's granddaughter, Arbella Stuart, secretly married William Seymour, she was put under house arrest and he was despatched to the Tower. Their attempt at escape came to naught. While William managed to flee to Flanders, Arbella's ship was intercepted and she was sent to the Tower, where she remained until her death four years later. Even Elizabeth did not remain unscathed. As a teenager, she had lived with Katherine Parr, the widow of Henry VIII, and her stepfather Sir Thomas Seymour. From the age of thirteen she endured Seymour's unwanted advances and, it is believed, sexual abuse. On Katherine's death, Seymour continued to pursue Elizabeth, seeing her as his gateway to the crown. There were rumours of a liaison, of a pregnancy.

## Two Dolls' Dresses Made of Grey Damask Threaded in Gold

In 1549, when she was sixteen, Elizabeth became implicated in a conspiracy, orchestrated by Seymour, to seize the throne. She was interrogated and imprisoned in the Tower for over sixty days in the apartments her mother had been held in before her execution. She pleaded with her half-sister, Mary Tudor, then queen, to be allowed to meet with her and prove her innocence in person. But Mary Tudor refused her request. Although Seymour was executed, Elizabeth escaped further censure, but she was seared by the experience. Thereafter she remained over-cautious of being caught up in other peoples' tragedies, wary of being blamed as the architect of the downfall of others. This reticence impinged on the relationship she had with Mary. It made her more hesitant to meet her, to over-play their sisterhood. Guided by her male advisers, Elizabeth often let them bear the brunt of decision-making, a burden they accepted – at times even connived to shoulder – to enable her to live in the fiction of a clear conscience.

At the French court, Mary had enjoyed a culture in which women had prominence, despite the ancient French Salic law that excluded women from monarchy. Women in France and other European courts found different ways to exercise their power and political influence through mentoring, diplomacy, hospitality, material propaganda, royal patronage and largesse.

Isabella d'Este designed her own clothes, which were so arresting they generated international emulation and brought her a cultural importance beyond her own borders.[33] Catherine of Aragon used the power of dress to emphasise her dual Spanish and English identity and promote her role as the mediator between two competitive realms. She wore gowns of green and white – the colours of the Tudor dynasty and her own mother – to simultaneously reference both her marital power and her own dynastic significance.[34]

During the sixteenth century Europe was in the grip of female rule, with an unprecedented rise in women becoming queens, female consorts, regents and governors. Isabella I of Castile, Mary of Hungary, Margaret of Parma, Anne of France, Catherine de' Medici, Mary Tudor and Catherine of Aragon were just some of the women who wielded power. Some of these women inherited their political authority; others assumed it in the absence of husbands, whose deaths or departure from court during warfare, left them as widows or wives, mothers or daughters, in charge of kingdoms. At court, women were responsible for domestic harmony and took on the role of intermediaries and pacifiers in times of division. They were expected to be maternal role models, mentoring the young aristocracy in their care, acting as surrogate mothers to their husbands' illegitimate children and arranging marriages between dynastic families. Through such roles they could strengthen their own political power base. They were simultaneously rivals and supporters of each other. If unmarried, they could find themselves vying for the same prestigious suitor; if widowed, fighting to retain their influence under the rule of a new queen. But as well as fashion intelligence they also exchanged recipes, herbal remedies, gifts and advice. In 1497, Anne of Brittany published *Lessons for My Daughter* for her daughter, Suzanne of Bourbon. It was written to equip her with the wisdom necessary to survive life at court. While most of her guidance concerned manners, etiquette, demeanour, clothes and conduct, she also explored women's relationships:

Furthermore, my daughter, you must attend to other women in times of childbirth, misfortune, and illness and, if you have it, send them something you think they might need or that might please them; you should do this at the very least for the women you know, especially for your own relatives and those of your husband, because whether they are rich or poor, you owe them more than anyone else, as long as they conduct themselves honestly.[35]

Renaissance queens, consorts and regents were educated,

literate and multi-lingual, the creators and consumers of material culture. They straddled the worlds of art and science as readily as their spouses. They patronised poets and artists, created their own libraries, collected maps and globes, studied astrology and invested in new discoveries. Catherine de' Medici had more than thirty maps and over 750 books in her library, written in Latin, Greek, Hebrew and other languages, ranging in subject matter from philosophy to medicine.[36] More than their husbands or sons, these women combined modern thought with age-old superstitious practices. They cultivated their own networks, garnering allies, advisers and admirers – men as well as women – and many had their own disposable incomes gleaned from pensions, land revenues and dowries.

Benefactors to the poor, mentors to the children of the rich, these women hunted and had babies, danced at banquets, flew their hawks and strummed lutes. They made proclamations and ordered executions. They were astute, accomplished and ambitious. In the courts they ruled over, they introduced a distinct female culture, separate from that of men, one which other women could appreciate, respond to and benefit from. This female culture was collaborative and supportive, and was expressed through alternative mechanisms – such as textiles, sewing, gifts and dolls – mediums whose emotional potency went unrecognised by their male peers.

Women of power also made their own gestures of political theatricality. Anne of Brittany sent James IV a glove as a challenge when Henry VII invaded France at the end of the fifteenth century during the War of the Holy League. The glove was a taunt to spur on the Scottish king to support his French ally. In 1517, Catherine of Aragon and Margaret Tudor intervened in the proposed execution of boy apprentices involved in the May Day riots by appearing before Henry VIII with their hair loose, pleading that the boys be spared. And when Catherine was banished from the English court to make way for Anne Boleyn, she defiantly ordered new livery that sported her initials entwined with Henry's. After James IV of Scotland died, Margaret Douglas, his widow, remarried. She was instructed to vacate Stirling castle and give up her young son James V into the care of her nobility. Hers was a material protest. She dressed James in royal purple with a crown on his head and paraded him on the castle's esplanade, clutching the keys of the castle. With his hand in hers she pleaded for a reprieve and, while her appeal proved ineffectual, her dramatic gesture of maternal defence has remained part of her history.

The sixteenth century, moreover, saw a shift in how women were perceived. The *querelles de femmes* or 'woman question' was an intellectual debate played out in literary circles throughout Europe. It was provoked by two thirteenth-century publications. The *Romance of the Rose* was a popular and controversial medieval poem, written by Guillaume de Lorris and expanded by Jean du Meun. An allegory on the sensual and romantic pleasures of love, it attracted controversy because of its underlying belittlement of women. *The Lamentations of Matheolus*, a work by the poet and cleric Matheolus, bewailed the misery men suffered at the hands of their wives. These two manuscripts fanned a literary dialogue which explored the difference in nature between men and women, and re-assessed the hitherto assured place of men as women's superiors. The discourse was not primarily about gender equality; men's supremacy – economic, political and cultural – was never in question. What was under debate was the essence and extent of women's rational, physical and moral competence. Much of the argument focussed on what was seen as the innate female temperament. As descendants of Eve, the temptress, women were deemed to be the weaker sex, driven by passion rather than logic. They were thought to lack the emotional and physical robustness needed to withstand the travails of life without the shield of men. The counter-argument exposed the oppressive nature of men's dominance. It alleged that male regulation of women's behaviour and status allowed men to perpetuate their privilege at the expense of women's advancement and prestige. It further protested that the supremacy of male control gave licence for the abuse of women to take place without censure. It was a debate that had begun in the fourteenth century and was to continue over the next 200 years.

While most of its arguments were made by male exponents, there were rare female voices, notably that of Christine de Pizan, a Venetian-born poet and author. When she published her *The Book of the City of Ladies* in 1405, it became one of the most widely read and discussed books of its time. Pizan's book was a 'dream vision'. It was set in an imagined, allegorical, city ruled and inhabited exclusively by women. It celebrated the leadership and achievements of 200 women through time: female saints such as Agnes, Cecilia and Margaret, and women rulers including Isabeau of Bavaria and Helen of Troy. Esther the biblical heroine was represented as was Minerva the mythological goddess. De Pizan chose these women as exemplars of female fortitude and moral strength. At its heart were four heroines representing Virtue, Reason, Justice and Rectitude, through whom de Pizan defended the efficacy of women's co-operation, their benign influence on society and their capacity for diligence and learning. Manuscripts of the book, some of which were illustrated, entered the libraries of the elite women of her day and were passed on to their daughters. The woman question and its currency among the educated classes unsettled the secure fortress of male primacy.

It was in this context that John Knox published his *The First Blast of the Trumpet Against the Monstrous Regiment of Women* in 1558. His was not a lone attack on women's rule; rather, it was written within the critical context of the current debate. But his diatribe against women rulers was met with unease by many and downright censure by others, men as well as women. It was because of it that Knox was refused a passport into England by Elizabeth; and because of her refusal that he returned to Scotland and diverted his condemnatory attention towards Mary.

In the sixteenth century, it was women who were the custodians of the atmosphere at court. They monitored its morality and mood. And, as women took their place at the head of European courts, they began to assert not just their presence, but their growing confidence to challenge the male prerogative. When men sought to undermine their influence, women began to explore and initiate more emphatic expressions of female culture that communicated, circulated and consolidated female bonds. They adopted new tactics for female co-operation to claim a more public and participatory place in political life and exercise their power. And they developed their own networks of support, independent of the men around them. As a young queen in her own right, Mary was at the vanguard of that change.

# 4
# A Great Mourning Gown of Black

Sixteenth century court tailors and embroiderers were the makers of majesty. More important for a tailor than his expertise in sewing – an aptitude shared with most women of the time, and readily sourced – was his skill in the cutting out of garments. When fabric was such a precious commodity, every scrap mattered. The art of constructing garments to make the most economical use of treasured cloth was a coveted skill, and it demanded complex piecing. Gowns, doublets, bodices and breeches were created from an intricate jigsaw of fabric, with joins camouflaged by criss-crossing braid or an overlay of embroidery. Real ingenuity, however, lay in the patchworking of velvet or other cloth whose pile, pattern or ribbing posed the challenge of directional shift, where tone and sheen changed according to horizontal or vertical placement. Velvet, much loved by royalty, was particularly vulnerable to such alteration. When the highest grade of velvet was so expensive it was sold by the quarter-ell, dexterity in its piecing was paramount.

It was not just the art of cutting out, and the toil of seaming and hemming that tailors laboured over. Hose, codpieces, shoulder rolls and doublets were stuffed and shaped, and whalebones slid through narrow channels to create the hoops for farthingale petticoats. Garments had to be lined, sometimes with equally expensive fabrics: each piece of lining cut out, sewn up and oversewn for strength twice over. And tailors were not only responsible for the making of garments, but for their repair and 'translation': altering them to accommodate a pregnancy or adapt to a thickening waistline. The clothes a monarch donated to others also had to be refashioned to fit their new owners. While court tailors had at their disposal a substantial store of cloth, other fabric was purchased from merchants as the need arose. Tailors were also expected to be adept at recycling, removing braid from one gown to adorn another and unpicking worn garments to serve as patterns for new clothes. These tailors, invariably men, cared for the longevity of cloth, for exploiting its potential and extending its life.

It was the draughtsmanship of embroiderers that was most highly prized. They were responsible for the propagandist script of monarchy. Embroiderers illustrated and stitched down the messages on textiles for posterity and advised on the needlework undertaken by elite women at court. The privy purse accounts of Mary Tudor records the 6s 6d paid to John Hayes 'for drawing a pattern for a cushion for the queen'. Three months later, he received 10s for drawing out the design for another cushion.[1] Embroiderers had access to emblem books and botanical encyclopaedias to inspire content, knowledge of the symbolism of plants and animals. They drew their designs out on parchment that had been oiled to create translucency, then pricked the paper at small intervals following the outline of the drawing, and transferred the design onto the fabric by rubbing charcoal through the parchment's holes to mark the cloth in a technique known as 'prick and pounce', a technique still used by professional embroiderers today. If the embroidery was not urgent, the outline might be inked, or even sewn onto the cloth. Precision was vital. Court embroiderers handled the costliest of materials: the finest silk threads from Spain, gold and silver threads made from precious metal where narrow strips of ore were wrapped around a silk core. They worked closely with goldsmiths, and the materials they used were so valuable that sometimes the Lord High Treasurer would be present when embroiderers were entrusted with their allotted portion of metal thread.

Court tailors, while remaining in long service, were not as well remunerated as embroiderers. A court embroiderer could grow rich in his service to a king. Paid in instalments, his income could be supplemented by extra piecework. William Ibgrave, Henry VIII's embroiderer, was able to buy a large manor and its surrounding lands through his earnings as a stitcher. He managed to amass, if not a fortune, then a handsome dividend.[2] Both tailors and embroiderers were part of a network of textile producers and suppliers: goldsmiths, furriers, tapestry weavers, upholsterers and merchants. Working alongside them were others just as necessary for sartorial splendour: seamstresses, braid makers, milliners, shoemakers, hosiers and glovers. Mary's treasury accounts provide a glimpse of her wardrobe staff. They included her tailors Jehan de Compiegne, Jacques de Soulis, John Carwood and Gilbert Thomson, her embroiderers Pierre Oudry and Ninian Miller and her tapestry weavers Nicholas Carbonnier, David Lieger and Pierre Martin. These and more are names long forgotten now, but in their time it was they who crafted the Scottish queen's image.

Whether ensconced in palaces or in their own professional workshops, tailors and embroiderers were answerable not only to their employers, but also to their peers. There was strict governance over the nature and quality of what they wrought in order to safeguard prestige and prices. A long apprenticeship of seven to eight years was compulsory. Only then might an apprentice be admitted to guild membership, a necessary validation of their knowledge, skill and trustworthiness. Without such membership it was impossible to trade. The London Worshipful Company of Merchant Taylors received its royal charter in 1327, the London Company of Broderers in 1561, although its incorporation is thought to have been much earlier. These guilds protected their reputations fiercely through tight controls. All sewn work was examined before being passed for guild certification and stamped with the guild's seal. Those textiles that failed the test would be burnt. Workshops could be searched at any time to check that no materials of inferior quality were being used, and that the prescribed working conditions were being met. All stitching had to be done in daylight: a ban on sewing by candlelight ensured that standards were not compromised by its uneven flicker. And each workshop was only allowed one apprentice at a time to guarantee the thoroughness of their training.

I became a burgess and guild sister of Glasgow by default when, in 2009, I was commissioned to make a large wall hanging to celebrate 500 years since the inception of the Trades House in Glasgow. I recruited a group of other sewers as volunteers, women who had worked with me over many years on a variety of community textile projects. Week after week, we entered the hallowed chambers of the Trades House and stretched out our work-in-progress over its polished boardroom table to trace out the city's craft history in stitches. Designed in columns, one column for each century, it was exacting work, requiring ingenuity if we were to do visual justice to the talent and precarious survival of Glasgow's local guilds over the past five centuries. We mapped, illustrated and re-imagined the commercial creativity of the past. Once it was done, it was ceremoniously unveiled. As the women who helped me had sewn in the service of their city, I half-jokingly suggested that they should receive the accolade of being accepted as guild members. Those at the Trades House were delighted with the idea. So it was that, to the surprise of its stitchers, the unveiling saw applause not only for their endeavours, but also for each woman being presented with a framed certificate that declared they were now burgesses and guild sisters of Glasgow. I too was admitted, 'entitled to all the civil rights and privileges by law'. It is rumoured that, as well as being permitted to ply our trade as tailors in the city, we also have the right to keep sheep and hang out our washing on Glasgow Green, an inner-city

Portrait of Mary, Queen of Scots, aged 15, *c.*1557 by François Clouet.

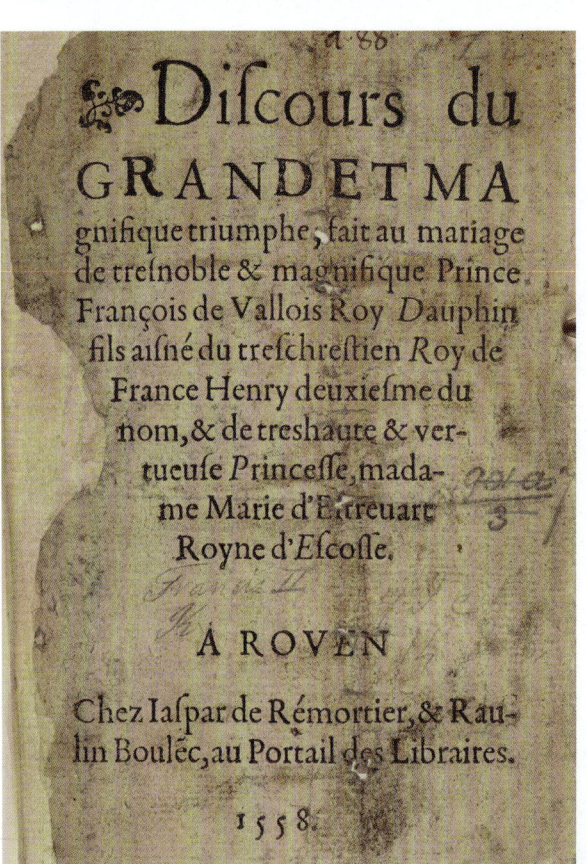

A pamphlet from 1558 describing Mary's marriage to François II and a double portrait of François and Mary at his coronation in 1559.

The coat of arms Mary adopted after her marriage to François, representing the royal houses of Scotland, France and, controversially, England.

An example of sixteenth-century French silk embroidery, c.1560.

The Scottish Fetternear Banner, *c.*1520.

A detail of the banner's central image of Christ as the Man of Sorrows, part of the cult of the Confraternity of the Holy Blood.

The Prayer Book of Mary, Queen of Scots, given to her by one of her Guise aunts in France, possibly as a wedding present in 1558. Its French inscription, penned by Mary herself and accompanied by her motto and monogram, reads 'since you wish that I remember you in your prayers, I want you first to remember what part you have in my affections.'

A portrait of John Knox, the spiritual leader of the Scottish Reformation. Woodcut, after Adrian Vanson c.1580.

The title page of John Knox's *The First Blast of the Trumpet against the Monstrous Regiment of Women* (1766 edition). It was a controversial diatribe against female rule, published in 1558, which was directed at Mary Tudor, Queen of England and Marie de Guise, Regent of Scotland.

Female leaders of the sixteenth century: Isabella d'Este (1474–1539), Marchioness of Mantua; Mary Tudor (1516–1558), daughter of Henry VIII and Catherine of Aragon and Queen of England from 1553 until her death; Catherine of Aragon (1485–1536), first wife of Henry VIII; Catherine de' Medici (1519–1589), wife of Henri II of France and Regent of France following his death in 1559.

Fashion dolls were an important form of female exchange and support in the sixteenth century. When they had served their purpose, some were handed down to children as playthings. Clockwise from top left: A doll made by Clare Hunter in 1962; a sixteenth century fashion doll in the Livrustkammaren Museum in Stockholm; Catharina van Warmondt with her doll, by Isaac Claesz Van Swanenburg, 1596; the granddaughter of Bess of Hardwick, Arbella Stuart (1575–1615).

Details of sixteenth-century women's and men's fashion. Sixteenth-century fashion was a vital marker of status, power and wealth and an expression of personal and political identity.

stretch of open land. None of us, to my knowledge, has ever dared to test the ancient prerogative.

A real understanding of the labour involved in sixteenth-century tailoring and embroidery is elusive to us now. We have become so accustomed to industrial and digital processes that it is almost impossible to envisage the number of hours required to construct even the simplest of garments. When everything was hand-stitched it was an achingly slow process, as much then as now. In the fourteenth century, the three counterpanes commissioned by the English King Edward III for his wife, Queen Philippa of Hainault, for her 'churching' (the mass held when she re-entered public life following the birth of her child), took 114 stitchers three months to complete the images of fantastical beasts and design of knots.[3] In 1352 Edward tasked his embroiderers with sewing 8,544 fleur-de-lis in just three months.[4] The costumes for Henry VIII's 1515 revels involved eighteen tailors working flat out for thirteen days at 8d a day.[5] No matter how adept or experienced a tailor, embroiderer or seamstress might be, this was laborious toil.

In an age yet to invent the roles of interior designer or couturier, it was materials that drove the changes in fashion. The secular circulation of confiscated, richly wrought, ecclesiastical textiles during the Reformation bred an appetite for material adornment both in clothes and furnishings. But at the start of the century, only the Spanish had the technology to forge fine hand-sewing needles suitable for delicate embroidery. The rest of Europe had to make do with hand-hammered needles, which blunted easily and snagged fragile fabrics. When Spanish needle-making technology migrated to the rest of Europe, access to high-quality steel needles increased. Elizabeth's wardrobe staff used to order 200 of them at a time. The availability of such needles fuelled a greater enthusiasm for embroidery. The repertoire of decorative needlework expanded to include lace-making, cutwork, drawn-thread work, tasselling and braid weaving. Such embellishments altered the surface of cloth and endowed it with a different dimension: a variance of weight and texture. Fashion changed to accommodate the new opportunity. Front petticoats became popular as they offered an unfolded, unpleated expanse that could be filled with sewn adornment. Sleeves became larger to provide a greater surface area to inscribe with stitching.

The art of fashioning majesty continues today under the creative direction of the world's top designers. Royal weddings, coronations and the rituals of British monarchy still furnish us with the material evidence of inherited power, manifested in the pageantry which accompanies them. In Britain, the fabric trappings of royal spectacles – ceremonial robes, banners, the vast cloth that hangs over the balcony at Buckingham Palace in London for celebratory events – still carry hand-crafted elements to honour tradition and reference a past magnificence that lingers. Celebrity culture has fostered another layer of public material performance. In celebrity fashion, embroidery is often used to connect modern-day glamour with historical splendour, promoting what artisan skills still survive. It features in the sartorial sensations worn by stars as they stroll down red carpets, by rock musicians in their sell-out concerts. And we experience it in the close-ups of characters in costume dramas and on the catwalks of couturiers searching out sensual flourishes of crafted glory.

Two prestigious bespoke embroidery companies are still practising today in London. Hand & Lock has been stitching for over 250 years, servicing royalty, the nobility and military as well as film companies and celebrities. The Royal School of Needlework was established in 1872 and by 1875 could claim Queen Victoria as its patron. It continues to supply the monarchy with ceremonial embroidery and, like Hand & Lock, provides bespoke embroidery for a range of other clients. The school has always provided training, ensuring that traditional needlework techniques are passed on generation to generation. Its embroidery classes and courses for the public, both in person and online, have, in recent years, become surprisingly over-subscribed.

I connect with Jessica Jane Pile, Hand & Lock's production director, and Dr. Susan Kay-Williams, the Royal School of Needlework's chief executive, on a zoom call to ponder on the changes in embroidery and for embroiderers over the past centuries. They, more than most, have witnessed its alteration, diminishment and revival first-hand. Both companies still stitch as embroiderers have always stitched, slowly. They agree that there is no other way to capture embroidery's unique presence. It is not a question, Susan explains, of how it looks, but what you see. When you look at an embroidered flower in which the tones of its petals have been executed in carefully graduated hues of the finest silk thread, you should not notice the stitches, but the flower; you should experience it so tangibly that you can almost inhale its perfume. Jessica also champions the lush, tactile quality of hand embroidery. There is something deeply satisfying, she feels, in being the guardian of tradition, of stitching as others have stitched for hundreds of years, of honouring their methods through replication.

Not much has changed since the sixteenth century. The basic requirements are still simple – cloth, thread, needle, thimble, scissors and frame – and while there was perhaps a greater variety of materials available in earlier centuries, the standard of what can be accessed now is comparable. With access to not only natural but synthetic dyes, the colour palette has increased. But embroidery continues to demand, at times, long hours, late nights and even all-nighters if an urgent order is to be completed on time. Susan shows me a newspaper photograph of Royal School of Needlework sewers busy at their frames in 1901, stitching the funeral pall for Queen Victoria. Nearly fifty embroiderers stitched for twenty-one hours without a break to sew the heraldic Royal Coat of Arms on its ivory white satin. Then, as now, death was no respecter of lead-in time. Jessica says they receive orders that require everyone, even her, to thread up a needle. While such commissions can be exhausting, there is camaraderie in the take-away pizzas and the shared sense of accomplishment that is remembered with affection once the pressure has passed.

We talk about the royal commissions today, either directly or through their designers, and it seems that scale and volume remain prerequisites of royal material spectacle. The so-called Elvis outfit – a gown and matching bolero with a high standing collar – that Princess Diana first wore to Hong Kong in 1989, and reprised for her appearance at that year's British Fashion Awards, was designed by Catherine Walker. It became so iconic that when she donated it to a charity auction it realised £3 million. The company that bought it went on to market a Diana doll wearing a replica outfit. Now classed as vintage celebrity memorabilia, the dolls sometimes appear for sale online – at a price. It was Hand & Lock embroiderers who hand-stitched the 20,000 oyster pearls onto the outfit. The effect, one journalist reported, was to make it seem as if the light literally shone around her. I think back to the spiritual luminosity of pre-Reformation ecclesiastical textiles, of how they were created to emanate God's radiance, and realise that in the secular celebrity culture of today the use of sequins, Swarovski crystals, rhinestones and other sparkles is as irresistible now as their equivalents were to Catholic prelates then. Sequins, pearls and other gems continue to play an essential part in the performance of public charisma, whether it is hereditary, earned or media-driven.

Royal weddings, of course, are and always have been a time of public celebration and enthusiasm, watched by millions on their screens. Not just because of the delight in the romance of the royal couple, but because deep down it makes a nation feel secure, safe in traditions still being enacted. Such celebrations offer the comfort of continuity. While not everyone approves of their pomp and circumstance, and many mutter disapprovingly about their expense, most will admit to a thrill in their pageantry and sartorial finery.

I was Arts Development Officer of Northampton Development Corporation when the wedding of Prince Charles and Princess Diana took place in 1981. I had promised Ken, a trainee in our department, that he could organise a community arts project of his choice and that I would participate in whatever way he chose, as his supporter. He contacted a local community centre and offered to run a day's workshop for children on the day of the royal wedding. Unbeknownst to me his plan was to get local children to replicate the entire event in paper with him and me as the bride and groom.

So it was that the children set to work with rolls of black and white paper. With an extensive use of Sellotape and staples, they outfitted Ken in a dress shirt, three-piece suit and top hat, and me in a vast crinoline with an excessive neckline frill and a veil concocted from bubble wrap. When all was made, I was duly married to Ken by a small, officious child-high vicar (I hope in a ceremony that could not in any way be legal). Fistfuls of confetti rained down on us in rainbow tissue paper shards, before the exhausted participants partook of juice and cake. I insisted that Ken swear that he would never, ever, whisper a word of what had taken place. I was not anti-royalist, but I had socialist credentials that I was eager to safeguard and my emulation of a royal princess, albeit in paper, was not something I wished to be broadcast.

The following year I left my job. A surprise leaving party was arranged. My team, other colleagues and a camaraderie of adults and children gathered over four years of local creative projects appeared. Near its end, there were short speeches – a farewell to me, my thank you to them, the usual niceties of such occasions. I was presented with a bouquet, a leaving gift and, lastly, with an enormous two-foot-high card which featured an eight-page cartoon storyboard that traced the highs and the lows of my tenure as arts officer. At its centre was a warning writ large in black felt-tip pen that advised anyone under the age of eighteen or suffering from a heart condition not to turn to the next page, as it contained explicit material. On turning the page, I discovered two black-and-white photographs of Ken and me on our wedding day with the caption '47 Children go to Mum's Wedding', and me sitting at our wedding feast in my paper-puffed sleeves and doily-frilled neckline, with my bubble wrap veil blowing skew-whiff in the wind. I was embarrassed to have found myself captured as the centrepiece of local celebrations for Charles and Diana's marriage but the photographs have become treasured reminders of the creativity, zeal and delight of the children involved.

When the Duchess of York married Prince Andrew in 1986, she chose to have her seventeen-foot-long veil embroidered with thistles and bees to reference her own heritage, while anchors and waves signified Andrew's naval career. Sophie, Countess of Wessex, sported 325,000 crystal and pearl beads. Kate Middleton, when she married Prince William in 2011, chose Sarah Burton of Alexander McQueen as her designer. Burton commissioned the lace specially, and it was the Royal School of Needlework that was tasked with cutting out its hundreds of floral motifs – among them shamrocks, roses, daffodils and thistles, the emblems of Britain's four nations – and applying them to her gown and veil. Such was the media frenzy of speculation that secrecy was vital. The embroiderers' windows were double netted to ensure extra privacy. A code word was issued to embroiderers to be used when discussing their progress and a passcode was devised for the door of the school itself. Brides' desire for emulation was such that it was barely a week before copies of the dress became available. And when Meghan Markle married Prince Harry in 2018, she incorporated the fifty-three floral emblems of the Commonwealth on her veil to mark their shared commitment, at the time, to Prince Harry's role as Commonwealth Youth Ambassador.

Hand & Lock and the Royal School of Needlework marry their traditional needlework with innovative approaches to embroidery. They both continue to sew the trappings of ceremony such as the insignia for the Queen's bodyguards, or the stitching of the Lord Chancellor's purse. But, increasingly, the demands of Netflix and other media channels to create alluring historical dramas, of modern haute couture to resonate with the power of craft and the desire of promoters to devise more unusual branding for their products, mean that the bespoke embroidery offered by Hand & Lock and the Royal School of Needlework has become more seductive. The restraints, however, of time and budget require ingenuity. Hand & Lock reproduced uniforms for *The Crown* and embroidered a costume for the feisty heroine of the TV series *Killing Eve*. The Royal School of Needlework fashioned the vast Buckingham Palace balcony canopy for the Queen's Diamond Jubilee in 2012, for which it successfully married the traditional technique of goldwork for Elizabeth II's monogram and the Royal arms, with the contemporary exuberant renditions of the Commonwealth emblems, stitched by today's children.

As the sixteenth century took hold, the dress of the nobility – for men as well as women – became more complex. It evolved into a form of personal architecture, its structure and ornamentation as revealing as the buildings and rooms which surrounded it. Courtiers' attire had to offer impact at a distance and reward exploration closer to hand. This was transformative fashion: appearance and identity purposefully manipulated through dress. In an age when portraiture became more important as a method of constructing and circulating a personal image, how the elite presented themselves gained greater traction.

This personal architecture was moulded by tailors, who created an underlay of stiffer fabric to shape the upper body and hold it taut in canvas, buckram or another densely woven fabric. Women wore 'brassieres' to flatten and raise their bosoms. They lacked elasticity but helped to contour shape. Shoulders were accentuated by rolls of fabric around the tops of arms and skirts were made wider by whalebone farthingales and sets of petticoats. Men's codpieces and hose were padded to offer a boast of virility, while women's waistlines were elongated to a point to make them appear narrower and their hips – the site of fertility – fuller. The rigidity of these garments' central panels was offset by the fluidity of the fabric that glided around them.

Such clothes had a spatial dimension: they took up room. Their expansive excess ensured that each person inhabited their own space, separated and shielded by what they wore. At the start of the sixteenth century, elite men's outfits were designed to add width and height, authority made palpable in vast collars lined in fur, grand velvet bonnets studded with jewels or decorated with feathers. Women's clothes suggested composure. Their hair was snared into close-fitting mesh hoods, and bosoms and shoulders were screened by modest partlets, cloth that hid their breasts. As the sixteenth century evolved, however, women began to claim more physical space. They adopted higher headdresses and the artifice of wigs. Their ruffs became wider, their skirts fuller. Veils flowed behind them; trains, some as long as three ells, trailed as they processed. While farthingales made their appearance in the fifteenth century, in the sixteenth century they were used more consciously to amplify women's personal space further and, through the century, grew ever more expansive, reaching up to 120cm wide in some instances.

There could be as many as five layers of clothing worn by

the sixteenth-century elite: components that were interchangeable, detachable and replaceable. Sleeves, kirtles, capes, front petticoats, hoods, shirts and more all proffered a flexible repertoire of colour and texture. Their attachment was often temporary, serviced by pins. Sleeves would be pinned to bodices, front petticoats to skirts. Pins allowed for the easy exchange of separate parts. Through them, the more sumptuous and expensive elements of dress could be transferred from gown to gown, from doublet to doublet, to create a different impact. The use of pins was extensive. The entries in the treasury accounts for 1562 record that Mary ordered them in their thousands: 2,000 in July, 15,000 in August and 10,000 in October.[6] Laces were another form of attachment. While such methods allowed for flexibility, they also made it virtually impossible to dress or undress without help.

Trimmings were an essential addition. They offered textural variety. Knots were popular. Tightly tied, they symbolised bonds that could not be undone. Hems of gowns, doublets and cloaks were bordered and banded in velvet or *passements* (narrow hand-wrought gold, silver or silk braids or bands of lace) and might be further adorned with jewels or other spangled flourishes, additions that sometimes cost more than the fabric they adorned. Such iridescent accumulations did more than add interest; they delineated human movement and traced out gestures as they caught the light. Then there were ribbons and laces, buckles and belts – conceits that were treated much like jewellery, viewed as changeable adornments to enhance this outfit or another.

Accessories were as important as clothes, and carried their own stitched declarations. Purses and bags, muffs and ear coverings, coifs and gloves, hose and footwear all offered sites for visual inscription. They could feature covert expressions of love and assertions of lineage. Men's stockings were decorated with intricate embroidery at the ankle called 'clocks'; handkerchiefs were stitched with emblematic motifs or monograms. Velvet slippers and mules were popular, as were heeled shoes. For Marie de Guise's arrival in Scotland, James V ordered three pairs of high heels for himself. It was reported that Marie de Guise was more than 5 feet 10 inches tall, and James had no intention of appearing to be dwarfed by his new wife.[7] Gloves had particular significance, and were often given as gifts of friendship. Thought of as extensions of the hand, they signified support. If exchanged between courting couples and embroidered with hearts, they acted as a reiteration of the marriage pledge.

In dance and in sports, clothes became provocative, revealing what lay beneath: the lining of a gown, the gleam of a petticoat, the reverse of a cape. This was a culture that delighted in secrets and their disclosure, that took pleasure in deciphering coded messages. The impresa was a personal device thought of as an 'unwritten thought'. Isabella d'Este, the marchioness of Mantua, devised one composed of the notation of a musical key which matched the pitch of her voice. Accompanying it was a pattern of rests and the musical symbol for repeat. It signified balance and silence and, with its accompanying motto 'In neither hope nor fear', was transmutable; able to be interpreted in different ways according to where and when Isabella displayed it. When her rival, her sister-in-law, Lucrezia Borgia – whose marriage Isabella disapproved of – came to visit, Isabella had the impresa embroidered on her gown. It might have signified that she was determined to keep her own counsel, or, alternatively, it might have signalled that she was adverse to any rapprochement between the two women.[8] Such ambiguities were entertaining and, when people were amused by hidden mechanisms, intrigued by espionage and fascinated by mazes and labyrinths, the display of such material puzzles was diverting. When Henry VIII held a summit meeting with François I in 1520 – an event which became known as the Field of the Cloth of Gold because of the extravagance of the attire, pavilions and other textile trappings – the French king wore purple satin enriched with gold embroidery. His outfit was embellished with small, slightly unravelled rolls of white satin on which, at the start of their encounter, just the first words of a motto were revealed. Each day, the scrolls were uncurled further until the motto 'Heart, fastened in endless pain, when she does not loose me from her bonds' could be read in its entirety, the scrolls now fully realised as little books.[9]

Surprising contrasts could also be revealing. The lining of a garment could add a textured commentary on whatever the main garment was designed to convey. With an increasingly rich variety of fabrics available, complexity could be realised by combining different kinds of cloth: the heavy folds of dark velvet offset by the delicacy of frilled white lace, for example, offered the drama of opposites. The shimmering underside of a silk cloak might reveal a burr of soft fur, the seductive gleam of a cloth-of-gold petticoat might be lined in virginal white. The fabric itself was also enthusiastically manipulated. In an age of exploration and experiment, cloth became another medium through which to show human ingenuity. It was slashed, razed, pleated, pin-tucked, gathered, stamped with designs and cut away to expose another layer. In this world of revelation, the deliberate alteration of cloth provided another intriguing dimension.

There is only one outfit that I have ever worn that had the impact of Renaissance glory. It was bought as a panacea for a lost love. In the months of my first true romance, I had spent the prerequisite hours locking eyes with my beloved over cooling cups of coffee, writing the necessary reams of bad poetry, and suffering – as is usual for first loves – the pain of its end. Shortly after our break-up, I was invited to an event that I knew he would be attending. Pride dictated that there had to be triumph: the hurt of rejection overcome, an ex-love regretful of his decision and, if possible, a garnering of attention from potential new loves eager to fill his shoes. It called for spectacular glamour, the gloss of a new me. As luck would have it, I had just received an instalment of my student grant and I took it – all of it – to Fraser's of Glasgow, then the most exclusive department store in the city. I scoured its rails, searching out the perfect redress to abandonment. What I found was a body-hugging midi dress made in the softest of velvets. It was patterned in swirls of the deepest pinks and ruby reds against a background of deep forest green and was graced with a hood lined in glowing crimson satin which framed my face and fell graciously to my shoulders. Its *pièce de résistance* was a row of tiny velvet-covered buttons that fastened at the front. They were caught in braided loops, arranged to leave just a sliver of flesh visible from neck to navel. To complete the outfit, I added teetering high heels in red crocodile leather and sheer burgundy stockings. I went to the event and made my entrance. The dress achieved all I could have hoped for it. It gathered around me a cluster of admirers, leaving my first love, my lost love, standing marooned on the edge, witness to my sartorial triumph.

The material wealth of royal wardrobes demanded constant vigilance, and courts employed a huge contingent of wardrobe staff to maintain it. Sturdy coffers, some padded to better protect their contents, ensured safe transportation from place to place, and canvas covers kept textiles free from dust. Cloth and clothes were infused with perfume and folded away with sprigs of herbs to protect them from insects and vermin and reduce the clinging tang of human sweat. The instructions issued to Henry VIII's wardrobe staff were to: 'gather for the king's gowns and sheets and other clothes, the sweet flowers, herbs, roses to make amongst them sweet fumes, things to make them breathe more seemly and delectable'.[10]

With the plague rife throughout the sixteenth century, scenting clothes with herbs was also thought to be a deterrent to infection. Washing was kept to a minimum. As textiles were hued with natural dyes, their colour fastness was never fully guaranteed. Rubbers or sponges were generally used to deal with stains. Personal linen – shirts, sheets and underwear, handkerchiefs and coifs – was washed more regularly by laundresses employed full-time at court.

The expense of the materials and the labour involved in the construction of the densely decorated garments of the sixteenth century gave them a value that warranted sentinel care. The royal wardrobe kept such textile treasures in separate locked storehouses, safeguarded by specialist staff who kept a strict tally of dispersals, repairs and alterations. Henry VIII had three such stores, which contained workshops, accommodation for artisans and storerooms. The largest was located near the Tower of London. Here, lengths of silks and velvets, cloths of gold and silver and other rich fabrics were stockpiled alongside garments. The master of the revels had charge of a separate storehouse for masque costumes, the trappings of tournaments and other court 'disguisings'. At Whitehall, Henry had 'a secret guarderobe' in which he squirreled away the most precious of the cloth he had accumulated.[11] In 1536, Mary Tudor had to rent a chamber at Greenwich to accommodate her clothes.[12] Never knowing when and for how long she might be welcomed at court, it would have been an impertinence to assume her clothes could be housed permanently in the royal wardrobe. Royal progresses, hunting expeditions and court migration to avoid the plague required complicated logistics. Wardrobe staff had to pack up a multitude of textiles, transport them by mules, ships or wagons to myriad locations, rehang tapestries, assemble bed furnishings, store away clothes and set up temporary workshops for ongoing maintenance.

A monarch's death created the dilemma of what to do with the vast array of garments they had amassed during their reign. Despite regular clear-outs of Henry VIII's clothes, he still left behind a mountain of attire. Elizabeth is said to have left nearly 2,000 gowns. Too old fashioned for her successor, the fashion-conscious Anne of Denmark, they were cut up, sold or donated to travelling players and court fools. Some sovereigns, however, kept the clothes of their dead loved ones for sentimental comfort. Henry VIII refused to part with the Parliamentary robes of his brother, Arthur, who died when he was fifteen. He also cherished the wardrobe of Jane Seymour, his young third wife, who died shortly after childbirth. In Scotland, James V cherished the clothes of his young French wife, Madeleine.

In the sixteenth-century courts of Europe, there was a penchant for wearing fashion that referenced international connection and cosmopolitan sophistication: the fashions of countries other than your own. Spanish farthingales, Lombard sleeves and French hoods all feature in the Scottish treasury accounts. One of the interviews Elizabeth conducted with the Scottish diplomat, Sir James Melville, of Halhill, which he recorded in his memoir, provides an insight into the queen's penchant for foreign fashion:

The Queen of England said she had clothes of every sort; which was every day, so long as I was there, she changed. One day she had the English weed, another the French, and another the Italian, and so forth.[13]

When Marie de Guise came to Scotland, James V appeared anxious to ensure that she did not find his court old fashioned or parochial. He spent large amounts of money to ensure that his household, key courtiers and court officials were dressed in the splendour of new livery, and he ordered new clothes and accessories for his illegitimate daughter, Jean Stewart. She was to have a headdress of Paris gold and a new gown and hood, which he stipulated were to be 'of the French sort'.[14]

Many foreign brides arrived at their new home accompanied by their own tailors and embroiderers. Mary brought her French embroiderer, tapestry weaver, tailor and upholsterer with her from France. These experts created the preferred clothes and furnishings that best suited the taste and style of their queens and brought with them techniques and skills honed in their own countries. And foreign brides often insisted on continuing to wear the fashion of home – not from a sense of nostalgia, but as a political act. New queens influenced court style. They could introduce fashions that were dominant in their own country as a form of cultural colonisation.

Catherine of Aragon, the first wife of Henry VIII, is thought to have introduced the farthingale and blackwork (a form of intricate monochrome embroidery) into English fashion.[15] As Spain was the most powerful of the European kingdoms at the time, Catherine persisted in wearing Spanish dress for state occasions, to mark out her heritage and her political importance. Marie de Guise and Mary, Queen of Scots similarly continued to dress in French fashion at the Scottish court. They sourced French fabrics and wore French styles, visually referencing the Franco-Scottish alliance through their clothes. Eleanor of Castile persisted in wearing Spanish dress at the French court when she married François I as a defiant reminder of the power of her native land.[16] And Anne Boleyn, who had been educated in France, continued to wear its fashions. It was only at her execution that she adopted an English gable headdress, as a last desperate conciliatory act when she was still hopeful of a reprieve.[17]

In the sixteenth century, new dye colours for fabric were constantly being devised. We know that watchet was pale blue, but cloud, horseflesh and maiden's blush have to be imagined.[18] Colour was symbolic: green signified rebirth, yellow hope and silver purity. Red, the colour of blood, was the symbol of strength, and was thought to be efficacious for physical health. It was often used to line garments and was favoured for petticoats, as advocated by the physician Andrew Boorde in his 1542 manual *A Dyetary of Health*, which advised: 'Next to your shirt you should wear a petticoat of scarlet'. On his recommendation, red became adopted by doctors as a form of treatment, with Elizabeth's physician instructing that her bed furnishings be changed to red curtains when she was ill with fever.[19]

The pairings of specific hues was significant. White and tawny orange-brown indicated patience; red and purple strength; blue and violet loyalty in love.[20] The combination of black and white posed a visual paradox, as black stood for constancy, a stable attribute, whereas white signified the moving energy of the spirit. Henri II's mistress, Diane de Poitiers, chose black and white as her emblematic colours. Her adoption of them gave her a dramatic and provocative presence among other rainbow-hued courtiers. While Mary adopted Diane's colours in France as a show of allegiance, she also made use of them in Scotland for theatrical effect when, at a Shrovetide masque in 1562, she and her ladies appeared dressed in black and white.[21] Elizabeth used a similar contrast of colour to accentuate her presence in the early part of her reign. She dressed her ladies in white and herself in colour to better mark her distinction as queen. It was for the same reason that, on a visit to Elizabeth's court, the Princess Cecilia of Sweden wore black and had her ladies all attired in crimson.[22]

Black was commonly worn in the sixteenth century, by men as well as women. The stability it signified, given that it could not be dyed any other colour, was an attribute much desired in a Europe assailed by political and religious change. It was in the sixteenth century that a 'true black' was devised, which was denser than any that had previously been available. Some believe that the increasing popularity of black clothing during the fifteenth and sixteenth centuries was a reaction to the Black Death, the pandemic that decimated populations in Afro-Eurasia from the fourteenth century onwards. The Catholic Church, believing the plague had been sent by God as a punishment for men's sins, called for mass penitence, and black clothing was widely adopted as a communal mark of repentance. Others point to its widespread use in the Spanish court as an outward manifestation of piety in its ultra-Catholic culture as a badge of sobriety and virtue. Still others name Baldassare Castiglione the author of its popularity. In his famous conduct manual *Il Cortegiano* (The Courtier) he recommended wearing black at court as it was 'more suitable for garments than any other colour'. Henry VIII owned hundreds of black garments and Elizabeth was also partial to it, possessing numerous black gowns in a variety of fabrics. The fact that black was a colour not subject to sumptuary laws meant it also became the colour of choice among merchants, lawyers and aspirational administrators who could mingle with the aristocracy without overtly betraying their more lowly origins.

Black was also the colour of grief, donned for mourning clothes not only by those directly bereaved, but also by their households and associates. In France, white was worn for mourning by a former queen who relinquished the throne on the death of her husband. Catherine de' Medici, however, broke with tradition and wore black because she stayed in power, becoming France's regent after Henri II's death. The collective wearing of black expressed kinship, a shared loss. It indicated the extent of the connections garnered by the person who had died. It was traditional for women to wear mourning black for the first year, sometimes more, following the death of a husband. Many women, however, continued to wear it long after the ritual mourning period had ended. Catherine de' Medici persisted in wearing black until she herself died, thirty years after Henri's death. Hers was a strategic choice: wearing black was protective and deflected the unwanted attention of men. Moreover, it provided widows with a unique and ambiguous status, neither virginal nor under male control which allowed them greater agency and independence. For queens, mourning attire acted as a reminder of their spousal connection to their husband's status, authority and lineage, and prolonged their political prestige. Mary chose to remain in black after the death of François II until her second marriage in 1565. According to the treasury accounts, she had an unremitting preference for black Florence stemming (a fine wool fabric), satin, taffeta, velvet and silk. The cost of her black fabrics was met through treasury funds, which suggests that the queen persisted in wearing black not only to emphasise her widow's status, but also to mimic male authority and adopt – for state business – the customary garb of male European courtiers and court officials. It indicates that Mary was deliberately reinforcing her role as head of government through her attire in order to counter any undermining of her ministerial authority.

Although status was an important element of sartorial performance, all this attention to clothes was not just about power dressing. Mary was alert to the performative theatricality of clothes, of dress as a spectators' sport. The robes she wore for the opening of her first Parliament, in May 1563, presented a heightened display of her monarchy as a public demonstration of her sovereignty. She spent approximately 175 Scots pounds (equivalent to over £11,000 sterling today) on her appearance. Of this, 124 Scots pounds (nearly £8,000 sterling) was spent on 16½ ells of purple velvet for her robe. The remainder covered the cost of white satin for its skirt and sleeves, violet and white taffeta and 25 ells of gold braid.[23] Her wearing of royal purple, the monarchical colour of power, was traditional. Mary processed through Edinburgh resplendent in a long train and sparkling in jewels. At more than 5 feet 10 inches tall, her appearance would have been particularly impressive among what was then a population of generally much smaller stature. In the procession, Mary's female entourage followed behind her dressed in sumptuous, if not quite equal, splendour in gowns with sweeping trains to amplify Mary's magnificence. Spatially, the use of trains expanded their presence. This impressive cavalcade of women was purposefully the most glamorous that had ever been witnessed in Scotland. Mary's intention was clearly political: through this parade of youthful, confident women she wanted to inspire a surge of hope. As a new female monarch she had much at stake. She needed to shore up her authority with an irrefutable and resolute show of majesty. As ever, John Knox remained unimpressed, dismissing the display and commenting that 'such stinking pride of women as was seen at that Parliament was never seen before in Scotland.'[24] Later, he followed this observation with a cautionary note:

O, Fair ladies, how pleasing were this life of yours, if it should ever abide, and then in the end that we may pass to Heaven with all this gay gear! But fie upon the knave Death that will come whether we will or not! And when he has laid on his arrest, the foul worms will be busy with this flesh, be it never so fair and so tender; and the Silly Soul, I fear, shall be feeble that it can nether carry with it gold, or garnishing, targetting, pearl, nor precious stones.[25]

With the Scottish Reformation, clothes became increasingly subject to moral judgement. Any excess of luxury fabric and embellishment was looked upon by zealous reformers as a sign of vanity, of placing temporal delight above spiritual worth. The reformers advocated sober, unadorned dress as a mark of virtue and respect for God.

As with Mary and her entourage's shared magnificence at the opening of parliament, visual cohesion created a stronger group identity. Livery was the emblematic uniform of court officials: it codified and quantified a royal household and visually separated people's roles and functions to clearly delineate their pecking order. While there would have been a linking theme of colour and emblems, the quality and detail of the livery of a trumpeter was superior to that of a page. A page's livery different from that of a dog keeper. When Marie de Guise became queen of Scotland, she chose to keep her own household in black livery rather than have them adopt the Scottish court colours of red and yellow. It marked them out as her servants and visibly accentuated the extent of her authority and the measure of support she had at her disposal. One of Mary's first actions on taking up her throne was to order sufficient fabric, thread and trimmings to outfit herself and fifteen of her ladies for their first progress through Scotland in September 1561. All still in mourning black, their collective material grief even extended to the trappings of their horses, whose bridles and reins were woven in black silk thread.[26] Such uniformity ensured that Mary's status was reflected in the swell of the women grouped around her. It manifested the extent of the loyalty and protection accorded to her. The queen, however, had to be perceived as the central and most powerful figure in the throng. To this end, while Mary's women wore black woollen cloth trimmed with wool braid, the queen was dressed in Florence serge trimmed with black silk ribbons.

Monarchs often chose to appear at ceremonial events dressed in matching cloth and colours. When Charles V of France and Henry VIII met in 1520 at Dover Castle they purposefully dressed 'both of one suite' in cloth of gold embroidered with silver. It reiterated their amity. For the wedding of James IV of Scotland and Margaret Tudor of England, they both wore figured cloth of gold lined with crimson velvet to visually reference their political as well as personal union.[27]

When Mary returned to Scotland from France, she brought with her the material triumph of her glory days as the French Queen Consort. As well as furnishings, there were gowns of cloth of gold and silver, yellow and crimson satin, crimson-violet taffeta, orange and blue damask and crimson and green velvet, all enriched with gold or silver braid or embroidery, often with both. An inventory compiled in 1561 demonstrates the richness of the wardrobe she imported:

> A gown of crimson satin ... covered in embroidery in roses and leaves of silver and the rest ordered with gold and banded with gold passement.
>
> A gown of green velvet ... covered in embroidery and corded [with] gold and silver and bordered with a passement of the same silver and gold.
>
> A gown of shot orange taffeta striped with silver and decorated with silver braid that was stitched all along it.[28]

Yet Mary, it seemed, made scant use of them in Scotland, eventually passing many on to her close circle of ladies-in-waiting and female associates. She removed only four gowns and three vasquines (petticoats) for her own use during her reign. Until 1565, the treasury accounts track Mary's relentless, almost exclusive, purchase of black cloth and trimmings. But the 1578 inventory of her wardrobe tells a different story. Here are gowns of green and purple velvet; yellow, orange and crimson satin; crimson and silver silk. One 'long-tailed' gown (in other words, with a train) is of incarnate taffeta decorated with silver braid and couched in blue and silver cord; another, low-necked, is of blue satin enhanced with gold braid; a third is of silver and purple silk with white satin sleeves wrought all over with silver work.[29] The sumptuousness of these garments offers a striking contrast to our image of the Scottish queen, portrayed in black. Only some of this splendour accompanied Mary from France; the rest she purchased during her reign in Scotland. It seems plausible that Mary chose to access treasury funds for her 'official' clothing: the black gowns she wore for political business, her ceremonial attire and the costumes required for diplomatic entertainments. The cost of her more elaborate and colourful clothes seems to have been met from her own resources, from the pension she received as queen dowager of France and what revenue she culled from her estates in Scotland. It pointed up Mary's dual role as the ruler of a kingdom and as hostess of a court. As a ruler, she wore clothes that emphasised her gravitas and responsibility for governance. As court hostess, she chose to array herself in garments that reflected Scotland's aspirations, sophistication, prosperity and vibrancy.

Despite her sombre garb of widow's weeds, Mary attracted admirers. A French poet, Pierre de Bocosel de Chastelard had been part of Mary's entourage when she came to Scotland in 1561 and, after a brief return to France, Chastelard returned to Scotland. There he found favour with the queen. They danced well together, shared a love of poetry and engaged in a seemingly innocent flirtation. Chastelard gave Mary a book of his poems; she lent him one of her finest horses. While their intimacy appeared merely coquettish fun, some found it troubling. In the new morality of Protestant Scotland, some viewed the French court as licentious and dissolute, and feared that it had had a corrupting influence on their own queen.[30] When, in 1563, Chastelard was discovered hiding under Mary's bed in the Palace of Holyroodhouse. he was severely reprimanded and banished. Two days later, however, he made a dramatic re-appearance in Mary's bedchamber, declaring his love and trying to embrace the Scottish queen. Mary was frightened. This was more than a romantic ruse – Chastelard posed a threat to the queen's safety. He was tried, sentenced to death and executed as Mary looked on in tears. Sometime later, the Scottish statesman William Maitland advised a Spanish diplomat that there was reason to believe that Chastelard had been sent as a Protestant agent from France to 'sully the honour of the Queen' and destroy her chances of marrying her potential suitor at that time, the Catholic Don Carlos of Spain.[31]

It was time for Mary to settle her own affairs. By the end of 1563, she became fretful and prone to sickness, and Randolph, the English ambassador, observed that 'some think the Queen's sickness is caused by her utterly despairing of the marriage of any of those who she looked for'.³² The question of Mary's marriage was an absorbing topic for monarchical conjecture, much discussed and debated in European diplomatic circles. At the onset of her personal reign, she had declared that when it came to marriage, she would follow the will of her people and her nobility, but Mary was aware that her choice of a husband would be dictated as much by foreign as domestic policy. Her decision would impact on the already fragile balance of power in Europe. It was a choice fraught with political pitfalls.

A Catholic husband would find favour in Rome but not in England, but a Spanish match would undermine Scotland's special relationship with France. A Protestant candidate might appease England and be welcomed in Scotland, but would not please a Catholic Europe already destabilised by religious division. A Scottish choice would be certain to incite jealousy among her own nobles and exacerbate factional disaffection. To marry a foreign monarch risked Mary becoming, once again, an absent queen. Each of the serious contenders – Don Carlos of Spain, Archduke Charles II of Austria, Eric XIV of Sweden and the French Duke of Nemours – had matrimonial merit, but none of them came unencumbered by some element of political risk.

To Mary's list of possible suitors, Elizabeth added her own: Robert Dudley, her Master of the Horse. While he was not of royal blood and had no estates nor titles, Dudley had risen to a uniquely privileged position at Elizabeth's court as her favourite and, many believed, her lover. Given the latter, Elizabeth's suggestion was outrageous. The English queen dangled a carrot to seal the match. Should Mary accept Robert Dudley she would be rewarded not just with a husband but with Elizabeth officially naming Mary as her successor. For Elizabeth, such a plan was masterful. In one fell swoop she could keep Dudley close, Mary under surveillance, dissipate English Catholic ambition and advance her alliance with Protestant Scotland.

As a further inducement, Elizabeth made Dudley the Earl of Leicester (henceforth known as Leicester). She pressed on with her plan, declaring:

And this also shall most content her that if she, Mary, shall be conversant with her, Elizabeth, in this realm, and living with her, she will glad to bear the charges of the family, both of the Earl of Leicester and her, as shall meet for one sister to do for another.[33]

What Elizabeth was proposing was a political and personal *ménage à trois*. While the idea seemed preposterous, Mary seemed prepared to entertain the scheme. Even so, she prevaricated.

In time, King Philip II of Spain abandoned the negotiations for Mary to marry his son, Don Carlos, due to his mental instability. Into the gap stepped Henry Stuart, Lord Darnley, who was already lurking in the wings. When Darnley was fifteen, he had been sent by his parents to France to convey their condolences to Mary on the untimely deaths of Henri and François. It was a pre-emptive strike. Darnley's parents wanted to parade their son's eligibility in front of the newly widowed queen. Here was a young, accomplished nobleman with his own royal credentials.

Darnley was the second son of the fourth Earl of Lennox, a great-grandson of Henry VII. His mother was Margaret Douglas, the daughter of Mary's grandmother Margaret Tudor by her second marriage, which made Margaret Douglas, like Mary, a claimant to the English throne. Margaret's royal ancestry ensured she had stayed close to the English court. She had been lady-in-waiting to three of Henry VIII's wives and to Mary Tudor, who viewed Margaret as her heir presumptive. She even gave Margaret precedence over Elizabeth at the Catholic queen's coronation. Margaret, herself a Catholic, had her successional hopes dashed, however, when the Act of Succession was revised. She diverted her monarchical ambitions to her son. Darnley was groomed in court culture and raised in the expectation of royal advancement. He entered Elizabeth's court and, in time, became one of the English queen's favourites. By July 1563, he was to be found there daily, soothing Elizabeth's frazzled nerves with the soft strains of his lute.

History has set Darnley down as a petulant youth, vainglorious and ambitious, a young man given to promiscuity, bisexual adventures and excessive drinking. Waywardness and drunkenness fuelled a malevolence that could erupt in vengeful violence; but there must also have been charm. Educated in France, tutored in all the graces expected of a high-ranking courtier, Darnley had cultural finesse. He was a skilled musician, a passionate huntsman and a fine dancer. He must have had a sufficient semblance of grace and refinement for him to find such a favoured place at Elizabeth's court.

It was Darnley's father, the Earl of Lennox, who paved the way for his son's arrival in Scotland. In 1564, Lennox was granted permission to visit his homeland. Elizabeth had originally championed his petition. When she realised, however, that he may have had ulterior motives lurking beneath his excuse of settling his affairs, and might be returning to Scotland to try to win the support of Scottish nobles for a marriage between his son and Mary, Elizabeth tried to withdraw her support. But it was too late. Mary had already agreed to his coming. Alarmed, Elizabeth had the presence of mind to prevent Darnley and his mother accompanying the Earl and, as a precaution, placed them under house arrest. In December 1564, Lennox requested his son's presence. Still wary, Elizabeth reluctantly agreed, on the advice of Cecil and Leicester. Mary had her own reasons for approving Darnley's visit. Her need to secure a suitable marriage had become more urgent. That December, Elizabeth had fallen dangerously ill. By the beginning of January 1565, it was said that she was near death. Now, more than ever, Mary had to boost her successional potential. She needed to arm herself with a union which strengthened her claim to the English throne. Darnley, with his royal pedigree, fitted the bill. His appeal was bolstered by a rumour that Elizabeth was considering naming him as her heir. While Mary still pursued the possibility of a marriage with Don Carlos, she now also entertained the idea of Darnley as a potential suitor, as an alternative strategy to strengthen her claim to the English throne.

Darnley was just twenty years old, three years younger than Mary, when he arrived in Scotland in February 1565. He met Mary at Wemyss Castle. When I stood in what remains of their trysting place, a thick-walled courtyard with seven enclosed spiral staircases leading to different parts of the castle, I tried to visualise their encounter there. It is said that Mary's first glimpse of him was from one of its narrow windows, watching as he arrived on his horse, calculating his promise. He made a pleasing impression. At over 6 feet tall, Darnley was well matched with Mary. He was graceful and well-proportioned. In the hours they spent together at Wemyss, he was to prove entertaining: he demonstrated prowess in hunting, agility at dancing and musical accomplishment. To those watching with eagle eyes, Mary seemed diverted but hardly enamoured. To Leicester's dismay, Elizabeth continued to press his suit.

The following month, as John Balfour Paul, the editor of the treasury accounts relating to Mary's reign, drily remarked in his preface, 'the queen had many more gowns this month'. He continued 'on the 10th is mentioned one of velvet … lined with grogram; a few days later she had another velvet gown lined with silk taffeta; and ornamented with no less than seven dozen long tailed buttons'.[34]

The treasury accounts chart Mary's increasing investment in her wardrobe. On 27 March she ordered three new gowns of silk camlet, grey damask and Florence serge; the damask gown was to be bordered in grey velvet and ornamented with 50 ells of red crimson braid. Ribbon was needed for cloaks and aprons, satin for new headdresses; a quantity of veils and buttons were required.

Three days later, 12 ells of white silk satin were purchased with sixty white buttons and some red silk taffeta. Gold thread was needed to set rubies in a collar and sleeves. Silk napkins were procured. More was added to the accounts in the days that followed: white and blue taffeta, green silk, crimson camlet, white velvet, incarnate satin and hanks of gold and silver for their embroidery.[35] After four years of only purchasing black, this sudden shift to colour was dramatic. It is interesting to speculate on the purpose of these purchases. If, as seems to be the case, Mary used treasury funds for expenditure she considered valid for affairs of state, it suggests she thought these March purchases essential political investments in Scotland's future.

In his memoirs, the Scottish diplomat Melville followed the trajectory of Mary and Darnley's relationship. Darnley, it seems, was over-eager to play his hand:

Her majesty took well with him and said that he was the lustiest and best proportioned long man that she had seen; for he was of high stature, long and small, even and erect, from his youth well instructed in all honest, and comely exercises. After he haunted the court for some time, he proposed marriage to Her Majesty, which she took in evil part at first, as the same day she herself told me, and that she refused a ring which he then offered to her.[36]

That March, the door finally closed on the proposed marriage with Don Carlos. Leicester, too, spurned the honour of becoming Mary's husband, much to Randolph's frustration:

He whom I go about to make as happy as ever was any, to put him in possession of a kingdom, to make him Prince of a mighty people, to lay in his naked arms a most fair and worthy lady ... nothing regards the good that shall ensue unto him thereby ... but so uncertainly deals that I know not where to find him.[37]

Faced with ever-decreasing options, Mary began to test the political temperature regarding a possible union with Darnley.

Although Darnley affected to be Protestant, as many of the nobility did in order to remain in political favour, he had been raised a Catholic. Like many of his generation, he exercised his religion on a needs-must basis. Mary's Guise uncle, the Cardinal of Lorraine, sent out a warning shot describing Darnley as 'a polished trifler'.[38] And, when the possibility of the marriage began to be whispered abroad, Elizabeth became unsettled.

In April, Darnley fell ill at Stirling Castle. Mary visited him regularly, sometimes staying until after midnight. What had begun as solicitude quickly became infatuation. Darnley's vulnerability must have rekindled for Mary memories of her vigil by François' side as he fought for life. It seemed to have sparked in her something deeper than her desire for a politically expedient union. Here was a life she could save. Darnley remained in his sick room at Stirling Castle for the next month. Some said that he feigned a prolonged lassitude, seizing the opportunity to eke out his illness and snare Mary into intimacy. What is certain is that by the time Darnley was released from his sick room and returned to court, Mary had become enamoured.

By Easter, Mary and Darnley were inseparable. Their proposed marriage, while not yet settled, was an open secret. Many were uneasy. Randolph was horrified:

She does so much that some report she is bewitched: the tokens, the rings, the bracelets are daily worn that contain secret mysteries. Shame is laid aside, and all regard of that which chiefly pertained to princely honour removed out of sight ... she has brought her honour into question, her estate in hazard, her country torn to pieces. Woe worth the time that ever Lord Darnley set foot in this country ... what will become of her?[39]

Elizabeth was furious, and gave vent to her wrath by instructing Darnley to return instantly to England. Mary demanded that he stayed. Darnley remained in Scotland. He was, however, an English citizen and Elizabeth's subject and his proximity to the English line of succession required him to secure Elizabeth's consent to any marriage. His defiance risked severe repercussions, and Elizabeth tried to force his hand. She imprisoned his mother, Margaret Douglas, in the Tower, confiscated her estates and movables and forbade her to have any communication with her husband or son. But it was ineffectual; Darnley stayed in Scotland. Margaret Douglas was to remain in the Tower for the next two years, becoming increasingly impoverished and in want of material comfort.

But why was Mary and Darnley's marriage such a threat to Elizabeth? The fact that their separate successional eligibility to the English throne was strengthened by their union certainly posed a challenge, but it was not insurmountable. As the law stood, Mary, having been born in Scotland, did not meet the conditions of successional rights, and Darnley's claim was at best tenuous. The real threat lay in their Catholicism. While Mary's Catholic faith was intransigent, Darnley's religious adherence was more mercurial. There was a fear that he would readily embrace Catholicism if it was to his political advantage. Together he and Mary could reignite the ambitions of English Catholics who, combined with what remained of Mary's Catholic Scottish forces and those of Catholic Europe, could usurp Elizabeth and put Mary in Elizabeth's place. Not only would Elizabeth be dethroned, but Protestant England would be returned to Rome. The marriage must be stopped.

The two queens exchanged bitter words, with Elizabeth declaring through her Parliament that Mary's marriage would be 'un-meet, unprofitable and perilous to the sincere amity between two queens'.[40] Mary was undeterred. In May, she knighted Darnley Lord of Ardmanoch and Earl of Ross, and fifteen others were also knighted, including some of Lennox's and Darnley's closest cohorts. It caused a shift of balance among the prevailing Scottish nobility, fostering a stronger Catholic contingent. A serious rift developed between Mary and Moray (her half-brother James Stewart who had been elevated to the Earl of Moray and will henceforth be referred to as Moray). He vehemently opposed the marriage. Like Elizabeth and her advisers, he was fearful of a Catholic insurrection. Moray refused to vote at the meeting of nobles convened to sanction the nuptials and absented himself from the second convention to ratify the match. This was not just disapproval, but opposition. He petitioned Elizabeth for support to sabotage the marriage, and she responded with £3,000. Moray's plan was to kidnap Mary, Darnley and his father and bring them to London. But Mary was forewarned, and escaped her pursuers flanked by an armed escort of 2,000 men. The collusion between Moray and England to destroy the union of Darnley and Mary, and thus disempower Mary, only made the Scottish queen more resolute.

By 18 July, it was rumoured that Mary and Darnley were 'handfasted' (a form of unofficial wedding pledge in Scotland in which a couple's hands are bound together in cloth to symbolise their union). Alarmed at Mary's public proclamation that the proposed marriage would not threaten the religious status quo, and seeing it as a declaration that masked a hidden agenda, Moray and the Lords of the Congregation (the Scottish nobles who had led the reformist rebellion), once more beseeched Elizabeth for financial aid to raise an army against the Scottish queen and her husband-to-be. More funds were sent. This was treason: a confrontation between Mary and her recalcitrant nobles was inevitable. With Darnley at her side, Mary steeled herself for battle.

July saw Darnley made Duke of Albany. The bans were called and Darnley was proclaimed King of Scotland. Without waiting for the necessary dispensation from Rome (this was required because Mary and Darnley were first cousins and fell outside the permitted degree of consanguinity), on 29 July 1565, the treasury recorded payment for 'the ordinary gunners within the castle of Edinburgh for their labours in shooting the artillery within the said castle this instant day at the solemnity of the marriage of her highness'.[41]

In the early hours of the morning, Mary entered the chapel at the Palace of Holyroodhouse accompanied by her ladies and her nobility. She wore, according to Randolph, 'a great mourning gown of black, with a great wide mourning hood, not unlike that she wore the doleful day of the burial of her husband'. It was a Catholic ceremony and, after Mary and Darnley had said their vows, they knelt to pray. Darnley, however, excused himself from attending the Catholic mass that followed. When it was over, Mary, as Randolph reported to Cecil:

was required, according to the solemnities, to cast off her care, and lay aside her sorrowful garments, and give herself to a pleasanter life. After some pretty refusals, more I believe for manner sake than for grief of heart, she suffered those that stood by, every man that could approach her to take out a pin, and so being committed to her ladies, she changed her garments.[42]

Subsequent historians have pounced upon this removal of pins as evidence of Mary's brazenness, an example of how Mary's marriage to Darnley was forged by passion rather than political discernment. But since garments in the sixteenth century were held together by hundreds of pins, the removal of a few was simply a ritual act and would not have resulted in the queen being immodestly dressed. The participation of the nobles was symbolic, marking their consent to her marriage and her transition from widow to wife. It was a performance of alteration.

The wedding masques organised for Mary's marriage to Darnley were performed over three nights and took as their theme the potency of marriage and love. One masque celebrated the return of Salus, the Roman goddess of safety and well-being. Diana, the goddess of love, appeared among a miscellany of Greek deities to lament the loss of one of her followers. There was also an equestrian masque which featured Ethiopian warriors, Knights of Virtue and Peace, Neptune's followers and a group of knights with Cupids embroidered on their breastplates, who extolled Mary's virtues and offered her fealty. In the contentious climate of their marriage, Mary and Darnley were careful to avoid any overtly political themes in its revelries.

Just three days later, Mary and Darnley began to dress their court and its king in a new magnificence. The treasury accounts for August 1565 make eye-watering reading. In just one month, the couple purchased over 1,000 ells of fabric. There was sumptuous new livery for members of their households emblazoned with a new coat of arms. Gifts were distributed. Mary's Italian secretary, David Rizzio, who had helped to broker the marriage, received black satin and taffeta and swathes of green taffeta and velvet for his bed furnishings. Bastian Pagez, thought to have masterminded the wedding festivities, was rewarded with new outfits and a string for his bonnet set with pearls and precious stones. For the most part, however, it was Darnley who was indulged. He was decked out in modish and lavish finery: 73 ells of holland cloth were procured for his shirts, ruffs, handkerchiefs and foot socks. There were new doublets of white silk taffeta, red crimson, black velvet and satin, adorned with silk and silver buttons. There were perfumed gloves lined with velvet. An under-jerkin for his armour was ornamented with silver lace at a cost of over 100 Scots pounds. In just one month, the queen and her king spent over 3,000 Scots pounds, the equivalent today of over £250,000 sterling. It was a political investment, a way of visibly elevating Darnley and proclaiming his kingship through a fabricated grandeur. This was Mary's court re-presented in material triumph, declaring its promise and its potential for glory in the years ahead.⁴³

Mary and Darnley's enemies still plotted to undermine their joint rule and destroy their power. With the funds from England, they mustered an army to overthrow them. Mary and Darnley remained undaunted and turned their attention to matters of war. They requisitioned fur and buffalo hides to cover saddles, 600 ells of canvas to construct pavilions, 200 more to erect temporary stables and 80 ells of buckram 'in their majesties' colours'.⁴⁴

On 10 September proclamations began to be shouted out in all the major towns in Scotland:

> charging all and sundry of our Sovereign Lord and Lady Liege between the ages of 16 and 60 years from town and countryside, regally and royally, that they and each one of them well bodied in pride of war with pavilions and other needful provisions to lie on the fields with twenty days' provisions, to meet our Sovereigns at Stirling the last day of September, instant, under pain of forfeit of life, lands and goods.⁴⁵

Bakers, brewers, butchers, fishermen and other merchants were commanded to prepare provisions for the army, and Mary started to gather around her those nobles loyal to her cause. She freed George Gordon, who had been languishing in prison since the Battle of Corrichie in 1562, the battle in which his father and brothers had died. Now, in need of his support and, more importantly, that of his followers in the north, Mary released him from captivity. She presented him with a set of green damask bed furnishings. It was a gift purposefully laden with emotional appeal to ensnare his allegiance. The green furnishings echoed those listed in the forfeited trove of textiles that had once belonged to his father, and their significance would not have been lost on Gordon. The queen was bestowing on him a restoration of sorts, the retrieval of his own lost heritage. Later, he would be allowed to reclaim his title of the Earl of Huntly and his estates would be returned. For the moment, however, the bed furnishings acted as her bond of reinstatement.[46]

On 14 October, another proclamation was made to search, seek and apprehend the goods, gear and grain of the rebel lords. Moray and his associates were to be made outlaws. By November, what became known as the Chaseabout Raid, the martial confrontation between Mary and Darnley and their detractors amongst Scottish nobles, led by Moray, was over, and the rebels had been routed. Even Mary's most condemnatory critic, Knox, admired her strength: 'albeit the most part-waxed weary, yet the Queen's courage increased manlike so much, that she was ever at the foremost'. Darnley and Mary had outwitted their adversaries, who fled and became exiles in England.[47]

There is an English nursery rhyme, popular in the eighteenth century, although some believe its origins could be much earlier:

> Mary, Mary, quite contrary
> How does your garden grow?
> With cockle shells and silver bells
> And pretty maids all in a row.

For those, like me, who are diverted by apocryphal tales, there is a myth that it refers to this period of Mary's life and her seemingly wayward choice of Darnley. He was given the unwarranted honour, the following year, of being granted the French Order of St Michael, which in Scotland is called the Order of the Cockle; Mary's Catholicism is referenced through the silver bells, an allusion to the small Sanctus bell rung during the Catholic mass, and, of course, the four Marys would be the pretty maids. Nursery rhymes were often political in their origin, beginning their life as satirical ditties which captured the prevailing public opinion of a person or event. There is something in the poignancy of this rhyme that makes me want its association with Mary to be true: that it originated as a contemporary note of political caution and public unease at Mary's choice of her husband, conveyed through the haunting simplicity of a children's rhyme.

# 5
# A Suit of Savage Attire

My sewing skills were called upon during the early years of what I optimistically called my 'theatre career'. There was the actor-sized banana costume I fashioned from an old yellow bedspread which, once unzipped, revealed the wicked witch (a witch thought long dead by the tiny tots who screamed in terror at her reappearance). There was the human Christmas pudding who graced the Mad Hatter's Tea Party in a festive version of Lewis Carroll's *Alice in Wonderland*. The actor's face peeped out from a brown towelling dome topped with a scrap of white satin to mimic brandy sauce. For each performance, the dome would be smeared with a smidgen of paraffin. When it was lit, it earned a satisfying gasp from the audience – although it was somewhat more alarming for the hapless actor playing the part, who had to sing his jolly pudding song to the accompanying aroma of singed hair. At Bracknell Arts Centre I dressed a cast of over 100 people for a community production of Richard Crane's *The Quest*. In those cash-strapped days this reimagining of the magnificence of King Arthur's court had to be realised on a sixpence. Merlin appeared almost wind-blown in floaty translucent nylon curtains, while an assembly of medieval rustics were suitably garbed in recycled potato sacks.

The sixteenth century entered my costume-making repertoire when I was a student at the Bristol Old Vic Theatre School. Designated wardrobe assistant for a production of Ned Sherrin's musical adaptation of Caryl Brahms' *No Bed for Bacon* – an irreverent romp based on the life of Shakespeare – I was tasked with fashioning its accessories. The school's experienced wardrobe mistress inducted me in the intricacies of ruff making, an art I found both absorbing and frustrating in equal measure. More yards of starched white lawn than one would have thought possible were pleated with mathematical precision in repetitive figures-of-eight, their even undulation only achievable through a multitude of tiny stitches. It was a rare insight into what was demanded of the seamstresses and tailors in Mary's day.

The Scottish court was hosting a variety of theatrical and spectacular entertainments long before Mary's return. Its kings participated in the amusements: the treasury accounts record outlay for their 'play coats' and masquing costumes. In 1506, jubilant after the birth of his son, James IV organised a chivalric extravaganza, *The Knight and the Black Lady,* a tournament in which a knight (the king himself) rescued the Queen of Beauty, a Black Moor. Its setting was allegorical. A Field of Memory featured silk pavilions and a Garden of Pleasure containing a Tree of Hope with leaves of Delight, flowers of Nobleness and fruits of Honour, all crafted from the richest of fabrics. In the 1550s, Sir David Lyndsay's *The Satire of the Three Estates* was performed. It was a nine-hour outdoor dramatic marathon, a morality play that lampooned the Catholic clergy and explored – albeit through the screen of satire – the political and religious tensions in Scotland at the time. Much of what was enjoyed at court, however, was lighter entertainment. As well as Morris dancers and tight-rope walkers there were visits from guisers at Christmas: courtiers dressed in exotic costumes and masks who appeared disguised as strangers to challenge those present to a game of dice or offer to perform a dance in return for hospitality.

Like their English counterparts, Scottish monarchs had their own personal fools to provide irreverent commentary on contemporary political events and personalities. Fools were cherished members of the royal household. Mary had two female fools, Janet Musche and Nichola La Jardiniere. La Jardiniere had accompanied the queen from France. Her wardrobe included a blue gown trimmed in yellow and a red petticoat, a gown of English blue, another of grey and green and a gift from Mary of one of the queen's own gowns bordered in white satin. She was provided with green wool bed furnishings and linen sheets and seemed to require a regular supply of handkerchiefs, some of which were made from embroidered cloth.[1] On Mary's marriage to Darnley, his two male fools, Foyser and James Geddie, joined the court and Geddie was decked out in red and yellow and Servais recorded the dispersal of 'an old silk of green velvet with two feathered blue bonnets all to be given to the king's fool'.[2]

Mary was to introduce a more emphatically French veneer to Scottish court diversions organising, as a contemporary chronicler recorded, 'marvellous sights and shows [and] singular devices'.[3] The repertoire of tournaments, spectacles and masques continued but these entertainments were designed with greater attention to the glamour of costume and the ingenuity of sets to emulate those Mary had witnessed in France. When Mary's wardrobe was inventoried in 1578, a cache of the remnants of her court revelries was discovered: feathers of different colours; fringed masking costumes; golden shields; headdresses of silver and red-and-yellow Egyptian hats.[4] Her court was characterised by a greater indulgence in masques and the dancing and banqueting which accompanied them. Unsurprisingly, the spiritual leader of the Scottish Reformation, John Knox, castigated Mary for her delight in such fun: 'her common talk was, in secret, [that] she saw nothing in Scotland but gravitas, which was repugnant to her nature, for she was brought up in 'joyouestie', so [she] termed her dancing and other things'.[5]

There was another reason for Knox's dismay. With the plague taking hold, there were calls for mass gatherings to be suspended and playhouses to be closed. Mary's persistence in continuing to host festivities must have seemed, for some, unwise but her revelries continued. By 1563, even Randolph was becoming sated: 'I have nothing to write, for we had so little to think in, that we passed our time in feasts, banqueting, masking and running at the ring and such like'.[6]

It was masques that lay at the heart of such festivities. They combined extraordinary spectacle with music, song, dance and verse to explore political relationships and the health of the realm. They comprised a series of interludes performed at intervals during court banquets where the drama lay in the revelation of extraordinary tableaux rather than in character or plot. Masques paraded an eclectic cavalcade of living emblems: personifications of ideas and ideals interpreted through costume and set. They were visual feasts in which fantasy universes were ruled over by gods and goddesses, inhabited by supernatural spirits and allegorical beings.

The costumes for masques were elaborate, alluring and daring. Performers had licence to appear in more effervescent garb than would have been countenanced in daily or even ceremonial life. Women's skirts were shorter, fabric often translucent, girdles were tied under women's breasts to emphasise their fullness. Feet were shod in footwear bedecked with jewels and flowers. Diadems were haloed in stars that trembled on slender wire and diaphanous veils were made from fine silver tissue. There was a liberal use of spangles and tinsel to ensure that, in the glow of candlelight, performers were suffused in glimmering light and appeared glorious in gold and silver ornamentation. One description of the costume for Juno's aerial spirits, in a later masque by Thomas Carew called *Coelum Britannicum*, captures the luminosity of their presence:

The upper part of white cloth of silver, wrought upon Juno's birds and fruits, a loose under-garment, full gathered of carnation striped with silver and parted within gold zone. Beneath that, another flowing garment of watchet cloth of silver laced with gold ... Their shoes were azure and gold, set with rubies and diamonds; so were all the garments and every part abounding in ornament.[7]

Ingenious sets were engineered to transform a court's great hall into an Elysium grove or a velvet forest. These were wonderlands in which a mountain might disgorge a galaxy of magical creatures, where the great feats of architecture – castles, towers, battlements – were recreated in fictional splendour. Onlookers were transported to worlds where the extraordinary was credible. Innovations of mechanical invention enabled fantastical beasts to wander, angels to descend from heavenly clouds, vistas of stormy seas or pastoral fields to suddenly appear and just as quickly vanish. Dreamscapes of harmony and sensual illusions of perfection transported audiences to idealised worlds.

Masques were devised as intellectual challenges for the educated and privileged few. Redolent in complex allusion, the unravelling of their layers of artifice demanded visual sophistication. A masque audience needed to be well versed in classical and mythological literature to fully understand the significance of each personification, to detect the deliberate deviances from an original story and appreciate the connection between a performer and the role they played. Each prop carried a symbolic significance: the inclusion of a star, a sword or a palm branch held underlying meaning, as did the colours of costumes. White and crimson signalled desire; tawny (an orange-brown) represented sadness.

Although accounts of masques were widely circulated, they were designed to be intimate, private productions conceived for the court. Their audience was composed of courtiers and visiting dignitaries. Moreover, court masques were participatory. It was the nobility and, at times, the monarchy who played the starring roles. Through the parts they played the elite could be loosed from their established and constrictive personas to present to their peers a transformed self. They could adopt or be assigned roles that revealed characteristics beyond their public identities, which could be surprising, provocative, sensual or playful.

This 'joyouestie', as Knox described it, belied the more serious purpose of the masque: to salve court fractiousness and, through drama, explore and release political tension. In them, performers and their audience could experience, however transiently, an accord of sorts. There are few detailed accounts of masques at the Scottish court in the mid sixteenth century, but a description of the three-day masque prepared for the proposed meeting between Mary and Elizabeth, which was planned to take place in the late summer or early autumn of 1562, survives. Its purpose, as Mary wrote to Elizabeth in January of that year, was to 'present to the world such an amity as has never been seen'.[8] It was William Cecil, Elizabeth's chief adviser, who oversaw the production and fine-tuned its content. Designed to transmit a message of political peace between England and Scotland and the hope of personal friendship between the two queens, it was a symbolic distillation of the barriers to Mary and Elizabeth's political rapport and a celebration of the promise that lay in their lasting amity. Although it was not performed at the time, it was reincarnated later at the English court, and the description of this production provides an insight into the original plan.

The first night was to have been set in a prison at the Hall of Extreme Oblivion, guarded by Circumspection. Pallas (the virgin patroness of Athens and goddess of wisdom) was to appear riding a unicorn to signify Scotland (the unicorn being a device on the Scottish royal arms). Pallas was to carry a standard which featured two women's hands 'knit one fast to the other and over their hands written the word 'Loyalty'.[9] She was to be followed by two crowned queens: Prudence, riding a golden lion to signify England, and Temperance astride a red lion to represent Scotland. Behind them, a band of masked women dragged their captives, Discord and False Report, personifications of the obstacles which stood in the way of Mary and Elizabeth's mutual trust.

On the second night, Peace was to make her entrance on an elephant accompanied by Friendship with banners representing Ardent Desire and Perpetuity. She was to be reunited with the two queens at the Castle of Plenty. On the final night, Peace, having triumphed over Perpetual Malice and Disdain, was to call upon Prudence and Temperance to join her carrying symbols of their future alliance: a banner inscribed with 'Ever' and a sword engraved with 'Never'. The masque was to end in a garden filled with dancing and singing 'as full of harmony as might be devised' and each night, after each interlude, there was to have been dancing: Scots and English courtiers partnering each other in a choreographed celebration of reconciliation.

While the subject matter and its personifications appear somewhat laboured to our modern sensibilities, for a sixteenth-century audience the masque's multi-layered meanings would have been clear. The characters would not have been named, but onlookers would have identified them from their costumes, props and symbolic colours. The jewellery worn would have been real and the costumes lavish, guaranteed to elicit admiration and astonishment. While the unicorn was obviously fake, Cecil had planned for a real elephant, the first many of the attendees would have ever seen.

The meeting never took place. In the spring of 1562, Mary's uncle, the Duke of Guise, was involved in a massacre of the Protestant Huguenots in France, and the Scottish queen was tainted by association. When Mary heard that the meeting had been abandoned, she was devastated. The news so distressed her that she took to her bed. While other attempts were made to arrange a meeting, they came to naught. Much to Mary's, and perhaps Elizabeth's, frustration, the cousin queens never met.

## A Suit of Savage Attire

During Mary's reign there was a greater emphasis on dressing up. According to the French chronicler Pierre de Brantôme, when Mary was in France she sometimes donned 'the barbarous fashion of the savages of her country'.[10] On her progress to the north of Scotland in 1562, Mary ordered plaids (wool cloth, the forerunner to tartan as we know it now) for her and her ladies to wear and she had her male courtiers don saffron shirts, the traditional male dress of the highlands. There were other reports of Mary adopting disguise. Days before her marriage to Darnley, the queen and her ladies-in-waiting caused something of a scandal in Stirling when she 'and divers of her women apparelled themselves like burgesses' wives, [and] went upon their feet up and down the town, and of every man they met they took some pledge for money towards the banquet'.[11] This tradition lives on in Scotland. Brides-to-be, accompanied by a gaggle of female friends, take to the streets at night banging saucepans. They demand money from passing men and, these days, a kiss for the bride.

Cross-dressing was an intrinsic and, for us today, intriguing feature of sixteenth-century court revelries. Its roots lay in age-old pagan rituals but it was appropriated in the fifteenth and sixteenth centuries as a sophisticated vogue among courtiers. Men dressing as women and women as men was not only a simple reversal of roles but an act of liberation and a flaunting of convention. It was a theatricalisation of self. A portrait of François I of France sees him dressed for a masque in a costume that borrows the draped robes of Mars, Mercury, Minerva and Diana, an amalgam of gods and goddesses. Here was a king unabashed about adopting a female persona if it helped strengthen his claim to classical glory.

Mary liked to escape from her queenly decorum. That she did so outside of the convention of masques led to scandal. She was recorded on several occasions dressed in men's attire. In France, Catherine de' Medici had introduced Mary to breeches to wear under her gown for riding. They offered comfort but also ensured protection of her modesty should she take a tumble. In Scotland, shortly before her marriage to Darnley, Mary decked herself out in male attire to stroll with him through the streets of Stirling, causing, as one chronicler reported, 'tongues to chatter fast'.[12] Lennox, Darnley's father, later also stated that the queen, dressed as a man, took to the streets with Darnley on more than one occasion. Mary and her Marys also appeared 'all clad in men's apparel' at a farewell masque given in honour of the French ambassador when he visited in 1566.[13] At the Scottish court, men also cross-dressed. In a tournament in November 1562, 'the Lord Robert, the Lord John, and others ran at the ring on the sands at Leith, six against six, disguised and apparelled, the one half like women, the other like strangers, in strange masquing costumes'. The women won the ring.[14] Such cross-dressing was frowned upon by the Protestant reformers. They viewed any form of disguising with distrust, seeing it as unnatural and immoral, a rejection of the human form that had been bestowed on man by God.

While cross-dressing caused gossip, rumours of homosexuality were more potentially slanderous. In the sixteenth century, sodomy was a sin. Men sleeping with men, however, was an inevitable consequence of limited bed space, especially during hunting expeditions and warfare. While it was accepted that kings and other high-ranking courtiers surrounded themselves with young bloods whom they would favour with gifts, and who would accompany them on excursions and adventures, such relationships were not thought of as sexual liaisons – although some undoubtedly were. David Rizzio, Mary's private secretary, was reported as having shared a bed with Darnley, but the underlying criticism in the account is of sycophancy, not immorality: 'To strengthen himself against those who hated him he insinuated himself into the favours of Lord Darnley, so far that they would lie sometimes in one bed together'.[15]

David Rizzio was an Italian Catholic who had arrived in Scotland in 1561 as part of a diplomatic mission. He stayed on as Mary's valet before joining her consort of French musicians as its bass singer. Initially, his position was lowly and his remuneration basic, with 50 Scots pounds recorded in January 1561.[16] Rizzio, however, impressed Mary with his musical accomplishments. He was invited to accompany her on hunting expeditions and to attend private suppers in her apartments. Before long, Rizzio had become the queen's intimate.

At first, the Scottish nobility tolerated Rizzio's rise to favour. Mary and Darnley certainly acknowledged the supportive role he seemingly played in their marriage negotiations, prioritising him in the gifts they bestowed after their wedding. He was chosen as the first recipient of their largesse, gifted black taffeta and satin for clothing, and nearly 150 ells of the finest green taffeta, silk and velvet for bed furnishings.[17] But, amongst the Scottish nobility, he was beginning to be viewed as an upstart and an unworthy foreign interloper. Rizzio exacerbated their jealousy by flaunting the royal favour bestowed on him. He wore expensive and flamboyant clothes and installed an arsenal of weapons on the walls of his chambers at the Palace of Holyroodhouse in a quasi-baronial boast of power and privilege.[18]

There was an intriguing exchange of gifts between Rizzio and the Scottish queen. Rizzio presented Mary with a brooch in the shape of a tortoise, adorned with diamonds and rubies. The tortoise was a symbol of protection against predators. As a creature able to defend itself on its own, it was a talisman of endurance, an apt and considered gift for a queen who was constantly being challenged by the male culture that surrounded her. In response, Mary gave Rizzio six pieces of cloth of gold taken from the royal store which, unusually, were patterned with scales, like a tortoise.¹⁹ Such an exchange suggests that the tortoise held a special and private meaning between them. The use of symbolic imagery permeated the visual culture of the Renaissance; it was an intrinsic part of its crafted rhetoric. Depictions of animals, birds, flowers and fruit held moral or emotional significance. Catherine of Aragon chose the pomegranate as her emblem. Signifying fertility, it also represented a unifying authority, as its outer shell harbours inner compartments filled with many seeded clusters. Marie de Guise made use of the phoenix, the symbol of the resurrection and of singularity, an image adopted by Mary in her later years. Symbols accrued deeper significance when repeated across generations. Elizabeth sometimes chose to sport a falcon, the emblem of her mother Anne Boleyn. It symbolised superiority. And Mary adopted the marigold, the emblem of her sister-in-law, Marguerite de Valois, to register her Valois connection.

The distrust and dislike of Rizzio by Mary's nobility turned to overt hatred when the Scottish queen elevated the Italian to the privileged position of her private secretary. Now it was Rizzio who was privy to Mary's private correspondence, and had charge over the arrangements for the queen's audiences with her nobles. He used his role as Mary's gatekeeper to control her nobility's access to her, and exploited his power by accepting bribes from those who wanted him to intercede with Mary on their behalf. Even the exiled Moray (Mary's half-brother, James Stewart) was reduced to offering Rizzio a substantial bribe to persuade Mary to stay the threatened forfeiture of Moray's lands and titles, imposed because of his rebellion against her in the Chaseabout Raid. He sent Rizzio a diamond ring as a further inducement, but Rizzio dragged his heels.

As Rizzio's influence increased, the loathing of him escalated. It was exacerbated when he was appointed Keeper of the Mint and when there began to be talk of him being given a title and lands. Melville recorded in his memoir the mounting tensions:

'Some of the nobility would glower upon him and some would shoulder him and shove him when they entered the chamber and found him always speaking with Her Majesty'. Randolph feared for Rizzio's safety, confiding in Cecil that:

David now works all [at court] and is my Governor to the King and his family. Great is his pride and his words intolerable. People have small joy in this new master and find nothing that God must send him a short end or them a miserable life.[20]

Other rumours began to fly about the court. It was whispered that Rizzio was a papal agent, a Spanish spy, a Catholic priest. Mary's dependency on him and the frequency of his visits to her private apartments, not to mention his overnight stays, fanned gossip that they were lovers.

In January 1566, Mary announced that she was pregnant. While there was rejoicing at the news, there was also concern at the rapid decline of Darnley and Mary's marriage. Darnley's veneer of charm had slipped all too quickly. Heady with royal advancement, spoiled by Mary, triumphant at their victory in the Chaseabout Raid, he pushed for the right to the Crown Matrimonial, which would mean he would reign equally with Mary and, should Mary die, be king of Scotland. But Mary hesitated to make him her political equal and risk his dominance. Darnley punished her for her lack of trust. He drank more excessively, frequented brothels and became abusive and aggressive to the queen. His profligate carelessness was paraded as a calculated humiliation of Mary. The court grew restless in the face of the couple's discord, with the Scottish politician, Sir William Maitland, observed that Darnley 'For she has done him so great an honour, contrary to the advice of her subjects, and he, on the other part, has recompensed her with such ingratitude and misuses himself so far towards her that it is heartbreak for her to think he should be her husband'.[21] There were public quarrels. Mary and Darnley began to sleep apart and go their separate ways. Randolph wrote to Leicester to say 'I know for certain that this queen repents her marriage: that she hates Darnley and all his kin'.[22]

At the Scottish court the already fragile political coalition was at breaking point. There was growing opposition to Mary who, it was felt, had elevated the base-born Catholic Rizzio to unwarranted power. There were fears that his advancement was the precursor to a reinstatement of wider Catholic privilege in the realm. Furthermore, those rebel lords who had been exiled after the Chaseabout Raid – Moray among them – now faced not just banishment but the threat of forfeiting their titles and lands, scheduled to be considered at Parliament that March. They resolved, with other nobles at the Scottish court, to eliminate Rizzio and seize back power. It was time to act.

The nobles exploited Darnley's resentment of Rizzio's intimacy with the queen and fed him rumours of an affair, of Rizzio being not just in Mary's favour but in her bed. Worse, they suggested that the child that Mary was carrying was Rizzio's not Darnley's. Darnley was more than susceptible to the bait. Jealousy, ambition and vanity coalesced and Darnley agreed to join them in a plot to be rid of the Italian. A deal was done and a bond signed. Darnley bartered a pardon for the rebel lords and a stay of the forfeit of their titles and lands in return for him being granted the Crown Matrimonial. While the plan to eliminate Rizzio was not committed to paper, the bond avowed that the nobles would not 'spare life or limb in setting forward all that may bend to the advancement of his [Darnley's] honour'.[23]

The plan to eradicate Rizzio was a secret that was hard to keep. By the end of February, Randolph had apprised Leicester of it:

> I know there are practices in hand contrived between father and son [the Earl of Lennox and Darnley] to come by the crown against her will. I know that if that take effect which is intended, David [Rizzio], with the consent of the King, shall have his throat cut within these ten days.[24]

Shortly afterwards, however, Randolph's days as the gossipy chronicler of Mary's reign were over. His agent was caught supplying funds to the rebel lords and Mary banished him from the Scottish court. It is our loss: there are no more colourful insights into the social and political machinations of the court, nor insights into Mary's emotional state. What we are mostly left with are the opinions and biases of Mary's detractors.

The story of David Rizzio's murder has a central place in Scotland's bloodthirsty history. On my visit to the Palace of Holyroodhouse, I trace the much-debated events of 9 March 1566 with Deborah and Emma, the past and present curators of the palace. We stand in the cramped supper room that barely has space for a table, never mind the company of the seven people that Mary, now over five months pregnant, was entertaining that night. The fire and candles would have been lit and, in such a small space, the air must have been stifling. There might have been music. There was certainly card-playing and a game of dice. Standing in that supper room I imagine the sound of the rebel lords pounding their way up the narrow staircase one after the other. While I find it impossible to picture the scene, I can hear its commotion. The supper room jammed with men shouting down women's cries, Rizzio pleading for his life. As Darnley and his cohorts pulled out their daggers, Mary tried to intervene and Rizzio snatched at her skirts, begging her to save him. But the queen was stilled by the cold steel of a pistol held at her swelling stomach. Rizzio was seized, dragged into

Mary's outer chamber and there stabbed fifty-six times. Darnley, who that very afternoon had played tennis with Rizzio, was among those who drove their daggers home. They heaved his body to the stairwell and threw it down; it was then bundled into a makeshift grave by a porter.

The three of us go into the outer chamber and stare at the red stain on the floor by the window, said to be of Rizzio's blood. It has persisted for nearly five centuries, despite claims that every effort has been made to wash it away. It is very red and seems a little larger than the last time I was here, but none of us mention that. Some myths are not worth dispelling.

As I stood in the room where the horror happened, I ponder on Mary's fear in its aftermath. She was now held captive in silenced chambers in a palace guarded by men other than her own. The queen was at that stage of pregnancy when she could begin to feel her baby move. She must have yearned for its restlessness, some evidence that it had survived the trauma. One thing is certain: these chambers would never again provide the tranquillity they had once offered. Their sanctuary had been ruptured.

Rizzio's murder was not an impulsive act by a group of hot-blooded, drunken nobles, but a premeditated grab at survival and power. Assassinating Rizzio in Mary's presence was a deliberate choice. It was planned with the knowledge that the horror of the carnage, in the claustrophobia of the supper room, with all its attendant and frightening hullabaloo, might provoke Mary's death through miscarriage. But why should Darnley and these recalcitrant nobles wish to cause the death of their queen and Scotland's future heir? The aim of these men was not only to safeguard what they were due to forfeit at the forthcoming Parliament but, by granting Darnley the Crown Matrimonial, make him their puppet and seize political control, a control which would be more assured should Mary also be eliminated. Darnley's ambition to become king outweighed any desire to protect his wife and child. His unborn child was a potential rival should the rebel lords renege on their promise to grant Darnley the Crown Matrimonial. If both mother and child died, it was indisputably Darnley who would be crowned king.

It was a brutal plan which had been plotted with little thought of the consequences beyond Rizzio's murder. By assassinating Rizzio, Mary's closest adviser, the rebel lords hoped, at the very least, to shatter the queen's confidence and weaken her authority. They had other nobles loyal to Mary in their sights that night, others who they planned also to murder. The queen's network of support was to be destroyed. But their proposed victims evaded capture.

Mary was ignorant of the extent of Darnley's involvement, and unaware that he had signed papers sanctioning the pardoning of the rebels in return for him being granted the Crown Matrimonial. When Darnley came to her, contrite and scared, Mary appeared to accept that his part in Rizzio's murder was fuelled by personal jealousy. She effected a reconciliation and included Darnley in her plan for escape and survival. Declaring that she would pardon the rebel lords and those others who had participated in Rizzio's murder, Mary feigned a miscarriage to gain access to her supporters. With their help, the couple managed to flee. Nine days after Rizzio's murder, Mary and Darnley re-entered Edinburgh with 3,000 men. Mary had Rizzio's body removed from its makeshift grave and reburied in the chapel royal. She then installed Rizzio's brother as her private secretary. This was a queen on her mettle, sending out an unequivocal message to those who sought to undermine, betray or endanger her: that she and her child would survive against all the odds.

For any monarch, the birth of an heir is a surety against loss of power and carries the reassurance of continuity. For queens in centuries past, a male child was not a guarantee but a ballast against political and personal insecurity. It was, however, an era fraught with uncertain dynastic survival and successional frailty, since barren queens, infertile kings, stillborn babies and infant deaths were common. Henry VIII's first wife, Catherine of Aragon, bore him six children in nine years. Three were stillborn, two died in infancy. Only one survived babyhood, their daughter, Mary Tudor. Jane Seymour, the mother of Henry's only male heir, died shortly after childbirth and their son, Edward, only lived until the age of fifteen. It took ten years for Catherine de' Medici to conceive; she imbibed a punishing cocktail of remedies and, some said, resorted to black magic before she became pregnant. Of her ten subsequent children, three died in infancy and only two survived her.

For a remote and impoverished country like Scotland, it was only its political worth that safeguarded its independence. The Stewarts had striven to reach the pinnacle of royalty and sustain their power since the eleventh century. Heirs were vital to its dynastic and monarchical survival: they were a political resource. It was through the marriages of their children that the Stewarts brokered alliances with other powerful kingdoms. The 1503 Treaty of Perpetual Peace with England was designed to shield Scotland from English predatory ambitions by uniting the Tudor and Stewart blood lines. It brought the Stewart dynasty and Scotland nearer to the touchline of the English throne, and it was consolidated by James IV's marriage to Margaret Tudor. Married when she was just fourteen years old, Margaret became pregnant two years later – an endorsement of her political value.

Through the treasury accounts we can revisit the excited preparations for the birth of Margaret and James's first child. Florentine taffeta and green ribbons were bought for the cradle and soft woollen fabric for baby blankets. Fine Holland cloth was stitched into cradle sheets and luxurious ermine procured to cocoon the baby in warmth. A purple velvet pillow was sewn to cushion the small royal head. Since it was believed that the clothes of others could transfer their spirit and strength, the king donated one of his own gowns of cloth of gold lined with fur to be reworked as a cradle cover for his child. More fringes, taffeta and white ribbons were purchased for the baptismal font as well as a length of cloth of gold to wrap around the baby when it was carried from the palace to the chapel for its baptism. The nursery was made ready. Ten pieces of arras were hung around its walls and a canopied feather bed furnished for the wet nurse. Its accompanying linen was requisitioned, along with new beds and bed linen, for the appointed chamber children, the valets who would serve the child.[25] James Stewart, Duke of Rothesay, was born on 21 February 1507 at the Palace of Holyroodhouse. It was a moment of dynastic triumph: a son born, a wife assured of her fertility, a peace secured, a Stewart king vindicated.

Prince James died the following year, when he was just one year old. Both James and Margaret were devastated. Margaret was to give birth to five more children, two daughters and three sons: the daughters were stillborn, two more sons died in infancy. Only one child survived: Mary's father, James V. For him, they commissioned a cradle, purchased a scarlet cover, some blankets and three small coats. It was a paltry outlay compared to the exuberant investment that had been made for their first son.[26]

The importance of women's fertility was manifested in the elaborate textile rituals that surrounded childbirth: ceremonies of withdrawal and reappearance that were exclusive to women. They centred on the queen's body as a political site. The birthing chamber was lavishly redecorated to envelope the mother in material power. In 1486, Elizabeth of York, the wife of Henry VII, chose cloth of gold and velvet trimmed with furred ermine and embroidered with Tudor roses for her bed furnishings. Her birthing chamber was hung with blue arras adorned with gold fleur-de-lis. Margaret Tudor had yellow damask, which required thirty-six double hanks of gold for its fringing. Catherine of Aragon's birthing bed had a counterpane of crimson and purple embellished with powdered ermine and it was hung with blue silk.[27] Mary also chose blue. In May 1566, she ordered blue velvet and silk taffeta – over 180 ells in all – for her bed furnishings, plus ells of white ribbons and pounds of blue silk fringing. A staggering 350 ells of linen and holland cloth was requisitioned for chemises and sheets.[28]

In the later months of her pregnancy, a queen retired from court life to begin her 'lying-in'. Her period of exclusion was marked by a ritualised ceremony of retreat. First there would be a torchlit mass and communion attended by the king and courtiers. The queen, seated on her chair of state, would be brought spiced wine. She would process with her women to her inner bed chamber which, newly hung and scented, had its windows draped with cloth to screen out light, which was thought to be harmful in childbirth. With all made ready for her labours, and a midwife and wet nurse appointed, the queen would stay sequestered until the child was born, attended only by her women. After the birth, the queen would remain in seclusion for another month, during which time, when she was deemed strong enough, an upsitting feast was held. This was a ritual event, a gathering of the queen's friends, diplomats and courtiers to witness the health of her newborn baby. At the end of the month, the queen's churching or purification took place, her ceremonial attendance at a church service. Such ritual events were celebrations of a queen's fertility in which she, the begetter of dynastic and monarchical continuity, played a central role. They honoured queens at the pinnacle of their power, an elevation expressed in the textiles that surrounded them.

The preparations for childbirth and its aftermath, however, demanded that queens be absent from court life for a prolonged period. It was a risky necessity. It allowed time enough for a king to return to a mistress, or find a new one. After the birth of Mary, which came so soon after the death of her father, Marie de Guise found herself removed from political power by the traditions of

## A Suit of Savage Attire

seclusion giving her nobles time to foster their own ascendancy. By the time she was able to leave her chamber, she had been usurped. Queens did what they could to maintain their presence vicariously during such absences through the continued display of their textiles. Their embroidered ciphers and emblems, their choice of court furnishings and the modes of court dress they had introduced acted as reminders of them. In 1511, during Catherine of Aragon's lying-in, her ladies re-animated the queen's presence by dancing at an entertainment wearing Spanish gowns brocaded with a pomegranate motif, Catherine's personal emblem.[29]

At Easter in 1566, with Mary's pregnancy far advanced, she risked a stronger promotion of her Catholic faith and encouraged her nobles to return to the mass. She petitioned the Pope for a papal subsidy, money granted by the Pope to assist European states during warfare or other periods of financial need, intimating that she was in the process of championing the Catholic cause in Scotland. The chapel at the Palace of Holyroodhouse was becoming a mecca for Scottish Catholics, with hundreds – some said thousands – attending mass there. Mary's immediate household had always been largely Catholic, but now she appointed officials with more overt Catholic credentials. Darnley also appeared to have embraced Catholicism more enthusiastically. It heralded an unsettling shift in religious focus and a dangerous fragmentation of delicate political alliances. The Protestant nobles became uneasy as they witnessed this resurgence of Catholic influence.

Mary's lying-in began on 3 June 1566 at Edinburgh Castle, where she had moved for reasons of security. Preparing herself for death – an all-too-common outcome for pregnant women at the time – she drew up a will to distribute her wealth of jewels. Her priority were her French Guise relatives, whose bequests she listed first. There followed her women at the Scottish court, Darnley, and others with whom she had a special relationship. On 16 June, the appointed midwife, Margaret

Asteane, was provided with sufficient Paris black cloth and black velvet for a gown, a pre-emptive gift from Mary to ensure that the midwife gave her the best of care.[30] Two days later, Mary went into labour. The relics of Saint Margaret were brought from Dunfermline to Edinburgh Castle to assist her in her travails, as was the custom of Scottish queens. Margaret Fleming, the Countess of Argyll, who was knowledgeable in sorcery, attempted to transfer Mary's labour pains onto the wet nurse, but it proved ineffectual. On 19 June, after a prolonged and difficult labour, Mary gave birth to a son who was named James after Mary's father and grandfather. With a healthy boy born, bonfires were lit, cannons were fired and missives were sent out throughout Europe to proclaim that Scotland and the house of Stewart had an heir.

At the end of July, Mary left her birthing chamber. Her relief at having borne a son was tinged with fear. She was beset with anxiety about her baby's safety, terrified that he might be seized by Scottish nobles and that she might now be considered redundant, and therefore vulnerable to imprisonment or even assassination. She kept her baby at her side until August, when he was moved to the guardianship of the Scottish noble, John Erskine, the Earl of Mar, at Stirling Castle, in keeping with tradition. For the prince's new abode, Mary ordered 'necessities as are needful and requested for my Lord Prince's Chamber': ten hanks of gold and silver thread, 'the finest that could be got'; 42 ells of blue cambric for a covering and canopy for his wet nurse's bed. Fifteen ells of blue plaid were purchased for a bed canopy for the 'rokkaris' (the women employed to rock the baby's cradle), and a further 120 ells of linen bought for sheets and bedding for the servants who slept in the prince's outer chamber.[31]

Preparations for the prince's baptism began almost immediately after his birth and taxes were raised to cover its costs, the only extra taxes Mary ever imposed during her reign. She was

## A Suit of Savage Attire

determined to put on an extravagant display of lavish hospitality and spectacular celebration. The baptism presented a rare opportunity to reposition Scotland at the heart of European politics and Mary was alert to its potential. It was to host the most illustrious band of international guests that had ever visited the Scottish court. There was even a possibility that Elizabeth herself might attend. As ever, for Mary interior splendour was vital, as much an indication of sovereign worth as bricks and mortar. Her enhancements were an investment in Scotland's future, a chance to demonstrate its confidence and prosperity. Mary now had a son who was not only heir to the Scottish throne but, potentially, to that of England, too.

In July, she began her material offensive. This was to be a sumptuous renovation, and she focussed on beds. In the sixteenth century, the number of opulent beds a host provided signalled status and wealth. Henry VIII owned eighty sets of bed furnishings, fifty of them embroidered.[32] Beds were the most important and expensive piece of furniture in any home and the bedchamber was the site of business as well as repose and pleasure. At court, the monarch's state bedroom was a political as well as a personal space. Public reception chambers led through galleries to the sovereign's presence chamber, which in turn led through to their private chambers, within which the inner sanctum was the state bed chamber. Being invited to progress from a court's public rooms to a monarch's private realm, signalled favour. Intimate proximity to sovereign power was granted only to those deemed worthy of the privilege. There, the monarch's bed was festooned in layers of embroidered cloth: there were curtained drapes, an overhanging canopy, a headpiece, under-panels, valances and a cloth of state as a backdrop. Fringed and tasselled, braided and beribboned, the grandeur of the bed's material presence was continued in its linen, where sheets, pillowcases and bolsters were patterned and bordered in telling stitchery and coverlets boasted not just the finest of fabrics but intricately embroidered claims of lineage and symbols of aspiration.

Some beds were constructed as tented pavilions with fabric suspended from the ceiling to fall around a large hoop and fall again to the ground, their undulating drapery pulled back on each side like folded wings. Sometimes called 'chapel beds', their pavilion-like structures echoed those in religious art in depictions of the Annunciation as in Hans Baldung Grein's woodcut, *The Annunciation*, of 1514.[33] By the middle of the sixteenth century, however, a more modern style of construction was in vogue. Four-poster beds were adopted, their carved cornered pillars topped in decorative finials, between which curtains fell in thick folds of fringed luxury cloth. These too might be canopied, valanced and lined with inner curtains. Such beds could be startling in scale, some reaching as much as ten feet square. They were designed to dominate the room. As much as 150 ells of fabric could be required for their hangings, with even more ells of braid and fringing to ensure a unique resplendence. These beds were not just impressive, but imposing; they encapsulated power. It was the bed's dramatic presence that reminded visitors they had entered the exclusive stage of political majesty.

Mary liberated bed furnishings from the royal store, among them some that she had brought from France five years earlier, furnishings that were embroidered with Stewart, Valois, Guise and Tudor emblems: imagery which conveyed Mary's dynastic power. A bed of crimson velvet, stitched with golden phoenixes and another of black velvet embellished with coats of arms were shaken from their folds and installed. Bed furnishings that narrated the history of Hercules in gold thread and a set with embroidered moral fables were also removed from storage, as was one stitched with lovers' knots and another called 'the bed of amity'.[34] They were all reclaimed to play their diplomatic role and argue against any accusation of Scotland being a country lacking in sophistication or ambition.

This repair and replenishment of the court furnishings would also have been, for Mary, a metaphorical act. In the symbolic world of the Renaissance, when actions as well as objects held meaning. She was not only enhancing her interiors but also, metaphorically, restoring Scotland to glory. Her renewal of court furnishings represented Mary's nurture of Scotland.

Feverish activity ensued in the palace workshops from July to December 1565, the month of Prince James's baptism. To fashion a dais and canopy for a chair of state, 45 ells of crimson velvet were removed from the wardrobe store. Although some new silver and gold embroidery thread had to be purchased, the fringing from an old set of incarnate damask bed furnishings was still serviceable and was added with other embroidery from the Huntly textiles, those forfeited to the Crown on Huntly's defeat at the battle of Corrichie in 1562, to further embellish the dais and chair. Another gold and silver cloth of state, ornamented with knots, had its silver panels replaced with crimson velvet. Gold cushions were reclaimed. Figured black and crimson velvet was smoothed over banqueting tables and each bedchamber was serviced with newly upholstered chairs, folding stools and soft rugs fabricated from redundant velvet bed hangings.[35]

To amplify the care Mary was taking over her visitors' comfort and delight, colours and textures were harmonised room by room. The renovations bear witness to Mary's political intent. They may seem like indulgence, a queen's penchant for beautiful surroundings let loose, but for Mary, as for other women of her era, textiles were a potent visual currency of power. While the baptism was the centrepiece of the festivities, she wanted to ensure that wrapped around it was the inescapable diplomacy of solicitude, which would honour and encourage political accord.

The baptism of Prince James was Mary's triumph. It was a declaration of religious tolerance, domestic unity and international amity set within the dramatic enclosure of Stirling Castle.

It sought to revive the cult of Scottish monarchy, elevate the status of its Stewart dynasty and effect a reconciliation between Scotland's nobles. The Frenchman Bastian Pagez was appointed as the impresario for its entertainments and Servais dutifully tracked the distribution of the red, white, violet and black taffeta, cloth of gold, white satin and black velvet required for the revelries. The dominant colour was crimson: the symbol of celebration, energy and courage. The Chapel Royal altar in Stirling was hung with the crimson velvet hangings Mary had brought with her from France and that she had used for her marriage to Darnley. The same velvet covered its cushions, robed the Catholic prelate who officiated and dressed its sumptuous chair of state.[36] Although she had consented to becoming James's godmother, Elizabeth did not, in the end, attend in person. Instead, she sent a handsome gift in her stead, a font 'of massive gold. Of sufficient proportions to immerse the infant prince, and of exquisite workmanship, with many precious stones, so designed that the whole effect combined elegance with value'.[37]

A cradle and ornate silver coverlet were commissioned for the prince, and the presiding nobles were outfitted from the treasury purse: for the Earls of Mar and Huntly, red silk camlet striped with gold; for the Earl of Argyll, cloth of silver; and for Lord Bothwell, white camlet striped with silver.[38] They officiated at the event, with Bothwell, Moray, the Earl of Mar and other lords, in respect of their Protestant faith, staying outside the chapel during the Catholic ritual. This was a baptism which had, at its heart, the themes of political peace and religious harmony. The Protestant Earl of Argyll and the Catholic Lord Seton carried white staffs as symbols of reconciliation.

In the three days of action-packed entertainments that ensued, the masque was written by George Buchanan, the Latin scholar. In it, performers welcomed and honoured their Scottish prince, the wellspring of continuing Stewart kingship. There was a procession of rural nymphs and spirits to represent the natural bounty the prince would inherit: Scotland's waterfalls and lochs, its hills and glens. Mary was eulogised as the mother of their fealty. At the banquet, the foreign ambassadors were served by Scotland's Protestant and Catholic nobles in a spirit of political and social friendship. The principal guests sat at a round table to echo that of the fabled chivalric court of King Arthur. And Buchanan wrote, as Merlin's prophecy, that 'A royal nymph will set sail from the fields of France ... she will resume sovereignty and, by the virtue of her ancestors, for many years she will reign successfully'. The guests were served from a moving stage by a dozen satyrs and musicians dressed like maidens. The stage setting changed – at times confusingly – from course to course. There were tailors cutting out silk in one tableau, a boy angel descending from clouds in another, a rocky hill, a fountain. The satyrs proved controversial. As they wove their way in and out of the feasting audience, they cracked whips and waggled their tails, which was a mischievous challenge to the English visitors. To those readily acquainted with English satire, such tail-wagging referenced an irreverent myth, that the backsides of Englishmen had been endowed with tails in God's revenge for the murder of the Archbishop of Canterbury, Thomas Becket, in 1170. Others said it was an insult traded between the French and the English. Whatever its origin, some of the English contingent were not amused. They turned combative, and an uneasy atmosphere lingered until the English revellers were placated.

After the masque and banquet, the company gathered on the esplanade of Stirling Castle to watch a spectacular fire drama. Bastian Pagez had borrowed elements of the extravaganzas he and Mary had witnessed at the Valois court in France. Its costumed magnificences and entrées involved dramatic scenes of combat, rescue and victory: enactments whose exotic and thrilling theatricality differed from the Scottish chivalric tournaments. For the baptismal finale, a cast of culturally diverse warriors fought to gain control of a fabricated fort ringed with fire. Savage Highlanders were dressed in goatskins, Moors costumed in animal hides and false hair. Mary's soldiers posed as knights, horsemen and devils with battle weapons of incendiary balls, hand-held fireworks and flaming spears. This was a transportation to something more primal, adventurous and dramatic than had ever been seen in Scotland. As its audience watched explosions of light canopying the sky and heard them whoosh to the heavens, they must have felt they were witnessing their triumphant future, that Scotland was on the brink of glory.[39]

Although Darnley was in residence at Stirling Castle, he did not attend either the baptism or its attendant celebrations. No reason was given, and few questioned his absence. Contemporary and future historians have long conjectured on the reason for his non-appearance. Some concluded that he might have been excluded and not invited to attend. Some suggested it was his decision, in vengeful pique at not having been given a central role in the proceedings; others submitted the possibility that he had stayed away to diminish Mary's reputation as a virtuous queen and dutiful wife and deliberately cast doubt on Prince James's parentage; still others cited his disgruntlement at the inadequate finery of the attire with which he had been furnished, believing it insulted his status as Scotland's king. Whatever the reason, there are no reports that his absence was lamented. It made clear to those who attended, however, that Mary and Darnley's marriage had reached an impasse. Just six days after the baptism, Mary's French ambassador found her 'pensive and melancholy', lying on her bed 'weeping sore'. He confided to the Scottish ambassador in Paris that:

I do believe the principal part of her disease to consist in a deep grief and sorrow, nor does it seem possible to make her forget the same, still she repeats the words 'I could wish to be dead.'[40]

## A Suit of Savage Attire

In her final will before she died, Mary bequeathed Pagez 'a suit of savage attire', one of the goatskin costumes worn by the Highlanders in the fire spectacle that he had helped to organise for Prince James's baptismal festivities. It was a keepsake that Mary had treasured. She gifted it to Pagez as a reminder of their shared moment of triumph when Mary experienced her greatest moment of sovereign power.[41]

# 6

## *Three of the Fairest*

In 1566, James Hepburn, Lord Bothwell, emerged from the shadows 'unlooked for, uninvited, the evil spirit of the storm' to become a central figure in Mary's drama.¹ He is somewhat of an enigma. While we know some of the facts of his life, we know frustratingly little about his motives. Bothwell was an outsider, not attached to any specific faction. Although he was a member of Mary's privy council, he rarely engaged with court life, and despite being Protestant, he did not bind himself to the Protestant cause nor ally himself with its leaders. He seems, in short, to be a man who forged his own style of nobility: loyal to his country, savage in his dealings with those who crossed him and strategic in adversity.

Bothwell was no sudden champion who emerged late in Mary's reign. He had long been a significant, if at times vexatious, figure in Scottish affairs. His earldom – realised when he was just twenty-one – bestowed on him the duties and offices of Lord High Admiral of Scotland; Sheriff of Berwick, Haddington and Edinburgh; Bailie in Lauderdale; and the governorship of castles in Hailes and Crichton. Two years later he became Lord Lieutenant of the Borders and – for all his reputation as a forceful man – he was well educated, fluent in French and the possessor of an extensive library. Moreover, he had proved loyal to Marie de Guise, even when his fealty was not in his best political interest. In July 1561, it was Bothwell, as Mary's Lord High Admiral, whom the Scottish queen had summoned to France to help arrange her voyage back to Scotland. Mary and Bothwell also had a personal connection

## Three of the Fairest

– Lady Fleming, Mary's governess in France, was Bothwell's half-sister; Mary Beaton's aunt had been his mistress at one time, and his father had been a suitor to Mary's mother.

But his relationship with the Scottish nobles was volatile. There were confrontations, one so grievous that it led to him being banished from court. In 1563 he was even imprisoned for disloyalty. Mary, however, was unconvinced of his guilt and delayed his punishment. Bothwell managed to escape to England and journeyed on to France. There, on Mary's nomination, he became captain of the French court's Gardes Écossaises (Scottish Guards). In 1565, Mary recalled him to Scotland once more to assist in dealing with the Chaseabout Raid, and Bothwell was grudgingly accepted back at court. When he married Jean Gordon, the daughter of the dead Earl of Huntly, Mary supplied the bride's wedding dress of cloth of silver.[2] After Rizzio's murder, it was Bothwell who helped Mary and Darnley escape, and it was to his castle that they fled. Later, Mary was to say of his support: 'we must confess that service done at that time to have been so acceptable to us we could never to this hour forget it'.[3] And, in the will Mary made before the birth of Prince James, she left Bothwell a diamond and ruby brooch in the form of a mermaid. Bothwell had been by Mary's side at many of the key turning points in her life, and they had shared some of the most dramatic moments in her history.

In October 1566, just five months after the birth of her son, Mary travelled to Jedburgh, a small town in the Scottish borders. She was there to preside over a series of assizes (local courts convened to pass judgement on local affairs). Shortly after Mary and her council arrived, they heard that Bothwell had been seriously wounded in an affray and it was feared his injuries were fatal. Contemporary chroniclers and later historians have milked what they could of Mary's journey to Bothwell's side once her duties at the assizes were over, making of it not a mercy dash, but a pilgrimage of passion. There is nothing, however, in the facts to justify this version of events.

On her return to Jedburgh, however, Mary fell so violently ill that she asked for bells to be rung in Edinburgh calling on her subjects to pray for her recovery.[4] The queen's condition deteriorated. She suffered multiple fits of vomiting and bouts of unconsciousness. Her body became so cold and rigid that her servants thought she had died and opened the windows to free her spirit. They ordered their mourning clothes. Mary's physician, however, made a last desperate attempt to resuscitate her: he swaddled her body tightly in bandages, forced wine down her throat and administered an enema. His drastic action saved her life.

In the haze of illness, Mary tried to put her affairs in order. She entreated her nobles to 'have charity, concord and love amongst yourselves'.[5] Her priority was to safeguard the succession to the Scottish crown. She commanded that Darnley was to be bypassed in favour of Prince James under the charge of Moray. The king had been on a hunting trip when Mary's illness struck, and was hard to trace. However, his apparent lack of haste, and the brevity of his visit when he eventually arrived, demonstrated a lack of concern that was unforgivable. Mary regained her strength as quickly as she had succumbed to her sickness and, by the end of October, was sufficiently recovered to order fabric: white plaiding and taffeta, fine black velvet and 20 ells of red silk cloth. A messenger was sent that day to the supplier and a horseman was despatched to Jedburgh 'with diligence' bearing the queen's purchases.[6] It would seem that Mary was hastening her recovery by enveloping her bed in red, the colour advocated as efficacious for restoring vigour in Boorde's dyetary manual, the guide to how to maintain good health published in 1542.

For the final meeting of Mary's council in Jedburgh, Bothwell arrived in a litter. His attendance seems to have marked a change in their relationship. While there was no indication of romance, there appeared to be a deepening of mutual dependency. A pattern was beginning to emerge in Mary's attachments: her loyalty and affection being sparked by male vulnerability. It was evident in her devotion to the frail François. Her so-called infatuation with Darnley had been kindled during her tending of him when he fell ill in Stirling. Now that Bothwell, her martial leader, was struck down by injury, it seems her compassion transmuted into care. It is possible that her own recent brush with death might have intensified her empathy.

Mary's separation from Darnley was already being considered by Mary and her councillors. The king had become a loose cannon. He had taken to firing off letters to the pope and the sovereigns of Spain and France, undermining Mary's – and Scotland's – authority and integrity. He had even threatened to leave Scotland and go to France. His self-exile might have been welcomed were it not for the fact that, given his ambition, his motives were suspect. In France, Darnley could attempt to rally foreign support to help him gain the Crown Matrimonial, or even usurp Mary. He was becoming a liability.

Barely a month after Jedburgh, there was a convention of Mary and her chief nobles, Bothwell and Moray included, at Craigmillar Castle. The possibility of divorce, or at the very least the removal of Darnley, was debated. While expressing her desire to be free of her husband, Mary was adamant that the legitimacy of her son had to be protected and that her honour could not be compromised. Divorce, therefore, was not an option. Mary's nobles took things into their own hands. They signed a bond that they would dislodge Darnley by some means or another.

In January 1567, Darnley fell ill. He relocated to Glasgow, the traditional seat of Lennox power. Aware of the growing antagonism towards him, he felt safer among his own kin. There was another reason. For months, what is now known to have been syphilis had been festering. While only twenty-one, and three years younger than Mary, Darnley's hedonistic lifestyle was beginning to take its toll. He was suffering from fevers and aching joints; his skin had erupted in pustules. Urgent treatment was necessary. His physicians prescribed hot baths of mercury and recommended he wore a face mask of cambric. Mary remained concerned but distant, sending her own physician to his aid and ordering the cambric.[7]

But Darnley's political activity remained dangerously capricious. Rumours of his intrigues continued to circulate. When Mary was told that he was plotting to abduct Prince James and have him crowned in Mary's stead with himself as regent, she brought her son from Stirling to be under her protection at the Palace of Holyroodhouse. She also brought Darnley back to Edinburgh, where a closer eye could be kept on his movements. His agreement to the move is surprising given the circumstances, but it is possible that Mary feigned the hope of a marital rapprochement in order to win his trust. Darnley returned to Edinburgh on 1 February. Six days later, he was reporting to his father, the Earl of Lennox, that Mary 'doth use herself like a natural and loving wife'.[8] Meanwhile, behind closed doors, nobles continued to debate the nature of Darnley's disposal and Mary continued to refuse to be drawn into their deliberations.

On Darnley's return to Edinburgh he spurned Mary's proposal to take up residence at Craigmillar Castle and chose instead a mansion known as Kirk o' Field, just three-quarters of a mile from the Palace of Holyroodhouse. There he sequestered himself with a small contingent from his household. Having been vacant for some time, the house required refurbishing and Servais de Condé, the keeper of the royal wardrobe store, dutifully issued and recorded the removal of items: tapestries, cushions and coverlets, a black velvet cloth of state. There too was taken a bed of violet-brown velvet embroidered in gold and silver with flowers and cyphers that had once belonged to

## Three of the Fairest

Marie de Guise, and which Mary had given to Darnley the previous August.[9]

At 2 o'clock in the morning of 10 February, the citizens of Edinburgh were awoken by the reverberating boom of an explosion. People ran towards the source of the blast in Kirk o' Field. There, they found Darnley's lodgings reduced to rubble. In its garden lay the dead bodies of Darnley and his valet, William Taylor. Beside them, laid out in a tidy row, were a chair, a rope, a dagger and a furred cloak. Given the force of the explosion, the bodies were strangely unmarked. When it was discovered that they had been strangled, another scenario unfolded. It was deduced that the king and Taylor had been disturbed by the noise of intruders and had tried to escape using the rope and the chair to break their fall, but that they had been pursued and murdered as they fled. A sketch was made of the scene and sent to Elizabeth's adviser Cecil in London. It was a montage of the explosion and its aftermath: the ruined rubble, the two dead bodies, Taylor's body being interred on site, Darnley's being carried away. A small group of onlookers have gathered. In the uppermost corner of the sketch, there is a portrayal of Prince James praying for justice for his dead father. The sketch depicts the manner in which the king's and Taylor's bodies were left, and it is disturbing. Taylor, lying on his side, has his shirt rucked up to reveal his naked buttocks. Darnley is lying on his back. His shirt is drawn up above his navel to expose his private parts. His left hand is resting on his genitals. For the bodies to have been left so dishonourably exposed is strange.[10]

The sketch so intrigued me that I contacted Jim Fraser, Professor of Forensic Science at the University of Strathclyde and a member of the Scottish Criminal Cases Review Commission. I sent him a copy of the sketch and asked him what he made of it. He too was puzzled. He told me that, in the sixteenth century, there was no forensic examination in the aftermath of crimes, no objective or systematic inspection of a crime scene. Decisions on guilt were based on received information and anecdotal evidence, from what people said they saw or heard. Such testimonies might be extracted under duress, through physical torture or threats of forfeiture of goods, reputation or position. The status and character of suspects was all too often the determining factor in reaching a guilty verdict. Given this, why was such a graphic depiction of Darnley's murder sketched out if it was not to be used as evidence in law?

It was Cecil, Elizabeth's advisor, who commissioned the sketch. The identity of its author is unknown. What Jim Fraser was confident of was that the sketch did not offer a neutral viewpoint. Neither a pictorial eye-witness account nor a reconstruction of the scene as described by others, in his view it was a partial and possibly even fabricated version of the scene itself, likely with a political motive. While murder victims were, in his experience, sometimes purposefully arranged to satisfy some fetish of their assassin, there was no sexual motive behind the murder of Darnley and Taylor and their exposed nudity had none of the ritualistic hallmarks of a psychotic killer. But there must have been a reason to either leave their bodies in such a manner or to draw them as such. There was no certainty that the bodies were discovered in the poses shown, or that the accompanying props were present. The fact they were laid out in such an orderly fashion pointed more, perhaps, to the choice of the sketcher and what they wanted to show rather than the veracity of the scene when it was first discovered.

If it was intended for wider circulation, then the exposed nudity of Darnley and Taylor would serve to fan greater horror at the deed, the king's subjects appalled to see their king so humiliated in death. The sketch emphasised the lack of respect shown to the king by his assassins. As it was, this sketch – which was to play a key role in Mary's later disgrace – was highly suspect.

No matter how often the final hours of Darnley, King of

Scotland, have been pieced together in a patchwork of conjecture, vital clues are missing. The night of 9 February seemingly began well: a king in recovery, his return to health celebrated with wine, music and playing at dice. Mary and other courtiers, including Bothwell, had come to join him after a day celebrating the marriage of Bastian Pagez, the member of her household who had masterminded the prince's baptismal festivities. The queen had provided the bride with black satin and velvet and green ribbons for her gown.[11] After the wedding, Mary and other guests, still dressed in their finery, came to Kirk o' Field to keep Darnley company for his last night there, arrangements having been made for him to return to the Palace of Holyroodhouse early the following morning.

At around 10 o'clock that evening, so the story goes, Mary was reminded that she had promised to grace Pagez's wedding masque with her presence. When Darnley became petulant at her departure, Mary presented him with a ring to placate him. It was late when they left the masque, so Mary and her party decided to return not to Kirk o' Field but to the Palace of Holyroodhouse, where Darnley was to join them the next morning. In the early hours, Mary was woken by the sound of the blast and was told that Darnley's lodgings had been decimated by gunpowder and that the king had been killed in the explosion. It was only later that it transpired he had been murdered. Later that day, Mary wrote to the Scottish ambassador in Paris saying she believed the explosion had been meant to cause her death as much as Darnley's, and that its perpetrators would be sought with due alacrity, whereby 'we hope to punish the same with such rigour as shall serve for example of this cruelty for ages to come'.[12]

In the days that followed, Mary's chamber was shrouded in black and the queen oversaw the preparations for Darnley's interment. The necessary spices and perfumes were purchased for the embalming of the king's body and Darnley's corpse was laid out in state before being buried in the royal vault at Holyrood Abbey beside Mary's father. There was no grand state funeral – instead, it was reported that his burial took place 'without any decent order, cast in the earth, without any ceremony or company of honest men'.[13] Mary ordered her mourning attire, but it was a surprisingly modest request – less than 20 ells of serge and silk camlet – and it compared uncomfortably with the 246 ells of mourning black that Marie de Guise had ordered for herself and her attendants following the death of Mary's father.[14]

The traditions of mourning required the queen to be secluded in her chambers for the next forty days, as Mary had done after the death of François II. But, after Darnley's death, Mary did not observe the ritual. The day after the king's murder, she acted as a witness at the wedding of her chamber woman, Margaret Carwood, albeit briefly. Then, as so often happened with Mary, she became overwhelmed by emotional distress and fell ill. Given that it was only four months since her last, almost fatal, collapse, her physician advised Mary's council that she should leave her 'close, solitary life' and 'repair to some good wholesome air'.[15] Putting Prince James under Bothwell's protection, Mary left for Seton Palace with her household and members of her nobility. In time, Bothwell joined her there and his increasing prominence in Mary's life, fuelled speculation that they had become lovers.

The search began for Darnley's assassin. A substantial reward was offered by the privy council to anyone who could identify the perpetrator and bring him to justice. But while witnesses were questioned, Mary failed to order a formal investigation. She was in a state of nervous collapse, unable to act. She undoubtedly suspected the involvement of some of her own nobility in the king's murder and was wary of exposing their guilt. Elizabeth became so alarmed by Mary's inertia that she wrote to the Scottish queen to question her tardiness in 'not wanting to avenge the murder or apprehend the guilty party'.

## Three of the Fairest

She advised Mary that, in regard to Bothwell, the Scottish queen should be 'in fear to touch him whom you have closest to you, if this thing touches him'.[16] But still Mary did not act.

People took matters into their own hands. Placards, a relatively new way of disseminating public censure, began to appear in Edinburgh, pinned to the doors of key buildings in the city. Most named Bothwell and his associates as the king's murderers. Mary's foreign servants – Bastian Pagez, Joseph Rizzio and Francesco Busso – were also targeted, an opportunistic act of racism. In the quiet of the night, the city's streets resounded with condemnation and the calling out of Bothwell's name. Mary's apparent neglect in observing the traditions of mourning, the nature of Darnley's burial with scant pageantry and her defection to Seton in Bothwell's company, all fanned suspicion that Mary had been Bothwell's accomplice. The claim by the Earl of Lennox that the Scottish queen had bestowed his dead son's armour, horses and clothes on Bothwell only served to feed the speculation. It was being muttered that Darnley's death was not just a crime of regicide but of passion.

On 1 March, a more ominous and salacious placard greeted the people of Edinburgh, pinned to the door of St Giles Church. A sketch of the placard, made at the time, still exists and is kept in the National Archive in London.[17] It depicts a bare-breasted mermaid wearing a crown. She is waving what some think is a sea anemone – the symbol for female genitalia – and others interpret it as a feathered lure used in falconry; either way, it insinuates seduction. Written alongside the mermaid are the initials M R to stand for Maria Regina. Below the mermaid is a crouching hare enclosed by three circles. The outer circle has seventeen daggers around its rim. Above the hare are the initials J H for James Hepburn, Bothwell's birth name. The sketch is hurried, with little attempt at refinement: the mermaid's hair just a squiggle of lines, the circles roughly drawn. However, this quick drawing preserves an audacious act: the public conjoining of Mary and Bothwell in an accusation of adultery. In the febrile climate of Edinburgh at the time, it was a calculated smear on Mary's reputation. For those with even a minimal grasp of the meaning of symbols, its message would have been clear.

The hare was a device on Bothwell's coat of arms, but it also symbolised fear, and its portrayal was intended as a threat. A mermaid was a familiar symbol denoting temptation, but the mermaid in this sketch had a forked tail, which was a slanderous alteration that denoted prostitution. The circle of daggers has a more obtuse origin. It had featured in Claude Paradin's book *Devises Heroïques*, published in 1557, the first publication to illustrate and explain the heraldic devices adopted by the aristocracy. Paradin's book showed the same image but paired it with a motto taken from the book of Deuteronomy: 'The sword shall destroy them from without, and terror within'.[18] The seventeen daggers might originate in an even more rarefied source. In ancient Rome the number was deemed unlucky. An anagram of its Roman numeral spells out the word VIXI, or 'I have lived'.[19]

Whoever created the original placard was educated. They needed to be conversant with Paradin's book and knowledgeable of the symbolism of Roman numerals. They might also have known of Mary's gifting to Bothwell of the jewelled mermaid in the will she made before the birth of Prince James. Mary and Bothwell would have been in no doubt of the placard's defamatory intent and its inherent threat. The choice of the cathedral door for its display suggests that it was an attempt by Mary's Protestant detractors to damage her reputation irreparably. Mary acted quickly: amid the pressure to seek out Darnley's murderers, she convened a gathering of the city's painters and writers to try to identify the placard's author. Suspicion fell on a certain James Murray but he fled the city before he could be arrested. Mary had an act passed in Parliament that anyone found distributing slanderous material in the future would face prosecution and execution. But the damage had been done.

Over the next few weeks, rumour and counter-rumour continued to circulate. It was to continue over months and then years, as suspected conspirators and reliable and unreliable witnesses were brought in for interrogation, some questioned under torture. One of Bothwell's associates, Captain William Blackadder, who had been first on the murder scene, was apprehended and charged with the king's murder. He was summarily hung, drawn and quartered at the Mercat Cross, his body parts distributed to Scotland's main cities in a show of resolute retribution. Although he had been in the vicinity of the crime, there was no substantial evidence of his guilt. Still, justice had to be seen to be done. The testimonies collected were confusing and conflicting. A woman said she had heard the king crying out for mercy from his kin, which implicated the Douglas clan, to whom Darnley was related. One of Bothwell's servants said that in the early hours of the morning of the king's murder he had seen his master change from his wedding finery to don a plain canvas doublet. Even more sinister was the rumour that Mary had murmured to Darnley just before she left for Bastian Pagez's wedding masque 'it is about this time of year that David Rizzio was killed'.

In the interrogations that followed, more accounts inferred Mary's involvement. Witnesses spoke of her removing costly furnishings from Kirk o' Field in the week before the king's death, insinuating they were taken to protect them from damage or loss in the explosion. One of Darnley's servant stated that:

Because there was a bed and some tapestry of valour in that lodging set up for the King before his coming there, she caused the same to be removed to Holyrood by the keepers of her wardrobe on the Friday preceding the murder, and another worst one set up in its place.[20]

A key witness, Nicholas Hubert, one of Bothwell's servants, confessed that he had been sent on the Saturday before the murder to fetch an expensive furred coverlet from the Queen's chamber at Darnley's lodging, and that the next day Mary had checked that it had been done.[21]

However, the tapestries appear in the list Servais compiled of what was lost in the explosion, so they could not have been removed by Mary. Later the Latin scholar George Buchanan was to write that 'the bed (where) the queen used sometimes to lie, was taken from there, and a worse put in its place'.[22] This too – the set of yellow and green damask bed furnishings – was, according to Servais' records, destroyed in the blast.[23] The evidence mustered against Mary, and which was later repeated, focussed on textiles. It is as if they were chosen, with witnesses schooled to cite them, as evidence of female complicity, a plausible confirmation of Mary's guilt. The stories, however, were contradictory. Different witnesses cited different textiles: tapestries, a fur coverlet, the queen's yellow bed furnishings. The conflicting accounts reinforce the probability that the testimonies were fabricated.

Sometime in March, Mary did remove a number of ecclesiastical textiles from the royal store, part of those claimed by the Crown on the forfeiture of the Earl of Huntly's belongings. Servais had noted their addition in 1562, detailing that they were made of cloth of gold, that three were figured in red and the others in yellow and white. He had added that the three figured in white were old. When Mary came to withdraw them, Servais deviated from his usual terse annotations and described their dispersal in unusually expansive prose:

In March 1567 I delivered three of the fairest which the Queen gave to the Lord Bothwell and she took more for herself – a cope, a chasuble, four tunics to make a bed for the King which were all broken up and cut [up] in her presence.[24]

## Three of the Fairest

The 'bed for the King' was likely to have been a memorial bed for Darnley, his bed of state re-draped to serve as a commemoration. The recycling of the cloth of gold would suit such a purpose, ensuring that the bed was of sufficient richness to honour the dead king. Her gift of the church vestments to Bothwell is, however, more intriguing. As a resolute Protestant, Bothwell would have had little interest in Catholic finery. While the vestments had value, no ecclesiastical textiles – apart from those Mary brought from France – had been removed from the royal store for any purpose until now. The cloth of gold Mary had given to Rizzio had been pristine and there was still enough of it in the royal store to bestow some on Bothwell. That she chose to give him 'three of the fairest' from Huntly's collection is illuminating. 'Fairest' does not necessarily mean that these were the most beautiful, but that they were, in some important way, the most precious. Were these the vestments from St Machar's cathedral, made from the cloth of gold that had once graced the pavilion of Edward II at the Battle of Bannockburn, which were imbued with the spirit of a king, cloth considered talismanic by the Scots? If so, Mary's gift had a deeper resonance. What the queen was gifting Bothwell was something far more valuable than old cloth: she was bestowing on him the spirit of victory.

Used textiles can have a significance beyond the sentimental, believed by some to conserve the aura of their original owner. Cloth can be imbued with emotional, even spiritual, value if it is thought to be impregnated with a person's essence, still carrying their emotions, memories and traits of character. Many cultures harbour talismanic cloths, not necessarily as mediators to the divine or the supernatural, but because they connect the past to the present, one person to another. Such cloth is thought to be capable of transferring the spirit of its owner to whoever takes possession of it. Trophies of battle such as standards, pavilions and uniforms were coveted not just as tangible spoils of war but because they were thought to transmit the human spirit inherent in them to those still living. So it was with the St Machar's vestments recast from Edward's pavilion, which, appropriated by the Scots, consigned the English king's power to the Church and to Scotland itself. In them lay the battle glory of Bannockburn, the triumph of victory and the strength of a powerful king.

Servais' annotation conjures an uneasy image of the careless camaraderie of Mary and Bothwell in the middle of a personal and political crisis: Mary selecting 'three of the fairest' and presenting them to Bothwell, explaining their significance; Servais' assistants, at the command of the queen, cutting up those she has procured for Darnley's bed while Bothwell cradles his talisman of power. Murder and memorialisation coalesce in what seems like the innocent reclamation of old textiles. Was Servais prompted by a sense of unease to write up his accompanying narrative so fulsomely? Or was it the preciousness of the textiles themselves that compelled him to detail their dispersal?

In the sixteenth century, gifts were the currency of favour, allegiance and reconciliation. Clothing was particularly potent, and especially the clothing that had been worn by a monarch. It signalled connection, a special relationship. Mary gave her four Marys, the women she was closest to, her own clothes from the royal store. Such redeployment was not subject to the same control or scrutiny as the gifting of other textiles. The queen's clothes were hers to dispose of as she chose. The gifted clothes these women wore created a tangible link to the queen and reinforced and declared their intimacy with her. Mary Livingston was given the most, marking her out as Mary's favourite. She received gowns of black velvet, cloth of gold and silver, and crimson satin. The other Marys received gowns, cloaks and petticoats: the Countess of Mar a gown of crimson figured velvet; Mary's half-sister, Jean Stewart, a gown of violet-crimson satin damask and a mourning robe of black on the death of her husband. These gifts were designed to celebrate and reiterate the bonds between women. They gave female friendship tactility.[25]

It was not only their own clothes that a king, queen or regent could bestow. They also gifted clothes of monarchs who had died. When the Earl of Arran became regent on the death of James V in 1542, he distributed the king's clothing as well as his weapons to nobles whose allegiance he wanted to secure: a robe of black silk lined with sables to the Earl of Rothes, another of purple velvet to a Norman Leslie, a cloak 'transit with gold' to James Hamilton of Haggs, and more.[26] At the English court, Elizabeth donated a cloak that had once belonged to Edward VI and some of Mary Tudor's clothes to costume a play.[27] She also commandeered the coronation robes of her half-sister Mary Tudor to wear at her own coronation. Theirs had been a conflicted relationship, and Elizabeth's appropriation of Mary Tudor's robes was a material seizure of her power as much as a statement of Elizabeth's own political and religious victory at her half-sister's death. It was also a visible reiteration of Elizabeth's legitimacy, an expression of the material continuity of the Tudor dynasty in the ceremonial robes of office passed down from one Tudor queen to another. Mary removed many of her mother's clothes from the royal store. Apart from the fur from one of her mother's gowns which she later gave to Bothwell, the five gowns and doublets and ten cloaks she reclaimed were for Mary's own use.[28] Cloaks had a deeper significance than other garments because they were thought to possess magical protective properties. Marie de Guise's cloaks furnished Mary with her mother's shield, a palpable consolation and comfort to bolster her resolve in the challenges she faced as Scotland's queen.

When I was young, I was dressed in 'hand-me-downs': clothes I inherited from my two older sisters when they had outgrown them. I remember how eagerly, and critically, I used to view the dresses that were bought for my sisters, knowing that one day they might be mine. If they received something particularly pretty I used to pray that it was not ruined before I had a chance to wear it. One dress sticks in my mind as being especially coveted. It was red and the bottom of its skirt was appliquéd with an undulating sea with embroidered fish swimming and leaping through its waves. I loved that dress. When it did eventually come to me, it had lost some of its crispness and its red had faded, but its fish still swam with their original exuberance and still filled me with delight. Others of my sisters' clothes were less appealing. There were drab beige school uniforms and serviceable skirts that my mother would alter to fit. I had to slowly pirouette as she puffed chalk from a wooden contraption to mark out a new hemline or stand still, my arms raised wearily, as she stuck in pins to track the position of a new seam. As I and my sisters grew older and developed different tastes in fashion, the tradition of passing on clothes ended. There were rare exchanges, sister to sister, the gifting of something that did not fit or did not suit, but they never had the excitement of the sartorial transference of our younger days when we had fewer clothes and when the anticipated joy of a hand-me-down was thrilling.

In the aftermath of Darnley's death, his clothes were packed away. A valet de chambre was provided with sponges, rubbers and cleaning cloths to prepare the king's clothing for storage. White fustian was purchased to make protective wraps and two large trunks were acquired in which to fold Darnley's indulgent outfits of velvet hose, satin doublets and embroidered cloaks.[29] On 23 March, a requiem mass and solemn dirge was held at Holyrood Abbey, but it was scarcely afforded more pomp than the king's funeral. Mary ensured that the musicians and Darnley's pages and lackeys were appropriately attired in new outfits of mourning black.³⁰ But, by the end of March, William Drury, an English statesman who was then Marshall and deputy-governor of Berwick-upon-Tweed, was reporting to Cecil that 'the judgement of the people is that the Queen will marry Bothwell'.³¹

After much pressure, Mary had agreed that Bothwell should face trial, but through a private suit raised by the Earl of Lennox, not one brought by the crown. The Scottish queen continued to be frail, and Drury reported Mary's mental and physical state to Cecil: 'She has been for the most part either melancholy or sickly ever since, and specially this week upon Tuesday or Wednesday often swooned ... the Queen breaketh very much'.³² In a letter to the Bishop of Dunblane, Mary described her turmoil:

> this realm being divided in factions as it is, cannot be contained in order, unless our authority be assisted and forth set by the fortification of a man who must take upon his person in the execution of justice ... the travail thereof we may no longer sustain in our own person, being already wearied, and almost broken with the frequent uproars and rebellions raised against us since we came to Scotland.³³

Her admittance that she needed 'the fortification of a man' seemed to indicate that Mary was already considering Bothwell as her consort. Moray, Mary's half-brother, had left for France early in April, without waiting for Bothwell's trial. His departure was not welcomed by Mary. Despite his acts of betrayal, it seemed she still depended on his presence to keep her nobles in check. When Bothwell's trial convened, Lennox did not appear. He had received alarming threats to his safety. Elizabeth, wanting to see the crisis resolved and Mary's name cleared by a fair trial, sent a messenger to try to delay the proceedings but it was to no avail. Bothwell arrived in Edinburgh flanked by 4,000 men, a show of strength which saw him acquitted. Triumphantly, he sent a town crier into the streets of Edinburgh to proclaim his innocence and posted leaflets emblazoned with his coat of arms to announce the verdict throughout the city.

The opening of Parliament that followed saw Bothwell bearing the ceremonial sceptre in processional splendour. When it closed, it was Bothwell who carried the sword of honour back to the Palace of Holyroodhouse. The sceptre, the oldest of the Scottish royal regalia, symbolised royal power, virtue and justice. It was used during the proceedings of parliament to signal royal assent to any acts passed, with the monarch ritualistically touching the paper copy of the relevant act with the sceptre. The silver sword signified warrior strength and the protection of liberty.[34] By assigning Bothwell the privilege of being the bearer of such potent symbols of royal authority and justice, a role only entrusted to the most senior members of government, Mary was publicly declaring his importance to the Crown. Ever quick to seize the advantage, at the end of the parliamentary proceedings Bothwell gathered together the country's chief nobility and clergy at Edinburgh's Ainslie Tavern, ostensibly as a celebratory finale to parliamentary business. A lavish meal was served and excessive quantities of good wine poured. By the end of the evening, Bothwell had secured what he had hoped for: a bond signed by those present, twenty-eight nobles and churchmen, in support of his plan to marry the Queen.

Meanwhile, Mary concentrated on her son's welfare. She ordered Holland cloth, white Spanish taffeta and Florence ribbon for 'my lord prince' and visited Stirling Castle to see her ten-month-old son, now returned to the care of the Earl of Mar.[35] On her way back to Edinburgh, Mary's entourage was suddenly halted by Bothwell and 800 of his followers. He told the queen that Edinburgh was unsafe and that her life was in danger and that he had come to escort her to the security of his castle. Some of those in Mary's company objected and urged caution but, not wishing to cause an affray, the queen acquiesced to Bothwell's request and accompanied him to his castle in Dunbar.

Mary later recounted that it was only when she reached Dunbar that she realised that Bothwell's interception was not a rescue but an abduction. It is reported, however, that there was advanced intelligence of the plan. The Spanish ambassador wrote to his king, Philip II: 'It is believed that the whole thing has been arranged so that if anything comes of the marriage the Queen may make it that she was forced into it'.[36] The Earl of Lennox, William Drury and others also appeared to have prior knowledge.[37] But when hand-written documents could be so readily doctored and dates of correspondence changed, it is impossible to verify whether rumours of the abduction was circulated before its enactment.

That evening, Bothwell came to Mary's chamber and, in her own words, 'albeit we found his doings rude, yet were his words and answers gentle'.[38] Melville was more candid, reporting: 'The Queen could not but marry him, seeing he had ravished her and laid with her against her will'.[39] While it is plausible that Mary and Bothwell conceived the ambush to enable Mary to place herself under Bothwell's protection, it is highly dubious that Mary's rape was feigned or that she was already Bothwell's lover. The pretended ambush might have been a necessary ploy to ensure that the queen was not seen to initiate Bothwell's support: an action which insinuated an intimacy that compromised the queen's honour and which would have exacerbated the hostility of Mary's nobility. Without any male defence to ward off the very real threats to her liberty and life, Bothwell was her only safeguard. Her rape, however, is a separate issue. It was an abuse of not just Mary herself but of her trust in Bothwell. Accompanied, as she was, by other nobles loyal to her, including Melville and George Huntly, Mary would not have expected such a violation.

But Bothwell's rape of Mary sealed her compliance to their

marriage and paved the way for him to become King of Scotland. It was undoubtedly a brutal act, and one that Mary – made fragile by illness, distressed by slander and emotionally unmoored by Darnley's murder – seemed to accept as her fate. At Dunbar, Bothwell would have told her of the Ainslie Tavern bond – of the agreement, if not approval, of her nobility and churchmen to their marriage. Despite Bothwell's abuse of her, Mary stayed at Dunbar Castle for the next twelve days, refusing any proffered offers of rescue. Thinking her nobles sanctioned the match, and with her honour now compromised, Mary agreed to the marriage. It was, it seemed to her, her only means of survival. Here was a man capable of securing her safety. Bothwell was an experienced soldier, loyal to the crown, a political shield. She and Bothwell rode back to Edinburgh together, with its castle's artillery sounding in salute. But for Mary it was hardly a celebratory return. As she rode through the city streets with Bothwell leading her by her horse's bridle, it must have seemed to some that she was returning as his captive.

There was still a major obstacle to their marriage: Bothwell's wife, Jean Gordon. An annulment was sought in haste, with Jean's agreement. On 12 May, Mary made a formal declaration to the Lords of Session concerning her ambush and subsequent imprisonment, describing how Bothwell 'partly exhorted, and partly obtained our promise to take him as our husband but would not be satisfied with all the just reasons we could allege to have the consummation of marriage delayed. We cannot dissemble that he has treated us otherwise than we would have wished, or what we have deserved at his hand'.[40]

The wedding gift that Mary bestowed on Bothwell has been dismissed as meagre and tokenistic by most of her historians and biographers: furs from Marie de Guise's informal robe of black velvet.[41] But more than the love tokens, expensive jewels and fine clothes that Darnley received, this gift to Bothwell was imbued with hope. It was a present of trust. Through it, Mary

## Three of the Fairest

transferred the care of her mother to Bothwell and claimed her mother's protection. The marriage might have been an enforced political accommodation, but it seems that Mary was still hopeful of kindness.

Bothwell was made Duke of Orkney, Lord of Shetland and Marquess of Fife. Mary ordered black and white silk taffeta, black satin and velvet for her wedding attire as well as Florence ribbon, hanks of gold and silver thread and quantities of gold braid for its adornment.[42] On 15 May, little more than three months after Darnley's assassination, just three weeks after Bothwell had raped Mary at Dunbar, they were married in a lack-lustre Protestant service. Mary's acquiescence to forgo Catholic rites seems to imply that she was hopeful that, at some point, she could secure an annulment on the grounds that the marriage was not lawful in the eyes of God. Few nobles attended. Already regretting their drunken assent to Bothwell marrying their queen, and with many now believing he had secured her consent by force, Mary's nobles expressed their disquiet through their absence. There was no grand procession or celebratory masque, no sailing ships with sails of silver.

On the evening before her wedding, it was reported that Mary had become suicidal and had demanded a knife to kill herself. When those around her remonstrated, she threatened to drown herself.[43] It is easy to dismiss Mary's emotional upset as histrionics. It is clear, however, that although she had agreed to the marriage, she was in a state of deep despair. There could be another reason for her extreme distress, that Mary suspected she was pregnant.

The scholar and historian Lesley Smith is currently working towards a PhD in obstetrics and gynaecology in early modern Britain. She is a member of the Association of Medical Writers and a performer who adopts the personas of historical figures, Mary, Queen of Scots among them. Who better, therefore, to discuss the controversial subject of Mary's pregnancy by

Bothwell? In Smith's view, Mary's mental crisis, in the months following Darnley's murder, was triggered not just by his assassination and the subsequent accusations of her complicity, it was also provoked by pregnancy. Some historians and biographers have suggested that the reconciliation Mary effected with Darnley might have been a ploy to pass off a pregnancy resulting from an adulterous affair with Bothwell. It is more likely, however, that Mary's pregnancy was a result of her rape. The symptoms that Mary displayed at the time of her marriage to Bothwell – her suicidal tendencies – mirror those caused by prenatal and postnatal depression. She had experienced similar symptoms when she was pregnant with Prince James: then, too, she was prone to uncontrollable fits of weeping and, after his birth, had wished she was dead.

Mary was trapped. There was no question of an abortion. Not only was it a mortal sin, one which would see you damned in hell, but abortion was illegal in Scotland. In the early period of Mary's reign, one of her chamber women had embarked on an affair with the queen's apothecary and had fallen pregnant. The couple planned an abortion. When their affair and their intent was discovered, it was Mary who authorised their execution. It was April, perhaps earlier, when Mary discovered that she was pregnant with Bothwell's child. Since it was untenable that she could bear a child out of wedlock and imperative to legitimise her unborn baby, marriage to Bothwell was her only option, but it was one she railed against.

According to Drury, the kindness Mary had hoped to find in Bothwell was not forthcoming:

There has already been some jars [quarrels] between the queen and the duke and more looked for. He is jealous and suspicious and thinks to be obeyed ... The opinion of many is that the queen is the most changed woman of face that in so little time without extremity of sickness they have seen.[44]

Mary became a virtual prisoner under Bothwell's control. Her women were replaced by those of Bothwell's choice, his men guarded her door. She was unable to send or receive private correspondence without Bothwell's sanction. Drury tersely observed that 'Bothwell does all at court',[45] and a Scottish noble reported that 'from the day of the marriage there has been no end of Mary's tears and lamentations; for Bothwell would not allow her to look at or be looked on by anybody …'.[46] Mary admitted that 'Bothwell has us in his puissence [his power].[47]

Bothwell took up the reins of government with alacrity. He arranged meetings of the privy council and with it ushered in currency reform, established a more efficient system of royal revenue collection and revoked religious permits. It was Bothwell who now took charge of international correspondence, Bothwell who penned diplomatic missives and wrote letters to Elizabeth and Cecil. Mary's nobles became ever more marginalised, their power usurped by a man whom most believed had murdered their king and ravished their queen. Those who had conspired in Darnley's removal and who had agreed to Mary's marriage to Bothwell, regretted their compliance and now were determined to destroy Bothwell's power. The rumour that Mary was pregnant fanned fears for Prince James's safety. Bothwell had already attempted to take charge of the prince and had been deflected. But there was a real possibility that he might kill Prince James to ensure that it was his child who became heir to the throne. Mary's nobility – past rebels and some of the queen's supporters – became united in open revolt. They raised an army. On 11 June they issued a proclamation at the Mercat Cross in Edinburgh 'charging all subjects, specially the burghers of Edinburgh, to assist them in delivering the Queen, revenging the late king's murder, and preserving the prince's person'.[48]

Mary's monarchy was in jeopardy, and with it the Stewart dynasty. On 30 May 1567, Bothwell and Mary summoned their followers to gather at Melrose and take up arms. They installed themselves at Borthwick Castle, only to find it encircled by armed rebel forces. A proclamation went out to citizens to come to rescue their king and queen, but before armed help could be marshalled, Bothwell managed to escape and set off to muster support for the inevitable confrontation. Mary contrived her own escape, disguised as a man, and the couple were reunited at Dunbar Castle. Having left her belongings at Borthwick, Mary had to resort to borrowing clothes from a local country woman. She was lent a short red gown with sleeves tied in bows, a velvet bonnet and a muffler.[49] The queen, Bothwell, 600 horsemen and a large phalanx of infantry marched towards Edinburgh. That day the rebel lords justified their insurrection in a bond to:

take true part together till the author of the said murder and ravishing be condignly punished, the said unlawful marriage dissolved and annulled, the Queen relieved from the thraldom, bondage and ignominy which she has sustained, the person of the prince reposed in surety, and justice restored to all the subjects of the realm.[50]

At 2 o'clock in the morning on 15 June the rebel lords and their supporters rode out of the city to meet Mary and Bothwell's troops at Carberry Hill, just outside of Edinburgh. Saltires and the yellow and red of the Scottish royal standards led the queen's troops. The rebel lords had devised their own banner for the encounter. It was a grim response to grievance: a large replica of the sketch of Darnley's murder sent to Cecil showing Darnley's half-naked body lying strangled in Kirk o' Field's garden, Prince James kneeling in prayer and a speech bubble voicing his lament: 'Judge and Revenge my Cause, Oh Lord'. Was the sketch intended all along to be the source of a banner of indictment? Had it been drawn with that in mind? Compared to the splendour of the embroidered heraldic banners that were usually carried into battle, the banner of the rebel lords' army was a flag of blame and protest. It was borne as a justification for their revolt and as a challenge to Bothwell's kingship.

The day was unseasonably hot. Negotiations were protracted and energies dissipated as demand followed counter-demand, with messengers riding up and down between the protagonists. In the heat of the sun, Mary and Bothwell's soldiers became dehydrated and began to fall away. Bothwell, realising that their armed strength was dwindling, suggested that honour be satisfied by one-to-one combat. More negotiations followed as Bothwell first refused a candidate of lower rank, then another and another. Eventually, Mary came to an agreement, against Bothwell's advice, that she would put herself under the protection of her nobility if he was allowed to go free. Bothwell rode away. They had been married for just one month, and would never see each other again. Mary gave herself up into the safekeeping of her nobles. There still exists a sketch of the encounter, a montage of what transpired: a gathering of the troops with their banners, the parley between opponents, Bothwell riding away on the horizon, Mary submitting to her nobles. While its anonymous artist might not have been aware of it at the time, what he was documenting was Mary's nemesis.[51]

Bothwell fled to Dunbar to raise support. Initially he met with some success, securing the allegiance of key Scottish magnates. But as his associates and servants were taken in for questioning and torture – as they were executed, and had their limbs distributed throughout the towns of Scotland – the support Bothwell had garnered became more hesitant by those fearful of reprisals. Commandeering a small fleet of ships, he sailed towards his dukedom in the Orkneys but he was prevented from disembarking. Still hopeful of securing troops to restore himself and Mary to power, he sailed onto Denmark and sought the protection of Frederick II, the king of Norway and Denmark. At first, Frederick was accommodating, thinking Bothwell a useful tool with which to negotiate the return of the Orkneys and Shetlands to Norwegian rule. He gave Bothwell a generous allowance for clothes and invited him to place a regular order with a merchant in Odense for silks and velvets at Frederick's expense.

However, a Danish-Norwegian noblewoman, Anna Throndsen, reappeared in Bothwell's life. She and Bothwell had been involved previously, and had possibly married. She had lived with him as his wife in Scotland and in France but had returned home when the relationship foundered. Now, with Bothwell back in her sights, she raised a complaint against him for abandonment, suing him for the depletion of her dowry and his sale of her movables. Bothwell was taken into custody at Copenhagen in 1573 and, by now deemed devoid of political value, he was imprisoned in Dragsholm Castle in Denmark, an isolated and notoriously austere fortress. It is said he was kept there for the next five years in a tiny cell, chained to a pillar with insufficient room to stand. At Dragsholm he eventually went mad, and died in April 1578. His mummified corpse and coffin were interred in the crypt at the church at Färevejle, near Dragsholm, where, in 1858, his body was exhumed and put on show as a macabre exhibit, where it remained until 1976.

Queen Mary's House in Jedburgh – a sixteenth-century fortified tower, neither grand nor extensive – has become a popular tourist attraction and is now the Mary, Queen of Scots Visitor Centre. It was where Mary stayed when she came here in the autumn of 1566 to preside over the local assizes, and where she nearly died. Through the centuries, the house has remained much as it was in Mary's day. In the 1920s it was turned into a museum, its appeal boosted by thrilling reports of paranormal phenomena: the mysterious perfume of flowers in the second-floor chamber where Mary reportedly slept, the ghostly rustle of her skirts sweeping up its empty stairs.

## Three of the Fairest

The museum's *pièce de résistance* is its penny-in-the-slot machine – now, with pennies obsolete, a receptacle for gratefully received donations. Much to the delight of children, when fed money it allows a choice between a mechanical re-enactment of Mary's coronation to the sound of cheering crowds or Mary's execution to the sound of communal booing. There are exhibits on display that profess a connection to the queen: a pretty thimble, a scrap of silk, a lock of her hair and the remains of a high heeled slipper she is reputed to have worn. There is also a particularly grisly relic of her past: a black-and-white photograph of the mummified head of Bothwell reduced to skeletal ravage. Even allowing for the processes of mummification and decay, his debasement is palpable. What was photographed is what remained of him in the nineteenth century when his body was exhumed. What is left to us is horror.

Bothwell's mummified corpse, however, is not the only grisly remnant of this dramatic period in Scotland's and Mary's history. Darnley's skull also exists. It was scavenged from a raid on his tomb in the late eighteenth century and in 1865 was sold to a collector by the auctioneers Sotheby's for 6 shillings. The collector donated it to the Royal College of Surgeons in London. In 2016, a forensic student at the University of Dundee, Emma Price, crafted a 3D reconstruction of Darnley's head using his skull as reference. This recreated image of Darnley reminds us of his youth. The twenty-one-year-old Darnley is fine-featured with bright blue eyes but, in his re-imagined self, there seems a hint of evasion, as if he is unsure whether he condones his resurrection and is wary of our judgement.[52]

There is another memorial to Darnley's murder and the debacle of Carberry Hill. After Darnley's death, the Lennox family commissioned a large commemorative painting from the Antwerp artist Livinus de Vogelaare. It is displayed in the Palace of Holyroodhouse, in the very apartments that Darnley used to occupy. It depicts Darnley's effigy dressed in armour lying on a stone tomb, his head flanked by the unicorns of Scotland's armorials surmounted by a golden crown. Above him are suspended the heraldic banners of Scotland and the Lennox dynasty. The Earl and Countess of Lennox and Darnley's brother, Charles, dressed in mourning black, kneel beside the tomb, their hands clasped in prayer. In front of them is the small praying figure of Prince James wearing state robes edged in ermine, with the gold chain of the Order of the Thistle lying heavy on his collar.

This might have been a conventional family portrait, a pictorial lament depicting Darnley's family united in grief, were it not for other more unusual elements. Inserted alongside Darnley's heraldic achievements are two oval paintings. One illustrates Darnley and his valet, William Taylor, being dragged from their beds. The other is of their corpses lying in the garden of Kirk o' Field. On the bottom left is another painting – a painting within a painting – framed in wood. At first glance it seems to be a rural idyll with blue skies, green hills and figures gathered in the fields. What it depicts, however, is a denouement: the battle at Carberry Hill at the moment of Mary's surrender and Bothwell's departure. The banner of blame is there, triumphant among the rebel troops.

In the larger commemorative painting, Prince James's head is haloed by a scroll on which is written: 'Arise O Lord and avenge the innocent blood of the king my father and, I beseech you, defend me with your right hand'. The heads of Darnley's family are encircled by another undulating scroll with a legend bearing similar sentiments. On the wall of the painted mausoleum is an inscribed tablet that exhorts the prince to seek vengeance: 'If they, who are already old, should be deprived of this life ... the King of Scots ... should not put out of memory the recent atrocious murder of the king his father, until God should avenge it through him'. This may be a memorial painting, but what it commemorates is a crime as yet unpunished, its perpetrators not yet brought to justice. The inclusion of the depictions of Darnley's murder and the Battle of Carberry Hill are intended as evidence of Mary's and Bothwell's part in the king's death. It is a painting of accusation and a declaration of retribution yet to come.[53]

# 7
# A Dozen and a Half Little Flowers Painted on Canvas

One crisp morning in early autumn, I decide to take a trip to Lochleven Castle. It stands marooned on a small island in the old county of Kinross-shire and is only accessible by boat. When I arrive and buy my ticket, I discover there is still time before the next sailing and I lurk in the warmth of the booking office, perusing its selection of Mary, Queen of Scots memorabilia: guidebooks, key rings, bookmarks, the usual fare of tourist consumerism. Among them, however, I discover a more comical memento. It is a rubber duck of the queen herself: her lips pouting red, her black headdress adorned with plastic pearls and her ruff moulded in undulating white around her duck neck. Simultaneously hideous and seductive, on my trip to explore the next doomed chapter of Mary's life, it feels like a consolation. For it was at Lochleven Castle that Mary had her first taste of captivity. Here, in a place exposed to the elements, her sovereignty began to unravel. This jolly, irreverent duck seems as incongruous a touchstone of her grief here as would be possible to find. And yet there is a tang of defiance in its brash colours and spirited red-lip pout, and it appeals to my sense of humour. I buy it because, in writing about Mary's life, there is precious little to laugh about.

The boat trip across to the castle is surprisingly rocky but thankfully short. The castle, perched on a picture-postcard green lawn, gathers more texture as it comes into focus. While most of it is in ruins, the framework of its external structure still stands, stolid and compact. Once disembarked and adrift from

## A Dozen and a Half Little Flowers Painted on Canvas

the mainland, it seems that the breeze has free rein. It slices through the air in a splintered chill that snatches at you, whichever way you turn. It is too cold to linger. Instead, my exploration has to be brisk, with head down against the wind.

When Mary left Carberry Hill after striking her deal with the rebel nobles, she believed she was returning to Edinburgh to resume her reign and be reunited with her son. But when her nobles dismissed the women who were with her, leaving her flanked by a close press of soldiers, she must have become uncertain, suspicious that what she had brokered at Carberry Hill was not a compromise but a capitulation; that she was not in the company of her nobility, but under their control. Still wearing the borrowed clothes she had worn for battle, she entered Edinburgh dishevelled and defeated, 'her face so begrimed ... that it looked as if it had been daubed with dirt'.[1] And as she progressed through the city streets, it was not to glad hurrahs, but to the taunts of her subjects, who lined the narrow streets eager to witness the drama of her downfall, shouting 'Burn her, burn her, she is not worthy to live, kill her, drown her.'[2]

Rather than returning to one of her royal residences, as Mary had expected – and as she had been promised – the queen was taken to the Provost's house on Edinburgh's High Street. Armed guards had been posted outside, and two of them were instructed to keep watch on Mary inside her chamber. Without the shield of her women, deprived of the dignity of privacy and lacking basic necessities – not even a change of clothes – Mary feared for her life. The battle at Carberry Hill was meant to have resolved the crisis, to have seen Bothwell captured or dead. Instead, he was still at large, still King of Scotland. Bereft of the guidance of Mary's half-brother Moray, who had removed himself to France to distance himself from the ensuing drama and safeguard his innocence in the event of any retaliation,

Mary's nobles were unsure of how to proceed. With Mary threatening to expose their treachery and their complicity in the bond to remove Darnley and the bond approving her marriage to Bothwell, they felt it best to keep Mary captive and prevent her from summoning help. Mary demanded her release, a hearing, her reinstatement but when there was no response, the queen grew hysterical. Outside her lodgings a crowd had gathered. Among them was yet another betrayal: the banner of the Trade Guilds of Edinburgh held aloft as a flag of condemnation.

The Blue Blanket, as the banner was called, was a material declaration of sovereign fealty. The right to bear it had been granted to the Edinburgh Trade Guilds when they had risen up in defence of Mary's great grandfather, James III, when he was held captive by the English at Edinburgh Castle in 1482. Their support of their king had been rewarded with the granting of the right to carry their own banner as a badge of fealty. The privilege was enshrined in its scripted legend: *Fear God and Honour the King with a Long Life and a Prosperous Reign and we that is Trades shall Ever Pray to be Faithful for the Defence of His Sacred Majesty's Royal Person till Death*'. Now their banner had been unfurled not to protect their queen, but to accuse her. It was a declaration that she was no longer worthy of civic support, that she had lost the loyalty of her people.[3] But, as recorded in the history of the Blue Blanket by Alexander Robertson: 'The honest crafts; joined with other loyal citizens, pierced with pity to see their sovereign thus used, and their ensign displayed, where the ensign of the Blue Blanket used to be erected in the cause of loyalty, crowded to the place and compelled the conspirators to restore her to the Palace of Holyroodhouse'.[4]

The pernicious banner that the rebel lords had carried into battle, and which had accompanied Mary back to Edinburgh, was now hung across from her window as a reminder to her and the assembled throng of what lay at the heart of the queen's disgrace and the rebels' revolt. When Mary came to the window the following morning and heard the crowd still jeering, she exposed her desperation. She appeared, as a chronicler recorded, in 'so miserable a state, her hair hanging about her ears and her breasts, the most part of all her body, from the waist up, bare and discovered'.[5] This was a newly pregnant queen, only twenty-four years old, who, just six years earlier, had been queen of France and Scotland. Since then, Mary had lost her mother, witnessed the death of her first husband, relinquished her French crown and faced insult, betrayal and assassination. Her attempts to quell the disaffection of her recalcitrant nobles had been thwarted. Now, with her second husband murdered, her complicity in his death suspected, and Bothwell no longer by her side, she became desperate. Moreover, it was believed that Bothwell, as he left Carberry Hill, had given Mary the bond signed by the queen's nobles and churchmen endorsing Bothwell's marriage to Mary. It was evidence of their betrayal. She was now at the mercy of some of those same nobles. No wonder she begged for deliverance. Yet while some of the crowd were moved to see their young queen so wretched, others, believing that Mary was party to Darnley's assassination and alarmed at the alacrity with which she had married Bothwell, continued to bay for her blood.

That same day a warrant was issued to legitimise Mary's imprisonment citing Mary's 'inordinate passion to the final confusion and extermination of the whole realm'.[6] It was endorsed by just nine lords, including some of those who had put their names to Bothwell's bond. Bastian Pagez, her valet and the impresario who designed the revelries for Prince James's baptism, was arrested on suspicion of involvement in the king's death. Some nobles seized the opportunity – quite illegally – to destroy the furnishings of Mary's private chapel. They also looted the royal wardrobe, ransacking and removing clothing and textile furnishings.[7]

It took until evening for Mary to be returned to the Palace

of Holyroodhouse. Her journey there was hardly triumphant. The queen was marched back to the palace under the guard of 1,000 soldiers with the banner depicting Darnley's murder leading the way.

At the palace Mary was reunited with her women and allowed to change her clothes. She was served food, the first she had eaten in two days, while Lord Morton, one of Rizzio's assassins and a key player in the nobles' rebellion, watched over her. Her meal was interrupted by the arrival of two other rebel lords who had also participated in Rizzio's murder. To Mary's alarm, she was instructed to make all speed for departure. Her entreaties to have a little time to pack a few necessities – a few clothes – were disregarded, as was her plea to be allowed the company of a few of her women. Attired only in an informal loose gown and cloak, with no other belongings, Mary was escorted to her horse. She set off for an unknown fate 'conveyed, and with haste ... stripped out and spoiled of all her princely attire'.[8]

Instead of being taken to Stirling Castle and a reunion with Prince James, as had been intimated by Morton, Mary's small entourage turned north towards Kinross. It was a hard ride, a journey of thirty miles and more. In the early morning they reached the shores of Loch Leven, the seat of Sir William Douglas, Moray's half-brother. It was a destination decided on in haste. It was felt that William Douglas could be trusted as a guardian while Mary's nobles worked out what would be best for their, and Scotland's, future. They had no intention of reinstating the queen while Bothwell remained at large. She had to be persuaded to break with him. Only then might she be allowed to resume her throne. With Mary safeguarded at Lochleven Castle, her nobles now had time to deliberate on their course of action and consult with Moray. They were wary of Mary enlisting the martial support of France or England, of her exposing their treachery and, given the rumours of her pregnancy, they were increasingly fearful for the safety of Prince James.

## A Dozen and a Half Little Flowers Painted on Canvas

For Mary, the choice of Lochleven as a place of captivity was bittersweet. The castle had once been a respite, a place where she could retreat from the volatility of court politics in Edinburgh. Her visits had been frequent enough to warrant the furnishing of apartments worthy of a queen. The royal wardrobe had contributed to their finery, providing green-fringed curtains, tapestries and a chair of state canopied in crimson satin. But Mary was not taken to these apartments. Instead, she was conducted to other rooms that were sparsely furnished and where 'little or no effort had been made to lessen their discomfort'.[9]

Lochleven was to manifest Mary's humiliation, where she was purposely and literally divested of her power. In a culture where a monarch's authority was marked out by the size and status of their entourage, the magnificence of their dress and the material splendour of their surroundings, the absence of Mary's ladies-in-waiting, the want of proper apparel and the paucity of her accommodation were deliberate erasures of her sovereign identity. She was – as she later described in a memoir dictated to her secretary Claude Nau – 'despoiled of sceptre, crown and all the goods of this world, with nothing remaining but life itself'.[10]

Her debasement intensified the following week when she received a letter from Elizabeth. In essence, it was a reprimand:

To be plain with you our grief has not been small: for how could a worse choice have been made for your honour than in such haste to marry such a subject who, besides other notorious lacks, public fame has charged with the murder of your late husband, besides touching yourself in some part, though we trust in that behalf falsely! And with what peril have you married him, that hath another lawful wife alive, whereby neither by God's law nor man's, yourself can be his lawful wife nor any children betwixt you be legitimate?

It ended on a more conciliatory note: 'For your comfort, in such present adversity, as we hear you are in, we are determined to do all in our power for your honour and safety'.[11] Elizabeth had been advised not to attempt to rescue Mary by force, as her intervention might precipitate Mary's assassination. Instead, she despatched Nicholas Throckmorton, an English diplomat, as her emissary to glean intelligence of Mary's situation. Throckmorton was not allowed to see the Scottish queen but was reassured by Mary's nobles that 'they did not intend to touch her surety of honour; for they speak of her with respect and reverence and affirm that ... they will restore her to her estate'.[12] He was less than convinced and feared that 'such double faces and such treacherous minds' were plotting to eliminate the captive queen.[13]

On 26 June, the lords issued a proclamation to justify their actions. It declared that their intent was:

to punish the author [Bothwell] of the said cruel murder and regicide, to preserve the person of the innocent infant, born King of the Realm, from the bloody cruelty of him that slew his father, and to restore and establish justice abused in this corrupt time to all the citizens of this Realm.[14]

Unlike the wording of their earlier proclamation of 15 June, the protection of Mary was not mentioned. To prevent the queen making contact with Bothwell or having news of him, Mary was not permitted writing materials. Any correspondence she received was intercepted and read. Bothwell's followers were rounded up and some were executed, their remains exhibited in towns throughout the kingdom, as was customary in the sixteenth century, to dissuade any thought of a counter-rebellion in support of Mary and Bothwell.

Mary was so terrified of being poisoned that, for two weeks, she refused both food and drink. She succumbed, as she did under extreme stress, to physical debility and mental distress. On 18 July, Throckmorton told Elizabeth that, when he had conveyed to Mary the English queen's advice that she should divorce Bothwell, 'she sent me word she will in no way consent to it, but rather die, giving this reason that taking herself to be seven weeks gone with child, by renouncing him, she would acknowledge herself to be with child of a bastard, and forfeit her honour'.[15] But Mary's political, emotional and physical turmoil had taken its toll. Later that month, it is said, Mary miscarried twins. However, in the sixteenth century it would have been impossible to detect twins at such an early stage of their development. Either Mary was much further along in her pregnancy and was using the excuse of twins to justify her increased size, or there were no twins. Her claim of such a pregnancy at seven weeks would confirm that conception took place after her marriage to Bothwell and would exonerate Mary from any charge of adultery. As there seems to be little advantage to recording the miscarriage of twins unless it was to mask a more advanced pregnancy, it is likely that it was a self-protective deception. Moreover, given her distress at the time of their marriage, it seems likely that Mary knew by then that she was pregnant which, with Bothwell's rape of her, compelled her into a marriage she had not chosen.

After her miscarriage, Mary became afraid for the safety of Prince James, whose first birthday was just days after she had arrived at Lochleven. She had good reason to be alarmed. Her son was in the care of the Earl of Mar, one of the chief rebel lords and Moray's uncle. With her incarceration, James's importance as a political pawn was heightened. France was already offering its guardianship and, wary of a renewed Franco-Scottish alliance, Elizabeth schooled Throckmorton to relay to Mary, on her behalf, the English queen's willingness to become Prince James's custodian:

she [Elizabeth] thinks it is good, that besides dealing with the lords in charge of the young prince to commit him into her realm, he can also assure the Queen, looking to the troubles there, her own danger, and the child's peril, that such is her best course, for he will be treated as Elizabeth's own child, and become acquainted with her country. So dealing, it will stay her from inclining to the French practice which is notoriously to convey him to France.[16]

Moray had now returned from France to Scotland. When he eventually came to see Mary, he lectured her on the foolishness of her actions and threatened her with execution if she would not renounce Bothwell. But Mary refused. One of the Scottish nobles, William Kirkcaldy of Grange, reported that Mary had declared that she would follow Bothwell 'to the world's end in a white petticoat ere she leave him', but as one of the rebel lords, his testimony is suspect.[17] While Mary's miscarriage left her with no reason to stay married to Bothwell to legitimise their child (or children), she had to trust that Bothwell was marshalling support to liberate her, and she believed he had the capability – both of martial expertise and strategic acumen – to restore her to the throne.

At Lochleven Mary continued to be deprived of necessities. Her household was limited to just two women attendants, a physician and a cook. In July, Throckmorton advised Elizabeth that Mary 'required some other gentlewomen about her ... to have her apothecary and some modest chaplain, also an embroiderer to draw out such work as she would be occupied on, and a valet for her chamber'.[18] There is no evidence that the apothecary, chaplain or embroiderer were ever sent but, later in September, Mary Seton was allowed to join her.

Lacking possessions and clothing, Mary repeatedly dispatched what letters she could, most covertly, pleading for supplies. Not only did she have a paucity of clothes, but the little she had hardly reflected her status as queen. Moreover, her inability to adequately clothe her women undermined her role as their protector. Her authority had become so eroded that even modest requests were ignored or delayed. In June and July, Servais de Condé, the keeper of the royal wardrobe, sent her small parcels that included basic items such as pins, soap, slippers, shoes, a quilted manteau, a chemise and handkerchiefs.[19]

By July, the royal silver was being melted down to make coinage to augment the funds of the rebel lords. On 24 July, a small delegation of nobles appeared in Mary's chambers with a mandate to force her abdication. Given her refusal to renounce Bothwell, who had now been declared an outlaw, they were resolved to claim governance of Scotland in the name of Prince James. Moray was to be installed as regent and Mary – a woman with a damaged reputation, of questionable innocence in regicide – was surplus to requirements, no longer deemed fit to be Scotland's sovereign. It was a political coup. The queen was outraged at the proposal and demanded the right to appear in front of Parliament to answer for her supposed misdemeanours. Their riposte was to threaten to cut her throat if she did not sign. Throckmorton, hearing of their threats, secretly messaged Mary, reassuring her that anything she signed under duress could not be upheld. In her own words 'vexed, broken and unquiet', Mary signed away her crown. She agreed to her son becoming king and Moray regent and to a consortium of nobles to rule on Prince James's behalf should Moray die. Once she had signed, Mary collapsed.

On 29 July, on the second anniversary of Mary's marriage to Darnley, one-year-old Prince James was declared James VI, King of Scotland. The treasury accounts chart the preparations for his coronation and the ordering of crimson and blue velvet, red and blue silk taffeta, crimson thread, gold braid and fifty-four fur skins for the prince's tailor, James Inglis, to make the child-king's coronation robes.[20]

Mary knew nothing about it. It was only when she asked why bonfires were being lit below her window and why people were dancing in the castle garden that she learned that she was no longer queen. A thousand bonfires were lit that night throughout Scotland. Edinburgh Castle boomed with the discharge of its artillery. While it was reported that the people 'made great joy, dancing and acclamations so as yet appear they rejoiced more at the inauguration of the new Prince, than they did sorrow at the deprivation of their Queen',[21] the lack of attendance by most of the nobility at the prince's coronation was testament to the lie of the report of widespread celebration. While the rebel lords had taken control of the council, they did not have the unqualified support of the wider nobility, and many felt uneasy at the coup. Despite their reservations, on 22 August, Moray was declared regent.

Moray, as the illegitimate son of Mary's father, James V, had come close to becoming heir to Scotland's throne when his father had petitioned the Pope to annul the marriage of Moray's mother to William Douglas and approve her marriage to the king. However, his petition was rejected. On Mary's return to Scotland, it was Moray she chose as her chief political adviser. As a Protestant, he had engendered the support, if not the trust, of England. But his efforts to make Mary his puppet had failed. She had ignored his counsel, married Darnley against his advice and elevated Catholics to positions of political influence. With Darnley dead, Mary had chosen the outsider Bothwell as her consort and Moray had found himself marginalised. While recognising that the position of regent was challenging, it nevertheless presented him with the opportunity to safeguard the Protestant stranglehold over Scotland he had fought so hard to establish.

In August 1567, Mary wrote to her uncle, the Cardinal of Lorraine in France, to say that her messenger:

will tell you of my miserable state and present himself and these letters. He will tell you more because I have no paper to write much and ask the king and queen to burn my letters because if they know that I have written it will cost many lives and put mine in jeopardy and they will guard me more closely. God keep you in his care and grant me forbearance. From my prison …[22]

Mary's overthrow, however, was not solely based on the political disquiet of rebel lords, but on the threat to their property and land posed by Mary remaining queen. In December 1567, Mary would become 25, the age at which, as queen, she could, if she chose, revoke the grants of lands and properties made during her minority. Should she be released and restored to her throne before then, the rebel lords were likely to face forfeiture. It was another reason to keep Mary in captivity, but it had to be justified politically. At the Parliament that convened on the fifteenth of that month, the rebel lords pronounced Mary's abdication 'lawful and perfect', confirmed Moray's appointment as regent and validated the coronation of James. The rebel lords also introduced a new thread of vindication: that of Mary's guilt in the murder of Darnley. They declared that the queen had been 'privy and a part of the actual device and deed of the forenamed murder of the King her lawful husband'.[23] For that same Parliament, a further invidious proposal was drafted that 'in no time coming should any woman be admitted to the public authority of the realm or function in public government within the same'.[24]

When I contacted Dr. Alastair Mann, Senior History Lecturer at the University of Stirling and research fellow in the Scottish Parliament Project at the University of St Andrews, seeking clarification of this proposal, he advised caution. This denouncement of women's role and influence in Scotland's political affairs was never actioned. Its status remained that of a draft proposal. Moray, Mann suggested, was too eager to see his regency recognised by Elizabeth – an acknowledgement which remained elusive – to ever have sanctioned it. The proposal never resurfaced. Mary's son, James, also left it lying as a draft, unwilling to resuscitate anything that might further damage his mother's reputation and contaminate his own. When William and Mary secured joint rule of Scotland and England in 1689, it remained a footnote in parliamentary history. The fact that it was drafted at this point in Mary's downfall, however, demonstrates the strength of some male attitudes against women's rule.

That September, Mary wrote to the Scottish diplomat, Robert Melville. Her letter captures her growing frustration at the parsimonious delay in receiving supplies:

You shall not fail to send with this bearer to me half an ell of incarnate satin and half ell of blue satin. Also, Servais my concierge, send me more twisted silk if any remains; and sewing gold and silver; a doublet and skirt of white satin, another of incarnate. And another of black satin and a skirt of the same … also a loose gown of taffeta, also you shall send the gown and other clothes that I had Lady Livingston send me and also you shall not fail to send my maidens clothes for they are naked, and I marvel that you have not sent them some since departing from me, together with the cambric and linen cloth of which I gave you a reminder.[25]

This was not just neglect. Her want of necessities reflected Moray's lack of care. It was designed to be chastening: Moray wanted Mary humbled, resigned, not to harbour any hope of restoration. As regent, it was now Moray who signed the precepts for orders of livery, for fabrics to dress the court and his family. Eventually, he approved the dispatch of provisions to Mary:

by my Lord Regent's special command to be sent to Lochleven and delivered to Robert Melville to the Queen's Grace 3 ells of fine black … 2 ells double Lisle worsted, 2 ells of cambric, 3 ells fine stemming,

## A Dozen and a Half Little Flowers Painted on Canvas

1½ ells of satin, 4¾ ells fine English cloth to be a gown, 12 ells of gold passement, ¾ silk taffeta, 4¼ ells of red braid, 3 ells of canvas, 6 ounces of silk, 1 ell linen grey, 2 ells buckram, 2 ells camlet, 2 ells black velvet.[26]

One has to wonder if there was something deliberately humiliating in Moray's choice of English cloth for a gown rather than the foreign fabrics Mary favoured. Mary would have certainly recognised its provenance and his choice must have felt like a rebuke.

In July 1567, Servais had sent Mary 'a dozen and a half little flowers painted on canvas and traced out in black silk'. It was a small consolation for the lack of the professional embroiderer the queen had requested. But Servais had done what he could. He had arranged for a court embroiderer to trace out the flowers ready for sewing, and sent Mary silk and gold and silver thread for their stitching.[27] His record of this despatch provides us with our first insight into how and what Mary sewed. The canvas cloth and the outlined flowers indicate that she stitched in the French fashion, embroidering 'slips' (small pieces) bearing different motifs which were to be applied onto larger cloth. It was a method that allowed control over the final design, enabling images to be juxtaposed to complement, contrast or amplify the meaning of one another.

At Lochleven, with little opportunity for outdoor exercise, Mary was forced into a more interior life. In the vacuum of court activity, royal progresses, revelry and the business of government, she turned to embroidery. There is only one previous report of her sewing during her reign in Scotland, in a missive sent by Randolph to Elizabeth's chief adviser, William Cecil, in October 1561, in which he tells Cecil: 'Next day I was sent for to the Council chamber, where she herself ordinarily sits most part of the time, sewing at some work or other'.[28] That Mary sewed when the council was in session, or perhaps when she conducted formal audiences with governmental officials, may seem strange to us now. But in the culture of the sixteenth century, when women were attempting to assert their right to authority, it assumes greater significance. Was Mary's sewing an act of female confidence or was it simply a way for her to concentrate on what was being said? Was she using it to emphasise her female conformity, docility and industry, or was her sewing a provocative act, a strategic offensive to accentuate the gendered shift in power?

There are other indications that Mary sewed during her reign in Scotland. Embroidery frames and small boxes containing sewing silks are listed in the 1578 inventory of her belongings kept at Edinburgh Castle. Among them are over sixty pieces of canvas either drawn out ready for sewing, or partially embroidered. It is impossible to disentangle which of these were the work of professional embroiderers, Marie de Guise or Mary. Indeed, some might have been started by Marie de Guise and continued by Mary, as is common practice among needlewomen of the same family. Two small samplers 'penned for sewing' appear in the 1561 inventory of Marie de Guise's possessions, so they can confidently be ascribed to her, as can the length of blue velvet stitched with the heraldic arms of Longueville, the dynastic house of her first husband. While it might not have been embroidered by her, it was surely needlework that she commissioned.

One group of unfinished embroideries have a more plausible connection to Mary. It comprises a set of ten large canvases sewn in silk and metallic thread, materials much in evidence in Mary's later needlework. The canvases bear the arms of Brittany, Orléans and France, each a place of significance in Mary's life. Roscoff in Brittany was where Mary landed when she came to France at the age of five. Orléans was where François II died, and where Mary's days as France's queen ended. France was her cocoon, the place of family, friendship, girlhood and marriage.

## A Dozen and a Half Little Flowers Painted on Canvas

Places of arrival, settlement and departure: threads of memory, stitched so that Mary could hold them fast in cloth and preserve a sense of self.[29]

As well as the flowers outlined on canvas, Servais sent other cloth and other thread during her captivity at Lochleven. Throughout history and across cultures, people who are confined – held prisoner, or trapped by mental or physical frailty – have often turned to embroidery as a salve. Sewing is tactile. It has a rhythm. It steadies the mind and calms the spirit. In worlds robbed of comforting textures, the softness of cloth and the slip of thread is therapeutic. What is more, for those marginalised from the flow of life, needlework can act as a bridge to others, a way to communicate. It marks their presence. And, through the centuries, needlework has been a refuge for female royals cloistered within the confines of the court or when exiled, a medium through which they can remain emotionally and politically connected to the wider world.

There are many accounts in history of queens sewing. In the eleventh century, Matilda of Flanders, the wife of William the Conqueror, was renowned for her piety and skill with a needle. She stitched in God's name. So did Queen Margaret of Scotland who, that same century, established a school of embroidery at the court in Edinburgh, where 'her chamber was so to speak a workshop of sacred art in which copes for the cantors, chasubles, stoles, altar-cloths, together with other priestly vestments and church ornaments of an admirable beauty were always to be seen either made or in the course of preparation'.[30]

Henry VIII's first wife, Catherine of Aragon, is said to have introduced the technique of blackwork embroidery to England, a form of monochrome embroidery where just one colour of thread, usually black, is used to create intricate patterns on a white or cream background. It was commonly adopted to furnish shirts, sleeves and coifs with delicate and intricate embroidery. Through Catherine's introduction of it, blackwork became a prominent feature of sixteenth-century stitchery. In preparation for the battle of Flodden with Scotland in 1513, Catherine is thought to have helped to stitch the standards and badges that were carried into the fray. She also embroidered Henry's shirts as an act of care, a practice she persisted in even after they were separated, until his subsequent wife, Anne Boleyn, protested. On a visit to Catherine by Cardinal Wolsey – the unwilling, and unsuccessful, negotiator of Henry's divorce – he found the queen sewing with her ladies, 'at work, like Penelope' (Homer's heroine from the *Odyssey* who spent years weaving on her loom to hold would-be-suitors at bay). Catherine came to greet him wearing a skein of red embroidery thread around her neck. It was a grim joke, a reminder to them both that even she, Henry's queen for twenty-three years, could be executed. When Henry finally divorced Catherine in 1533, she was sequestered at Kimbolton Castle. Cut off from court life, she spent her final years of exclusion embroidering for the Catholic Church: a defiant gesture in the newly Protestant England of which Henry claimed to be the protector. An altar cloth in St Peter's Church in Windcombe in the Cotswolds is reputedly a survivor of her needlework. Made from recycled vestments and celebrating saints, Catherine signed it with her emblem, a pomegranate, as if to ensure that through it, at least, she would leave some trace.[31]

Catherine and Henry's daughter, Mary Tudor, was also a keen needlewoman. On her father's marriage to Anne Boleyn, Mary Tudor refused to acknowledge their union or adopt the Protestant faith. She was declared illegitimate, removed from the succession and kept distant from the court. In 1536, however, when Anne Boleyn was executed, Mary Tudor was welcomed back. She used gifts of embroidery as acts of reconciliation. An embroidered coat of crimson satin was sent for her three-year-old half-brother Edward, the heir to Henry's throne. Elizabeth, her half-sister, the daughter of Anne Boleyn, received a box covered in embroidered cloth wrought by Mary Tudor in silver thread. She gifted Henry a chair but bestowed its embroidered cushion on Katherine Parr, Henry's sixth wife, to signal her approval of their marriage.[32]

Elizabeth also embroidered. In John Taylor's book of needlework patterns and designs, published circa 1631, *The Needle's Excellency: A New Book wherein Diverse Admirable Works [are] Wrought by the Needle*, he composed an introductory set of verses within which he extolled the needlework talents of queens past and present. He praised the embroidery of Catherine of Aragon and Mary Tudor, and devoted one of his verses to Elizabeth:

> Yet how so ever sorrow came and went,
> She made the Needle her companion still:
> And in that exercise her time she spent,
> As many living yet, cloth knew her skill.
> Thus was she still a Captain, or else Crowned
> A Needlewoman Royal, and renowned.[33]

Like her half-sister, Elizabeth had been removed from the succession and declared illegitimate on the execution of her mother. Elizabeth used embroidery not only as a gift of reconciliation, but also to emphasise her royal credentials as a king's daughter. In 1544, the year she regained her rights to the succession, the eleven-year-old Elizabeth translated a religious work penned by Queen Margaret of Navarre, *The Mirror of the Sinful Soul*, from French into English. She wrote the text out in her own hand as a New Year present for Katherine Parr and embroidered the book's cover. At its centre Elizabeth stitched Katherine's monogram surrounded by a complicated interlaced pattern to signify her everlasting loyalty. Its four corners were decorated with pansies or heartsease, the floral symbol for thoughts. It was a carefully considered gift that referenced Elizabeth's Protestant faith, her fealty and her desire for connection, all of which Henry and Katherine would have understood from its embroidered vocabulary.

The following year, Elizabeth developed her theme. She presented her father with a book of prayers that Katherine had composed, accompanying it with a self-effacing note declaring it a gift from 'a humble daughter ... to prove what I could do'.[34]

Again, she embroidered its cover, which featured a white rose. In its simplest form, the rose stood for love; a white rose, however, signified purity and, as the emblem of Elizabeth of York, Henry's mother and Elizabeth's grandmother, its choice was designed to tug at Henry's heart as well as reiterate Elizabeth's heritage, her dynastic and royal provenance. Through crafting and presenting such gifts, Elizabeth was displaying not just her affection but, more importantly, her industry, intellect, virtue and creativity: her worthiness to be recognised as the daughter of the king. By embroidering them herself she was gifting Henry and Katherine the time she had spent in their making and her associated thoughts of them that its making entailed. The techniques she employed were purposely difficult, chosen to emphasise her devotion and her skill. Moreover, by choosing texts written by queens and copying them out in her own hand, she was putting herself in their company as an aspirant and deserving female monarch.

Through the centuries, queens have continued to embroider. Queen Victoria embraced the needlework she had learned as a child to salve her grief on the death of her beloved Albert. Queen Mary, the wife of George V, used her love of needlepoint to contribute to the post-war reconstruction. In 1941, after the death of the king, when she was nearly seventy years old, she spent eight years embroidering a series of twelve panels, each autographed by her, which, when joined together, created a carpet of flowers made up of over one million stitches. Once it was completed, Queen Mary presented it to the British nation to be auctioned off to raise money to offset Britain's war debts. It raised $100,000. Her grandson Edward VIII, who abdicated in 1938 to marry Wallis Simpson and was exiled in France, was also reputed to be a devotee of needlepoint.[35]

My own sewing began, not in captivity, but in social isolation. My brother, sisters and I were brought up on the fringes of Glasgow with a mother ever-anxious as to our safety. Her nervousness was understandable. She had experienced the Blitz in London during the Second World War when German bombers had tried to decimate the city night after night. One never knew who or what would survive. Our childhood was also, for a time, haunted by the existence of the serial killer Peter Manuel, who was on the loose near where we lived. The body of one of his victims, Isabelle Cooke, was found in a field not far from our home. No wonder our mother wanted to keep us safe, but her zealous protection put limits on our childhood. Apart from going to school and church on Sundays, we rarely met other people and, even more rarely was anyone invited to visit us at home. We lived in a family bubble, relying on each other for company and pursuing the different hobbies our mother encouraged. Mine was embroidery, a skill she taught me. Through it I could divert my yearnings for activity and sociability towards something quietly absorbing. Embroidery soothed my solitude. It became an escape from the tensions that were inevitable in a household thrown in on itself with little outside stimulus and few opportunities for self-expression. It allowed me to discover an inner rhythm, an individual creativity and practise an independence of sorts. It allowed me to find myself.

Those who kept company with the queen at Lochleven were closely watched. When Moray heard of a growing intimacy between Mary and his half-brother, George Douglas, he acted decisively. Suspecting that Douglas's ambition was fixed on a royal alliance, George was summarily banished from the castle.

Mary was still young, attractive and fertile. Were it not for the obstacle of Bothwell, she could remarry.

For Mary, the betrayal of Moray and the rebel lords cut deep: these were men she had once danced and hunted with, whose marriages she had celebrated, whose loyalty she thought she had earned. Moray, in particular, represented family. In her later memoir, dictated to her then secretary, Claude Nau, her distress at Moray's lack of compassion is palpable:

> The same persons laid hands on all the remainder of her most valuable movables, as well from her cabinet as her chambers, as also her entire wardrobe, from which she could never obtain one single garment, or even a chemise, until the return of the earl of Moray, who caused his wife's tailor to make the queen a dress of violet cloth, which he sent to her, along with some beggarly old clothes, for which he could find no other means.[36]

When an attempt at escape dressed as a washerwoman failed in March 1568, Mary was held in even stricter security, as she herself reported: 'I am so closely watched that I have no leisure but during their dinner, or when they sleep, that I get up: for their daughters sleep with me'.[37]

As Mary's movements became more circumscribed, Servais continued to send her cloth, thread and clothing but, in the lists he compiled on Moray's instructions, one can see him becoming more nervous, more judicious in his choices. Wary of being seen to despatch too much, he tried – given his limitations – to send things which Mary would find appealing and through which he could, covertly, convey sympathy and loyalty. Among the supplies he sent her was a vasquine of red satin trimmed with fur and a little casket with the letter F embroidered in silver. Mary, as Servais intended, would have interpreted the red of the satin as a medicinal spur to increase her vigour. The little casket with its F for François was a reminder of love and of France. While most of what Servais dared to parcel up was to cover Mary's basic needs – sleeves, coifs, shoes, gloves, thread and canvas – he included, where he could, other items that held sentimental or sensory comfort. He sent her Scottish pearls, the finest Spanish silk thread and perfumed gloves. There was a box of dried plums and pears harvested from the orchard at Stirling Castle. It was Mary's mother, Marie de Guise, who had introduced them to Scotland. She imported three varieties of pears and two of plums from her family estate at Joinville. Their inclusion would have been sent as a nostalgic memento and a touchstone of family.[38]

As the months dragged on, there was little sign of Mary's release. On 1 May 1568, Mary wrote to Elizabeth:

It is less wearyful to me than to be unable to tell you of the truth of my evil fortune, and of the hurts which have been done to me from many parts ... You know how my brother Moray has all I that own. Those who have anything agree to send me nothing: I beg you ... to have pity on your good sister and cousin, and to be assured that you will never have a more near and loving kinswoman in this world ... I beg you to have care lest anyone should know that I have written to you, for that would cause me to be worse treated.[39]

She was not to know but, that very day, Elizabeth was perusing Mary's rings and other jewels, including her coveted black pearls. Moray had sent them to London in the hope of selling them to the English queen to raise funds to replenish Scotland's coffers. When Catherine de' Medici heard of the availability of the pearls, she expressed an interest in procuring them for herself. Her French ambassador in England sent her their description: 'six cordons of large pearls, strung as paternosters, but there are about twenty-five separate from the others much larger and more beautiful than those which are strung'. A few days later, he reported that it had been impossible to buy them. They had become Elizabeth's prize.[40]

The very next day, on 2 May, Mary escaped. It was a plot planned with cunning and courage by Willie Douglas, the orphaned cousin of George Douglas, whose allegiance Mary had won – along with his heart, some said. The day was spent enjoying traditional May Day celebrations with Willie concocting the ruse of masquerading as the Abbott of Unreason, a central figure in the festivities. Tradition dictated that someone of high status was demoted for the day to act as the Abbott's servant. Willie purposefully chose Mary. The role required her to follow Willie wherever he went, thus setting up a plausible reason for Mary to be in his company. Earlier in the day, Willie had secured all the boats, bar one, on the castle shore. A pearl earring was to act as the signal for escape, its 'discovery' and 'return' to Mary a sign that all was ready. When she received it, Mary retired to her chamber on the pretext of seeking solitude for prayer. There, she and Mary Seton donned matching red kirtles and long, hooded mantles. With the revelry well underway, Willie managed to spirit the castle keys away from the guard of his father. Meanwhile, Mary Seton replaced Mary in her chamber and the queen made her escape. She simply left the tower, crossed the courtyard and walked out of the castle gate as Willie locked it behind them and threw its key down the mouth of a cannon. Mary was ferried across the loch to horsemen on the other side and sped to freedom. History relates that although she was recognised by local people, no one betrayed her.

Mary made for Hamilton Palace, where she was reunited with those nobles who had stayed loyal to her cause. When news of her escape reached Elizabeth's ears, she sent Mary a letter of support:

But this is time for congratulations, and pardon my affection, leading me to consider your present needs, and give the advice which I should wish for myself in this case. I pray you give ear to what the bearer will say and remember that those who have two strings to their bow may shoot stronger but they rarely shoot straight.[41]

## A Dozen and a Half Little Flowers Painted on Canvas

On 8 May 1568, nine Earls, nine bishops, eighteen lords and 100 others signed a proclamation in defence of their queen, declaring that they would 'serve and obey her with their bodies, lands, goods and friends'. Mary must have been heartened by their response. The Marian Party, as it became known, quickly attracted support and troops were rallied. After nearly a year of incarceration, separated from her people and erased of her power, Mary was able, just two weeks later, to lead an army of 6,000 men into battle against the rebel lords, her troops far outnumbering those Moray had managed to marshal.

The Battle of Langside took place on 13 May. It should have been Mary's moment of triumph. But, as ever, fate went against her. Lord Argyll, the leader she had appointed to command her forces, collapsed mid-battle, some said 'for fault of courage or spirit '.[42] Since he was Moray's brother-in-law, there were later mutterings that it was a pre-arranged betrayal. Leaderless, Mary watched from a hillside as her troops fell into disarray. It is said that she tried to rally them herself, and rode spurred and booted down from the hill to take Argyll's place, only to find her men fighting among themselves. With defeat beckoning, Mary yet again had to flee.

The roads back into the heart of Scotland, however, were blocked by Moray's followers. Mary and her small entourage were forced to go south. Now a fugitive, in imminent danger of recapture, and in fear of her life, the queen skirted the main highways and journeyed through Scotland's hinterland. She experienced what she had craved during that 1562 progress to the north of Scotland: the chance to lie at night in the open with a dagger by her side. But, as she later reported to the Scottish ambassador in Paris, there was no joy in it:

I have endured injuries, calamities, imprisonment, famine, cold, heat, flight, not knowing whither, ninety-two miles across country without stopping or alighting, and then I have had to sleep upon the ground, and drink sour milk, and eat oatmeal without bread, and have been three nights like the owls, without a female in this country where, to crown all, I am little else than a prisoner. And in the meantime, they demolish all the houses of my servants, and I cannot aid them.[43]

It was a 70-mile ride to Terregles Castle in Dumfriesshire and a further 20 miles to reach Dundrennan Abbey, her chosen sanctuary. There, her next course of action was debated. Isolated and lacking communication with others in Scotland, Mary was unaware that her supporters were already re-grouping to defend her. Her small loyal band of nobles advised her to go to France, where she had political allies, family and revenues. In France she could surely muster an army and return to Scotland to reclaim her throne by force. But Mary had set her heart on England. While it offered her nothing by way of intimates or funds, it promised her Elizabeth. The letter Mary had received from the English queen after her escape had convinced her that she had in Elizabeth a trustworthy champion, a soulmate who understood the limited choices that a woman, even a queen, had in the face of betrayal. Mary later admitted that the decision to set sail for England was hers alone, and that she had 'commanded my best friends to permit me to have my own way'.[44]

In borrowed clothes and with her head shaved to avoid recognition, Mary set sail for England at 3 o'clock on the afternoon of 16 May. A small fishing boat had been commandeered to carry the queen and sixteen of her followers. During the four-hour voyage, when they were halfway across the Solway Firth, Mary became uncertain and asked the boatman to change course and make for France. But the tide was against them. The only way forward was England.

Later that day, Mary arrived at Workington under the assumed guise of a Scottish heiress. Her cover, however, was soon broken and Sir Richard Lowther, the deputy governor of

Carlisle Castle, arrived with 400 of his men to escort the queen to the castle. They travelled via Cockermouth, where a local merchant named Henry Fletcher, recognising the paucity of Mary's attire, presented her with a length of black velvet and instructed a black gown to be made for her. Mary wasted little time in writing to Elizabeth to appraise her of her plight:

> It is my earnest request that your Majesty will send for me as soon as possible, for my condition is pitiable, not to say for a Queen, but even for a simple gentlewoman. I have no other dress than that in which I escaped from the field.[45]

She signed it 'your loyal and affectionate good sister and cousin, an escaped prisoner'. That she was in dire straits was confirmed by a letter written two days later by Sir Richard Lowther to Cecil, in which Lowther observed: 'Her Grace's attire is very mean, and, as I can learn, has none better, nor the wherewithal to change, so as I doubt that her highness's treasure did not much surmount the furnishing of her robes I not only ordered her charges at Cockermouth to be defrayed but provided geldings to convey herself and her train.[46]

In her straitened circumstances, Mary had little choice but to appeal for help. She petitioned Catherine de' Medici:

> Madame, I beseech you to have regard for my necessity. The King of France owes me some money, and I have not a penny. I am not ashamed to make my plaintive appeal to you, as to her who has brought me up; for I have not the wherewithal to purchase a shift (chemise) but am reduced to a plight which the bearer will tell you.[47]

She wrote to her Guise uncle, the Cardinal of Lorraine, saying 'Have mercy on the honour of your poor niece and provide the help that the bearer will acquaint you with and the need for money. I have nothing with which to buy bread, a chemise, or a gown. The queen has sent me hither a little linen and provided me with one dish. The rest I have borrowed but I cannot find anymore'.[48] Later, in the memoir Mary dictated, the Scottish queen was a little more circumspect. She recalled that Elizabeth had sent her a little box, a foot and a half square, which contained 7 yards of taffeta, as many of satin, some lawn and a few shoes of black velvet to set her up having heard that she brought nothing with her from Scotland.[49] In the months that followed, Elizabeth sent Mary more cloth including 'sixteen ells of black velvet, sixteen ells of black satin [and] ten ells of black taffeta ... to be delivered by our commandment to our trusty and right beloved counsellor Sir Francis Knollys [Mary's first guardian in England], knight vice chamberlain of our chamber, for the Queen of Scots.'[50]

While her need was in no doubt, it seems that Mary was exploiting the sparseness of her wardrobe to make a gendered appeal to Elizabeth. The English queen's response would furnish Mary with an indication of how she stood in her favour. For Elizabeth, the request presented a challenge. To have sent Mary some of her own clothing would have been a statement of intimacy, signifying a closer relationship than she wished to convey at this juncture. More troublingly, it could be interpreted by Mary as a sign of Elizabeth's desire to see her regain her throne through the symbolic queenly investment such a gift might seem to represent. With Mary's innocence in Darnley's murder still unproven and Elizabeth's advisers warning against any hasty action until the circumstances of the king's death and the rebellion by Mary's nobles was fully understood, Elizabeth had to be seen to be impartial. Her decision to send a gift of cloth enabled her to be responsive but remain emotionally and politically neutral, while the nature of the gift – cloth of the highest quality – was an acknowledgement of the royal status they both shared. It is a demonstration of how nuanced and delicate the art of gift-giving was in the sixteenth century.

Under the care of Sir Francis Knollys, a courtier and a member of parliament, and she was moved to Bolton Castle. Knollys

## A Dozen and a Half Little Flowers Painted on Canvas

felt compelled to advise Elizabeth of Mary's straitened circumstances reporting that the Scottish queen had no more than 'three or four women, and those not of the best or finest sort' and asking if ' furniture of wardrobe stuff [and] cloth of state might be borrowed'.[51] In those early weeks in England, Mary's greatest limitation was her lack of financial and material resources. With no access to her French pension and unable to retrieve her clothing and furnishings from the Scottish Royal Wardrobe, she had to turn to others for assistance. Material possessions were important not only for comfort, but also because they equated to status and agency. To have any influence required the ability to gift money or possessions. It was through them that support could be garnered and loyalty rewarded. Mary was sorely hampered by their lack. In July 1568, Moray arranged for three coffers of necessities to be sent to the Scottish queen but their contents, as Knollys reported, were hardly adequate comprising 'but one gown of taffeta, the rest being cloaks, coverings for saddles, sleeves and partlets and such little trinkets [that] they have sent again to Moray for her own apparel from Lochleven'.[52] Eventually Moray arranged for Servais to send more generous supplies: grey and black taffeta, fine black velvet, sewing silk, jet buttons, twelve pairs of shoes and four pairs of mules.[53] Meanwhile, he was attempting to sell off Mary's belongings. At Mary's request, Elizabeth issued a warrant to detain the Scottish queen's apparel, textiles and jewels that Moray had had conveyed to England to be sold.

Mary's letter to the Cardinal of Lorraine demonstrates the despair the Scottish queen felt at her situation:

If you have any pity on me now, I may say with reason that it is all over with my son, my country, and myself, and that I shall be as ill off in another quarter of this country, as in Lochleven … either I shall die or they shall confess that they have invented all the villainies which they have cast against me …[54]

Growing impatient, she castigated Elizabeth for her prolonged confinement: 'I have been kept as if a prisoner in your castle for 15 days'. At the same time, Mary entreated the queen to meet her 'if it please you ... without ceremony or in private'.[55] She told the English queen that 'I sent you my heart in a ring, and now I have brought to you both heart and body, to knit more firmly the tie that binds us together.[56] She sent Elizabeth a poem:

> One thought that is my torment and delight,
> Ebbs and flows bittersweet within my heart
> And between doubt and hope rends me apart
> While peace and tranquillity take flight.
> Therefore, my dear sister, should this letter dwell
> Upon my weighty need of seeing you,
> It is that grief and pain shall be my due
> Unless my wait should end both swift and well.[57]

Elizabeth had not expected Mary to throw herself on her mercy, and her advisers – chiefly Cecil – were horrified at having a Catholic Scottish sovereign thrown into their midst. However, Mary did not expect to foist herself on the English for long. On 20 May she had written to the Earl of Cassilis, a Scottish peer, to say that she expected to be back in Scotland at the head of English or French troops by 15 August.[58] Cecil, in an effort to forge a plan for Mary's future, listed the disadvantages of her presence: the boost to English Catholic fervour that Mary's proximity might engender; the possible rekindling of the political ambitions of Catholic Europe now that Mary was physically closer to the English Protestant seat of power; the repercussions of supporting or not supporting the perpetrators of Mary's downfall. She was, he concluded, a political liability.[59]

But, among the political complexities presented by Mary's arrival in England, for Elizabeth there was a more troubling emotional dilemma. How best to protect and honour the bond with her kin and fellow queen, a bond based on affection but unrequited due to circumstance and the recommendations of her male counsel? She neither wanted to raise Mary's hopes that England would use force to effect the Scottish queen's restoration, nor did she want to welcome Mary at her own court. And she was growing weary of receiving so many of Mary's long, self-pitying letters. She requested that Mary 'have some consideration of me, in place of always thinking of yourself'.[60]

Although in many ways Mary and Elizabeth seemed mirror images of each other, nature and nurture had shaped them differently. Elizabeth had lost her mother to the axe when she was two years old and had grown up in the flux of royal religious adherence and paternal volatility. Deemed illegitimate as a child, her grasp on the English throne remained elusive until her coronation. She was raised as a princess but her childhood was anxious, unmoored in the tidal ebb and flow of her father's, Henry VIII's, favour. She knew how easy it was to remove, imprison and execute a queen on trumped-up charges. She had witnessed Henry's disposal of four of his wives. While Mary had been cocooned in the French court, trailing her fingers over the raised knotwork on her gown of cloth of gold and dancing across a polished floor under silver sails in the embrace of Valois power, Elizabeth's governess was writing to Lord Cromwell to plead for clothes for her, 'for she has neither gown nor kirtle, nor petticoat, nor no manner of linen, nor smock, nor kerchiefs'.[61] Elizabeth had to construct her queenship strategically step by step, ever vigilant of her questionable legitimacy, ever cautious of her political vulnerability. Her early experiences had made her wary of making choices. She preferred to let her advisers act on what they interpreted as her desires so that, should they prove unpopular, she could not be cited as their author.

Even Elizabeth could not protect herself against slander,

however. When the rule of women was seen as unnatural, and the ambitions of men were constantly snapping at the heels of queens and female regents, any opportunity to prove a female ruler was prey to her passions rather than motivated by political acumen was seized upon. Female rulers had to remain alert to the danger of becoming the target of male censure and defamatory reportage. Elizabeth's close relationship with Leicester had bred rumours and slurs. It was said she had had a child by him, some said two, others three. The rumours persisted throughout her reign. Her much-heralded virginity was one tactic adopted by the English queen to avoid male criticism and deflect male control. It ensured she was largely free of the kind of vitriol that beset Mary. Elizabeth would have understood and sympathised with Mary's situation. What she did not know was how best to balance her empathy for the Scottish queen with her need to safeguard her own political realm.

In an early missive to Elizabeth, Knollys reported that he found Mary to be of 'eloquent tongue and discreet head.' He informed the English queen that Mary wished to go to France, and advised her that she could not keep Mary a prisoner indefinitely without it blemishing Elizabeth's honour. He warned that Mary's agility was such that it would take little for her 'with the aid of towels or other such devices' to escape, and that her incarceration so close to the Anglo-Scottish border – where there was a concentration of English Catholics – risked inciting a religious uprising.[62]

Cecil advocated that Mary be moved and recommended further strictures. Mary – already forbidden to correspond with anyone in Scotland – was not to be allowed to receive any private letters, and only be permitted access to people outside of her own household with her keeper's permission. To circumvent any possibility of Mary going to France – given that she had already requested safe passage through England – he advised political intervention. The French were to be asked not to respond to Mary's appeals for support. Instead, he advised, Elizabeth should devise a way 'to cover the dishonour of the crime and settle her [Mary] in her realm, secure from the tyranny of France'. He suggested that Mary should either be restored – with restrictions placed on her sovereignty – or be allowed to rule jointly with Prince James, with Moray continuing as regent. If she were returned to Scotland then the incipient enthusiasm of English Catholics would be blunted and, in Cecil's estimation, 'The young prince shall have but a short time' and Mary herself 'would not have long continuance'.[63]

Under the care of her early guardians, the treatment of Mary was liberal, in keeping with her status as a fugitive guest. She was allowed to establish a mini court and had a sizeable household of her own with six waiting women, although only Mary Seton was of any standing. Although she was under the strict guard of over 100 soldiers to 'maintain her safety', she was allowed to hunt and ride under armed escort. But she was put under strict surveillance with the nature of her correspondence controlled, her activities monitored and her visitors vetted. All of which was reported upon regularly to the English queen and Cecil.

Another complication emerged. Mary, it now seemed, was willing to consider a divorce from Bothwell and was exploring who she might marry next. Prospective candidates were being approached and tentative negotiations begun. In her frustration at being kept captive, neither securing the support of England or France to hasten her liberty nor enforce her reinstatement, Mary became duplicitous. She purposefully spread intelligence that the Spanish ambassador had opened up discussions with Philip II of Spain, Elizabeth's main adversary, and that three possible suitors had been suggested – Philip himself, his son Don Juan and the Archduke Charles of Austria. It demonstrates how manipulative Mary was prepared to be to realise her liberty. In deliberately choosing to flaunt the possibility of a marital alliance with Spain, Mary hoped to galvanise Elizabeth and Cecil to release her and return her to Scotland, or, at the very least, grant her a passport to France. But her strategy misfired. Mary's intention to remarry, her consideration of a liaison with one of England's key political Catholic rivals, only served to harden Elizabeth's heart against the Scottish queen.

Elizabeth decided that the only way forward was to demand that Mary clear her name of the accusations made against her, of 'the great slander of murder, of which she was not yet purged'.[64] While a trial would not be appropriate, as Mary was not Elizabeth's subject, an enquiry would serve just as well. Mary was adamant that she would not commit to any investigation and Elizabeth had to use her utmost diplomacy to get her to agree, assuring the Scottish queen that 'I will do nothing to hurt you, but rather honour and aid you'.[65] With a promise that, should Mary prove innocent, Elizabeth would see to it that Mary was restored to her throne – by force if necessary – Mary consented.

It took until October 1568 for the enquiry to get underway. English and Scottish commissioners and Mary's representatives were appointed. York was chosen for the initial hearing, although the enquiry later reconvened at Westminster and then at Hampton Court. Mary chose not to appear in person, rejecting the authority of the tribunal to try her: a Scottish subject and a queen. She was unaware that Moray was busy not just gathering, but fabricating evidence against her. The rebel lords – fearful that their bonded conspiracy to remove Darnley and their support of Bothwell's marriage to Mary would be exposed – needed as much ammunition against Mary as they could muster to deflect any condemnation of themselves.

The main evidence of Mary's guilt rested on what are called the 'casket letters'. As ever in Mary's narrative, the story is convoluted and contradictory. In the aftermath of Darnley's assassination, Bothwell's tailor, George Dalgleish, was taken in for questioning. He had led his interrogators to a casket of letters that he said Bothwell had asked him to safeguard. On opening the casket, incriminating correspondence between Mary and Bothwell was apparently discovered. Dalgleish was never questioned about their contents and was hanged before anyone else could investigate his story. The number of documents the casket was claimed to contain varied over time, but in total there were said to be eight love letters, twelve love poems and two marriage contracts, one made before Bothwell's divorce. Their contents were damning. These were letters between lovers and murderous accomplices, and included a plan for Mary to poison Darnley. The dubious authenticity of these documents, which were undated and unsigned, has exercised historians and biographers over centuries. There are certainly anomalies. There are suspiciously clumsy insertions, inconsistencies in both the writing style and the handwriting. When Mary heard of their existence she delivered a spirited riposte, declaring 'there are divers in Scotland, both men and women, that can counterfeit my handwriting and with the like manner of writing which I use, as well as I use myself'.[66] The originals were never produced, only copies and their provenance remains controversial.

The documents were presented as proof by the Scottish commissioners that Mary had 'fore-knowledge, counsel, device, that she was the persuader and commander of the said murder to be done, maintainer and fortifier of the executions thereof'. More insidiously, they further claimed that Mary and Bothwell had conspired 'to cause the innocent prince, now our sovereign lord, to shortly follow his father and so transfer the crown from the right line to a bloody murderer and godless tyrant'.[67] They produced what was called a *Book of Articles*. It was an indictment of Mary, penned by George Buchanan, the Scottish Latin scholar and author who, just two years earlier had written the eulogistic verses about the queen for Prince James's baptismal masque. It had five sections, the first four tracked Mary's rejection of Darnley, her 'inordinate affection' for Bothwell, their complicity in the king's murder and the events that led to their marriage where, as their 'ungodly filthy usage continued, they devised a counterfeit ravishing'. The last section was a defence of the rebel lords' subsequent imprisonment of the Scottish queen.[68] This vindictive work, based on allegations, insinuations and conjecture, was presented to the English commissioners. As it was an enquiry rather than a court trial, no witnesses were cross examined, and the evidence could not be challenged. One of the English commissioners was appalled at the Scottish rebel lords' malevolence, declaring that 'they cared neither for the mother or the child ... but to serve their own ends'.[69]

Mary, while not present at the enquiry, countered the rebel lords' accusations through her representatives saying that the Scottish commissioners were a 'pretended authority', motivated by the desire to usurp 'their sovereign's authority and to possess themselves with her great riches and her true subjects'.[70] She protested that Moray had been allowed to meet Elizabeth privately, a privilege that she had been denied. When her request to be allowed to defend herself in Elizabeth's presence was refused, Mary's representative commissioners boycotted the proceedings. It is curious that Elizabeth would not permit Mary to meet her, given that the English queen had suffered the same frustration at the hands of her half-sister, Mary Tudor. She knew what it was like to be a prisoner unable to defend oneself against the accusations of others. She had experienced the distress of powerlessness and exclusion. But Mary's attempt to force Elizabeth's hand by nurturing an alliance with Spain had bred mistrust and, for the moment, the English queen was not willing to risk falling prey to Mary's charisma before the Scottish queen's innocence was confirmed.

The enquiry ended in an *impasse,* with Mary declining to answer the accusations against her unless she could speak directly to Elizabeth, and Elizabeth saying that she could not 'without manifest blemish of her own honour in the sight of the world' agree to such an audience until Mary was proved innocent. With the outcome unresolved, Mary's fate remained in limbo.

When the enquiry reached its inconclusive end, Moray prepared to return to Scotland. To Mary's outrage, Elizabeth presented him with eighteen horses, two dozen yew bows, sheaves of arrows and a £5,000 loan to ensure that Scotland's Protestants remained indebted to England.[71] Mary responded by exhorting her followers, the Marian party, to prevent Moray from returning home. She arranged for malicious rumours to be spread in Scotland that Moray's regency – as yet unrecognised by Elizabeth – was to be acknowledged by the English queen, and that England was planning to establish its own garrison at Edinburgh Castle. Through her efforts, the Marian party gathered more support in Scotland and Catholic Europe. But Mary's vengeful scaremongering served only to exacerbate and prolong the civil war that had erupted in Scotland following Mary's flight. Elizabeth retaliated. She warned Mary that she would publish 'the whole canvas and doings to the world' – meaning Buchanan's *Book of Articles* and the contents of the casket letters – if Mary did not leave off her slander.

At the start of February 1569, the queen was relocated 'with an evil will, and much ado' to Tutbury Castle, a property belonging to the Earl and Countess of Shrewsbury. Tutbury was more isolated and, more importantly for English security, further from the Anglo-Scottish border and more distant from England's Catholic northern counties. That summer Elizabeth discovered that Mary had diverted her marital intentions from possible Spanish candidates to the English Duke of Norfolk, then the richest man in the land. She put Norfolk in the Tower and instigated stricter controls over the Scottish queen. Elizabeth suspected that, behind the idea of their marriage, lay a much more treacherous scheme, to overthrow Elizabeth herself and return England to Catholic rule. Mary was forbidden to see anyone outside of her immediate retinue. She became guarded more closely. Her status as a protected queen began to metamorphose into that of a dangerous conspirator and with it came a lessening of her liberty.

In November 1569, a plot to rescue Mary was revealed. The Northern Rising, as it became known, was led by northern English Earls loyal to the Catholic cause. While Mary was aware of the conspiracy, she had refused to participate in it. She still had her hopes pinned on Elizabeth pressurising the Scottish rebel lords to restore their queen. But as the Catholic rebellion had managed to advance very near to where Mary was being accommodated another move was mooted. It was the start of what were to become innumerable relocations during Mary's years of imprisonment. And in the inertia of captivity, the Scottish queen turned to intrigue. In the absence of a voice, she turned to embroidery.

# 8
# A Catte

Hardwick Hall sounds like a name conjured up for pantomimes, somewhere where Baron Hard-Up is hen-pecked by his bullying wife. The early historians and biographers of Elizabeth Talbot, Countess of Shrewsbury – commonly known as Bess of Hardwick – would have her fit the bill as the harridan. She was lambasted as rapacious, selfish and self-seeking, a gold digger who rose up the social ranks through her entrapment of men. At a time when ambition was viewed as a flaw in women, Bess was denounced as 'masculine-minded'. But history has exonerated her. Bess of Hardwick has emerged, over time, as a woman of redoubtable qualities: generous, industrious, resourceful and creative, an able entrepreneur and an innovative property developer. Married at fifteen, likely in an arrangement to safeguard family property, by sixteen she was a widow. Her second husband, Sir William Cavendish, by whom she had eight children, died after ten years of marriage leaving substantial debts to the Crown. Bess felt she was entitled to the sum of his property and doggedly persisted with a lawsuit until she won her claim. When her third husband, Sir William St Loe, died a few years after their marriage, he left Bess his fortune. With that and her own revenues, Bess became the second-richest woman in England after Elizabeth I. She invested her riches in architecture and their interiors to become the matriarch of some of the grandest houses in the country. By the time Mary came into her life, Bess was newly married to her fourth husband, the sixth Earl of Shrewsbury, one of the foremost aristocratic magnates in England.

It was Bess who built Hardwick Hall. It was completed in 1597, ten years after Mary's death. She designed it as a showcase of female capability and a landmark of female ownership. It acts as a physical rejoinder to the trivialisation of her accomplishments and the character assassination she had to endure during her lifetime. In its time, Hardwick Hall was the most beautiful building yet seen in England. It neither borrowed from Italianate conceits nor aped French Renaissance elegance. Instead, it was firmly rooted in an appreciation of the English vernacular: a modern masterpiece of English magnificence.

It is 2019, and I am visiting Hardwick Hall for the first time with my friend Tina, who lives nearby in Derbyshire. Tina has cancer and our visit is to mark a friendship that has lasted for over forty years. We had decided on Hardwick Hall as a good way to explore somewhere new together and reinvigorate a closeness that we have both been too busy to nurture regularly over the decades. While the weather is not glorious, it is kind enough.

As we stroll along the path leading to the Hall itself, we pass its previous incarnation: the old Hall, Bess's ancestral home, where she was born and lived until her first marriage. It is now a shell, but it still holds traces of its cultural aspiration in the plaster reliefs of hunting scenes that cling to its dilapidated walls. They have refused to surrender to the erosion of time and stubbornly persist as evidence of an earlier sophistication.

The interior of Bess's Hardwick Hall unfolds like lengths of cloth, revealing itself bit by bit, a textural adventure of considered taste. Stone avenues curve to deliberately settled points of pause. The upward promise of a sweep of stairs allows a breathing space, a moment to stop, reframe yourself in the space around you and refocus on what lies above and below. This is a house designed for revelation. Narrow hallways lead to sudden grandeur, to the Long Gallery and the High Great Chamber, or reveal more private chambers including Bess's office where, from floor to ceiling, wooden filing drawers once held her documents. Bess designed Hardwick Hall around her textiles – they even dictated the scale of its rooms. In her Withdrawing Chamber the 'tapestries of personages with my Ladies Armes' are still in their original position, wrapped around its upper walls in a vividly coloured frieze. The dimensions of the High Great Chamber were determined by the size of the vast set of tapestries Bess commissioned from Flanders which tell the story of Ulysses. And the Hall's stone staircases and wood panelling are punctuated, softened, by the miscellany of needlework which is displayed among them: Turkish table carpets, velvet cushions appliquéd in gold cloth, wooden screens inlaid with embroidered octagons, each stitched with a single flower, each accompanied by a Latin motto as a visual anthology of moral principles. While small embroideries are unexpectedly encountered, hung on a side wall or decorating a mantlepiece, the sensation is one of being enveloped in textiles: vast vibrant tapestries, embroidered hangings and sewn panels line the stairwells and chambers. And there is a gift of unexpected reverie, a darkened gallery walled in stitched female portraits. They are a spectacular homage to women, a stitched assertion of their worth through time.

Tina and I are enthralled. We snap photographs on our phones and stop to watch the video that tells us about the life of Bess. Its strapline 'I am Bess' is repeated in its final frames, in which woman after woman from different ages and cultures hold up placards to tell, in a few hand-written words, of their experience of marginalisation and achievement. When we reach the portrait gallery, we discover an ingenious contemporary extension of the video's theme in an exhibition also called 'I am Bess'. Accompanying the usual ornately framed portraits of poised women of noble rank are twenty large colour photographs of contemporary women who have made their mark in different fields: women who have overcome the obstacle of their gender. Mary Beard, the eminent classics scholar, is there, paired with Bess herself.

In the room that follows, the National Trust has created a more participatory exercise. It invites you to write on a post-it note what you, as a woman, have done to contribute to the world, to the lives of others or to progress. Tina becomes mournful. She confesses that one of the things she fears – given that her cancer is terminal – is that she will leave nothing behind, that there will be no trace of her when she dies. She suspects her contribution will be ephemeral, forgotten. I take a post-it note and write: 'We were early community artists who used our creative talents to help local people express themselves in ways that were noticed. We are Bess'. We both sign it and I pin it to the board. The small act cheers us.

On we go through the great hall, where exquisite frescos stretch above and around our heads. We are entranced by their detail, by the way a hound pricks up its ears to the soft sound of a stag or how wildflowers dance along a hedgerow. But we are searching for Mary's embroideries. I know the Hall has two. At last we spy one on a stand at the entrance to a room roped off from the public. It is framed behind glass, understandably protected but nevertheless made separate. It was designed as a cushion. Its central image illustrates a moral tale, and at each of its four corners are more stitched fables, instructive stories whose cautionary warnings are largely lost on us now. When a guide passes, we intercept her and enquire as to the whereabouts of the second cushion. She is hesitant, uncertain. Perhaps it's in storage, she says.

That day, we discover that we can have access to the attic for an extra £1. We drop our coins into the attendant's hand and climb the narrow winding stairs to reach what would have been the servants' quarters, now requisitioned as storerooms. On shelf after shelf, labelled cardboard boxes are piled high, one on top of the other. They contain the embroideries and other textiles that Bess collected through her life, evidence of her compulsion – and her financial facility – to accumulate a wealth of material possessions. Bess, it would seem, was a gatherer and hoarder rather than a dispenser or distributer. What she harboured was not put into wider circulation but remained in her ownership until her death, when it was bequeathed to family members as dynastic wealth with instructions that it was to be kept together in its entirety and continue to be displayed in her various residences. Her love of acquisition, the familial partisanship she displayed in the preservation of her textiles and her cherishing of what she amassed, are our gain. They ensured that one of the best collections of sixteenth-century and earlier embroideries and tapestries has remained largely intact, conserved through family guardianship, generation upon generation. It is because of Bess's stewardship that the embroideries of Mary still exist.

In one of the rooms of the attic, casually leaning up against a chair leg, I think I recognise the second of Mary's embroidered cushions. It is unboxed and unwrapped, framed behind glass like the other. I squat down to study it more closely and, to my amazement, realise that it is indeed Mary's other embroidery. Like its counterpart, it has a central oval and four smaller ovals at each of its corners and, as with its companion, each oval contains a moral tale. Its background is also similar, embroidered in repeats of thistles, roses and lilies, compartmentalised within a pattern of knotted trellis. The floral emblems reference the kingdoms that harboured Mary: Scotland, England and France. I know the moral of its central medallion. It depicts frogs at a well, an illustration of one of Aesop's fables, which warns against leaping before looking, advising its readers to consider the consequences of their actions. I am astounded by my chance encounter and by the embroidery's abandonment, and I am sorely tempted to pluck it from its indignity and put it under my protection. I wonder how long it will lie there before its absence is noticed and it is returned to a curator's care.

That was my moment of empathy with Mary, a moment when I fleetingly grasped the humiliation of her powerlessness. I mourned her long, tedious, hours spent sewing, trying, through her stitching, to counter a world in which her critics maligned her, her rivals demeaned her, and in which she was made politically mute. It is through her embroideries, such as the one that now lay carelessly on the floor, and its partner on display in Hardwick Hall, that we can still hear what Mary had to say more than four centuries later. These embroideries and their stories – of the cat and the cock, the crown and the snake, the fox and the eaglet, a cat shut in a cage with mice running free outside and the frogs trapped at a well-head – dwell on themes of capture and liberty. The Scottish queen had a host of emblematic images and over 700 of Aesop's fables to choose from as inspiration for her embroidery. She carefully selected those which best voiced her sense of injustice. The story of a fox eating a young eaglet was aimed at Elizabeth. It carried the moral that a betrayer of friendship would be punished. The image of a cat devouring a cock implied that excusing actions in the name of justice was no deterrent to those prepared to use force to win what was rightfully theirs. It served as a challenge to Mary's political detractors. Those who viewed Mary's embroideries would have known the moral fable they depicted. Stitching these cushions was, for Mary, a form of emotional release, a way to voice her anger and resentment, to castigate Elizabeth and others who denied Mary her freedom and refused to acknowledge her power. In them she takes the moral high ground. The cushions show Mary at her most artful and defiant, not just in the tales she tells, but also in their framework of embroidered flowers which act as reminders of the powerful countries which shaped the Scottish queen's destiny.[1]

I left Mary's embroidery drowsy in its shaft of sunlight and came away saddened. I was too caught up in the poignancy of its neglect to remember to inform one of the attendants; its fate seemed to sum up Mary's life as a prisoner in England.

Tina and I left Hardwick Hall less joyfully than when we had arrived there. As we meandered through its gardens we felt chastened by the reality of this extraordinary and beautiful building and the spurious criticism Bess encountered, a belittling that still echoed in our own lives. While we had appreciated the Hall's magnificent presence and its glorious challenge to Bess's critics, and been heartened by the women in the exhibition whose achievements had surpassed any expectation even Bess would have had, we still felt pessimistic. The loneliness of Mary's stitched lament seemed to encapsulate what still needed to be done to assert women's worth. We walked on in silence, no longer feeling we were on a journey of discovery, as we had been when we first met, but older now and more fixed: sensing time running, like sand, too quickly through our fingers.

Mary's guardians, the Shrewsburys, were ideal custodians. They were rich enough to provide comfortable hospitality and an extensive guard. Loyal to Elizabeth, they were politically astute and understood the sensitivity of their charge. Their care came with instructions to Shrewsbury:

Not to allow her [Mary] to rule over him, or plot for her escape. To allow none about her but her retinue. Should she be sick or wish to speak to his wife the Countess, he should permit the latter to come to her but rarely, and no other gentlewoman shall be suffered to come to her presence or sight.[2]

It seems cruel that Mary was denied the company of other women except those of her household who, apart from Mary Seton, shared little of her culture. The motive behind such an order is difficult to understand. Could it be that Cecil – who would have imposed it – was intent on heightening Mary's isolation, excluding her from a female network of support which might have provided succour? If so, it indicates the progress women had made in threatening male supremacy, that he so feared Mary's access to female companionship.

With little warning of the arrival of their royal guest, there was scant time for the Shrewsburys to make preparations. Tutbury Castle had been used primarily as a hunting-lodge and was poorly furnished, so Bess sought the assistance of Elizabeth. The English queen duly instructed the removal of appropriate furnishings and furniture from the royal store. She was judicious and generous with her dispersals, not just in their volume, but in their spirit. She authorized Rafe Rowlandson, the groom of her removing chamber, to send tapestries narrating the Passion and the exploits of Hercules with another set called *The History of Ladies*. Over a dozen Turkish carpets were requisitioned and with them went feather beds and bolsters, embroidered counterpanes, chairs upholstered in crimson and gold, cushions and footstools covered in gold and silver. Rowlandson had the presence of mind to include 2,000 hooks, two hammers and a bolt of cord to truss the beds as aids to Tutbury's workmen tasked with refurbishing at speed. The richness of the furnishings reflected Mary's royal status. They were intended to reassure Mary that, although she was being kept under strict watch, she would be treated in a manner that befitted her station.[3]

The suite of tapestries known as *The History of Ladies* was inspired by Christine de Pizan's *The Book of the City of Ladies*. In the sixteenth century, this woven affirmation of women's social and political worth adorned the walls of the most powerful courts of Europe, and Mary was familiar with it. One set had graced the walls of the French court and another was displayed in Scotland, purchased by Mary's father, James V. Elizabeth's dispatch of them to Mary was no idle choice. While it seems thoughtful to provide Mary with a reminder of the palaces she had once frequented, Elizabeth's gift could also be interpreted as a reproach, given the tapestries' emphasis on the female qualities necessary for women to rule effectively. Equally, Elizabeth might have chosen them to bolster Mary's resolve to reclaim her throne, a sisterly act of empathy. In all likelihood, Elizabeth gifted them precisely because the motive behind her choice was ambiguous. Through them she could simultaneously message support, censure, sympathy and her own monarchical superiority. The closing passages of De Pizan's book are particularly pertinent to Mary's situation:

all you women, whether of high, middle or low social rank, should be especially alert and on your guard against those who seek to attack your honour and your virtue. My ladies, see how these men assail you on all sides and accuse you of every vice imaginable ... O my ladies, fly, fly from the passionate love with which they try to tempt you! For God's sake, fly from it. No good can come to you of it.[4]

None of the tapestries inspired by de Pizan's book exist today, not even in fragments, so we have little idea which were illustrated in those Elizabeth sent to Mary. But it is tempting to speculate that Elizabeth, the virgin queen, sent them to deflect Mary from thoughts of re-marriage, particularly a marriage that either spawned a closer alliance with Spain or, if with Norfolk, threatened Elizabeth's own sovereignty.

Tutbury Castle was hardly salubrious and Mary came to hate it saying 'the sun never shines upon it ... nor any fresh air come to it; for which reason it is so damp that you cannot put out any piece of furniture ... without it being covered with mould in four days'.[5] At Tutbury, Mary was allowed to set up her chair of state. When Elizabeth's envoy, Nicholas White, came to the castle to assess Mary's situation and report back to Elizabeth and Cecil, he was puzzled by the significance of its embroidered emblem, which depicted a phoenix rising from the ashes with the stitched motto 'In my end is my beginning'. White later confessed it made little sense to him.⁶ The phoenix, however, was a Catholic symbol that signified the resurrection, and it had been adopted by Marie de Guise as her personal emblem. To the visually literate Elizabeth, it would have been seen as provocative. Not only did the image reference Mary's Catholicism, but its accompanying motto carried the threat that should anything untoward happen to the Scottish queen, her Catholic allies would claim her as a martyr and that she would live on through their fervour. It was an early example of Mary using embroidery as a political weapon. As her years of captivity wore on, Mary stitched her own sewn statements: protests of lineage, vindications of virtue, challenges to her captors and sorrow at her loss.

By 1569, Mary was much in need of the solace of sewing. She confided to Archbishop Beaton, her confidant in France who had once been her Scottish ambassador there, that without her embroidery she had nothing to do but 'weep and pray'. In imprisonment, needlework became not just the Scottish queen's occupation but an obsession. At Tutbury she found a companion and creative collaborator in Bess of Hardwick. Bess's age is uncertain, but she is thought to have been around twenty years older than Mary, and she was lively company. Although she was not Mary's peer and could not lay claim to any royal lineage, she was a frequent and welcome guest at the English court, and could keep Mary informed and entertained with its gossip. Bess was astute. She was aware of how quickly the political wind might shift; she was conscious that Mary could be restored to the Scottish throne and mindful that she could succeed Elizabeth. It was in Bess's interests to nurture an intimacy with the Scottish queen and her chosen medium for affinity was embroidery.

Bess was a keen needlewoman. She used embroidery to enhance her interiors and advance women's visibility, both in content and creation. Before Mary's arrival, Bess had embarked on a highly ambitious project to produce a series of large appliquéd panels that celebrated women. It is these that now grace Hardwick Hall. For their fabrics, Bess recycled the ecclesiastical spoils of the English Reformation reaped by her third and fourth husbands: vestments of the finest silk damask, brocade, velvet and cloth of gold. She reconfigured the remnants of spiritual male authority to applaud female knowledge and glorify women's achievements. Her large figurative panels have women personified as the liberal arts among them astrology, logic and music. Her Heroic Women of the Ancient World celebrate women through history. Penelope is flanked by her virtuous attendants, Patience and Perseverance. Cleopatra is accompanied by Fortitude and Justice. There are forty-eight smaller panels that personify virtues and vices, elements of the natural world, nymphs, women from classical mythology and more. Another series epitomises the Virtues and captures the attributes of Hope, Charity and Temperance. These intricately stitched portraits of women, some bigger than life size, were sewn onto a black velvet background with the women posed within archways cut from cloth of gold, which was inlaid with velvet and overlaid with embroidered arabesques. Their figures were subtly padded to endow them with a softness that accentuated their grace, and their drapery and facial features were delineated in embroidery and paint.

It is thought that Elizabeth is among them, depicted as Faith, and the historian, Susan Frye, identified Mary as the muse for Chastity. The Scottish queen stands in front of a white unicorn, one of the devices on the royal coat of arms of Scotland. The expert on the Hardwick embroideries, Santina Levey, was convinced that Mary was, at the very least, tangentially involved in the project. If this is true, her inclusion as Chastity – ironically or defiantly, depending on one's view of the Scottish queen's life – evokes the mischief of Bess and Mary's collaboration that can be detected in some of their other embroideries, most noticeably in those sewn by Mary.[7]

Although Bess, perhaps with Mary's input, devised these panels, she and Mary did not make them. The needlework is clearly that of professional embroiderers employed by Bess. That is not to say that the two women would not have contributed, lent a hand to sew down elements here or there. But they were undoubtedly Bess's masterpieces in conception and design. When Shrewsbury contested Bess's possession of some embroidered textiles in the 1580s, she countered his claim, retorting 'These are mine. I caused them to be made'. For her, her role as originator and producer validated both authorship and ownership.[8]

Bess and Mary devised and stitched countless other smaller embroideries. These works were neither anonymous nor private. Many of them were 'signed'. Both women used a variety of ways to register their authorship. Bess stitched her full name or its initials, her monogram or the Cavendish emblematic stag, sometimes even the Tudor rose. Mary 'signed' with her personal cipher, MA with the Greek letter Ο (ph) for F (Francois II) which, at times, she showed in the reverse or superimposed with a double M and added R for Regina. She also used her monogram surmounted by a crown, the royal arms of Scotland or the Scottish thistle to mark them as her work. Such autographs assigned the two women's embroideries a distinguishable provenance. Their needlework, like the large portrait panels, was intended and destined for public use. Among them were cushions, wall hangings, bed furnishings and table carpets, all made to be seen. But the most ambitious project was a collaborative one comprising over 100 embroidered pieces to be assembled onto larger cloth as a miscellany of the two women's memories, knowledge and expressions of their emotional and family identity.

This project spawned the creation of embroideries set within squares, octagons and cruciform panels. The idea of stitching differently shaped pieces which could be united in a cohesive arrangement was unique to English needlework of the time. It would seem, however, that its design was influenced by textiles belonging to Catherine de' Medici, textiles which Mary would have seen in France. Here too, small squares and octagons of embroidered canvas were destined to be applied to longer lengths of cloth as bed furnishings or valances. The process allowed a kind of visual map to be fashioned through which the eye could travel from one piece to the next, accumulating information and gathering meaning. Bess and Mary planned that a large embroidered square would be the centrepiece. It was to be surrounded by the other cruciform and octagonal panels. Each shape had a distinct theme. The cruciform panels illustrated birds, fish and animals – real and imaginary – their names embroidered on scrolls. The octagons harboured flowers, fruits, herbs, vegetables and trees with mottos or proverbs stitched around their borders. A series of other octagons was devised containing monograms. The novelty of the project demonstrates the closeness of the two women's collaboration. Shape, size, where text should be placed, its style and scale would all have been debated. Colour palettes would have been agreed: the central panels to be bordered in red brocade, the lettering of the octagons picked out in cream or blue.

The challenge Bess and Mary set themselves was considerable. The amount of stitching required for each individual piece made each one a major undertaking. It was not only the sewing of the main images and text. The large central panels had inner borders which contained a medley of other imagery. Others would have been recruited to help with the task, cajoled or invited to fill in a background here, finish off a motto there. Professional embroiderers would have worked alongside the children of the household, of which there were many. Pierre Oudry, Mary's embroiderer who had accompanied her from France in 1561, had five children; Bastian Pagez, her servant of long standing and producer of her court revelries, became the father of nine children, most born during Mary's captivity. Valets and grooms of the wardrobe would undoubtedly have contributed. This was a collective venture, with Mary and Bess acting as its overseers and its authors.

Bess was as much in need of the diversion as Mary. Her new role as Mary's guardian meant that she was compelled to neglect the management of her ambitious building projects and forsake her sociable sojourns to the English court. Used to industry and a plethora of matriarchal duties, her stagnation and seclusion at Tutbury and the Shrewsburys' other residences must have been hard to bear. In the sterility of their shared limbo existence, Bess and Mary channelled their energies and creativity into their needlework, but they exploited it to different ends. Bess found in it a medium through which she could amplify and personalise the textiles she displayed in her grand interiors. She used it to secure a material legacy. Mary's obsession, however, was not with the stitchery per se, but in the stimulus it offered her as a mental and emotional exercise. Sewing was a medium through which Mary could use her intellect, reconnect to the women whose company had been denied her and document her experience of captivity. Needlework became her means to reframe, preserve and promote her story.

And it was through their embroidery that Mary and Bess got to know each other. Stitch by stitch, they shared a curiosity in the world around them: its dynastic families, botanical discoveries, mythological and moral tales. More intimately, they learned about each other's relationships. Although the stitches they employed were conventional enough – largely tent and cross stitch – with them they sewed the stories of their lives, retold through symbolism. Their needlework was an exposition of who they were, what they had lost, and what they aspired to. The central panels were the most graphic. In these they documented their most significant attachments, tracked their advancement and setbacks and recorded their sorrows and their hopes.

Two large square panels, sewn by Bess, are illuminating. In one, the central image is of a crow who is patiently dropping stones with its beak into a water-filled vessel in order to slowly raise its level so it can drink from it. The image, originating in one of Aesop's fables, carries the moral adage that 'necessity is the mother of invention': an apt choice for Bess, whose advancement was largely due to her tenacity and ingenuity. Another panel features tears which are falling, like rain, from the sky into quicklime. Its motto 'tears witness that the quenched flame lives' was a motto adopted by Catherine de' Medici after the death of Henri II, when for her new palace, the Hôtel de la Reine in Paris, she erected the Colonne de l'Horoscope, a 28-metre high Doric column dedicated to Henri and her heartache. On its surface were carved motifs of loss: torn love-knots, a shattered mirror. And around the border of Bess's embroidery are love tokens – rings, a chain, a girdle, a mirror and a gauntlet – all broken or torn. These are interspersed with the monograms of Bess and her dead second husband, Sir William Cavendish. Her panel is a lament for a lost love and a symbolic portrayal of Bess's determination to persevere. It is both commemorative and aspirational. It would have been Mary who supplied Bess with the motto and, while Mary had left France before the installation of the Colonne de l'Horoscope, she undoubtedly knew of its design and furnished Bess with its details.

In Bess, Mary encountered a woman who was unencumbered by status and free from the strictures of a public role. Here was a woman of independent mind and means. After the trauma of the duplicity and debasement that Mary faced at Lochleven, to be in the company of a resourceful and spirited woman like Bess must have been liberating. The two women, despite their age and social difference, complemented each other. While Bess was sketchily schooled in arithmetic and literacy and had never set foot outside of England, she possessed acumen, wit, energy and drive. Mary, on the other hand, was extremely well-educated and her knowledge was extensive and cosmopolitan. She was well versed in the classics and conversant with emblematic imagery. Moreover, she had been immersed in the sophisticated material world of France and had witnessed its court fêtes, entrées, masques and ceremonial rituals and understood their attendant symbolic manifestations. It seems likely that Bess encouraged Mary to be more fearless in what she expressed through her needlework, emboldened her to put herself and her relationships at the heart of her sewing. Mary, for her part, introduced Bess to a repertoire of concepts that could not be gleaned from contemporary publications, but were borrowed from the visual culture of the French court, which itself was influenced by Italy. They inspired Bess to develop a sewn vocabulary of greater intellectual and emotional complexity, evidenced in the panel she stitched to commemorate her relationship with William Cavendish.

On the visit of Elizabeth's envoy Nicholas White to Mary, he had asked her how she passed her time, and he had reported back to the English queen and Cecil that: 'she said that all day she wrought with her needle, and that the diversity of the colours made the work seem less tedious and continued at it so long till the very pain did make her give it over'.[9] White also provided us with his assessment of the Scottish queen. He paints a sympathetic picture of Mary as a woman with 'an alluring grace, a pretty Scottish accent, and a searching wit, clouded with mildness'. Throughout her life, Mary is described as having charm. She attracted admirers, and even at Lochleven, in the direst of circumstances, won the loyalty – some said the love – of George and Willie Douglas, the latter willing to risk his life to help her escape. Elizabeth was alert to the seductiveness of Mary's charms, particularly on men, and was not prepared to take any risks. To her mind both Sir Francis Knollys, the Scottish queen's early custodian in England, and Nicholas White, Elizabeth's envoy, displayed unfortunate partiality to and sympathy for the Scottish queen. With the Shrewsburys newly married, Elizabeth hoped that their newly forged attachment would be a deterrent to the Earl succumbing to Mary's magnetism. But their close proximity and the pity of Mary's situation inevitably bred empathy.

White's account of Mary engrossed in the virtuous pursuit of sewing was reiterated by Shrewsbury who, in a letter to Cecil, reassured him that:

The queen daily resorts to my wife's chamber where with Lady Livingston and Mrs Seton, she sits working with the needle, wherein she much delights, and devising works – her talk altogether of indifferent and trifling matters, without any sign of secret dealing or practice I assure you.[10]

It was an optimistic view of Mary's resignation to her fate. The Shrewsburys' care of Mary was certainly relaxed. Instructed to keep constant watch over the Scottish queen, the only way the couple could maintain any semblance of their past lives – the hospitality and sociability vital to their status – was by including Mary in their activities. But it led to Shrewsbury being accused of using Mary as an attraction, of bringing his friends and the local gentry to meet her. And although Elizabeth, through Cecil, had issued the command that there was to be little fraternising between Mary and Bess, in reality Mary spent many hours of every day in Bess's company. And life was not without its comforts. Mary was allowed to continue hunting. She was permitted to acquire a number of little dogs. Maltese dogs from France were a particular favourite but terriers also made their appearance. The Scottish queen, with Elizabeth's permission, was also able to decant from time to time to the spa town of Buxton, to take its waters for the sake of her health. There, much to Elizabeth's chagrin, Mary encountered luminaries of the English court, Cecil and Leicester among them. The Shrewsburys were lax in their surveillance. The services of a priest were secured under the guise of being but another addition to Mary's household. If the Shrewsburys suspected his real calling, they turned a blind eye. Mary had a lifestyle, if not of luxury, at least splendid enough to require the acquisition of sartorial finery. She exhorted Mothe-Fénelon, the French ambassador for England with whom she corresponded, to arrange the dispatch of:

patterns of dresses, and of cloth of gold and silver, and of silk, the handsomest and the rarest that are worn at court ... a couple of headdresses, with a crown of gold and silver such as were formerly made for me, and ... procure for me from Italy some new fashions of headdresses, veils and ribbons with gold and silver ...[11]

If occasionally Shrewsbury fretted at the licence he accorded Mary, his sympathy for her wellbeing and her contentment outweighed his reservations. But he was right to be anxious. In time, his son's tutor and some of his servants were found to be acting as Mary's go-betweens, smuggling letters in and out between Mary and her supporters.

When a freak earthquake struck England in April 1580, Mary wrote of it in a letter to one of her goddaughters, saying that 'my women could not sit steady on their boxes and chairs, where they were working around me'.[12] It paints a picture of Mary, Bess and their women gathered together sewing, chatting as they stitched, as women have done through the centuries. There is camaraderie in sewing. With heads bent over stitching, confidences are more readily shared and topics can become more intimate. The pooling of equipment – scissors, threads, needles – necessitates small physical interactions that break down social barriers. Technical problems are communally solved, collective skill and achievement applauded.

In my work as a community textile artist, I have been privy

to such creative conviviality which, invariably, includes laughter. Put a group of women together and they will enter the fray of collaborative design and creation with jocularity and often ribald humour. A suggestion will lead to a story, a story to an idea, an idea to a more subversive, sometimes salacious, suggestion. There is no reason to believe it was any different in Mary's day. Those she sewed with were not her peers, but women and men who had a more seasoned take on life. Add Pagez into the mix and there certainly would have been irreverence. George Buchanan, Mary's Latin tutor in Scotland, described him as 'cunning in mind and merry jesting' and he was once reported as being 'in the Queen's good grace because of his jokes'. His contribution, not only to Mary's needlecraft but to her *joie de vivre,* was considered vital to the Scottish queen. In a letter she described him as 'a very necessary servant whom during these fractious times, has given me solace by his inventions for needlework, which is, for me, after my books, the only exercise left to me'.[13] Pagez had been with Mary since 1562. He was the author of the tail-wagging, whip-cracking costumed satyrs that had so infuriated the English guests at Prince James's baptism. His role in Mary's household was ambiguous. He is variously described as her 'chamber child, musician and valet' and latterly, in England, as her 'broderer'. It was a term used in sixteenth-century parlance as a catch-all for a deviser or maker. It seems Pagez also played an undercover role. When the Scottish queen was held at Lochleven, it was Pagez whom Mary entrusted to convey her letter to Elizabeth in London, and she sent him to Dieppe with missives for her French supporters. His nomenclature as 'broderer' probably masked his real purpose as Mary's courier, trusted with conveying her secret and sensitive political correspondence.

The main sources of Mary and Bess's needlework were the recently published anthologies of emblems and books illustrating flora and fauna. Among the latter were Conrad Gessner's

*Icones Animalium,* and his *Icones Avian* and *Icones Animalium Aquaticum,* compendiums of real and fantastical creatures which appeared 1553, 1556 and 1560 respectively. There was Pietro Andrea Mattioli's detailed study of plants and Pierre Belon's *La Nature et Diversité des Poissons.* These early naturalists included small woodcut illustrations in their publications and Bess and Mary adopted many of them, searching out those which were most pertinent to the sentiments and experiences they wanted to express in their needlework. There was more to their replication of woodcuts than their usefulness as a visual resource. In the slow, steady replication of them in stitches, their form could not only be better explored, but also memorised. They provided Bess and Mary with a storehouse of knowledge of what existed in the wider world.

While the two women borrowed from printed sources for many of their designs, they did not always copy them faithfully. Some were deliberately altered to realise a more personal or emphatic meaning, others augmented with a motto to provide a cryptic commentary and pose a greater intellectual challenge. Pairings of mottos or proverbs with images created abstruse puzzles, designed to tease. They were open to different interpretations. Emblems and impresa (personal emblems) could be reworked. A different motto could replace an existing one to provide a new twist to the significance of an image. Or the motto might be kept but a different image used to suggest another message, or even develop a line of thought in response to the original. The creation of emblems and impresa was a visual game between courtiers and Mary was an active player. An embroidery of marigolds turning their drooping heads towards the summer sun was the impresa, the personal emblem, of Mary's French sister-in-law, Marguerite de Valois, the Queen of Navarre; the flower's French name, *marguerite,* creating a visual pun. It was an image later adopted by Mary in her embroidery. It both honoured a familial connection and referenced her religious faith as marigolds were associated with the Virgin Mary, who is said to have used their golden petals like coins.

One of the most elusive symbols in Mary's embroidery is that of a tortoise climbing up a crowned palm tree. It is a replica of the image chosen for a silver coin, the Scottish ryal, which was minted to commemorate Mary and Darnley's marriage. The coin has puzzled emblematic experts over centuries, as has its embroidered counterpart that Mary stitched nearly a decade later. There is nothing in Scottish iconography to suggest an indigenous provenance. Generally, the image is interpreted as a sarcastic comment on Darnley, who is personified as the cumbersome tortoise venturing an ineffectual campaign to be granted the Crown Matrimonial. But that is almost too graphic and simplistic to serve as a visual conundrum. Some think it references the Catholic victory at the Siege of Malta in 1565; others that its meaning is more personal, signifying fertility, given Mary's pregnancy at the time that the coin was minted, and since both images are symbols of fecundity. The palm tree also symbolises strength and the tortoise endurance, so they might have also conveyed a moral message. Was it a veiled reference to Rizzio, with whom Mary is thought to have exchanged gifts that represented the tortoise, or did its meaning lie in Tarot cards, recently imported from Italy to the rest of Europe, which feature the tortoise and the palm tree? The fascination with Mary's needlework is that we can never fully unravel her meanings and intentions.

Through her embroidery, Mary also conceived aural puns. Her sewn dolphin is copied from a woodcut by Gessner. But Mary added a crown to it and relied on the word play of dolphin and *dauphin* to make of it a reference to François II. While this served as a commemoration of her past, other devices captured her present. One of her most poignant is her image of a bird in a cage with a predatory hawk hovering above it. Its motto reads: 'It is ill with me now I fear worse to come'.

The emblem expert Michael Bath has painstakingly unpicked some of the personal connections in Mary's embroidery. In his book *Emblems for a Queen*, he explores, among others, the provenance of her stitched 'byrd of America'. Bath traces the origins of Gessner's woodcut to reveal surprising links between it, Scotland, Henri II and Mary's father, James V. The 1578 inventory of Mary's possessions lists 'the beak of a fowl of India or Brazil': one of the curiosities that the queen treasured through time. Bath suggests it came with her from France to Scotland, and he identifies it as a trophy from an expedition made by the French explorer André Thevet. On Thevet's return from his voyage to Brazil, he presented Henri II with a cache of exotic specimens, one of which was presumably this beak. Thevet's expeditionary force had been under the command of Nicolas Durand de Villegagnon, who later captained the ships that brought Mary to France in 1547 and escorted her back to Scotland in 1561. There are further connections. Gessner had obtained a toucan beak to assist in his illustration of the bird that Mary later embroidered. It came from Giovanni Ferrerio, who was an Italian emigrant to Scotland. Ferrerio spent thirteen years in Scotland, four of them at the Scottish court during James V's reign. At some point in his life, Ferrerio sent the toucan beak to Gessner, presumably before he came to Scotland and, once in Scotland, he continued to send Gessner information on Scottish species of animals, birds and fish. Moreover, the entrée of Henri II into Rouen in 1550, which Mary had attended, had a reconstruction of a Brazilian village as its centrepiece. As Bath concludes, Mary's choice of the illustration encapsulates a matrix of connections to the Scottish queen's past. What appears on the surface to be a sewn duplicate of Gessner's woodcut of a bird is, in reality, a multi-faceted repository of Mary's personal memories.[14]

Together, Mary and Bess completed over 100 of their small, encrypted embroideries for their collaborative project, each one with thousands of stitches. The examples that survive are inventive and sometimes mischievous. Those that can be 'read' with certainty reveal the preoccupations of both women. Bess's are more explicit than Mary's, but still symbolic.

Bess and Mary would have had a scheme in mind for the project's final display, how it was to be arranged on larger cloth. Such a plan was a vital interpretative component of sixteenth-century textiles. Sadly, it was not realised during their lifetimes and their intent remains unknown. Without it, we cannot fully appreciate how the ordering of their chosen subjects would have amplified their meaning. Assembled as hangings and valances, Mary and Bess's embroideries would have been read like a storybook. In the sixteenth century, women's writing and embroidery were seen as interchangeable, each a medium of female thought and emotion, each carrying the 'hand' of their author. Embroideries such as those of Mary and Bess, like words, marked down characters and plots, sentiments and reflections, opinions and judgements. To the two women, embroidery would have been as valid a form of correspondence as their letters or other writings, replete with visual rather than literary allusion.

It is believed that Mary and Bess's needlework was passed down through the descendants of the Bedingfeld family and, at some point, mounted onto lengths of velvet as bed curtains and a valance. It was Alethea Talbot, Bess's granddaughter, who is thought to have assembled them. Now on permanent loan to Oxburgh Hall in Norfolk from the Victoria and Albert Museum in London, they are in the care of the National Trust, displayed as a triptych: three panels that encompass seventy-nine embroideries, all crowded onto a background of faded and patched green velvet. More are stitched on a valance. Authorship of thirty of them are verifiably Mary's, signed with her personal cipher, some with her crowned initials or identifiable through the presence of a thistle or some other Scottish reference. Bess's monogram of E S, for Elizabeth Shrewsbury, registers others as her work and one piece is dated 1570. The remainder are unsigned, but it is possible, through close inspection of the stitching and an understanding of their respective themes, to attribute, if not authenticate, their maker.

For Mary, living in an environment of surveillance and suspicion, with visitors monitored and conversations reported on, and where her correspondence was intercepted and read, verbal and written forms of communication had to be guarded, even when encoded. Such writings, therefore, cannot be assumed to be a true reflection of her thoughts and opinions. Mary's needlework, however, was uncensored. She could use it to express what she dare not commit to paper: her emotional state. Many of her embroideries are unsettling, containing images of destruction and violence. A scimitar (a sword with a curved blade) slices through a knotted rope, a vine is watered with wine to make it die, a snake falls into a fire of sticks, a leopard holds a hedgehog in its mouth accompanied with the motto 'It presses on it and it sticks'. There is a tree being cut down with a scythe, vines being pruned, a field growing spears and helmets instead of corn. One of the most disturbing is of a tree laden with motifs of power – sceptres, crowns, crosiers, precious stones, wallets and papal bulls. At its base stands a lone woman, her eyes bandaged. She is striking the tree's trunk with a rod. Its motto 'As chance will have given' and its imagery seem to encapsulate Mary's frustration at the choices she made, putting her power out of reach through a blinkered, or restricted, view of what could be done. Many of Mary's embroideries are redolent with images of destruction: splintered ships' masts, torn sails, felled trees, broken ropes, heaps of feathers from a dead bird. Her content, as Michael Bath reveals, was layered with her experiences and her memories, collected together like an album. Memory was also trapped in the way she stitched, replicating a style of needlework she had learned as a girl in France, sewing small embroidered pieces. Her needlework was a physical memorialisation, the canvas holding her touch through her handling of its cloth; capturing the tension of her stitches. It enabled her to leave a tangible imprint of her existence. In the sixteenth century, the needle held a number of symbolic meanings. It was thought to be synonymous with breath, the rhythm it produced being analogous to that of breathing. It also signified an arrow piercing a target or a gateway through which one could pass between the underworld, the temporal universe and the celestial heavens. Mary would have been mindful of the symbolism inherent in the act of sewing. It endowed her needlework with a deeper resonance.

The Palace of Holyroodhouse has two embroideries of Mary's and one of Bess's, which have been in its care since the 1950s. When I visit the palace in the company of its past and present curators, Deborah Clarke and Emma Thompson, they offer to take Mary's embroideries out of their glass case and let me see them close up. I am thrilled, of course. Emma lays a cushion of tissue paper on a nearby table and unlocks the case that contains the Scottish queen's needlework. As Deborah holds up its long glass lid, Emma slides her hands tentatively under the first of Mary's embroideries, entitled 'A Catte', and brings it out into the light. She sets it down gently on its tissue cushion and we crowd round to consider its detail. For many people, the interest in a piece of old embroidery lies in its antiquity and its provenance. Its fragility, the signs of its age, its wear and tear, validates its preciousness, along with the context in which it was made. It is such artefacts that seduce us to become cultural pilgrims. Mary's embroideries are endowed with added poignancy because they were made when she was in captivity in England.

My attention, however, is not focussed on the historical poignancy of her embroidery, but on its stitching, on Mary's tactile signature. I want it to reveal more than just her skill with a needle and thread: I want it to expose her temperament. In all my research on Mary, Queen of Scots, this is the closest I have ever come to being in her presence. Lying in front of me is a rare remnant of the Scottish queen, designed by her, wrought by her, purposed to serve as her voice. She had made it for others to see and she hoped we would understand her better through its viewing. But she could have had no idea that it would persist for nearly five centuries to speak to us, to me, now.

The embroidery, a cruciform, is larger than I imagined. Although I had seen its companion pieces at Oxburgh Hall, they were so tightly clustered with others that it was hard to distinguish their individual appeal. Now isolated, this embroidery seems magnified. Originating in one of Gessner's black-and-white woodcuts, Mary has coloured her cat with red-brown thread, to better personify it as the red-haired Elizabeth. She has inserted a little mouse scurrying by the cat's paws as its quarry, a personification of Mary herself. This embroidery was undoubtedly inspired by one of Gabriele Faerno's sixteenth-century fables, whose moral is that those who excuse their actions as just, still risk violence from those who believe their own is righteous. Although Mary's cat was copied from Gessner's woodcut, she has altered it to suit her political purpose. Her cat's tail is longer, its ears more rakish, its whiskers more aggressive and, tellingly, the cat's paw now traps the end of the mouse's tail.

Seeing it in the flesh is revelatory. Glass acts as a shield, deliberately distancing the viewer. The gleam of glass reduces shadow and diminishes contours. Such separation and alteration limits the opportunity for emotional connection. Now that I am just inches away from Mary's embroidery and able to see it unscreened, the mood of Mary's hand is more obvious. It is unsettled work. Mary's stitches run along rhythmically for a while, then miss a beat and grumble on unevenly before starting to flow again. Mary's cat – plumper, less sleek than Gessner's – is executed, as Deborah points out, in meticulous shading. It would have been slow work for Mary to continuously change the colour of her thread, to thread yet another needle, but she was determined to mimic and animate Gessner's original, to capture his highlights and his variance of tone. Such attention evinces more than a crafter's attention to detail; it conjures an act of yearning. It is as if Mary is stitching into her cloth her pangs of an unreciprocated attachment, as if she is willing each stitch to incrementally draw in Elizabeth. The little mouse is equally telling. It lacks definition and is depicted as lumpen, squat and stolid. It is poorly drawn, suggesting that it was sketched by Mary herself. If this is the case, it is a sad indictment of Mary's lack of self-worth. It is a lament on, and a recognition of, her increasing physical and emotional immobility.

The embroidery is worn away in parts and its eroded stitchery gives us a glimpse of its underlying drawing. But its colour has scarcely dimmed, despite its longevity. Emma gingerly turns the embroidery over so that we can examine its underside. It surprises us. Here there are unexpected traces of repair, roughly done. Perhaps, we conjecture, they were done by a child tasked with the chore in later centuries to ward off boredom.

With the embroidery carefully returned to its case, Emma removes the other one made by Mary. It features a crowned monogram in now barely decipherable letters. There is a lily and a thistle on each side of Mary's monogram and another flower lying below. I recall seeing similar panels illustrated in Michael Bath's book, and later I thumb through it, searching out companions. There are a few: some sewn by Bess, with a coronet rather than a crown and bearing her own, Cavendish's or Shrewsbury's names; others are Mary's. On one of hers the letters are flanked with thistles. Another spells out ELIZABETH MARY and is accompanied by the rose of England and the lily of France. Below them lies a broken thistle, its stem snapped in two. The motto, translated from Latin, states that 'The bonds of virtue are tighter than those of blood'. The flower lying at the bottom of the embroidery at the Palace of Holyroodhouse must be a broken rose. These monogrammed octagons appear to track the ebb and flow of Mary's fortunes through their flower placement: a broken thistle at the foot of one surmounted by an upright lily of France and rose of England, the broken rose of England in another surmounted by a thistle and lily. They are the only known representations of broken flowers in sixteenth-century embroidery, and are evidence of Mary choosing her own way to signal her plight.

Finally, we examine Bess's work. It too has a monogram, with 'George' and 'Elizabeth' sandwiched between floral motifs beneath a coronet. Bess's stitches are regular, the surface of her embroidery smooth. It indicates a more confident skill, a desire for perfection which eluded Mary. The irregularity of Mary's work might attest to its having been handed on, from person to person, during its making. But it might also evoke a distracted mind, the queen's lack of interest in the finesse of stitching. As a medium through which to channel her emotions, perhaps Mary was content to let it capture her agitation as a truer expression of her mental state.

With the embroideries returned to the protection of glass, I am surprised that I have not experienced any surge of empathy or affinity. What I feel is admiration for the countless hours Mary spent in her determined sewing. There are thousands of stitches in 'A Catte' alone, 10,000 at least, an embroidery made more complicated by its background of a diamond trellis carpet whose pattern is embellished with blue and edged in gold, an unnecessary if decorative addition. It is as if Mary wanted to linger in its sewing: stitching on and on with her stabbing needle, using it symbolically like an arrow to pierce its target. It is as if, through her embroidery, she could connect with Elizabeth and pull her in.

It was 1569 when a plan began to ferment for Mary to marry Thomas Howard, the fourth Duke of Norfolk, the most powerful man and the wealthiest landowner in England. Norfolk was England's Earl Marshal and Lord Lieutenant in the North, and he had been the chief English commissioner at the York inquiry. He was Elizabeth's second cousin. As an English Protestant and the only English Duke, Norfolk had credentials worth considering in the eyes of both Scottish and English nobles. Even Moray, Mary's half-brother and now regent of Scotland, entertained the idea of their marriage. Elizabeth, however, was less enamoured. When she confronted Norfolk, he denied any such ambition. Norfolk was a Protestant, but he came from a family with strong Catholic leanings and his sister was married to the Earl of Westmorland, one of the conspirators in the Northern Rising. Norfolk himself had been suspected of complicity in the rebellion, a suspicion that was never proven. Although the uprising had been quashed within weeks, it led to harsh reprisals. Hundreds of Catholics believed to have supported Mary's cause, albeit without her encouragement, were executed. In retaliation, the Pope excommunicated Elizabeth, denouncing her as a 'pretended title', and gave licence to Catholics to dispose of her without encountering papal – in essence, God's – displeasure. Despite having no proof of Norfolk's participation in the rebellion, Cecil, Elizabeth's chief adviser, began to monitor the Duke's movements closely. Norfolk and other English nobles were opposed to Cecil's power at court and his antagonistic policy towards Spain. Now Cecil marked Norfolk out as someone to watch. Elizabeth, too, had become wary of the English Duke and Norfolk found himself increasingly politically marginalised.

Mary and Norfolk had begun to correspond at the end of the 1560s. Although they had never met formally, Mary's letters to him demonstrated that she embraced him as a welcome saviour. Her letters bear witness to the hope she invested in him: 'And therefore when you say you will be to me as I will ... then shall you remain my good lord ...and I will remain yours faithfully', 'I am determined never to offend you but remain yours ... faithful until death'.[15] Still convinced that her best route to restoration was through Elizabeth, Mary was adamant, however, that she would not countenance a marriage with Norfolk without Elizabeth's approval.

By the early summer of 1569, three proposals were being considered for Mary's future: giving up her Scottish throne and remaining in England, ruling jointly with Prince James with Moray as regent, or being restored as Scotland's queen under Moray's regency. For a short while, liberty beckoned. But when, at the end of July, the Scottish Parliament, dominated by the King's Men, rejected any suggestion of Mary's return by a substantial majority, Mary was fated to stay in limbo in England. The civil war in Scotland – the power struggle between Mary's supporters, the Marian Party, and her son James's adherents who called themselves the King's Men – was escalating. Under Moray's leadership the King's Men were gaining ground, seizing garrisons and gathering support and strength. It was not in their party's interests to have Mary re-introduced to Scotland, just as they were making advances. But their rejection of Mary made a marriage with Norfolk more appealing to the Scottish queen, even more so when her secretary John Leslie, her Scottish ambassador in England, led her to believe that Elizabeth favoured the match.

As the relationship between Mary and Norfolk unfolded, they had exchanged gifts. Norfolk lent Mary money to help with her household's expenses. He sent her a diamond which she wore around her neck. And Mary sent him a cushion, one

Wedding double-portraits of James V and Marie de Guise in 1538 and Lord Darnley and Mary, Queen of Scots in 1565.

A portrait thought to be of David Rizzio and the stain of his blood at the Palace of Holyroodhouse in Edinburgh. Rizzio was murdered in the presence of the queen in her royal apartments. His bloodstain remains on the floor where he died nearly 500 years ago.

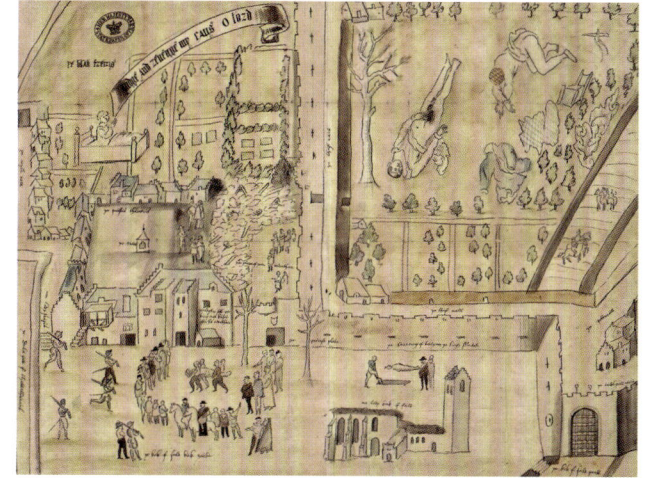

Sketched montage of the scene of Lord Darnley's murder in Kirk o' Field which was sent to Elizabeth's chief advisor, William Cecil.

Placard of the Mermaid and the Hare which was pinned to the door of St Giles Church after the murder of Lord Darnley as a scurrilous public accusation of Mary, Queen of Scots' intimacy with James Hepburn, the Earl of Bothwell.

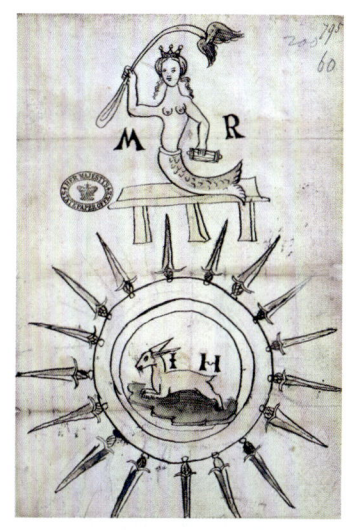

*The Memorial of Lord Darnley*, a painting commissioned by Darnley's family after his assassination in 1567.

Mary's embroideries of 'A Byrd of America' (left) and a tortoise climbing a crowned palm tree (below).

The monogram of Mary's captor, Bess of Hardwick, the Countess of Shrewsbury.

An example of Bess's embroidery at her house, Hardwick Hall.

The cushion Mary embroidered for the Duke of Norfolk c.1571 (top); 'A Catte': an embroidery by Mary thought to represent Elizabeth I as a ginger cat and the Scottish queen as a trapped mouse.

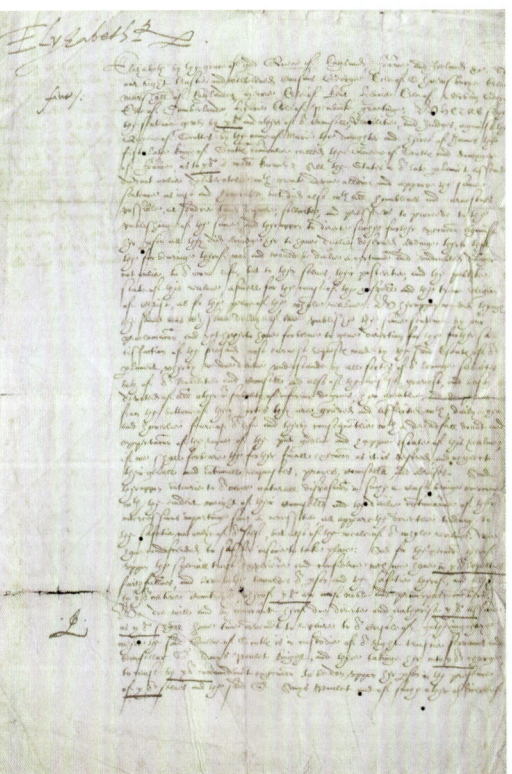

A sketch of Mary's execution (top); the warrant signed by Elizabeth I for Mary's execution (middle); the last letter Mary wrote in the hours before her death to her brother-in-law, Henri III, King of France (below).

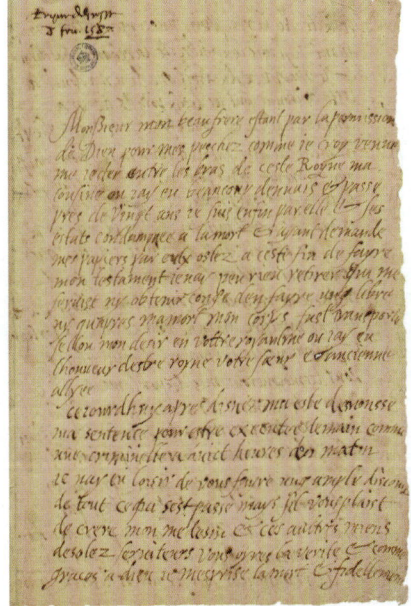

A memorial portrait of Mary, Queen of Scots commissioned by her lady-in-waiting, Elizabeth Curle, after 1603.

'Rainbow' portrait of Elizabeth I c.1601.

*Scotland as a Queen II*, limited edition print by Ashley Cook, 2020.

that she had embroidered herself. It was an appropriate gift for a man who owned one of the finest textile collections in Britain, but its content was hardly innocent. Mary's embroidered cushion was not merely subversive, but treasonable.

It depicted a lace-cuffed hand descending from the heavenly clouds, from the divine realm of God. The hand clutched a pruning knife with which it was cutting out the dead growth of an old vine to allow a younger fertile vine to flourish and bear fruit. It was a clear reference to the barren Elizabeth and the fecund Mary. Above the old vine was a windmill symbolising the vacillations of religious adherence that England had experienced under Tudor reign. Above the young vine stood a sturdy church flying a flag of triumph, signifying the stability and perseverance of the Catholic faith. There was a stag, the Catholic symbol of victory over non-believers, and a butterfly, the symbol of resurrection. Two birds were winging free across the sky, a possible optimistic allusion to Mary and Norfolk's future. The fabric frame which surrounded the embroidery was stitched with acorns and pomegranates, popular symbols of fertility. And in case its visual meaning was too complex for Norfolk to decipher, Mary had added text. On a scroll under the clouds she embroidered the motto *Viscerit vulnere virtus* – 'Virtue flourishes by wounding'. Its origin was biblical, a quote from John 15.2: 'every branch that beareth not fruit, he taketh it away, and every branch that beareth fruit, he cleanseth that it may bear more fruit'. It echoed the words of François II after the Tumult of Amboise: 'I desire nothing more than to exterminate them entirely and cut down their root so well there should be no future growth'.[16] Mary signed the cushion with her own monogram and the arms of Scotland to leave its authorship in no doubt.[17]

In July 1570, Norfolk wrote secretly to Moray to say he was resolved to marry Mary. It was reputedly Moray who alerted Elizabeth to the advancement of the couple's wedding plans, which had progressed without the English queen's sanction.

Elizabeth was furious. Leicester commiserated and gifted Elizabeth a jewel which depicted her on her throne with Mary chained to one of its legs and France and Spain drowning under waves.[18] There was more to Elizabeth's outrage than pique at not being consulted. Mary and Norfolk's marriage threatened the reigniting of English Catholic fervour, which would play into the hands of her predatory rival, Catholic Spain. It held the danger of the overthrow of both Elizabeth and English Protestantism. Mary's rooms were searched by men with pistols, her armed guard was doubled, and the liberties that had been accorded her were removed. She wrote to Archbishop Beaton in France to tell of the outrage:

I know not whether you are aware how uncivilly I have been treated, my writing desk and coffers ransacked, my servants menaced and driven away and myself prohibited from writing or receiving letters and all my people searched ... I am confined to my chamber, of which they wish to wall up the windows, and make a false door by which they may enter when I am asleep; and my people will no longer be permitted to come there, except for a few valets, and the rest of my servants will be removed from me.[19]

To Elizabeth's ambassador in France, Mary complained that 'Her people [were] not permitted to go beyond the gate of the castle, and Lord Shrewsbury's servants [were] prohibited from speaking to hers. She added that she was 'resolved to die Queen of Scotland ... a miserable captive ... [who is] much troubled by the intentions of the Queen of England toward the Duke of Norfolk'.[20]

Mary was right to feel troubled. Norfolk was apprehended and imprisoned in the Tower.

Whether she liked it or not, Mary had become the focus of English Catholic disaffection and a catalyst for their frustration. Conspiracies came and went, some without her knowledge, others without her consent or approval, all without her encouragement.

Now, however, her mindset changed. France had proved desultory in responding to her pleas for support. Elizabeth's reaction to the possibility of Mary's marriage to Norfolk and her imprisonment of him appeared impertinent and draconian. Mary had now been the English queen's prisoner for nearly two years and, at just twenty-seven-years-of-age, she was increasingly exasperated by her political impotence.

In January 1570, Moray was assassinated. Mary's main detractor was dead. The new Scottish regent was her father-in-law the Earl of Lennox, one of Mary's fiercest critics; his appointment, however, was not wholly popular in Scotland and caused some Scottish nobles to defect to the Marian party. The civil war in Scotland intensified. There was reason to hope that the Marian party might triumph. With the Pope and Spain beckoning Mary's liberty, the Scottish queen was primed for treachery. When Norfolk was released in August 1570, a more dangerous conspiracy, called the Enterprise of England, began to simmer. This time, Mary was prepared to be complicit.

The plot had been set in train by Roberto Ridolfi, a wealthy Florentine financier who had played a shadowy part in the Northern Rebellion. Now he orchestrated another plan to rescue the Scottish queen, one which combined the territorial competitiveness of Catholic Spain with the aspirations of English Catholic rebels. As well as liberating Mary, Elizabeth would be seized, Norfolk and Mary set up on her throne and England returned to Rome. Mary, although excited by its possibilities, was nervous of its consequences. It was better, she advised, that it not be carried out at all than that it miscarried. Mary's Scottish ambassador in England, John Leslie, became her go-between in the conspiracy. But access to each other was curtailed through the strictures placed on the Scottish queen and they could only correspond in code. They had to be very circumspect in what messages passed between them and their other key conspirators, Ridolfi and Norfolk. Distanced from one another, strategies became muddled and messages misconstrued. But, in time, the backing of the Pope was secured and Spanish support enlisted, as was the participation of English Catholics. Mary's strict regime of censorship meant that she, most of all, lacked intelligence of what exactly was being plotted in her name. When a letter from Ridolfi to John Leslie was intercepted by Walsingham, Elizabeth's chief spymaster, it linked Ridolfi to Mary. When a coded letter from Mary was discovered in Norfolk's house and deciphered, it linked her to the conspiracy. Norfolk was found to have funded the Marian party in Scotland, Mary to have borrowed money from Ridolfi. With their inter-connectedness exposed, Norfolk was arrested and sent back to the Tower. Leslie was also apprehended, interrogated and broke under torture to reveal all. As part of his testimony, he cited Mary's gifting of the cushion to Norfolk: 'one Bortycke [Norfolk's servant] brought the pillow which was wrought with the Scottish queen's own hand, with the arms of Scotland and with a sword in it cutting vines, with this sentence, "Viscerit, Vulnere, Virtus".'[21]

Given the notoriously mercurial interpretation of symbols, the content of the cushion was unclear, but it was still used as evidence of Mary's treachery. Mary was not the first woman of royal blood to have her embroidery cited in a trial for treason. Margaret Pole, Countess of Salisbury, the niece of both Edward IV and Richard III, had been caught up in an earlier conspiracy to depose Henry VIII after the Pilgrimage of Grace, an uprising in protest at Henry's proposed break with Rome. When the properties of family members were searched, it was said that a tunic embroidered with the five wounds of Christ – forbidden iconography in the now Reformed England – had been found among Margaret's possessions, presumed to have been stitched by her. It was used in court as evidence of her treason. Already incarcerated in the Tower, Margaret was executed in 1541.

Norfolk was sentenced to death, but Elizabeth prevaricated and delayed signing his death warrant. With Mary protesting that she had neither planned nor approved the conspiracy, that all she had ever sought was her liberty, Elizabeth also hesitated to bring Mary to trial. The English Parliament tried to force the English queen's hand, denouncing Mary in the most defamatory terms. It petitioned for her execution, but Elizabeth refused to countenance it. As Norfolk waited for Elizabeth to decide his fate, Mary took to fasting. She spent hours and days on her knees praying. But her hope of rescuing Norfolk through self-denial and prayer proved fruitless. In June 1572, he was executed. Mary's right to the English succession was revoked. She was warned that, if there was a hint of her involvement in any future plot, she would face trial. Elizabeth never spoke of Mary's restoration again. The St Bartholomew's Day massacre in August 1572, which saw 3,000 Protestant Huguenots murdered in Paris and a further 10,000 killed elsewhere in France, exacerbated concern in England that a treacherous Catholic Scottish queen was in their midst.

There were more attempts to help Mary escape. Each, when discovered, worsened the strictures of Mary's captivity. Not only were the number of her attendants decreased, but those of high status were eliminated until there were few left of any social standing.[22] The queen had to resort to subtler forms of deception to remain in illicit correspondence with her allies. Although her embroidery was no longer a safe medium for espionage, Mary continued to use the camouflage of textiles as a form of subterfuge. She wrote to Archbishop Beaton in France:

the best and most secret writing is in alum dissolved in a very little clear water four-and-twenty hours before you wish to write ... you can in this way write on white taffeta, or white cloth, especially lawn: and that it may be known between us when there is anything written, it would be necessary to cut from the piece of taffeta or lawn a small piece out of one of the corners ... but we must not use it except on occasion of great importance.[23]

She suggested other ruses. Half an ell could be added onto

a bolt of cloth so she would know that, if it was more than she had ordered, the package contained a secret communication. Green ribbons could be attached to books to indicate specific pages that held coded information, or a note could be secreted in the hollow of a shoe's heel.

As Mary's captivity continued through the 1570s, Shrewsbury became increasingly distraught by the financial burden he was having to shoulder, an anxiety which was aggravated by illness, some thought he had had a stroke. Shrewsbury bemoaned his 'careful burden', declaring that 'Surely no man of understanding can think that I or my wife wittingly should be glad of the tedious hourly attendance to the want of our own liberty, as we fain would have, where none of us can come or go without suspicion'.[24] Bess too was becoming frustrated at the curtailment of her life that Mary's care involved. The Shrewsburys' custodianship of Mary was a double-edged sword. While it gained them Elizabeth's gratitude, it also risked losing her trust. They were more vulnerable to royal criticism: chastised for being too liberal, berated for being over-intimate, rebuked for permitting the queen undue access to others and reprimanded for employing servants 'many of whom are reported to have been seduced to favour her [Mary's] practices,..'.[25] Shrewsbury had to defend Bess's intimacy with Mary saying 'It is no small grief to me and my wife that any fault should be imputed or suspicion had towards her, considering that no living creature could be more vigilant, more careful of mind, and fearful in this charge than she..' . But the threat of being accused of collusion hovered over them like a cloud.[26]

In 1574, Bess's standing with the English queen was severely tested when it emerged that Bess's daughter Elizabeth Cavendish had married Charles Darnley, the brother of Mary's murdered husband. As both bride and groom were connected by blood to the English throne, they required Elizabeth's consent to their marriage, an approval they had ignored. Bess was suspected of being the orchestrator of their union. Despite her protestations that the young couple had fallen in love, it was obvious that the match had been made with political intent. Moreover, the union brought the Shrewsburys uncomfortably close to Mary in kinship. Elizabeth Cavendish became Mary's sister-in-law and Prince James's aunt. There were successional implications, should the couple have children. Charles's mother, the Countess of Lennox, Mary's mother-in-law, was sent to the Tower. When Bess was summoned to London, she ignored Elizabeth's command, and instead laid low, waiting for the English queen's ire to dissipate. Mary was as outraged as Elizabeth. It brought the Cavendish dynasty – as had been Bess's intention – within touching distance of the English throne.

It looks probable that, with the Countess of Lennox in the Tower and Bess in disgrace, Mary seized the opportunity to ingratiate herself with Elizabeth through a gift of embroidery. She had received a favourable response to an earlier gift she had sent the English queen, an inkstand and some embroidery which Elizabeth remarked that she favoured because 'a great part thereof was wrought with her [Mary's] own hand'.[27] Mary had also sent Elizabeth an embroidered petticoat which she had commissioned. It came with a message to say that 'if the fashion pleases you... I will get him [her embroiderer], at more leisure, to make [you] more beautiful ones and ...I should wish to have a pattern of one of your bodies with a high collar'.[28] This was a gendered wooing. Mary was using a mutual interest in fashion to encourage a sense of empathy and connection. Now, with Bess discredited, Mary decided on a more seductive gift. In a letter to Archbishop Beaton in February 1574 she asked him to send her 'as soon as you can eight ells of crimson satin of the colour of the sample [of] silk which I send you a piece if you can find it in London but I should like to have it in fifteen days, and one pound of the thinner and double silver thread which you will be able to get soon, and soon I will give you an account of the work in which I think of employing it'.[29]

Another letter followed in quick succession It asked him:

> to send me, as soon as you can, four ounces more or less of the same crimson silk which you sent me some time ago, similar to the pattern which I send you ... The silver is too thick; I beg you will choose it for me as the pattern, and send it to me by the first conveyance, with eight ells of crimson taffeta for lining. If I do not have it soon my work must stand still, for which I shall be very vexed, as what I am working [on] is not for myself.[30]

The crimson fabric and silver thread were for Mary to embroider Elizabeth a skirt. Urgency was needed because Mary was aware of how fickle Elizabeth could be in her condemnations or approvals. She wanted to ensure that the English queen received her gift before pardoning the Countess of Lennox and Bess. The skirt was replete with material entreaty. It was embroidered with the intertwined floral devices of Scotland and England – the thistle and the rose – intermixed with honeysuckles, lilies and pinks. It was designed to remind Elizabeth of their shared sovereignty, with the red of its fabric symbolising their blood bonds. That it was sewn by Mary's own hand was its ultimate appeal. It manifested an intimate and gendered gesture of regard which, in the material etiquette of the day, demanded reciprocity. The skirt reached Elizabeth in the third week of May 1574. It was accompanied by a message from Mary that the skirt represented 'the honour with which I bear her and my desire to be employed in whatever she would find more agreeable'.[31] Later that month, the French ambassador of England, la Mothe-Fénelon, reported to the French king that:

> The Queen of Scots, your sister-in-law is very well and yesterday I

presented on her behalf a skirt of crimson satin, worked with silver, very fine, and all worked with her hand, to the Queen of England, to whom, the present was very agreeable, for she found it very nice and has prized it very much, and it seems to me I found her much softened towards her.'[32]

Having heard that the skirt pleased Elizabeth, Mary was emboldened to write again saying that 'it considers me happy that this little attempt at needlework ... [has] pleased you and that I will start by its means to recover something of your favour, and you would perhaps help me by some explanation of what disturbs you and what I can do to ... show you the honour and amity I have for you.'[33] Three little night head-dresses followed in March 1575. That same year, Elizabeth Cavendish gave birth to a daughter, Arbella Stuart. She was a viable claimant to the English throne, a rival to James's place in the succession. When Arbella's father died in the year following her birth, Elizabeth Cavendish and Arbella came to live with Bess, and Mary grew fond of her. But friction between Mary and Bess, after so many years cloistered in each other's company, was inevitable. Their relationship grew at first acrimonious and, latterly, vicious. Bess grew jealous of Shrewsbury's solicitude of the Scottish queen and accused him of having an affair with Mary, an allegation which she repeated to Elizabeth. It was a claim which both Shrewsbury and Mary vehemently denied. When a rumour that Mary was pregnant with Shrewsbury's child circulated, it fanned the flames of animosity with Sadler reporting to Walsingham that Mary was 'marvellously grieved with the Countess of Shrewsbury, for the foul slanders being raise about her by the said countess and some of hers, which have touched so near to her honour and reputation abroad'.[34] In retaliation, Mary wrote to Elizabeth. It was a vindictive letter in which the Scottish queen defamed Bess, saying that she often maligned and mocked the

English queen, detailing the unpleasant nature of Bess's comments which touched on Elizabeth's supposed virginity, possible lovers, her appearance and character. It is probable that the letter was never sent. There is no record of Elizabeth ever having received it or responding to it. But it survives among Cecil's papers, no doubt seized in one of the raids his agents made on Mary's apartments.

The Shrewsburys' guardianship of Mary had an impact on their marriage. With one or other of them required to be ever-present, they were forced to spend more time apart. They rarely had the release of going to court together and they shared, with Mary, the absence of friends. There were rows, separations and reconcilements. Their marriage reached breaking point. Despite Elizabeth's best attempts to effect a reconciliation, by 1585 the couple had become estranged.

The estrangement which caused Mary most grief, however, was that between herself and her son, James. It is in the embroideries that Mary made for him that we can see her vulnerability. Her loss of him was a constant theme in her petitions to Elizabeth. She wrote 'What advantage and honour can you hope for in allowing them to keep us, my son and me, so long separated, and him and me from you.'[35] James was fighting his own demons. His upbringing under the tutelage of George Buchanan – the Latin scholar who had become a fierce critic of Mary – was harsh. Moreover, James lived in the shadow of a supposedly murderous and adulterous mother: his rule was tainted by association. The slur that he was Rizzio's son still echoed. In a divided Scotland, there was no political stability and his early experiences of being unloved and kept in strict governance, stunted both his physical health and emotional development. In England, Mary was largely forbidden any contact with him, a son she had not seen since he was ten months old. She did what she could to signal her love. She sent him letters and gifts. Those which she addressed to 'the prince' rather than 'the king' were returned or remained undelivered. Lacking the means to directly communicate with James, or indirectly have news of him from a trusted source, Mary turned again to her embroidery. She made James a set of children's reins with its breastplate adorned with symbolic flowers that messaged protection and love. Its red ribbons were inscribed in thread with the text: *God hath given his angels charge over thee to keep thee in all ways.* Each word was separated by a pertinent motif: crowns, hearts and lions. Her gift was accompanied by a book of poems in her own handwriting, whose cover she had embroidered. Another letter to Elizabeth demonstrates the extent of Mary's grief at her enforced estrangement from James:

There remains still another request, of little importance to you, but of extreme consolation to me; it is that you will please, have compassion on a desolate mother, from whose arms has been torn her only child and hope of future joy in this world, to permit me to write at least open letters, to enquire into the real state of his welfare, and recall him to his sad mother.[36]

To counter their separation, Mary worked on a set of bed hangings, which were to serve as her explanation, her declaration and her testament for her son to inherit. They were the most revealing of the queen's embroideries, but sadly they no longer exist. However, when they were installed at the Scottish court after Mary's death, they were seen and described in detail by the Scottish poet, William Drummond of Hawthornden.[37]

The bed hangings contained not only the emblems of the royal dynasties to which Mary and James were connected – the houses of Lorraine, Guise, Valois and Stewart – but carried allusions to Mary's incarceration, documenting the deterioration of her power and conveying what she experienced in her relationship with Elizabeth. Some of its embroideries were accompanied with mottos, to amplify Mary's reason for their inclusion, and provide an instructive moral, political and personal subtext. Her experience of captivity was rendered through fables whose moral cautions James would have known: a bird in a cage, a lion in a net, a porcupine among sea rocks and, on a more hopeful theme, an apple tree growing on a thorn with the motto 'Her cause increased by captivity'. Mary's political and physical decline is captured in images such as a yellow rose eaten by canker, trees fallen into quicklime or a ship with a broken mast. To encapsulate her relationship with Elizabeth, Mary portrayed two women, one with a lance emblematic of war, the other holding the cornucopia of truth. For its motto, Mary stitched: 'Whatever fortune favours will prevail'. It contained images of an eclipse of the sun, two women on a wheel of fortune and, on its canopied roof, Mary kneeling before the cross, the Scottish regalia at her feet, praying to the heavens for release and salvation. It is impossible to fully interpret the complexity of the embroideries of these hangings. They distil, through their imagery and text, not just the experiences of Mary, Queen of Scots, but her deepest emotions.[38]

Bess's dreams of securing royal connection through her children was never realised. She tried to strengthen the royal rights of her granddaughter, but Arbella was not even mentioned by Elizabeth as a successional candidate when Elizabeth neared death in 1603. Bess continued with her projects, creating Hardwick Hall and her embroideries as her legacy. When Bess died in 1604 at the age of eighty-seven, she had already designed her memorial, an elaborate tomb which still stands in All Saints' Cathedral in Derby.

In December 2020, my friend Tina also died. She, like Bess, was a woman of indomitable energy who railed against any shortening of creative time and fretted over what she had to leave behind, not in the way of possessions, but in spirit. I think of Mary's 'A Catte' and realise that its mischievous spirit is what was most evocative of Mary, what made me come close to her, when I saw it at the Palace of Holyroodhouse. And Tina's mischievous spirit lives on too, in the hearts of those who knew and loved her.

# 9
## Red Petticoat and Sleeves

I have driven through the dark and left Scotland for what promises to be a unique experience: an audience with Mary, Queen of Scots. It was trumpeted online as a rare opportunity to meet the dead queen via Lesley Smith who, with her husband, promotes and programmes events at Tutbury Castle, the place of captivity that Mary most loathed. I find the castle almost in ruins. Having not been as assiduous as I might have been in my research, I had hoped for something more substantial. Still, I comfort myself that at least part of its structure is intact, and the tumbled down piles of stone are atmospheric in the night lights that guide visitors along its pathways. There are forty or so people gathered for the pre-show supper. While I wait to be seated, I survey the items for sale displayed by the counter. Among them is a mug whose legend reads 'Always be a mermaid unless you can be yourself! Then always be a mermaid!' Given the slanderous depiction of Mary and Bothwell on the placard posted in Edinburgh following the death of Darnley, it seems an apt souvenir, and I buy it just for that.

The staff are kind and accommodating. I find myself seated beside three cheery women who, as we devour our buffet of cold ham and coleslaw, pork pies and potato salad, regale me with stories of their lives. Supper done, we are summoned to the queen's presence, and as we climb the stairs I notice a headless mannequin at the top. I wonder if I am the only one here primed for irony. I also know that I am, quite unjustifiably, poised to ridicule. I am anticipating an am-dram tirade by a less-than-convincing enthusiast.

## Red Petticoat and Sleeves

Lesley Smith is magnificent. An hour passes in fabulous monologue. Here is a knowing queen, only too aware of her demotion to captive but still in possession of the power, charm and grace of the privilege she was born to carry. She relates the events and the emotions of her incarceration, her conflicted relationship with the woman who might have been her soulmate and saviour. She tells of the petty humiliations that she has had to endure, the mean-spirited theft of her joy, her lack of companionship. I sit, enthralled. At the end I applaud enthusiastically and with genuine respect. I am so glad I came.

Then it transpires that Lesley's performance as Mary is just the first part of the evening's entertainment. Our audience with the Scottish queen over, Lesley settles the skirt of her heavily embroidered black velvet gown around her and sits back in her chair of state. Moving out of character, she proceeds to tell us stories about her performances as Mary.

The best ones concern children, like the little girl who told her that her granny had a toilet roll cover that looked just like her. The schoolgirls bent on female solidarity, who entreated her to trust them and were convinced that they could smuggle her out if she could just crouch down low enough. They reassured her that, even if they were stopped, she could still evade recapture because no one would damage a child. There was the boy who, having clocked that there was a spare seat beside him on the school bus, offered her his hoodie as a disguise. And another boy who, teachers warned Lesley, could be disruptive. Lesley duly appointed him as her chief protector and champion throughout her monologue. He was to ensure that she was neither interrupted nor her audience distracted. When she had finished, she beckoned him to kneel and rewarded him with a knighthood for his good service. The best, however, was her story of being in Edinburgh itself, scuttling from one venue to the next during the Edinburgh International Festival in full costume. As she passed a building site, five workmen clambered down from the scaffolding, removed their hard hats and bowed while their gaffer declaimed 'Glad to see you back, Ma'am'.

Lesley Smith captures, in a mesmerising way, the duality of Mary's strength and vulnerability. She rekindles the human appeal of the Scottish queen. In affording her a contemporary presence, she connects her audience to a Mary who is not just a famous figure in history, but also a person and a prisoner. Through her stories of the children's responses to her plight, in their willingness to be Mary's champion, I discovered what I had been missing in the many books I had read: Mary's charisma.

The regular moving from one place to another for reasons of sanitation or security became increasingly irksome over the years of Mary's captivity. In the first eighteen months, under the care of the Shrewsburys, Mary was shuttled between their different properties: from Tutbury Castle to Wingfield Manor, from Chatsworth House to Sheffield Castle. Each relocation required the packing up of furnishings and furniture and their reinstatement elsewhere. During her nineteen years of imprisonment in England, Mary was to be moved over forty-five times. The disruption involved Shrewsbury, and subsequent guardians, in complicated logistics: the procurement and transportation of adequate supplies, the installation of suitable household necessities, and the provision of effective guard. Moreover, Mary's custodians were tasked with vetting and monitoring the comings and goings of visitors and tradespeople in different locations, as well as inspecting the queen's correspondence, and writing regular reports on Mary herself.

Textiles were seen as a particularly susceptible means of subterfuge and instructions were issued to 'be careful and foresee that no clothes, apparel or other folded [cloth] be suffered to be brought to the said queen, or to any of her people, without the same being first visited and searched by you'.[1] It was exhausting, time-consuming and sacrificial. Sir Francis Knollys, the first of Mary's guardians, was desperate for release from his duty telling Elizabeth that he was 'so wearied of this service, in a place where I have neither land, living, rule, friends, acquaintances, kin, nor alliance, that my wits are dulled'.[2] Ralph Sadler, a later custodian, went further, petitioning Elizabeth for his discharge, declaring 'I would to God some other had the charge … for I assure you I am weary of it … I would come home and yield myself to be a prisoner in the Tower all the days of my life, rather that I would attend here any longer'.[3]

Furthermore, Mary's care was expensive. Shrewsbury's accounts show that he was spending £4,000 a year just to secure the loyalty of those he employed.[4] Although the English treasury contributed to Mary's household costs, it was never enough to cover all that was needed. Since Mary refused to meet any of the expense herself as she was being held against her will, it was her keepers who had to meet any shortfall. Shrewsbury expended time and energy trying to recoup back payments and petitioning for more funds: endeavours which rarely met with success. When Elizabeth suggested that the Earl of Essex might house Mary at his residence of Chartley Manor, and contribute to the cost of her maintenance, he quickly gave directions that 'all bedding, hangings and like stuff' were to be removed, hoping that his lack of suitable furnishings would avert the possibility of his becoming the Scottish queen's guardian.[5] Furnishing Mary's accommodation, often at short notice, was a constant headache. In 1585, when Ralph Sadler was appointed to Mary's care, he reported that in Tutbury Castle 'there was nothing serviceable, saving the hangings and a chair or two, but it is worn and spent; besides much of the earls' stuff that is [here] is also wasted and worn.' He purchased coverlets and blankets, linen sheets, curtains, cushions and hangings for Mary's chamber protesting that 'fair words and promises will not keep folk warm'.[6] When the household goods of the disgraced Lord Paget were forfeited and taken to Tutbury for Sadler's use; Mary complained to Elizabeth at their state of disrepair, insinuating they had been deliberately chosen to make her life more uncomfortable. Sadler had to suffer Elizabeth's displeasure with the English queen rebuking him that because of his negligence 'our honour has been greatly touched'.[7]

While Mary possessed some tapestries that had been with her in Scotland, they often did not fit the walls of her ever-changing apartments. In a material world that was temporary, ever shifting and improvised, Mary clung to what familiarity she could: the fragments of her monarchical status. These included her chair of state, with its embroidered phoenix and portentous motto 'In my end is my beginning', and the tapestries of the Battle of Ravenna and the history of the Greek hero, Meleager. But the constant state of instability, of 'occupation', meant that she lacked any settled home.

In September 1584, after fifteen-and-a-half years, Shrewsbury was finally released of his charge. Mary was put in the care of Sir Ralph Sadler at Wingfield Manor, before being returned to Tutbury Castle where she was placed under the stricter watch of Amias Paulet. Paulet was a Puritan, and an anti-Catholic. He had served time in France as Elizabeth's ambassador before becoming one of her privy councillors. He was a man of honour, but also of moral censure, and had little patience for Mary's emotional and physical distress. He had scant tolerance of her faith. Uninterested in placating his captive or making her experience more palatable, Paulet was determined to fulfil his role as the Scottish queen's custodian to the letter and follow the instruction that Mary was not to find ' better usage, having given no cause for more comfort, rather less'.[8] One of Paulet's first orders was that Mary's cloth of state was to be removed, a cloth, described by Paulet as 'representing by letters the names of her father and mother, and furnished with the arms of

Scotland in the midst, and some quartered with the arms of Lorraine of every side'.[9] As a symbol of her sovereignty and her identity, it was one of the last remaining vestiges of Mary's power. When Mary vehemently protested, Paulet allowed it to stay but, as instructed by Cecil, he kept the Scottish queen under close surveillance. He even forbade her to give alms to the poor or bestow personal payments on members of Tutbury's household, as had been her practice. This was a lessening not just of Mary's liberty, but a restriction which prevented the queen from exercising her charm and garnering the affection of others. It was part of a tactical move by Cecil and Francis Walsingham, Elizabeth's spymaster, in their plan to entrap Mary. With dispassionate thoroughness, they had decided to isolate Mary and starve her of any communication with the outside world. Their hope was that the Scottish queen, cut off from her contacts and her allies, would become desperate and more reckless, ripe to lure into an incriminating plot against Elizabeth. Aware of Mary's vulnerability to stress, Cecil ensured that under Paulet's regime she endured incremental physical and emotional deprivation.

In 1584, Cecil and Walsingham introduced a Bond of Association which was later enshrined as an Act of Parliament. The Bond condemned to execution anyone found plotting to usurp Elizabeth and – most dangerously for Mary – anyone who stood to gain the throne through such a conspiracy, even if they had no knowledge of it. The Act further threatened the sentence of treason punishable by death to anyone, of whatever rank and nationality, who conspired against Elizabeth in thought or deed, who 'attempted, compassed or imagined anything tending to the hurt of our her Majesty's person'.[10] It legitimised their espionage. Elizabeth, recognising its direction, insisted on an amendment which ensured that any conviction had to be based on evidence heard in court.

Mary was now over forty. The spirited young queen who had

tried to rally her troops at the Battle of Langside in 1568 had become old before her time. As her physical health continued to decline and her rheumatism worsened, Paulet reported: 'The Queen has kept to her bed this six to seven days, being very much grieved with ache in her limbs, so as she is not able to move in her bed without great help and, when she is moved, endures great pain'.[11] Somewhat cruelly, Paulet told Cecil that 'the indisposition of this queen's body, and the great infirmity of her legs, which is so desperate as herself does not hope of recovery, is no small advantage to her keeper, who shall not need to stand in great fear of her running away'.[12] Paulet was also dismissive of her complaints about the discomforts of Tutbury:

She importeth to lameness, and all her disease, to this house, although indeed she brought some hither with her. But I told her that her passionate and discontented mind did more to increase her sickness than the coldness of this house, or any other thing whatsoever.[13]

Mary's frailty was not just physical. She had become, as Cecil and Walsingham intended, heartsore. Many of those who had played a significant part in her history were dead. Mary Seton – the last of the four Marys to stay by her side – had left the Scottish queen in 1583 to retire to a convent in France. There were few people around Mary now who shared her memories, apart from her servants. She kept in regular contact with Archbishop James Beaton who had been her Scottish ambassador in France before her captivity and who continued to manage her affairs there and she also maintained contact with Mothe-Fénelon, Elizabeth's French ambassador. John Leslie, the Bishop of Ross acted as Mary's ambassador in England. These men became the queen's main source of political intelligence, but now even their missives were largely denied her. After nearly sixteen years as a captive in England, Mary's mental and emotional health had become fragile. She described herself as not knowing 'what line to sail, nor how to lift anchor'.[14]

When the Scottish Parliament pronounced that Mary's marriage to Bothwell was binding, it ended the possibility of being granted an annulment. As Bothwell was still alive, achieving liberty through another marriage became increasingly unlikely. Mary was condemned to a life without sexual and emotional love. Moreover, the door to a possible return to power – a door which had been held ajar through the early 1580s, was slammed shut in the spring of 1585 when her son James – now twenty years old and a monarch in his own right – had rejected the proposal for their joint sovereignty. What was more invidious was that James, looking to his own successional potential, had aligned himself with England and Elizabeth. In a letter to Elizabeth, Mary poured out her distress: 'I am so grievously offended at my heart, at the impiety and ingratitude that my child has been constrained to commit against me'.[15] Elizabeth was less than sympathetic. Rather, she had encouraged James's defection and bought his loyalty. He was offered and accepted the proposal of a subsidy from the English treasury of £4,000, with a further £4,000 to be paid to him annually. Hoping to be named Elizabeth's successor, James sacrificed his mother to bolster his chances of becoming heir to the English throne. His treachery ended the prospect of a reconciliation between mother and son.

Mary also had to contend with financial difficulties. Her revenues in France had been badly managed and this left the Scottish queen with inadequate funds. She was forced to borrow money to resource her personal expenditure. The indignity caused tensions to simmer between her and James Beaton, who oversaw her affairs there. Their estrangement led to a distancing between the Scottish queen and her French allies, which intensified her isolation.

Mary's diminishment was reflected in her household. It had

once included members of the Scottish nobility and others who had served her in Scotland, it was now composed of fewer than forty people, the majority of whom were servants: laundresses, kitchen staff, stablers. She still had her own physician, surgeon and apothecary to provide for her medical needs, and two tailors and an embroiderer to maintain her wardrobe. But only a handful of her servants were women and there was no one of noble rank.

It was the Babington plot that did for Mary in the end, thanks to the twenty-four-year-old Anthony Babington and Elizabeth's spymasters. As a ten-year-old boy, Babington had been a page in Bess of Hardwick's household, and it was there that he would have first encountered the Scottish queen. A Catholic squire, rich, romantic and charismatic, Babington had gone to France and there assumed the role of courier to agents working on behalf of Mary's Catholic allies on the continent.

Catholic attitudes towards Mary had changed during her years of captivity. Although the conciliatory religious policies she had adopted in Scotland during her rule had disappointed domestic and foreign Catholic powers, Mary was now being hailed as a captive martyr. For a younger Catholic generation, uninterested in the earlier dramas of Mary's reign, she had become a muse, reinvented as a heroine of the Counter-Reformation. When Babington returned to England he was persuaded to become Mary's chivalric knight and participate in a plan for her rescue. He judged Mary's liberation 'a holy enterprise', one that would see the true faith restored in England. He was, however, a novice schemer, driven by passion but lacking in skill.

English Catholics were increasingly under siege. The decade had begun with a new law which carried the charge of treason for anyone found encouraging conversion to Catholicism. The Pope had retaliated by despatching undercover Jesuit priests to

England, which in turn led Parliament to pass an act that condemned to death any Jesuit found trespassing on English soil. Anti-Catholic propaganda continue to decry Mary's presence in England. She was seen as a threat to national security. The assassination of the Protestant William of Orange in 1584 generated more anxiety at the dangers posed by Mary remaining in England to fuel the zeal of disaffected English Catholics. When, in 1585, the Anglo-Spanish Wars began to flare up, alarm at the possibility of a coup by the combined force of domestic and foreign Catholics escalated, and with it Mary's unpopularity.

Unbeknown to Babington, another plot to free Mary was fermenting. It followed on from others – the Throckmorton Plot and the Parry Plot, to name but two – and while these had been quashed and their perpetrators punished, conspirators continued to lurk in the shadows. Cecil and Walsingham enlisted some of them to act as double agents. The nature of their double-dealing has never been fully exposed, but there was certainly engagement with the English secret services. What Elizabeth knew of her courtiers' exploits is debatable. She certainly would have known about the strategies they adopted in general, but whether she knew of the specific methods they used to bring about Mary's downfall is doubtful. Although not self-appointed, Mary was nevertheless the chosen figurehead of Catholic defiance, and with James now safely allied to England, Mary's death was not only desirable but expedient. Through it the brooding Catholic antagonism at home and Catholic support abroad could be diffused.

Cecil and Walsingham set their trap. They introduced a new member to Mary's dwindling household. Gilbert Gifford was a Catholic whom Walsingham had recruited as an agent provocateur. Now Gifford was tasked with making Babington his puppet and winning Mary's trust. He was to put himself forward as Babington's go-between and offer to ferry messages between Babington and the Scottish queen. At the same time, Gifford was to let Mary know that he was willing to convey messages for her in secret and access the pile of confiscated letters that had been accumulating for her at the French Embassy. So rigorous had Paulet been in following Cecil's instructions to forbid any communication that it had been over a year since Mary had received any such correspondence. Small wonder, then, that she accepted Gifford's offer with alacrity.

Gifford told Mary that he had conceived a foolproof system to smuggle letters in and out. They were to be secreted in the bungs of beer barrels that were delivered regularly by the local brewer. Little did Mary know that the brewer was in the pay of both Paulet and Walsingham. Overjoyed at the prospect of being reconnected to the world, Mary agreed to the subterfuge. She devised, with her secretaries Claude Nau and Gilbert Curle, a new set of ciphers for her coded letters. Her sheet of ciphers, written in neat, tiny handwriting by one of her secretaries, was organised into six tidy columns. It survives today, with each word accorded its coded symbol. The first two-and-a-half columns are devoted to key people, and begins with the Pope. Others include the queen of France, the Duke of Savoy and Sir William Cecil. There are place names, such as Italy, Scotland, Rome, London, and a list of words most expedient for espionage, among them desperate, soldiers, friends, enterprise, support and service.[16]

Mary duly received the letters that had been waiting for her at the embassy. She sent back her responses and she received replies via the beer barrels. The deception seemed to be working. She was not to know that Gifford was delivering her surreptitious missives straight to Walsingham's master codebreaker, Thomas Phelippes. He duly deciphered them and passed them to Walsingham, who forwarded them to Cecil. Once read and copied, the letters were returned to Gifford, who lodged them at the embassy for despatch to Mary's allies. The scheme functioned in reverse for letters sent to Mary:

intercepted, decoded, copied and resealed before being secreted in the barrels' bungs.

This was skilled work. At that time, letters were not just written and folded but sealed to prevent interference. Furthermore, they were often sent in bundles, purposefully grouped together in small packets so that their meaning would be amplified in relation to one another. Political correspondence was expected to be shared; to be read by both a monarch and their advisers. Sending letters, written by Mary, to Elizabeth, Cecil and others at the English court in the same packet, at the same time, allowed the Scottish queen to air a specific issue from different angles. Her views could be better modulated, expanded on, and appear ambiguous if necessary. It was similar to the way Mary and Bess planned to arrange their small embroideries on cloth: stitched down in a deliberate order to better amplify or make ambiguous their meaning. For particularly sensitive missives, the packets were stitched together in a complicated and personalised pattern. Phelippes's skill lay not just in deciphering coded letters, but also in replicating their seals and stitchery to ensure his tampering with them was undetectable.

Babington was next to be ensnared. Already thinking Gifford was his accomplice, he was duped into believing that the Spanish forces were battle-ready and poised for an invasion of England. Others in Walsingham's pay informed their counterparts in Spain that Catholic malcontents in England were well organised and more than capable of providing the necessary back-up for any insurgence. When Mary was told that Anthony Babington, who she might have remembered from his time as a page in Bess of Hardwick's household, had some letters for her from Scotland, she sent him a short reply: her confidence in his trustworthiness bolstered by his loyalty being verified from reliable sources. She used the tried-and-tested route. Babington had taken Walsingham's bait. He believed all he had been told about the strength of the Catholic plot mounting in England

and on the continent. He had met with the other conspirators. His and their plot now coalesced. Fired up with zeal for his venture, Babington recruited friends to join him: young bloods eager for adventure and seduced by Babington's ardour. The trap was set. With plans and people in place, Babington wrote Mary a long treasonous letter outlining the scheme.

Babington's original plan to free Mary had now expanded to include the ambitions of his other conspirators. Mary read how Elizabeth was to be usurped and face 'her tragical execution' at the hand of a trusty band of six gentlemen, how Babington and ten of his loyal accomplices would come to free Mary with 100 supporters at their backs. Walsingham and Cecil already knew the contents of his letter and they waited for Mary's reply. Her secretary, Claude Nau, advised Mary to leave it unanswered. Thomas Phelippes penned a note to Walsingham saying, 'we await her very heart in the next'.[17] They only had to wait a few days. Mary despatched a long letter of approval, tempered with caution. She was concerned that, without adequate foreign support, the enthusiastic young conspirators might 'ruin themselves in vain'.[18] Her letter was collected by Gifford in the usual manner and sent to Phelippes. When he had decoded it, he passed it to Walsingham, who wrote gleefully to Leicester that Mary would shortly be in their capture. To make certain of his prey, Walsingham added his own postscript which, once re-coded, Babington would assume came from Mary. His postscript asked for the names of the six gentlemen who were to be Elizabeth's assailants.

In the weeks leading up to Mary's agreement to Babington's plan she had been dealt a bitter blow. Eleven days earlier, James had signed a treaty with England, which cemented their alliance and confirmed the annual subsidy from the English crown which had previously been negotiated. Devastatingly for Mary, her fate was not mentioned. Her exclusion confirmed her political solitude and intensified the humiliation of her disempowerment.

Such was her fury that she wrote to the Pope requesting that he oversee the transference of her rights to the throne of England to Philip II of Spain should James not convert to Catholicism after her death. She had not seen James since he was ten months old and she had been prevented from forming any relationship with him over the ensuing years. He had been raised as a Protestant by Mary's enemies. When he reached his majority and become king in his own right, he made little attempt to rescue her. Now he had rejected Mary's only chance to recover, even if only in name, her God-appointed role as Queen of Scotland. It is unsurprising, therefore, that having given up any hope of her son's support, Mary leapt at what she felt was her last chance of freedom. She had little left to lose. While this does not fully justify her response, it goes some way to explain the provocation that prompted her treachery.

On the interception of Mary's reply, Babington and thirteen of his collaborators were arrested. Although Babington had taken the precaution of burning Mary's letters, he was forced to reconstruct them under torture. Elizabeth ordered that the execution of the first seven conspirators be slow and lingering. They were dragged behind horses through the streets of London before being hanged. Cut down while they were still alive, they were castrated, disembowelled and their bodies were quartered. The cruelty of their execution was designed to be a dire warning to others who might be considering following in their footsteps. But even fervent Protestants were disquieted by its brutality and the six others who had also been sentenced to death were allowed a speedier demise.

Unaware of their arrest, Mary was delighted when Paulet offered the unexpected treat of going deer hunting. Thinking she might encounter local gentry along the way, Mary dressed in her finest attire and was accompanied by her physician and her secretaries Claude Nau and Gilbert Curle. When she spied a group of horsemen riding towards her she assumed they were members of the local aristocracy. Instead, she and her small entourage were ordered to halt. They were confronted by emissaries from Cecil, who promptly arrested Nau and Curle. An accusation of conspiracy to overthrow and assassinate Elizabeth was read out. At the end of its recitation, when Mary was commanded to follow them, she fell on her knees and refused to move. Her protest was futile. She and her physician were taken directly to Tixall Hall. Once more, Mary was without a change of clothes and her female servants. Yet again she was in fear of her life.

In her absence, her chambers at Chartley Manor, where she had been in residence, were ransacked, her possessions trawled through and inventoried. Her jewels, letters and ciphers were gathered up and removed as possible evidence. When Paulet discovered 'a box full of abominable trash, as beads of all sorts, pictures in silk of all sorts, some Agnes Dei' he would have burned its contents if he could and was much aggrieved when he was prevented from doing so.[19] He compiled a somewhat chilling list of who among Mary's servants could be most easily culled from the Scottish queen's service. He surmised that her coachman and lackeys were dispensable, as the queen was unlikely to be allowed to venture abroad again. One of her two tailors and her sole embroiderer were also deemed to be redundant, as was Pagez and his wife and daughters.[20] After a fortnight at Tixall Hall, Mary was returned briefly to Chartley Manor, and was then taken to Fotheringhay Castle, which had been provided with additional armed guards. There, Mary was informed that she was to be put on trial.

On 15 October 1586, Mary's trial began. The Scottish queen entered to find thirty-seven male peers, among them eighteen earls, thirteen lords and the court's judges. Mary had dressed in her customary black, in a velvet gown with a train. A long, sheer veil billowed behind her. When she approached the chair of state, she was directed to the crimson velvet chair opposite.

The chair of state was there, she was told, to represent the absent Elizabeth. This material dishonouring was just one of the limitations the Scottish queen faced. Mary protested:

> I am alone, without counsel, or anyone to speak on my behalf. My papers and notes have been taken from me, so I am destitute of all aid, taken at a disadvantage ... My crimes consist in my birth, the injuries that have been inflicted on me, and my religion.[21]

Mary had little knowledge of the processes and tenets of English law, and had no legal representative to guide her. With no prior information about the nature of the proceedings and forced to conduct her own defence, she was at a major disadvantage. But she staged a spirited show. This was to be one of her last great performances as Mary, Queen of Scots, and she was determined to own the stage.

In her book *The Trial of Mary, Queen of Scots,* Jayne Elizabeth Lewis, the Professor of English at the School of Humanities in Princeton, offers an insightful critique of Mary's performance at her trial. She suggests that, in anticipation of the barrage of verbal accusations Mary knew she would encounter, she prepared a counter-offensive that played on her physical frailty. Her entrance, stooped and leaning on the arms of male stewards, introduced an aged queen much weakened by her captivity. To those present who knew Mary in her younger days, this sight must have come as a shock. Her long white gossamer veil accentuated her delicacy and was suggestive of innocence. When she addressed the court she purposefully drew attention to her incapacity, 'I cannot walk without assistance nor use my arms, and I spend most of my time confined to bed'. She wept copious tears and presented herself as a betrayed victim, rather than a vengeful assassin: 'I came into this kingdom under promise of assistance, and aid, against my enemies and not as a subject ... instead of which I have been detained and imprisoned'.

When Cecil castigated her on her use of the royal arms of

England during her later years in France, she countered his charge with the excuse of her youth, of the power Henri II and her Guise uncles held over her. It was they, she protested, who had claimed her as 'the legitimate and nearest heir' to the English crown. She insisted that their inclusion of the English arms did not represent any sinister intent towards Elizabeth. Mary, in turn, accused Walsingham of inventing ciphers and manipulating plots against Elizabeth. Denying any involvement in the Babington plot, she argued: 'Can I be responsible for the criminal projects of a few desperate men, which they planned without my knowledge or participation?' When she was shown copies of Nau and Curle's testimonies, she demanded to see the originals. Her performance as a wronged victim ended in an avowal: 'I do not desire vengeance I will leave it to Him who is the just Avenger of the innocent and of those who suffer for His Name under whose power I will take shelter'.[22]

The lords reconvened in the Star Chamber in London, the English court at the Palace of Westminster. In the ensuing debate, Mary's detractors used her gender to accentuate her iniquity, calling her – as Lewis records – 'the daughter of sedition, the mother of rebellion, the nurse of impiety, the handmaid of iniquity, the sister of un-shamefulness'.[23] The lords reached their verdict. It was agreed that, under the terms of the Act of Association, Mary was guilty of treason and should be sentenced to death. Despite the resolve of Elizabeth's councillors to have Mary executed, the English queen hesitated. At the Parliament at which the verdict was to be ratified, Elizabeth made two impassioned speeches. Her words were assiduously crafted, designed to be ambiguous and inconclusive:

If I should say that I meant not to grant your petition, by my faith, I should say unto you more perhaps than I mean. And if I should say that I mean to grant it, I should tell you more than is fit for you to know. Thus, I must deliver to you an answer unanswerable.[24]

Elizabeth was fearful of a political, and potentially martial, backlash from France, Spain or Scotland. She was concerned as to how she would be judged. Putting a monarch, her own cousin, to death could taint her carefully constructed image as a judicious queen, virtuous and protective. Moreover, sanctioning regicide might set a precedent that could threaten her own survival, and that of future sovereigns. She also had her conscience to examine. Mary was not just a monarch, she was a queen, a woman of her own blood, a reflection of herself. To execute Mary would be to undermine the rule of women. For all the vexations and dangers Mary represented, the Scottish queen had been a constant in Elizabeth's life, the closest she had come to having a sister, to having an equal. Her own mother's execution must have also haunted her: a queen put to death on spurious charges.

Through that autumn and into winter, Mary waited for Elizabeth to sign her death warrant. She penned what she believed were to be her last letters. She sent the Spanish ambassador a diamond, the one which Norfolk had given her, with a request that he use it to attend to the welfare of her household after her death. In a letter to James Beaton in France, she said that, as she wrote, she could hear the banging of workmen's hammers and presumed that they were 'making a scaffold to make me play the last scene'.[25]

On 4 December, the death sentence was announced, but Elizabeth did not action it. It could still be revoked, but its announcement allowed public opinion to be tested and the reaction of English subjects and the European and Scottish countries to be gauged. There was little doubt as to its popularity in England. Church bells were rung and bonfires were lit. At Fotheringhay, Mary's bed furnishings were replaced with ones of black. While the Scottish ambassadors and those of other European kingdoms were condemnatory and petitioned the English queen for a reprieve, there was little indication that

Mary's death would trigger an armed uprising, at home or abroad.

Elizabeth wrote to Mary, 'you have planned in divers ways and manners to take my life and ruin my kingdom by the shedding of blood'.[26] What concerned Mary, however, was not that she might be executed, but that she might be despatched covertly and be denied what she was now determined to have: her grand moment of martyrdom. On 19 December she wrote what would be her last letter to Elizabeth, petitioning the English queen 'not to permit that my execution take place without your knowledge, not for fear of the torment, which I am very ready to suffer, but for the rumours that would be spread about my death, without witnesses'. Calling herself 'an empty shadow, lost, unfortunate' she asked that she be buried in France, not Scotland, since there she would be assured of Catholic funereal rites. Mary ended her letter with a threat: 'I remind you that one day you will have to answer for your charge' and she signed it 'your sister and cousin, wrongfully imprisoned'. The letter was never sent. It was intercepted by Paulet and remained in Cecil's files.[27]

At first, Elizabeth sought a way to offer Mary a reprieve, and commanded Paulet to extract from the Scottish queen some expression of regret. But Paulet wrote to Walsingham: 'The lady continues in her former wilful and wicked disposition. No outward sign of repentance, no submission, no acknowledging of her fault, no craving for pardon'.[28] Elizabeth suggested that Mary's death might be contrived. On 1 February 1587, Walsingham reprimanded Paulet and Sir Drew Drury (who shared Paulet's guardianship of Mary at the time), accusing them of neglecting their duty to Elizabeth by not saving her from the necessity of 'dipping her hands in the blood of her sister Queen':

she notes in you both a lack of that care and zeal in her service that she looks for in your hands, in that you have not in all this time, (of yourselves, without other provocation), found out some way to shorten the life of the Scots Queen, considering the great peril she [Elizabeth] is subject to hourly, so long as the said Queen [Mary] shall live.[29]

As a postscript, Walsingham advised them to burn his letter once they had read it. Elizabeth exhorted Paulet, 'my most careful and faithful servant', to do her the service of despatching Mary quietly. Although Paulet deplored Mary and all she stood for, he was a man of integrity and was appalled at Elizabeth's proposal. He refused the mission, telling Walsingham that it would cause 'great grief and bitterness of mind' to do that 'which I am required, by direction of my most gracious sovereign, to do an act which God and the law forbids ... God forbid I should make so foul a shipwreck of my conscience or leave so great a blot on my poor posterity, as shed blood without law or warrant'.[30]

Mary's world shrunk even further. Her secretaries, Claude Nau and Gilbert Curle, were still in prison. Bastian Pagez and his family, her embroiderer and one of her tailors were dismissed. The three laundresses became two. Following his earlier plan, Paulet also got rid of Mary's coachman and stable lads and culled her kitchen staff. Mary seemed to accept these curtailments with equanimity. Her fate was now beyond her control. She entered a period of calm, enfolded in her faith. No longer having to engage with political intrigues and betrayals or fret over the political machinations of Scotland, England and Europe, she began to prepare for what she thought of as her martyr's death. It energised her. Her physician reported that he had 'not seen her so joyous, nor so constantly at her ease for the last seven years'.[31]

In her book, Lewis puts forward a convincing case to explain

Mary's incipient buoyancy at this tragic stage of her life. Within the Catholic faith, Lewis explains, exists the concept of *imitatio Christi,* a form of Catholic devotion which emerged in medieval times. It was a symbolic practice through which Catholics rejoiced in their sufferings, viewing them as opportunities to emulate Christ's tolerance of his torments. For Mary, her trial, the long wait for her sentence, the last petty indignities she encountered, were experienced as a form of religious sacrifice, almost ecstasy – both redemptive and liberating.[32]

On 1 February 1587, Elizabeth requested the death warrant. Cecil had taken the precaution of becoming 'ill' and it was his temporary replacement, William Davison, who inserted the warrant among a pile of more inconsequential papers that required the English queen's signature. His was a small, premeditated act of good service, allowing Elizabeth the reprieve of being able to later claim that she had been unaware of what it was she was signing. Under this screen of innocence, Elizabeth committed Mary to death.

Without waiting for a change of heart or for Elizabeth's instruction to despatch the warrant, her councillors affixed their own seals to it and had it conveyed to Fotheringhay with all speed. Preparations began for Mary's execution, but she was not informed: it was thought best not to risk the chance of any attempt at rescue or escape. On receipt of the warrant, Paulet summarily ordered the embroidered canopy of Mary's chair of state to be removed, saying, according to Mary in one of her letters, that she was 'now only a dead woman, without the dignity or honour of a Queen'.[33] For Mary, the canopy, stitched with its phoenix rising from the ashes, symbolised her defiance and survival. When Mary's servants refused to dismantle it, Paulet had his own men take it down. The next day, Paulet, in uncharacteristically conciliatory mode, offered to seek official permission for the canopy to be reinstated, but for Mary it had served its time. With martyrdom in mind, she had already replaced it with black drapes, a crucifix and pictures of Christ's passion.[34] Its transformation marked a shift in Mary's material propaganda. If her days as a queen were over, she had no further need of sovereign magnificence. Rather, for this, her last sacrifice, she chose the visual props of a Catholic martyr.

On 7 February, Paulet, Shrewsbury and other officials came to Mary's chambers to inform her that she was to be executed the following morning. Elizabeth's warrant was read out. Cecil reported that 'she seemed not to be in any terror … but rather, with smiling cheer and pleasing countenance, digested and accepted the said admonition of preparation to her unexpected execution, saying that her death would be welcome to her'.[35] Mary thanked them and requested a priest but, as Paulet later recorded, 'we utterly denied her that'.[36]

That evening, Mary dispersed the contents of her wardrobe among her household: to her apothecary, a cloak of figured velvet and two hats; to Janet Kennedy, who had served her through a generation, gowns of taffeta, violet and black satin and the bulk of Mary's linen: her sheets, smocks, handkerchiefs, coifs and veils; to Hannibal, her valet, a short serge cloak lined with figured velvet and a velvet hat. The under-cook Hamilton received a gown of russet damask furred with grey coney. It is possible to discern Mary's care and thoughtfulness in these material dispersions: serviceable clothes were given to the cook, her own gowns to Janet Kennedy, an embroidered velvet gown adorned with pearls and a pretty taffeta hat to Pagez's young daughter, and the suit of savage attire she bequeathed to Pagez himself as a reminder of their shared moment of triumph at Prince James's baptism revelries.

Mary's bedding, furniture, musical instruments and other small possessions were also distributed among her servants. Some other rich garments, bed furnishings, tapestries and three cloths of state, one of which was embroidered with true lover's knots, were all, along with her horses, left in the charge of her steward, Melville, and her physician to be sold. The money they realised was to be put towards the expenses of the queen's household 'in their journey homewards'. Melville was also to deliver personally 'to the King of Scots' a bed 'wrought with needlework of silk, silver and gold, with diverse devices and arms, not thoroughly finished' and 'a cloth of state garnished with arms'. Mary wanted to be certain that James received the bed furnishings she had spent so many hours of her captivity stitching. They held her truth.[37]

It was in the early hours of 8 February 1587 that Mary wrote her last letter to the king of France and enclosed with it two jewels thought to be talismanic for health. In her heart, it was Catholic France, not Protestant Scotland, that she claimed as home: the place of family. Charles had shared her girlhood, her glory days. He was the person she felt closest to in death. At 6 o'clock in the morning Mary handed over her will and gave out keepsakes and money to her servants, before retiring to her oratory for private prayer. At around 8 o'clock they came for her. She asked that her Catholic chaplain be permitted to be present, a request that was refused. The small procession descended the stairs to the Great Hall with Hannibal, Mary's valet, leading the way holding a crucifix. But as they reached the hall, Mary's servants were held back. She protested, but was told that their presence could not be countenanced for fear of their behaviour, the likelihood of unpalatable emotional scenes, the possibility of impromptu speeches, the danger of them taking liberties by dipping their handkerchiefs in the queen's blood to secure some relic of her. Mary asked that she be allowed at least some of her women. It was hurriedly conceded that she might have two, Janet Kennedy and Elizabeth Curle, and four men from her household.

Shortly after 9 o'clock on 8 February, in the Great Hall of Fotheringhay Castle, Mary appeared in front of the 300 men who had been invited to witness her death. They comprised the local gentry, court officials and English nobility. Local villagers who had heard talk of what was to take place had crowded into the castle's courtyard. The gates were locked behind them to make sure that no news be broadcast abroad before Mary had been executed.

A two-foot by twelve-foot platform had been erected in the hall, draped in black. On it stood the two executioners, dressed and masked in black and wearing white aprons, the customary garb of their trade. Three stools covered in black velvet had been placed on the platform, one for Mary and the others for the Earls of Shrewsbury and Kent. There were chairs for her custodians, Paulet and Drury. The executioner's block was also shrouded in black velvet and a great fire blazed in the fireplace. There was, however, no dazzle of jewellery or sequins for its flames to catch at, no glint of gold thread in surrounding tapestries to glimmer in its flare. For Mary's final moments, the material magnificence that had accompanied her throughout her reign was finally extinguished.

It was Sir Robert Wingfield, Cecil's nephew, who documented the Scottish queen's execution in a manuscript that still survives. It is a biased report. In his eyes, Wingfield was witnessing the death of a traitor, the would-be assassin of his queen, a woman of dishonour and disrepute. It is not the only eye-witness account, but it is the most detailed. Adam Blackwood, a Scottish Catholic, wrote an equally biased account of Mary's execution, which he entitled *Martyre de la royne d' Ecosse*. In it, he depicts Mary as a heroic defender of the Catholic faith facing the brutality of perfidious Protestant executioners with grace and courage. The truth, as is often the case, probably lies somewhere between the two.

When Mary entered the Great Hall, she was a woman much changed from the young, graceful queen who had danced 'high' at the Scottish court. Although only forty-four years of age, captivity and illness had forced alterations. Now almost lame, Mary had to lean on others even to walk the few steps to the scaffold. Around her were men who had played key roles in her life. There was Ralph Sadler, the English statesman, who had been her reluctant custodian for a while. He had first seen Mary when she was just born, when Marie de Guise sought to reassure him of her baby's strength to counter rumours that were circulating of a sickly child. Now he would witness her death. Paulet was also present, as was Shrewsbury, who had done what he could to make Mary's captivity more palatable.

For her final public appearance, Mary wore a gown of black figured satin with a long train and a transparent white veil edged in delicate bone lace, a form of fine lace made from thread wound on bone bobbins: dark and light, strength and frailty, body and soul. Her gown was adorned with buttons representing acorns, symbolic of the spirit. Her long black sleeves were underlaid with others of purple velvet, a small claim of royalty. Around her neck she wore an Agnus Dei (a wax disc etched with the image of the lamb of Christ) and around her waist she had wound two rosaries. In one hand she clutched a prayer book, thought to be her Book of Hours, in which over the years she had inscribed prayers and poems and collected signatures. In the other she held a small crucifix.

Mary proceeded to the platform and sat down on the stool, flanked by the two earls. The Commission of Execution was read aloud. At its end those present responded with 'God Save the Queen'. The Protestant Dean of Peterborough Cathedral began to deliver the lengthy speech he had prepared, but Mary interrupted him and reminded him that she was a Catholic. When urged to hear him out and join him in prayer, Mary refused. Ignoring her interjection, the dean knelt to pray. But Mary began to say her own prayers at the same time, reciting them in Latin. The dean fell silent. Mary continued praying, but now in English so that her words could be understood by everyone present. While the dean was not able to deliver his whole sermon, copies of it were later circulated. It made grim reading. Mary was to prepare herself for 'entry into a house of clay, where worms shall be your sisters and rottenness and corruption your father'.

Mary prayed for an end to her travails. She prayed for her son and for Elizabeth. She asked God to forgive England and excuse her enemies. When she had finished she held up her crucifix, declaring that it was in Christ's name that she shed her blood. Kissing the crucifix, Mary made the sign of the cross, saying 'even as thy arms, O Jesus Christ, were spread here upon the Cross, so receive me, I beseech thee, into thy arms of mercy and forgive me all my sins'. It was time. The executioners knelt before her and asked for her forgiveness.

In a reprise of her wedding to Darnley over twenty years earlier, her ladies-in-waiting, Janet Kennedy and Elizabeth Curle, began to unpin the queen's outer garments. As they did so, Mary's final material drama was revealed. Underneath her black gown she was wearing a petticoat and bodice of blood red, the liturgical colour of martyrdom: symbolic of human sacrifice. It is said that red was also the colour of Anne Boleyn's petticoat at the time of her execution. By wearing it, Mary was connecting her fate to that of Elizabeth's mother, to the tragedy of a queen put to death in order to further the ambitions of men.

Declaring that she 'never had such grooms before to make her unready, nor ever put off her clothes before such a company', Mary prepared for death. When one of her executioners made to remove the Agnes Dei from around her neck – as was common practice for executioners, who were entitled to claim the ornaments of their victims – Mary stayed his hand. Telling him that he would be recompensed for its loss, she bestowed it on one of her women. She then slipped on a pair of blood-red sleeves. It was Janet Kennedy who bound the queen's eyes with a white cloth edged in gold. The cloth was a Corpus Christi cloth, used to cover the chalice at mass to protect the blood of Christ. Mary embraced and kissed her women and made the sign of the cross as a final blessing in the direction of her other servants. Then, kneeling down on the cushion and groping for the block with her hands, she rested her chin down on it and recited Luke 23:46, Psalm 31: 1-5: 'Into your hands, O Lord I commend my spirit'.

It took two, some said three, blows of the axe to cut off her head. But when the executioner held up Mary's severed head, he held only her auburn wig in his hands. Wingfield wrote that:

> her dressing of lawn fell from her head, which appeared as if she had been seventy years old, cropped very short, her face being in a moment as much altered from its form when she was alive, as few could remember her by her dead face.

There was a shocked silence before the dean declared 'So perish all the Queen's enemies'. It was reported that Mary's lips continued to move in prayer for a quarter of an hour after her decapitation, as if her spirit remained among them in Catholic devotion. The Earl of Kent rose from his stool and stood over her body, declaiming 'such an end to all the Queen's and the Gospel's enemies'. The Earl of Shrewsbury apparently cried.[38]

There was a poignant codicil to the drama of Mary's execution. One of her little terrier dogs had crept under her clothes and, undetected, had stayed by her side and accompanied her to her death. After Mary was executed, the dog lay in the pool of her blood, between her head and her shoulders, and refused to be coaxed away. Eventually, it was removed, forcibly plucked from its vigil, and its coat washed clean of Mary's blood. Everything else that had had any contact with the dead queen – her clothes, the black cloth on the scaffold, the Corpus Christi cloth, the executioners' garments – were burned. There were to be no relics. Mary's severed head was shown to the waiting crowds from the castle window. It was later painted by Amos

Cawood, with Mary's name inscribed on a gold scroll which simply read: 'Maria Scotia Regina'.

Although I had followed Mary through her life, at her death I felt only a sense of waste, not of pity. I had pitied her long, wearisome years of captivity, the enforced lessening of her as a woman and as a queen. I had pitied the plethora of betrayals Mary had faced, the duplicity of Darnley, of her half-brother Moray and, at times, of her cousin Elizabeth. Mary had had to contend with the vacillation of her supposed European allies, with the detachment of her son, and with the political guile of Cecil – Elizabeth's chief adviser, the architect of the Scottish queen's downfall – and she lacked a capable, trustworthy mentor to advise and protect her. But I did not pity her in death, in the embrace of her faith and her sacrificial release. I was reminded of how I had felt when I saw her embroidery close at hand at the Palace of Holyroodhouse: admiration. Not because choosing to reframe herself as a martyr exonerated her: Mary might have chosen that persona to justify her actions to herself and her God, but she certainly emerges from history as a flawed woman and monarch. She was headstrong, emotionally naive, needy, manipulative and she relied over-much on her sense of sovereign entitlement to sustain loyalty and power. Many had died following her star: Chastelard, Darnley, Bothwell, Norfolk and countless others. But Mary was tenacious. Loyal to her servants, to her faith and, personally if not politically, loyal to Elizabeth. There was kindness in her, and a belief in the worth of others.

Mary was groomed in absolute power. She reigned with the privilege of total authority. But in the end, her determination to persevere did a disservice to Scotland. It exacerbated divided loyalties within the realm and engendered a civil war. It left her son unprotected and damaged. With her end, Scotland moved inexorably towards a fate it had fought against for so many centuries. Her son, King James, became what she had wished for, Elizabeth's successor, and Scotland became subsumed under English governance. Its independence became compromised, an independence that had been defended for hundreds of years and in whose cause thousands of Scots had died. Its diminishment cannot be blamed on Mary, but there is no doubt that her actions and decisions foreshadowed the events that followed. Even today, the nature of Scottish independence is at the heart of Scottish politics, its full reclamation robustly campaigned for by some, Scotland's inclusion in the United Kingdom defended by others. But the debate is ever-present.

After the execution, everyone dispersed. Mary's women, despite their entreaties, were not allowed to strip her body nor lay out her corpse. Instead, her servants were locked in their rooms. With no plans made for her burial, a surgeon was called to remove her heart and vital organs, which were hastily and secretly buried in the castle grounds. Her body was embalmed and wrapped in a wax cloth and a local plumber was recruited to encase it in lead.

When the news of her execution reached London, more bonfires were lit and church bells rung, there was even dancing in the streets. Elizabeth, on being told the news, feigned devastation. According to her contemporary biographer William Camden 'her countenance changed, her words faltered, and with excessive sorrow she was in a moment astonished insomuch as she gave herself over to grief, putting herself in mourning weeds and shedding an abundance of tears'.[39] She took out her fury on her advisers. Cecil was subjected to Elizabeth's tirades, but her outrage against him was temporary. He was too necessary a servant to dismiss. It was Davison, Cecil's hapless stand-in, who bore the brunt of Elizabeth's rage. Davison – who had so diplomatically secreted Mary's death warrant under a pile of other papers – was sent to the Tower for eighteen months. There were conflicting reports of King James's reaction. Some said he was impassive and politically pragmatic, registering scant emotion. Others have him silenced and reclusive in grief. Whatever the truth might be, James severed his contact with England. It was only when Elizabeth sent him a contrite letter absolving herself of blame, apologising for 'that miserable accident, far contrary to my meaning', insisting 'how innocent I am in this case' and claiming ignorance in actioning the warrant, that James responded.[40] He demanded that she pronounce him her 'lawful and nearest successor to the Crown'.[41]

In France, the French poet Pierre de Ronsard, who had tutored Mary in the joy of words as a girl, was much grieved when he heard news of her death, saying 'Ah Kingdom of Scotland, I think your days are now shorter than they were, and your nights longer, since you have lost that princess who was your light'.[42] A memorial service was held in the Cathedral of Nôtre-Dame and the Archbishop, Renaud de Beaune, said of Mary in his funeral oration:

For, besides that marvellous beauty which attracted the eyes of all the world, she had [a] disposition so excellent, an understanding so clear, and a judgement so sound, as could rarely be paralleled by a person of her age and sex. She possessed great courage, but it was tempered by feminine gentleness and sweetness.[43]

Mary's servants were kept incarcerated at Fotheringhay Castle for the next six months. They were only allowed to make their journey homewards the following August. The last letters Mary had written did not reach their recipients until the autumn of 1587.

Little now remains of Fotheringhay Castle apart from a mound of earth. They call the purple thistles that grow wild within its footprint 'Mary's tears'. In time, the Great Hall, the scene of her execution, was stripped out and reinstalled in a manor house in Connington, but, eventually, that house too was demolished, and with it went the backdrop to Mary's final hours. The staircase, however, that she walked down towards death, was salvaged. In the 1630s it was removed to grace the Talbot Hotel in Oundle, where it remains to this day. It is said that along with it came Mary's ghost, replaying her final descent, her rosary beads chinking against the velvet of her dress.

A debate ensued as to where Mary's other remains were to be buried. Even in death she posed a dilemma. While there was no desire to create a place of pilgrimage, there had to be an honouring of sorts. In the end, Mary was accorded a state funeral at Peterborough Cathedral, where Catherine of Aragon had been interred. On 30 July, her body was taken from Fotheringhay at night, as was customary, in a funeral carriage draped in black velvet and richly decorated with the royal arms of Scotland. Six cloaked gentlemen, forty horsemen, four knights and five heralds accompanied her. As her coffin appeared, the heralds donned their heraldic tabards to acknowledge that they were in the presence of a queen. The cortege made the journey of ten miles by torchlight. It arrived at the cathedral at 2 o'clock the following morning. The lead coffin, weighing 900 pounds, was too heavy to be carried far. It was therefore interred with speed in the vault.

Elizabeth spent a small fortune to assuage her guilt. Peterborough Cathedral was hung with 2,000 ells of black cloth. Its pillars were also swathed in black. In its nave, a bier had been erected. Its ornate canopied platform displayed an effigy of the Scottish queen, as was traditional for royal funerals. The effigy was dressed in a rich robe of cloth of gold trimmed with ermine and wore a bejewelled golden crown. Heraldic shields decorated the bier and were hung throughout the cathedral.

On the following morning, a river of black-clad mourners processed to Mary's funeral. Heralds brought up the rear, bearing embroidered gold silk banners emblazoned with the Scottish coat of arms, the Lennox arms and the Scottish saltire. Bothwell was not represented. Long black-hooded gowns had been distributed to the chief mourners. Elizabeth's Master of the Wardrobe had also furnished the small remnants of Mary's household, who had been kept captive at Fotheringhay, with similar mourning clothes, but they spurned the gift. They did, however, attend her funeral, processing to the cathedral behind Mary's Catholic chaplain, who carried a crucifix. One hundred poor women had been recruited to augment the 200-strong gathering of the great and the good.

It was a Protestant service. While Mary's household entered the cathedral, when the first Protestant psalm began to be sung, they left and remained outside, keeping faith with the religion of their dead queen. Afterwards, the mourners repaired to the Bishop's Palace for a lavish banquet held in rooms draped with purple and black velvet and cloth of gold.[44]

On July 18 1586, an inventory had been made of Mary's belongings at Chartley Manor, the penultimate place of Mary's imprisonment. There were over 300 embroideries that Paulet annotated as 'unfinished, not yet enriched, bands painted only, not completed, uncut, prepared for a design'.[45] Among them were fifty-two embroideries of flowers, 124 of birds, sixteen of animals and fifty-two of fish and a set of ovals depicting female musicians. Mary left her embroideries to Renée Rallay (also known as Beauregard), her chamber woman in Scotland and England.

Listed in the queen's inventory was a small piece of *point tresse*, a form of embroidery sewn with silver hair and fine silk 'worked by the old Countess when she was in the tower'. It was a gift of reconciliation, sent to Mary by Darnley's mother, the Countess of Lennox, as a peace offering in 1584. She had signed the short letter which accompanied it with from 'your Majesty's most humble and loving mother and aunt'. It was an absolution of sorts, an acceptance of Mary's innocence in Darnley's murder.[46]

On Elizabeth's death in 1603, Mary's son became James VI

of Scotland and James I of England, his succession to the English throne having been agreed with Cecil two years earlier. James arranged for the site of Mary's burial at Peterborough Cathedral to be marked with a saltire and a banner emblazoned with the lion rampant of the Scottish royal coat of arms. As an act of posthumous restoration, in 1612, he had his mother's remains reinterred in a majestic tomb in the Lady Chapel at Westminster Abbey, near her great-grandfather Henry VII. Across from her lies Elizabeth, who died in 1603, taking with her the direct Tudor line. It is ironic that they were united in death. While Elizabeth died childless; the monarchy of Scotland and England persisted through the Stuart line. All subsequent monarchs, from James until Elizabeth II today, have been descended from Mary, Queen of Scots. In 1867, when the vault containing Mary's coffin was opened at Westminster Abbey in a search for the body of James, it was discovered that Mary lay surrounded by her own dead grandchildren and great grandchildren: the tiny coffins of the many babies lost to Queen Anne, the daughter of James II and VII, and the coffin of their grandson, the Duke of Gloucester, who died when he was eleven years old. There, too, were the coffins of Mary's grandson Henry and her granddaughter Elizabeth, and her great-grandson Rupert. Elizabeth lies alone.[47]

It is 8 February 2017, the 430$^{th}$ anniversary of the death of Mary, Queen of Scots. I have come to the National Library of Scotland to view her last letter, the one she wrote at 2 o'clock in the morning, six hours before she died. Her final missive was to her brother-in-law Henri III, the King of France, and is now so fragile that it has not been displayed for nine years. In 2008, people had queued around the block to catch a glimpse of it and the library had to extend its viewing time by three hours to satisfy public interest.

I set off early, as it is a cold morning and I thought an early

## Red Petticoat and Sleeves

start would be a reprieve from the freeze of queuing. When I arrive, I find that there is only one other woman waiting, who had shared the same enthusiasm and foresight. We stand outside the massive closed wooden doors and talk of Mary and her tragedies. Other women join us, and we are all grateful when the library staff take pity on us and unlock the doors earlier than advertised to allow us to crowd into the library's warmth. There is still time to wait. The atmosphere is unusually frisky for a place normally so sedate and serene. Today, the staff are jovial, chatty even. There is a television crew waiting for sound-bites from what they hope will be a motley crew of Mary devotees. They are somewhat disheartened when they realise that the bulk of those present are women of a certain age, but they press on with those of us who have gathered. When the reporter asks me 'Why have you come today?' I improvise, saying something about tangibility, about the letter providing a rare chance to make a material connection with the dead queen.

Eventually, the doors to the boardroom where the letter is displayed, are flung open. There is a bristling of anticipation from what is now a respectably long queue of visitors. I step into the long room and spy at its end a podium topped by a glass case in which Mary's last letter lies nestled in curatorial care. For a moment I feel oddly foolish, exposed. I walk past the library staff – part welcome committee, part guardians of precious history – in a room which feels stilled in reverent silence. When I peer into the case and see the letter, I am not sure what I expect it to yield. Is it something of Mary, or something in me? Is curiosity a kind of honouring? Is honouring a kind of sentimentality? Is this a pilgrimage?

It looks old, as I had imagined it would – it has now become a document. Rightly protected from the damage of human touch, the grime and grease of fingers, it sits in a vacuum of history; an object separated from its context, a solitary remnant of its time. The letter is in French. I stare down at Mary's scrawl, willing the letter to offer up a tear stain, willing it to recompense my interest with insight. But it remains what it is, a very old letter written by a dead queen in the hours before her death: nothing more, nothing less. With only one person at a time allowed to peruse it, I move swiftly on, buy the memorial transcript in the library shop and read it on the train home.

Royal brother, having by God's will, for my sins, I think, thrown myself into the power of the Queen, my cousin, at whose hands I have suffered much for almost twenty years, I have finally been condemned to death by her and her Estates. I have asked for my papers, which they have taken away, in order that I might make my will, but I have been unable to recover anything of use ... Tonight, after dinner, I have been advised of my sentence: I am to be executed like a criminal at eight in the morning ... I have not been able to get permission for him [a priest] to come and hear my confession and give me the last sacrament ... have prayers offered to God for a queen who has borne the title Most Christian, and who dies a Catholic, stripped of all her possessions.

Wednesday at two in the morning. Your most loving and most true sister. Marie R Queen of Scotland.[48]

# 10
## *A Black Dress and White Veil*

In Blairs Museum in Aberdeenshire – the museum dedicated to Scottish Catholic heritage – there are two full-length portraits of Mary, Queen of Scots. One is thought to be a seventeenth-century copy of a small portrait made of the young queen before she left France. The other, painted a decade or so after Mary's death, was commissioned by Elizabeth Curle, who was the queen's chamber woman through much of her captivity, and who witnessed her execution. These two portraits mark the trajectory of Mary's adult life from the flourish of her sovereignty in Renaissance France to her execution in England.

In the seventeenth-century copy, Mary is poised and confident in her status, a self-possessed queen surveying her audience with equanimity. She is resplendent in black velvet, her gown decorated with bands of gold-embroidered leaves and flowers. Her front petticoat of white brocade is boldly patterned and jewels encased in gold cascade down its middle. Fine white lace frills around her wrists and neck and a decorous partlet, a covering for the neck and shoulders, screens her chest. Her hair, meticulously braided tight to her forehead, is haloed in a diadem of pearls. The background is a luminous and voluminous swathe of silver tissue cloth, its delicacy emphasising her power. This is a political portrait that proclaims Mary's youth, strength and composure. Its smaller original would have been painted with circulation in mind. It trumpets the promise of a queen who will produce heirs to continue the Stewart and Valois dynastic rule and preserve the Franco-Scottish alliance. Its gold inscription simply reads 'Marie Stuart'.

The memorial picture of Mary has a different intent. Elizabeth Curle commissioned it to fix Mary forever as a Catholic martyr and secure for her queen an honourable legacy. In it, Mary wears a high-necked black dress trimmed in brown fur. There is no embroidery or jewellery; her white cuffs and ruff are plain. Her heart-shaped headdress is bordered with a narrow strip of lace, and the capacious transparent cape that falls from her shoulders to the ground envelops her like a protective shield. Catholic imagery is intensified. The small book Mary holds is thought to be her Book of Hours, a Catholic devotional manuscript, her fingers marking a specific prayer among its pages. In her other hand she clasps a large crucifix, held out as if in blessing. Another crucifix and rosary hang around her neck, and a second rosary serves as a girdle. This is a queen who has abandoned temporal material opulence to embrace spiritual redemption. Mary no longer gazes out to the world, but has retreated into contemplation. The Scottish royal coat of arms, set against the portrait's dark background, glows with colour. Across from it is a lengthy Latin inscription in gold. It is a condemnation narrating how Mary's plea for Elizabeth's help was ignored, and how the Scottish queen was kept imprisoned for nineteen years 'on account of her religion' before being executed. Another inscription – thought to have been added later – claims Mary as 'a daughter of the Roman Church'.

What makes this portrayal of Mary more than just a commemorative portrait memorialising the Scottish queen as a martyr to her faith are the two vignettes inserted to the right and left of Mary's figure. One depicts Mary's execution, her bodice and sleeves fiery red against the sombre black attire of others present, her head bowed over the executioner's block. The executioner's axe is raised, ready for another blow. The first has already been struck. It has cut into Mary's neck to leave a trail of her blood that drips to the floor. That detail invests the portrait with truth. It identifies this as an eye-witness account, recorded and remembered. Below the scene of Mary's decapitation is another inscription naming her as 'queen, daughter, wife and mother of kings'. The other vignette portrays two women, both in black and both wearing crucifixes around their necks. Their heads are bowed towards each other. One has her hands clasped in prayer, the other is reaching out to touch the edge of Mary's veil in a final benediction. Their names are written above their heads: Janet Kennedy and Elizabeth Curle, Mary's chamber women. This is a picture of personal grief. It is a portrait of loss.

Portraits of Mary from life are rare. There are some sketches made of her as a young girl in France: chalk and crayon drawings by the artist François Clouet, who also painted a miniature of Mary and François II for Catherine de' Medici's Book of Hours. There is a full-length painting of Mary in her last years of captivity, signed by her embroiderer, Pierre Oudry. Known as the Sheffield Portrait, like Curle's commission it depicts Mary in her customary black dress and white veil with the ever-present symbols of her Catholic faith. A cameo, painted by the miniaturist Nicholas Hilliard around the same time, shows just Mary's head and shoulders. Here too the queen is wearing a gown of black, a white veil and a crucifix. That is all we have. Only the Sheffield Portrait and Hilliard's miniature are of the adult Mary, drawn from life. It is a meagre pictorial legacy. But these two portraits and Curle's memorial picture have left us with the iconic and enduring image of the Catholic queen dressed in black with a flowing white veil, proclaiming her faith through her Catholic adornments.

During the sixteenth century, portrait painting became more significant. It was adopted as a political tool. It was through their artistic representations that the monarchy and nobility promoted their marital eligibility and broadcasted evidence of their wealth and power. In portraits, the objects sitters held or were surrounded by were symbolic: a book for erudition, a globe of the world for exploration, a gillyflower for purity. And confirmation of their status could be garnered from their clothing and textile backdrops: the swathes of tapestries, emblematic embroidery and richly patterned carpets they were posed against. The volume and adornment of fabric was purposefully accentuated, even exaggerated, to boast quantities of luxurious cloth and ornamentation. It was these which messaged prosperity.

In the sixteenth century it was the artist who could best convey the gleam of expensive silk or the rich pile of velvet who was paid the most, more than the painter who captured the sitter's facial features. Exactitude in depicting material magnificence was paramount. The German portrait painter Hans Holbein the Younger kept notes on the precise nature of the fabric he was to paint, and drew the designs of embroidery or lace in the margins of his sketchbook. For him, these were expedient aide-memoires for an artist renowned for his verisimilitude. Moreover, when pigments varied in quality – with some so costly that their allocation, grade and colour was often specified in a commissioner's brief – the miniaturist Nicholas Hilliard reserved the highest grade of white for white satin and used it liberally to conjure the texture of lace, daubing it in thick layers to make the fabric more tangible. Painting textiles in portraits was an art of critical importance.

As consciously political statements, monarchs' portraits were designed to promote an identity – not to show the reality of a specific personage, but to transmit an idealised version of sovereignty, the idea of majesty. They were agents of propaganda made with replication and circulation in mind. Many were exchanged as gifts, monarch to monarch, court to court. While Mary and Elizabeth never met, they did exchange each other's pictures and Melville, the Scottish diplomat, tells in his memoir

## A Black Dress and White Veil

of an audience with the English queen when, as an act of favour, she shared with him her portrait of Mary:

> She appeared to be so affectionate to the Queen [Mary] her good sister that she had a great desire to see her; and because their desired meeting could not be so hastily brought to pass, she often delighted to look upon her picture, and took me to her bedchamber, and opened a little lectern wherein were divers little pictures wrapped in paper ... [and] she took out the Queen's picture and kissed it.[1]

The anecdote offers a rare insight into the private Elizabeth, a queen who kept Mary's picture in her innermost chamber, alongside – it transpires – one of Leicester, her supposed lover. We think of monarchs' portraits as grand full-length portrayals commissioned for gallery walls. But in the sixteenth century, there was a brisk trade in smaller, more portable paintings made as personal keepsakes: some fashioned as cameos, others integrated into jewellery. They were cherished as family and political mementos, as evidence of amity, secreted in cabinets of curiosities and private coffers among the most personal of belongings.

The painted images that exist of Mary and Elizabeth highlight the disparity of their sovereign style and intent. When a portrait was a deliberate act of monarchical image-making, the fact that these two queens chose to project themselves in such a different light is revelatory. In Mary's rare portraits, she is pared down to an essential authority. They are representations of a conscientious and pious queen wearing black, the colour of constancy, and white, the colour of spirituality. But within them lies poignancy. The later portraits of Mary reveal her reduction. Although she was raised in a cosmopolitan court of festivity and magnificence, the Scottish queen has become depleted. Her physical and emotional isolation have contracted her vision of her own sovereignty. The portraits betray an erosion of her sense of self, a diminishment exacerbated by the remoteness and insularity of Scotland and the solitude of her captivity in England. There are no props or symbolic embroidery to amplify her significance, apart from the symbols of her faith. As a captive, Mary lacked a public stage for the display and exercise of her authority. She had no court in which to promulgate her sovereign worth through her clothing and interior decoration, and she clung to the last material vestiges of her power: her chair of state, her tapestries and her embroidered bed furnishings. With no audience and no platform, Mary's performance of power had transmuted: no longer expressed through the material trappings of wealth and status but now declared through visual manifestations of her Catholicism.

Elizabeth, on the other hand, displays herself as a concoction. Her portraits show her festooned in finery: a riot of colour and adornments. This is a queen weighed down in embellishments that speak of her power. She inhabits rather than wears her garments and accessories, using them as a form of material architecture. This construction of her identity as England's queen serves not only to assert but also to legitimise her sovereignty. Her extravagant ornamentation is an armour. While Elizabeth never travelled outside of England, she depicts herself as expansive; she is determined to emphasise her spatial presence. In her portraits she fills the frame with the excessive width of her farthingale, the exaggerated puff of her sleeves, the height of her hair and headdress and the scale of her ruffs. As a virgin queen with no heir to continue the Tudor line, Elizabeth had to encompass more than her own personal identity and camouflage the physical reality of her barren female body. Rather, she had to manifest the grander idea of monarchical power: the body politic.

The English queen's Rainbow Portrait, of which there are different versions, is the ultimate portrayal of Elizabeth as she wished to be seen. It stands in direct antithesis to portraits of Mary. Elizabeth personifies herself as the sun who has brought forth the rainbow she holds in her hand. Her skirt and mantle are scattered with embroidered ears and eyes, a somewhat unsubtle reference to Elizabeth's ever-vigilant surveillance network, her rigorous attention to her duty to keep her kingdom safe. On her right sleeve coils a giant serpent studded with jewels: the symbol of immortality. On her neck ruff, an embroidered gauntlet is stitched to reference her martial prowess. Pearls – the symbol of purity, innocence and virginity – proliferate. They nestle in her hair, are wound in a long rope around her neck, encircle her wrists in bracelets, edge her veil, decorate the body of the serpent and adorn her headdress. Her bodice and sleeves are stitched with acorns, pansies, roses and other flowers, each one betraying a symbolic function: acorns for the immortal spirit, pansies for thoughts, roses for love and the emblematic Tudor rose signifying Elizabeth's dynastic heritage. The portrait is inscribed with the motto *Non sine sole iris*, translated as 'The rainbow [appears], but not without the sun'. Painted after England's defeat of the Spanish Armada, its naval victory over Spain, its theatrical exuberance is a celebration of Elizabeth the virtuous, the victorious, the all-seeing and all-hearing, the wise and immortal queen.

Elizabeth's portrait shuns any overt expression of faith. If anything, her attire is spectacularly secular. She is intent on identifying herself with her people, not with her God. The English queen's lack of religious ornament is pragmatic. The debate surrounding her sovereign legitimacy focused on her Protestantism, an adherence which made her succession invalid in the eyes of Catholic Europe. To minimise its relevance, Elizabeth avoided any display of religious iconography or show of spiritual piety. Instead, she emphasises her human credentials as a glamorous, vigorous and spirited queen. But ironically it is this representation – Elizabeth supposedly at her most triumphant – that betrays her insecurity.

Elizabeth was only too aware of the fickleness of her

subjects, remarking to the Scottish ambassador 'I know the inconstancy of the people of England, how they ever mislike the present government and have their eyes fixed upon that person who is next to succeed'. She added a Latin codicil: '*Plures adorant solem orientum quam occidentum* (Most adore the rising sun rather than the setting sun)'. Her rainbow portrait was designed to forever portray her as the rising sun.² In it the English queen appears miraculously rejuvenated but, when it was painted, Elizabeth was nearly seventy-years-old and she was frail. Such was the fiction of many sixteenth-century portraits: they were fantasies of sovereign survival, rather than realities of monarchical decline. Mary's portrayal of her moral authority is equally propagandist. It heightens her innocence and piety to leave for posterity the enduring image of a martyred queen.

Mary became a captive when she was twenty-five years-old, the age at which Elizabeth ascended her throne. Her personal reign in Scotland only lasted for seven years, compared to the forty-five years afforded to Elizabeth in England. Unlike Elizabeth, whose monarchy was contested, Mary's sovereignty was unequivocally her rightful inheritance. As a God-appointed monarch, she was a separate and superior being. Her singularity was amplified on her return to Scotland, where she had no direct family and no one of equivalent status. It was further exacerbated by her flight to England, where she became marooned in captivity, estranged from Scotland and distrusted by the English. For much of her adult life, Mary was an outsider: a solitary ruler turned lonely captive.

Mary's life was submerged in tragedy. And it is the events of her life, rather than her character, her sovereignty or the culture that surrounded her, which dominate her narrative. Despite the hundreds of books written about her, the dramas, documentaries, films and artworks produced over the centuries following her death, Mary remains elusive, dubbed by Elizabeth as 'the daughter of debate'. Her enigma strengthens her appeal. It is her very ambiguity that allows us to make of Mary what we choose – romantic heroine, tragic victim, naive monarch or manipulative woman – in a story which is complex, contested, contradictory and controversial. Her biography is multifaceted. It can be interpreted through myriad prisms: religious, royal, dynastic, Scottish, European, feminist, political. Its complexity mirrored the culture of her time. In an age characterised by religious and political upheaval, when society was feeling its way towards modernity, there was friction: a jostling between different classes and faith groups, between men and woman, all seeking advancement. Women, in particular, were attempting to recalibrate their status and assert their influence and authority. When women's right and capacity to rule was at the core of intellectual and literary debate, Mary inherited not only sovereign and dynastic responsibility, but also the challenge, as a modern queen, of confronting male supremacy and, along with other women of her status, attempting to forge effective and alternative forms of female power and agency. In the sixteenth century, women's lives were restricted by male control. Their reputations were vulnerable to male censure. Both of these factors hampered women's progress, narrowed their parameters and diminished the impact of their presence. In 1561 Moray, writing to Elizabeth about Mary, observed 'You are both tender cousins, both Queens in the flower of your age, much resembling each other in most excellent and goodly qualities. But your sex will not permit you to advance your glory'.[3] In 1585, Mary of Austria, the queen of Hungary and Bohemia, wrote to Charles V, the Holy Roman Emperor and King of Spain, of the dangers facing women rulers of her time:

Moreover, a woman is never so much respected and feared as a man, whatever her position ... And if things then do not go as expected, it is not difficult to make people believe that the woman who heads the government is to blame for everything, and for this reason she is hated and held in contempt by the people.[4]

It could have been written about Mary.

Until the nineteenth century, it was men who told Mary's story, who wrote her biography and published interpretations of her life. Her narrative was appropriated by male contemporaries who used the Scottish queen's downfall to buttress their own political and religious agendas. It was their prejudiced, and often spurious, representations of Mary that became the accepted view of the Scottish queen. Mary was characterised as flawed, weak and reckless: a woman derailed by passion. Subsequent centuries have led to modulation, a better understanding of the political challenges, duplicity and male vilification that Mary faced. Now a more balanced assessment of her capacity and culpability has emerged and, through it, a better appreciation of Mary's intelligence, courage, charm and kindness. She was a conciliatory queen. No wars were fought with other countries during her personal reign in Scotland where she strove to secure religious and political peace.

With historians and biographers largely focussing on her personal tragedies rather than on her political or religious policies, Mary has been relegated to the pages of our emotional rather than our political history. In her controversial book, *Mary, Queen of Scots: A Study in Failure* the historian Jenny Wormald argues that Mary's political reality was overshadowed by the dramatic legend of her life. Wormald tries to redress the balance, exploring Mary's legacy as a political leader. It is hardly a feminist tract; Wormald is highly critical of Mary's lack of resolve to restore Catholicism in Scotland, the inadequacy of her political control and her misguided fixation on being named as Elizabeth's successor. It is a thought-provoking book. But, most importantly, it reinstates Mary as a ruler worthy of assessment, as an equal among her male counterparts. While there will be many who disagree with the stance Wormald takes, she accords Mary her rightful place in Scotland's political history.

Although, apart from Wormald, there has been scant assessment of Mary's political competence, our fascination with the Scottish queen has persisted. She has been reimagined and reinterpreted through time. Each generation rediscovers her anew, each reclamation revealing more about the culture in which Mary is rehabilitated than about the queen herself. Vilified, pitied and celebrated in equal measure through her life and in her afterlife, Mary appeals to different audiences – popular, scholastic, political – each finding an aspect to investigate and debate. Her very ambiguity and the uncertainties in the truth of her story, enables her to be reshaped over and over again as martyr, victim, mother, queen. Nearly five centuries on, Mary remains magnetic. In the decades following her execution, it was Catholic Europe who claimed Mary, enshrining her as its martyr. As the centuries unfolded, Mary was returned to secular hands and, by the nineteenth century, had become a romantic heroine. For the Georgian and Victorian marketeers of history and culture, Mary – wife and mother – was a better fit than the virgin Elizabeth. She could be moulded more easily to suit a sentimental promotion of femininity, more readily conform to the ideal female stereotype of a passive, vulnerable woman who possessed moral strength. Moreover, the events of Mary's life were redolent with melodrama, a boon to entrepreneurs keen to sell stories of sensation and passion.

In eighteenth- and nineteenth-century art, Mary weeps and swoons, slumps in chairs and gazes longingly at faraway vistas from barred windows; she is grouped with her ladies prostrate in melancholia, or encircled by men – sometimes gallant, often menacing. Nineteenth-century literature also depicted Mary as a fragile victim. Much of her appeal was spawned by the Scottish novelist Sir Walter Scott, whose chivalric novel *The Abbott*, published in 1820, fictionalised Mary's escape from Lochleven. It is a dramatic tale filled with Scott's signature tropes of brave laddies, bonnie lassies, mist-gloomed hills and heathered glens: all grist to the romantic mill. When Agnes Strickland, the historical writer and poet, published her *Life of Mary, Queen of Scots* in two volumes in 1823 and followed it with translations of Mary's letters, most of which were written in French, Mary's heroic credentials were established. Strickland's deployment of extensive archival material endowed her biography with an authenticity that was not only disarming, but misleading. Hers was not a dispassionate critique of Mary's life and reign, but a partisan and sentimental invention of a Mary guaranteed to tug at the heart strings.

Mary's rehabilitation into the hearts of the British public was cemented when Queen Victoria and later Queen Alexandra, the wife of Edward VII, repossessed the Scottish queen as one of their own. They searched out and bought up what they could of Mary memorabilia to add to the Royal Collection. Queen Alexandra went further still in her devotion: she dressed as Mary for the Waverley Ball in 1871, and her calling card survives to record her impersonation of the Scottish queen for posterity. Her red velvet gown is draped over an embroidered gold petticoat, its bodice excessively bejewelled. There is a ruff, a veil and what became known as a Mary Stuart cap – the heart-shaped headdress that Mary wore in her Sheffield portrait – but aside from her headgear, Queen Alexandra's costume bears little resemblance to the sartorial reality of Mary's wardrobe. Tightly corseted and wasp-waisted, it accommodates a nineteenth-century vision of sovereign glamour. In a society with a penchant for dressing up in historical costume, emulations of Mary became so popular that the society columnist Ardern Holt despaired. He declared that he was almost moved to tears by the sight of four versions of 'poor Marie Stuart' at the same ball. And personifications of Mary became so ubiquitous that, at the Great Exhibition in Glasgow in 1888, a temperance café dressed its waitresses as the Scottish queen. The Irish artist Sir John Lavery was there to record the homage, calling his portrait A *'Mary Stuart' Waitress (Thoughts Afar)*.

For the first cinematic experiment in historical drama, horror film and stop-motion editing, it was Mary who Thomas Edison – the inventor of the motion picture – chose as his heroine. He had a male actor, Robert L. Thomae, dress in a suitably capacious skirt for his eighteen-second film that dramatised Mary's execution. And Madame Tussauds, the waxworks museum in London, chose to reconstruct Mary's execution for one of its earliest gruesome tableaux. These manifestations were a response not to Mary herself, but to a Victorian fascination with tragedy and death. It was not Mary's role as queen which held allure, but her loss: the loss of her crown, of her son, of her country and her life.

In the late nineteenth century, Mary's apartments at the Palace of Holyroodhouse were opened up to the public. They became – and still are – one of the most popular tourist attractions in Scotland. In the apartments, curious Victorians found all they could have wished for: walls hung with faded tapestries, Mary's bed draped in crimson hangings. All of it was a sham: a stage-set of Mary's intimate life. Nothing, except the remnants of the original architecture, was genuine. This was a fabricated poignancy. Mary's apartments had been kitted out with old – but not that old – furniture and furnishings to give the impression of rooms untouched by time. The floor of the outer chamber was thrillingly stained with the red of Rizzio's blood, Mary's supposed love affair with Bothwell evoked in the sheen of a seductive silken bedcover. A 1902 souvenir postcard of Mary's bedchamber that I found in an antique shop captures the allure. It features a pretty, large-hatted Edwardian lady. She is clutching the wire frame barrier that encloses Mary's bed, looking wistfully at this relic of passion.

The nineteenth-century reclamation of Mary was an attempt not just to humanise and sentimentalise the past, but to assuage guilt. Elizabeth's regicide had been a troubling blight on the glorious story of England. By transforming Mary from helpless victim into tragic heroine, it served to ease the troubling taint of injustice. In a rewriting of history, it was fate, not the English queen, that had brought about Mary's downfall. This was a queen who was not only young and beautiful, but who epitomised moral and emotional courage in the face of adversity, her flaws recast as female frailty.

In the 1950s, curators cleared Mary's apartments at the Palace of Holyroodhouse of their bogus historical clutter. They kept Mary's red bed, however. It had proved too much of a draw to be discarded. The stain of Rizzio's blood also persisted. When two pieces of Mary's embroidery came up for sale at a Sotheby's auction, they were purchased by the Amenity Trustees of the Palace of Holyroodhouse at a cost of £1,050 – a major investment in historical heritage for the time. By the 1970s, opinions as to how history should be presented had changed again. Authenticity became key. Practically everything in Mary's chambers was removed, including the red bed. It was the walls that were to speak. In time, more objects were displayed to kindle Mary's presence: a lock of her hair, some jewellery, her crucifix. A cavalcade of portraits of those who had played a significant role in Mary's life – Darnley, Elizabeth and Henri II among them – were hung around the walls. Today, there are fewer objects. Those that are displayed act as signposts to the narrative of Mary's life: tactile punctuations to the rooms themselves, unobtrusive but informative, triggers to thought rather than emotion.

What is left of Mary's material world provides curators with a limited but eclectic repertoire for interpretation. It includes her letters, jewellery, coins and scraps of fabric. Of Mary's textiles and clothing – whose use, dispersal and loss was recorded so assiduously by Servais de Condé – nothing remains. All has been lost. The two small embroideries at the Palace of Holyroodhouse are all that remains in Scotland to tell of her sewing; the lion's share of Mary's needlework is displayed at Oxburgh Hall in Norfolk, Hardwick Hall in Derbyshire and the V&A Museum in London. There is still in Scotland, however, a pair of extant curtains to summon up the splendour of Mary's court, one of which is on permanent display in the National Museum of Scotland in Edinburgh. They were not stitched by Mary herself, as some had believed in the past, but by professional embroiderers, and they possibly date from slightly later than Mary's personal reign, but they guide us nonetheless to the elegance and sophistication of the sixteenth-century Scottish court. On a red background, black velvet appliquéd embroideries are sewn in gold and blue silk braid and thread. The intricacy and boldness of their patterning and the striking contrast of their colours display a surprising confidence of design.

Replication has potential. On display in Edinburgh Castle's Royal Apartments are thirty-seven facsimiles of Mary's embroideries produced by the School of Ancient Crafts. It took thirty-three volunteers over 7,000 hours to embroider them. And, as part of the most recent renovations of Stirling Castle, reproductions of its lost sixteenth-century tapestries and embroidered wall hangings were commissioned. The Unicorn Tapestries, listed in Marie de Guise's inventory of belongings, now hang in replicated vibrant glory in the queen's Inner Hall. And hangings depicting the Scottish Coat of Arms grace its Great Hall. But why are such reproductions so essential? It is necessary as evidence of the efforts of James IV and V, and of Mary herself, to dress their courts' interiors in Renaissance magnificence. Without them, Scotland's palaces and castles would appear deceptively grim, bereft of the tactile splendour which was their reality. While it is impossible to create all that once adorned the Scottish court, these modern textiles provide at least an indication of what Scotland's royal material aspiration looked like.

There have been claims, of course: hopes that other textiles, thought to be related to Mary and safeguarded through centuries, are authentic. Most have proved spurious. A few are considered doubtful but possible. The catalogue for an exhibition held at Fotheringhay in 1837 to commemorate the 250$^{th}$ anniversary of Mary's death demonstrates how fiercely owners of Mary memorabilia clung to the belief that their possessions had a Marian provenance. The exhibit listings include lengthy avowals of authenticity, some tracking the trajectory of ownership, others linking textiles with key moments of Mary's life to boost their significance: the Flemish lace she was wearing when Rizzio was murdered; embroideries she stitched at Fotheringhay; an embroidered glove she gifted to an attendant at her execution; the veil she wore at her death.[5] These, and other claims, expose people's eagerness to be seen as the guardians of Mary's legacy. Her untimely end placed a greater value on the little she left behind, not simply as historical objects, but as tangible connections to Mary herself in this place at that time. By preserving the small, tactile fragments of her life, the people who owned such objects were keeping faith with her.

This is also true of members of the public and museums today who believe they have Mary's textiles and other Marian objects in their care. Coughton Court in England has a chemise which is said to have been worn by Mary at her execution, stained with her blood. Someone, at some time, has stitched in red below the neckline a resolute assertion that it was worn by 'the holy martyr, Queen Mary'. Its owners, the Catholic Throckmorton family, have an unassailable historical connection to Mary. It was Nicholas Throckmorton who Elizabeth sent to Scotland in 1567 to assess Mary's situation when she was at Lochleven, and where he offered the Scottish queen advice and succour. But it is recorded that everything that Mary wore at her death was burned to prevent them being appropriated as precious relics. Although the authenticity of the chemise is doubtful, the family attachment to it is authentic. For nearly 500 years, they have preserved it and its story as an act of loyalty, of Catholic solidarity. Given the history of Catholic persecution and the Reformist proscription of Catholic iconography, the vigilant guardianship of such a relic represents an adherence to a defiant faith.

Textiles associated with Mary might still exist, lurking in attics or folded away in cupboards, unrecognised. Others might remain in private hands, covertly cossetted by owners unwilling to declare their safeguarded possession for fear of it being commandeered to augment public collections. Since so many of Mary's textiles went into wider circulation – gifted, sold, or purloined – it is plausible that some might have survived. There were the textiles which, after Mary's flight to England, were seized by members of the Scottish nobility keen to enhance their homes with royal finery. Even Francis Walsingham, Elizabeth's spymaster, could not resist the illicit acquisition of some rather pretty decorated hoods which, he confessed, so pleased the ladies of his acquaintance that he took 'the liberty to detain a couple'.[6]

And connections persist. When I visited Wemyss Castle, where Mary met Darnley, I also visited the Wemyss School of Needlework. It was established in 1877 as part of the enthusiastic revival of the artistic and monetary value of art needlework. This enterprise, along with the Royal School of Needlework and others, provided creative and lucrative employment to women who were otherwise dependent on seasonal agricultural labour or low-paid servitude. At the Wemyss School of Needlework, its current curator, Fiona Wemyss, showed me round its workroom and gallery, where historical textiles line the walls and are boxed, piled high, below its long worktable. It reminded me of the attic at Hardwick Hall, where much of what Bess collected remains unseen but curated. The Wemyss

School of Needlework has no public funding; it is not considered a vital resource in the storehouse of Scottish heritage. Yet for nearly 150 years it has gathered and conserved embroidery patterns, techniques and embroideries themselves, to create a unique archive. More than that, it has a genuine association with the Scottish queen through its family connection. Their aristocratic credentials have allowed them access to textiles that chime with their collection, a few of which have tangible links to Mary and other noble families of the sixteenth century.

The school continues to champion Mary's needlework, producing high-quality kits that reference her designs and patterns, but its expertise and care goes unacknowledged and unassisted. This neglected hidden gem of Scottish heritage struggles to survive. It is a salient example of how, even today, there is a limited appreciation of what is important in Scotland's history. Perhaps more of Mary's textiles might have been preserved if needlework had been accorded collectable value earlier. As it was, embroidery was not considered to be a significant feature of cultural heritage until the revival of interest in needlework art in the late nineteenth century. It took until the 1950s for Mary's embroideries – and then only two of them – to be purchased by the National Museum of Scotland. Moreover, the professionalisation of textile conservation came very late to the heritage table. It was considered neither a vital component of museum curatorship nor a viable subject for academic study until the 1970s. By then, many historical textiles had already disintegrated through lack of proper care. It is a sad indictment of the low value placed on women's creativity, on an expressive medium that reveals their skill and embodies their experience.

Mary's legacy, however, continues to resonate with popular culture, and its complexity is gaining more recognition from curators and academics. The University of Glasgow initiated a two-year research project called 'In my End is My Beginning': The Memorialisation and Cultural Afterlife of Mary, Queen of

Scots, to explore the use and purpose of Mary's surviving materiality and the myriad representations of the Scottish queen. A blog has contributions on subjects as diverse as Singing about Mary, Mary, Queen of Drag and Mary, Queen of Strips (which traces Mary's afterlife in comic books), and there have been online presentations and discussions by and with Marian experts. The idea of how an object's worth is evaluated is shifting. Whereas authenticity was once paramount, now other objects – made in homage, remembrance or even comical irreverence – are increasingly viewed as insightful and instructive. Their role in disseminating Mary's story, in maintaining her popularity and broadening our view of her has earned them a valid place in the queen's history. They are also illuminating markers of the thought, emotion, craft, skill, wit and nostalgia that has been invested in Mary in the centuries following her death.

The most fascinating discussion in the University of Glasgow's project considered how to display what is absent: not just the absence of objects – textiles being an obvious gap – but the absence of peoples' understanding of the multi-layered physical and emotional significance of what remains of the Scottish queen. Here lies the challenge. We are schooled to look at historical objects, as the word suggests, objectively. We regard them from the narrow assessment of their worth placed on them by their original collectors, who deemed authenticity key. It was that, and only that, which entitled them to care and display. But although such objects are exhibited and described – sometimes with a note on the nature of their connection to an event or person – their crafting and conservation, the impetus behind their design, their purpose and their impact is rarely explained. Today, however, we are less exercised by ownership and the genuineness of an object and more interested in what can enhance our experiential discovery and emotional understanding. The potential of Marian objects to reveal more than their physical form is gaining traction – a realisation that, while what exists of Mary might be limited, what has survived has more of a story to tell.

It is Alison Wiggins, a lecturer in English Language at the University of Glasgow, who brings to life for me the potential of objects to yield more than their physical properties and provenance, and cogently illuminates how a single object can expose multi-layers of history. Using Mary's letters, she explores the challenges faced by museum staff keen to exploit curated objects as triggers for visitor insight and engagement. The Scottish queen's letters, she explains, represent much more than paper and text. They are redolent with textural properties that are revelatory. Each of Mary's 900 or so letters has its own distinct appearance and history. The neatness or scrawl of Mary's handwriting and the way it is arranged on the page can expose intimacy, mood or urgency. Like her embroidery, it is not a settled script. To unravel its full meaning, an understanding of its context is vital. The time and place of its writing, correlated with knowledge of Mary's situation at the time, can disclose her mental agitation or physical frailty. Postscripts and marginalia are significant. Whether one of Mary's letters was handwritten, dictated, copied, written in code, or even forged by others is meaningful. Some are in Thomas Phelippes hand, the master-forger who worked for Cecil and Walsingham. While he decoded them we will never be certain to what extent he stayed true to their original content. Whether a letter was written to be sent individually or grouped with others in a packet is also pertinent. Mary's letters also had their own afterlife: read or intercepted, responded to or ignored, archived or lost for years, rediscovered, treasured. Within Mary's letters lie the physical trace of her feelings and relationships. They are a visceral residue of the Scottish queen. Yet for most of us, too impatient to peer at Mary's impenetrable handwriting and decipher the close scrawl of her sixteenth-century script, an exhibited letter tells us little. And I remember my reaction on viewing Mary's last letter – 'an old letter from a dead queen' – and how different that experience was from seeing her embroidery close up. Needlework was a medium I could 'read' with knowledge, empathy and understanding. What to others might just seem like a piece of sewing, for me conjured Mary. It created a bridge between us to allow me, at last, a sense of connection.

Proximity to an object and being able to see it without the screen of glass or, even better, be allowed to touch it, even hold it, undoubtedly offers a greater sensory experience. But, given the fragility of much of Mary's tangible legacy, such opportunities are rare. The answer might lie in digital media. The Unlocking History Research Group has reconstructed how Mary 'locked' the last letter she ever wrote to her brother-in-law, Henry III of France, to keep it safe from prying eyes. A narrow strip was cut from its margin but left attached to the letter itself. The letter was folded into a small rectangle and a hole made through its layers. The paper strip was then threaded through the letter to secure it. Anyone attempting to see the document would have had to tear its paper fastening. The group not only reconstructed the process but filmed it and posted it on its YouTube channel. It provides a fascinating insight into the preciousness of the letter and the methods Mary used to safeguard its privacy. Perhaps, through digitally replicating such processes greater fascination can be kindled in objects of the past.[7]

And how is Mary portrayed in more recent times? In 1973, the American feminist artist Judy Chicago included Mary in *Great Ladies,* a series of lithographs in which she combined etching with kiln-fired acrylic spray paint to literally fuse the materials of art and craft. At a time when craft was excluded from, and denigrated by, the male-dominated art world, Chicago sought to confront their prejudice through the power of her work. This series was envisioned as an abstract portrayal of each woman's burgeoning energy and power, and the male repression which shadowed it. For each woman there are spiralling rippled rays that emanate outwards from a vivid central core along a darkening path; for each there is a palette of specific colours, a difference in the tone and breadth of the shadow that follows them. Mary's core is golden. Her rays mutate from yellow to peach to red, but always rimmed in gold. Their background deepens to dark. Chicago says that she wanted to express Mary's quiet ambition, an ambition compromised by male power.

The Scottish artist Helen Flockhart's 2018 series *Linger Awhile* illustrates Mary's experiences as a woman in the sixteenth-century. Her *Men of Vision* has Mary dancing exuberantly in spilled light as seven dour Calvinists sing a psalm. In the title work, Mary lies curled up on a large bed, tenderly holding a diminutive François II in her arms. Her dress is of cobweb lace, worked in the floral emblems of England, Scotland and France. Flockhart combines bold and delicate colour and texture to reflect the contrasts of Mary's material and emotional world.

The contemporary artist Ashley Cook repositions Mary as a Scottish icon. *The Lament of Mary, Queen of Scots,* depicts Mary against a backdrop of a map of Scotland, its place names running across the canvas like rivulets of water. Sentinel giant thistles grow around her, shadowing her gown. On the queen's front petticoat of vibrant pink, Cook has superimposed the scene of Mary's execution and sheathed the petticoat with a skirt of bright silk tartan. In her *Scotland as a Queen*, Cook has Mary posed against images of Edinburgh, her petticoat patterned with the Scottish map. Around Mary's waist is a giant sporran, its downward-facing purple tassels mimicking thistles. There are bright blue bagpipes and a Scottie dog among an assemblage of popular Scottish motifs. Through her work, Cook pulls Mary into the tourist trail of a reinvented Scottish heritage, the nebulous world of modern tartanalia.

Although Mary was denied a stage for much of her life, her afterlife has made up for the deficit with the many operas and dramas inspired by her through the centuries. In 1987 a new play was premiered by Liz Lochhead, the Scottish poet, dramatist and former Makar of Scotland (the Scottish national poet). *Mary, Queen of Scots had her Head Chopped Off* is a perceptive, witty and compassionate drama in which Mary's experiences are used to channel Lochhead's investigation into the challenges facing a modern Scotland. In theatricalising the tension between Mary and Elizabeth, sixteenth-century Catholics and Protestants, and Scotland and England, Lochhead correlates Mary's narrative with contemporary Scottish issues: equality, sectarianism, independence, nationalism and domestic abuse. She makes Mary relevant.

Making Mary relevant has been a feature of the Scottish queen's more recent manifestations, in which Mary has been reinvented yet again to appeal to younger audiences. The Netflix series *Reign* (2013–17) ran for seventy-eight episodes and largely covered Mary's girlhood in France. The young Scottish queen and her posse of Marys were characterised as independent and sexually active young women who possess an almost feral survival instinct. Its costumes were transgressive. Their designer, Meredith Markworth-Pollack, deliberately avoided sixteenth-century replication. Instead, she devised contemporary interpretations of Renaissance styles to transmit their purpose and impact. While Mary's off-the-shoulder and halterneck dresses might have raised the hackles of period aficionados, the continuing online postings of *Reign*'s costumes demonstrate the appeal of its revisioning of Renaissance splendour.

Innovative, too, are the costumes devised for the 2019 biopic *Mary, Queen of Scots*. The costume designer, Alexandra Byrne, controversially dresses Mary in denim as a material metaphor for the energy of the young queen. As Mary becomes battle-weary, her denim costume is over-dyed in orange to suggest the rust of armour. Elizabeth's costumes are also modulated and, as the film progresses and the English queen's confidence wanes, the colour of her garments drains away to symbolise her emotional decline. For a Renaissance audience, the subtleties of alteration in the costumes of both *Reign* and *Mary, Queen of Scots* would have had resonance. Perhaps even more than us, they would have paid attention to the sartorial nuances and readily deciphered their meaning with relish.

Mary's most recent reincarnation was on *Ru Paul's Drag Race*, the American reality TV series that has spawned a British equivalent. In series thirteen of the American version, the Scots-born Ross McCorkell (alias Rosé) appears costumed as Mary, resplendent in a brocaded braided gown, shoulder rolls and ruffs. Said to be 'snatched from the pages of history', Rosé's portrayal of Mary proved so popular that it was reprised for a YouTube video shot in New York. And Mary is making a re-appearance on the drag queen circuit more widely. Lawrence Chaney, the Scottish winner of the second British series, and Paris Ettamol, a contestant in the American version, portray Mary and Elizabeth on stage with Ettamol wearing Mary's iconic black dress and white veil, complete with crucifix. While the language they use is not for the faint-hearted, and their portrayals of Mary are pantomimic and deliciously mischievous, they have kindled a Marian revival in young popular culture. Other drag queens have also adopted Mary's persona, presenting their versions of her through digital and social media, where she is reclaimed as a woman with a voice whose presence and power is expressed through what she wears. Watching *RuPaul's Drag Race,* I am surprised at my leap of enthusiasm to see Mary so distanced from her traditional image as a pious queen. These drag queens' portrayals of Mary are undoubtedly subversive, but they are presented with affection and provide the Scottish queen with something more important: they give her breadth.[8]

When Mary was on trial at Fotheringhay, she declared 'look

to your consciences and remember that the theatre of the world is wider than the realm of England'.⁹ This was a queen who began her reign looking out into the world, and who was born into an age of exploration and change. Her ambitions were challenged by the parochialism of sixteenth-century Scotland, its mercurial nobles, the petty vindictiveness of its clans and the moral tyranny of its Calvinistic reformers bent on eradicating Scotland's sensuality. She claimed the right to use her female culture to paint Scotland on a broader canvas and expand its vision of itself. Her form of cultural governance was not misguided, but it was misunderstood, misrepresented and, in the end, ineffectual.

I find that I have come to care for Mary, but not because I feel I understand her. Mary's unique status, the complexity of her relationships – political and personal – and her culture lie way beyond the reach of my comprehension and empathy. But I can catch at her charm and intelligence, and acknowledge her as valiant. When I think of her, denied privacy and companionship, prevented from exercising her sexuality from her mid-twenties onwards, forbidden contact with her son, deliberately excluded from affairs and discussions relating to her fate and, most insidiously, set up to betray her own moral code in Cecil's and Walsingham's trap of isolation and the duplicity of his agents, I admire her tenacity. She might have been refused a stage, denied a voice, but she sewed. She used the female culture of needlework to safeguard and ensure she left behind her her own testimony. Mary's needlework was not a pastime; you can see from her stitching that it was a labour. When we remember that 'A Catte' contained over 10,000 stitches, and add the 300 or more embroideries which she left behind at Chartley, those we know she gifted, the bed she made for her son with over fifty images and those of her embroideries which have survived, her sewing becomes a crusade. It encapsulates an extraordinarily lengthy testimony, the equivalent to thousands of pages of writing. It is threaded through with memory, documentary, allegory and symbolism: each separate piece requiring thought, design, ingenuity and time. Mary's sewing was a practice, a physical as well as emotional protest. When both Scotland and England wanted to erode her from their conscience and their consciousness, she insisted on her presence and preservation, asserting her worth and power through her needlework.

In June 2021, I receive an email from my agent telling me that Maria Grazia Chiuri, the Creative Director of Dior's Women's Collection – the first woman ever to be appointed to this prestigious role – wants to connect with me via Zoom. She has read my first book, *Threads of Life: A History of the World through the Eye of a Needle* with interest and wants to discuss it. A call is duly arranged. It seems an unlikely combination, surreal even: me a banner-maker and community textile artist with the marginalised and disenfranchised; her the designer of some of the most expensive frocks in the world for the inordinately rich and the world of celebrity glamour. But when we link up online we find ourselves inexplicably and surprisingly empathetic. We are kindred. We share a belief that fabric and thread has much to say, if only people took the time to savour its hand-written artistry. We recognise that clothing and textiles have been forces of social and political expression since time immemorial, particularly for women. We know that the textiles we wear, display, make and gift are potent mediums to register women's culture and female solidarity, and that their makers are an integral part of what they impart. It is the process as much as the product that engages us. Sewing is a conscious activity, not just an object. It is what we put into cloth, the time, care, thought, the evidence of self that we invest in it that makes it potent. This is not mere surface decoration; needlework is layered in emotional meaning.

## A Black Dress and White Veil

Maria Grazia Chiuri sends me an invitation so that I can view the launch of her latest collection live online. As I sit in my shed and watch it, I realise that time encircles us. While I am writing about the sensory, symbolic potency of Renaissance textiles, describing how they are infused with the purposeful use of texture, luminosity and flow, and imbued with concepts of discovery and exploration, models in Paris claim the stage. Each one, like the women of the Renaissance court, is separate in their own space and, like them, their clothes parade assertions of female power. As a backdrop, the gallery of the Rodin Museum in Paris has been walled in embroidery. The models are flanked by colossal stitched murals that, like their Renaissance counterparts, have been designed to interact with the figures that move past them. The fluidity of the processing fashion is heightened by the tactile and textured landscapes that surround it. It is a conversation between the human world and the world of nature. Commissioned from the French artist Eva Jospin, the murals reveal the deep-rooted complexity of nature that humanity cannot emulate. In strands of threaded colour, rivers travel, divert, reach settled points and evade the shore. Densely stitched patchworks evoke the solidity of rock formations that have stood through time. It is the artisanal skill of women from the Chanakya School of Embroidery in India that has recreated this portrayal of the power of nature. Past centuries and present culture coalesce in a connected design.

In the solitude of my shed, I gasp at this unexpected contemporary revelation of Renaissance sensory materiality. The fluid cloth, the glimmer of light-reflective silk, the encrusted embroidery and the intricate interlaced strapwork all resonate with what I have discovered about the material world of the Renaissance. And I think of how history can be interpreted not simply chronologically, but in layers: that we are touched and shaped as much by the past as the future, and that both linger in our psyche to insist on presence and absorption.

The revelation of Maria Grazia Chiuri's launch reminds me of a moment I had forgotten about. I am transported back to Strathclyde Arts Centre in Glasgow, decades earlier, where I was hosting the unveiling of community banners and wall hangings. For the past year I and a group of women known as the Thursday group, who have worked with me on community textiles in the city for years, have been supporting local groups throughout the region in their creation of large-scale textiles that express their cultures and creativity. Throughout the evening – to the accompaniment of poetry, dance and songs – each new work is revealed. The arts centre, revamped from an old school, is an empty and depersonalised space, activity hidden behind the doors of what were once classrooms. Its vast central atrium is a void. As the evening progresses, however, the centre's walls are gradually covered in embroidered and appliquéd textiles: the memories of elderly people on the small Scottish island of Mull, the bold assertions of Glasgow teenagers, the wistful recapturing of traditional festivals by women of different cultures. Rows of embroidered bunting are strung across an entire wall, each triangle representing a family, a neighbourhood, a culture or a campaign. Textiles cling to the rails of the balcony, they stretch up and on to the walls of the upper floor to display a tactile evocation of disability and a series of futuristic self-portraits made by 100 children. The finale sees the tumbling down of an enormous textile mobile. It fills the atrium's void with images of Scottish multicultural creativity: an Indian embroiderer, South African wellie dancers, gamelan musicians, pensioners at a tea-dance. Like the Fetternear banner, each mobile image is double-sided and can be seen from either side during its slow-twirling motion. Fashioned from translucent fabrics, with each image connected to the next, they shadow one another. By the end of the evening the centre is filled with human stories. It brims with history and memory, culture and community, loss and hope.

This is how it must have felt in Mary's day: how it must have been to live in a world in which you were surrounded by material voices that told of history and learning, morality and ambition. Renaissance textiles messaged power, but they also expressed aspiration, spirituality, human frailty and ingenuity. The female rulers of Mary's generation embroidered because it was predominantly, if not exclusively, their medium: their way of promoting their presence and orchestrating their public and political identity. Most importantly, through their display and creation of textiles, they reached an audience. Mary exploited the versatility of her textiles to honour the traditions of the past, mark her emotions and allegiances in her present, and preserve her testimony for the future. Her use of them crossed the boundaries of time to encompass contemporary issues of power and heritage, female agency and immortality. When so much was lost to her after her abdication and flight to England, she clung to her material world as evidence of what lay in her heart.

# Endnotes

## Abbreviations and Note on Sources

In researching the life and times of Mary, Queen of Scots two sources have proven essential and I have therefore referred to them a number of times in these endnotes: the *Accounts of the Lord High Treasurer of Scotland* and the *Calendar of State Papers*. For the sake of brevity, I will refer to them by abbreviation as *T.A.* (*Accounts of the Lord High Treasurer of Scotland*) and *C.S.P.* (*Calendar of State Papers*).

The *Accounts of the Lord High Treasurer of Scotland* were public records of the final audited accounts of the royal household, while the *Calendar of State Papers* are the accumulated papers of the secretaries of state and are made up of a wide range of documents, including private and official letters, reports, proclamations and memoranda.

### INTRODUCTION

1  *Hamilton Papers*, 2, 326 (LP, xix (1)), no 324
2  Mackenzie, *Scottish Pageant*, p. 162
3  Hale, *The Civilization of Europe*, p. 179
4  Hayward, 'Repositories of Splendour', p. 151
5  Wikipedia.org: list of countries by population in 1500
6  Pitscottie, *Histoire*, p. 358; cited by Fraser, p. 168

*Endnotes*

7  *Calendar of State Papers: Elizabeth*, 1, 581,1053
8  National Records of Scotland SP13/7

## 1. BIRDS, FLOWERS, FRUIT AND OTHER EMBROIDERED MOTIFS

1  *Accounts of the Lord High Treasurer of Scotland*, 9, p. 219
2  *Records of the Parliament of Scotland*, 1430/12–14
3  Cox, *Tudor Sumptuary Laws*, p. 26
4  Brewer, *Letters and Papers*, 3, 2214, p. 20
5  Hayward, 'Repositories of Splendour', p. 151
6  Monnas, *Inventory of Henry VIII*, pp. 264–267
7  Brewer *Letters and Papers*, p. 52
8  T.A., 7, pp. 5, 55
9  T.A., 7, pp. 4, 23, 33, 57, 58
10 Campbell, *The Inventory of Henry VIII*, pp. 27–32
11 Levey, *The Inventory of Henry VIII*, p. 154
12 Campbell, 'Tapestry Quality', p. 29; Jourdain, *The History of English Secular Embroidery*, p. 24
13 Watkins, *Mary, Queen of Scots*, p. 52
14 Further Reading: Guidicini, *Performing Spaces*
15 Bonnaffe, *Inventaire de Catherine de' Medicis*, p. 101
16 De Farcy, *La Broderie de XIc Siecle Jusqu'à nos Jours*, p. 81
17 Swain, 'The Needlework of Mary, Queen of Scots', p. 3
18 Labanoff, *Receuil des Lettres*, 1, p. 42
19 Watkins, *Mary, Queen of Scots*, pp. 58,61
20 St Clair, *The Secret Lives of Colours*, p. 99
21 Wardle, 'The Embroideries of Mary, Queen of Scots', p. 9
22 Further Reading: LaBouffe, 'Embroidery and Information Management: The Needlework of Mary Queen of Scots and Bess of Hardwick Reconsidered'
23 Clausse, *Comptes de la Royne D'Ecosse pour l'Annee 1551*. pp. 283–289
24 Clausse, *Comptes*, p. 305
25 *Balcarres Papers*, 3, no. 19, 30 March, 1548

26 Clausse, *Comptes*, p. 301
27 Labanoff, *Receuil des Lettres*,1, pp. 199, 283–289
28 Further Reading: Van Scoy, 'The Marriage of Mary Queen of Scots and the Dauphin'
29 *T.A.*, 10, p. 360
30 Eastwood, 'In the Shadow of the Queen', p. 12
31 de l'Aubespine, *Négociations, lettres et pièces diverses relatives au règne de François II* p. 342, 3757
32 *C.S.P., Foreign, Elizabeth*, 1, 179, March 1559
33 *C.S.P., Relating to English Affairs in the Archives of Venice*, 7, 215, 8 December 1560

## 2. THE FETTERNEAR BANNER

1 Mackenzie, *Scottish Pageant*, pp. 89–90
2 Inventory of Glasgow Cathedral, 1422, pp. 313–322
3 Inventory of Glasgow Cathedral, 1422, pp. 298–9
4 *The National Archives*, SP 59/1, f.212v
5 *Inventaires de la Royne Decosse*, pp. xxiv–xxvi
6 Thomson, *Collection of Inventories*, pp. 242–248
7 Labanoff, *Recueil des Lettres*, 1, p. 29, 28 December 1555
8 Further Reading: McRoberts, 'The Fetternear Banner'
9 *T.A.*, pp. 3, 35, 59, 65–68, 75, 290–1, 293
10 Knox, *History of the Reformation*, 2, pp. 267–71
11 *C.S.P., Foreign, Elizabeth*, pp. 4, 180
12 Marwick, *Extracts from the Records of the Burgh of Edinburgh*, pp. 104, 137
13 *T.A.*, Vol. 11, p. 63
14 Further Reading: MacDonald, 'The Entry of Mary Stewart into Edinburgh'
15 Knox, *The First Blast of the Trumpet*, p. 22
16 Knox, *History*, 1, p. 286
17 Knox, *History*, 2, pp. 369–70
18 *Inventaires*, pp. 145–41
19 *T.A.*, 11, pp. 216, 224

20 *Rutland MSS.*, pp. 467–468
21 Cited by Digby, *Elizabethan Embroidery*, p. 68
22 Jones & Stallybrass, *Renaissance Clothing*, p. 192
23 Staniland, *Medieval Craftsmen: Embroiderers*, pp. 65,66
24 Mackenzie, *Scottish Pageant*, p. 65
25 Chambers, *Domestic Annals of Scotland*, 1, p. 103

### 3. TWO DOLLS' DRESSES MADE OF GREY DAMASK THREADED IN GOLD

1 *Collection of Inventories*, p. 238
2 *Inventaires*, p. 139
3 Further Reading: Croizat, 'Living Dolls' and Pearce, 'The Dolls of Mary, Queen of Scots'
4 Pearce, 'The Dolls of Mary Queen of Scots'
5 Lezio, *Isabella d'Este et Leone X*, pp. 75–6, 92, 102
6 Bonnaffe, *Inventaire des Meubles de Catherine de' Medicis*, pp. 93–9
7 Hayward, *Dress at the Court of Henry VIII*, p. 158; Alford, *Needlework as Art*, p. 16
8 Further Reading: Payne, 'Pandora's Box: Replica of a 16th century Extant Fashion Doll'
9 Harrison, *The Wardrobe Inventories of James V*, pp. 5–8
10 Knox, *History*, 2, pp. 390–2
11 Maitland, *Miscellany*, 2, pp. 390–2
12 Teulet, *Papiers d'Etat*, 2, p. 31
13 *T.A.*, 11, pp. 24–27
14 Marshall, *Queen Mary's Women*, p. 158
15 Strickland, *Letters*, 1, p. 7
16 *C.S.P., Scotland*, 2, 41, 13 December 1561
17 *C.S.P., Scotland*, 1, 1048, 7 December 1561
18 *C.S.P., Scotland*, 1, 1125, 15 July 1562
19 *T.A.*, 11, p. 66
20 *C.S.P., Scotland*, 1, 1107, 29 May 1562
21 *C.SP., Scotland*, 11, 3 June 1562

22 Melville, *Memoirs*, p. 43
23 *Collection of Inventories*, pp. 237–242
24 *T.A.*, 11, pp. xlix, 83, 95, 103, 226–7
25 Calderwood, *History of the Kirk*, 2, p. 248
26 Mackenzie, *Scottish Pageant*, p. 177
27 *C.S.P., Scotland*, 1, 18 September 1562
28 *C.S.P., Scotland*, 1, 649, 1 August 1562
29 Creighton, *A History of Epidemics*, p. 305
30 Colthorpe, *Elizabethan Court Day by Day*, p. 102
31 *C.S.P., Scotland*, 1, 1023, 24 September 1561
32 Beer, 'Practices and Performances', pp. 33–56
33 Matheson-Pollock, *Queenship and Counsel*, p. 40
34 Cockram, *Sartorial Politics*, pp. 33–56
35 Anne of France, *Lessons for my Daughter*, p. 48
36 Bonnaffe, *Inventaire de Catherine de' Medicis*, pp. 169–210

### 4. A GREAT MOURNING GOWN OF BLACK

1 Madden, *Privy Purse Expenses of the Princess Mary*, pp. 150, 157
2 Hayward, *Dress at the Court of Henry VIII*, p. 326
3 Staniland, *Medieval Craftsmen: Embroiderers*, p. 23
4 Staniland, *Medieval Craftsmen: Embroiderers*, p. 30
5 Hayward, *Inventory of Henry VIII*, p. 112
6 *T.A.*, 11, pp. 183, 191, 203
7 *T.A.*, 6, p. 411.
8 Cockram, *Sartorial Politics*, pp. 39–41
9 Alford, *Needlework as Art*, p. 166
10 Public Record Office, E315/235. F.71r; cited by Hayward, 'Repositories of Splendour', p. 144
11 Hayward, *Inventory of Henry VIII*, pp. 71–74
12 Madden, *Privy Purse Expenses of Princess Mary*, p. 16
13 Melville, *Memoirs*, p. 38
14 *T.A.*, 6, pp. 399–406
15 Alford, *Needlework as Art*, p. 166

16 Cleary, 'Fabricating an Image', pp. 11–12
17 Ives, *The Life and Death of Anne Boleyn*, p. 357
18 Arnold, *Queen Elizabeth's Wardrobe Unlock'd*, p. 90
19 Mikhaila & Malcolm-Davies, *The Tudor Tailor*, pp. 40–41
20 Arnold, *Queen Elizabeth's Wardrobe Unlock'd*, p. 90
21 *C.S.P., Scotland*, 2, 60, 22 February 1564
22 *Elizabethan Court Day by Day*, p. 27
23 *T.A.*, 11, pp. 228–9
24 Knox, *History*, 2, p. 381
25 Knox, *Works*, 2, p. 389
26 *T.A.*, 11, pp. 65–6
27 Hayward, *Dress at the Court of Henry VIII*, p. 228
28 *Collection of Inventories*, pp. 219–236
29 *Inventaires*, pp. 61–2
30 Tweedie, *David Rizzio*, p. 55
31 *C.S.P., Relating to English Affairs in the Vatican Archive*, 1, 1558–71, No 278, 2281
32 *C.S.P., Scotland*, 2, 42, 21 December 1563
33 *C.S.P., Elizabeth*, 7, 723, 7 October, 1564
34 *T.A.*, 11, p. L
35 *T.A.*, 11, pp. 350–351, 362, 367
36 Melville, *Mémoirs*, p. 134
37 Wright, *Queen Elizabeth and Her Times*, 1, p. 199
38 Cited by Guy, *My Heart is My Own* p. 198
39 *C.S.P., Scotland*, 2, 191, 3 June 1565
40 *C.S.P., Scotland* 2, 172, 1 May 1565
41 *T. A.*, 11, p. 374
42 Wright, *Elizabeth*, p. 199
43 *T.A.*, 11, pp. 381–393
44 *T.A.*, 11, pp. 404, 406–7
45 *T.A.*, 11, p. 413
46 *Inventaires*, p. 33
47 Knox, *Works*, 2, pp. 500–501

## 5. A SUIT OF SAVAGE ATTIRE

1. T.A., 11, pp. 420, 473; *Inventaires*, pp. 126–7, 130, 137
2. *Inventaires*, pp. 64, 126, 127, 130, 156; T A. 11, pp. 85, 159, 357, 420-1, 473, 405
3. C.S.P., Scotland, 2, 60, 21 February 1564
4. *Collection of Inventories*, p. 237
5. Knox, *Works*, 2, p. 294
6. C.S.P., Scotland, 2, 294
7. Nicholl, *Stuart Masques*, p. 162
8. C.S.P., Scotland, I, 1060, 5 January 1562
9. Evans, *English Masques*, pp. xxiii–xxvi
10. Mackenzie, *Scottish Pageant*, pp. 167–168
11. C.S.P., Foreign, Elizabeth, 7, 348
12. Stevenson, *Selections*, pp. 119–120
13. *Diurnal of Occurrents*, p. 87
14. C.S.P., Scotland, 1, 1049, 7 December, 1561
15. Calderwood, *History*, 2, pp. 285–286
16. T.A., 11, p. 102
17. T.A., 11, pp. 381, 387, 462
18. Tweedie, *Davd Rizzio*, pp. 116, 119
19. *Inventaires*, p. 161
20. Keith, *Papers*, 2, p. 259
21. Tytler, *History of Scotland*, p. 400
22. Tytler, *History*, 5, p. 334; cited by Fraser, *Mary, Queen of Scots*, p. 306
23. Keith, *History*, 3, p. 404
24. Tytler, *History*, 5, p. 334; cited by Fraser, *Mary, Queen of Scots*, p. 306
25. T.A., 3, pp. 272–277
26. T.A., 4, pp. 208–9
27. Matheson-Pollock, *Queenship and Counsel*, p. 198; T.A., 2, pp. 215–5; T.A., 10, p. 360
28. T.A., 11, p. 501
29. Matheson-Pollock, *Queenship and Counsel*, p. 183

30 *T.A.*, 11, p. 512
31 Hay Fleming, *Mary, Queen of Scots*, p. 501
32 Levey, *Inventory of Henry VIII*, p. 147
33 Pearce, 'Beds of "Chapel" Form', p. 3
34 *Inventaires*, pp. 40–41
35 *Inventaires*, pp. 29, 31–36, 44–5, 50, 164–173
36 *Inventaires*, pp. 40–41
37 *C.S.P., Foreign*, 7, pp. 387,426
38 *Inventaires*, p. 166
39 Further Reading: Bath, 'Rare Shrews and Singular Inventions'; Lynch, 'Queen Mary's Triumph'
40 Keith, *History*, 1, p. 96
41 Labanoff, *Recueil des Lettres*, 7, p. 269

### 6. THREE OF THE FAIREST

1 *T.A.*, 11, p. li
2 *Inventaires*, p. 162
3 Gore-Brown, *Lord Bothwell*, p. 245
4 *Diurnal of Occurrents*, p. 101; cited by Hay Fleming, *Mary, Queen of Scots*, p. 417
5 'Proceedings of the Society of Antiquaries', 3, (1881) p. 228
6 *T.A.*, 12, pp. 27–8
7 *T.A.*, 12, p. 37
8 Cited by Fraser, *Mary, Queen of Scots*, p. 364
9 *Inventaires*, pp. 29, 33–4, 39, 47, 49
10 *National Archives*, MPF 1/366
11 *T.A.*, 12, p. 41
12 Cited by Fraser, *Mary, Queen of Scots*, p. 380
13 Hosack, *Mary, Queen of Scots*, 1, p. 539; cited by Hay Fleming, *Mary, Queen of Scots*, p. 441
14 *T.A.*, 12, pp. vii, 41; *T.A.*, 8, pp. 141–147
15 Anderson, *Collections*, I, p. 24. Cited Fraser p. 382
16 *C.S.P., Foreign, Elizabeth*, 8, 971, 24 February 1567
17 *National Archive*, SP 52/13 f.60; *C.S.P., Scotland*, 2, 518

18 Further Reading: Bath, 'Placardes and Billis and Ticquettis' pp. 223–246
19 Chevalier & Gheerbrant, *Penguin Dictionary of Symbols*, p. 867
20 Hosack, *Mary, Queen of Scots*, 1. p. 537 Cited Hay Fleming, *Mary, Queen of Scots*, p. 434
21 Hay Fleming, *Mary, Queen of Scots*, p. 435
22 Buchanan, *History*, 2, p. 493
23 *Inventaires*, p. 177
24 *Inventaires*, pp. 177–8
25 *Inventaires*, pp. 62–73
26 Harrison, 'The Wardrobe Inventories', pp. 5–8
27 *Elizabethan Court Day by Day*, p. 27
28 *Collection of Inventories*, pp. 130–132
29 T.A., 12, p. 43
30 T.A., 12, p. 45
31 *C.S.P., Foreign, Elizabeth*, 8, p. 198
32 *C.S.P., Foreign, Elizabeth*, 8 p. 198; cited by Fraser, *Mary, Queen of Scots*, p. 387
33 Labanoff, *Recueil des Lettres*, 2, 31; cited by Fraser, *Mary, Queen of Scots*, p. 404
34 Mann, 'The Role of Ritual and Procession', pp. 13–18
35 Hay Fleming, *Mary, Queen of Scots*, p. 508
36 *C.S.P., Spanish Elizabeth*, 1, 639, cited by Hay Fleming, *Mary, Queen of Scots*, pp. 140–151
37 Cited by Fraser, *Mary, Queen of Scots*, p. 392
38 Labanoff, *Recueil des Lettres*, 2, p. 31
39 Melville, *Memoirs*, p. 149
40 Cited by Hay Fleming, *Mary, Queen of Scots*, p. 451 and Guy, *My Heart is My Own*, p. 357
41 *Inventaires*, p. 176
42 T.A., 11, p. 52; cited by Hay Fleming, *Mary, Queen of Scots*, pp. 511, 567–8
43 Teulet, *Papiers d'Etat*, 2, p. 155; cited by Hay Fleming, *Mary, Queen of Scots*, p. 463

44 *C.S.P., Foreign Elizabeth*, 8, 1566–68
45 *C.S.P., Foreign Elizabeth*, 8, p. 198
46 Hay Fleming, *Mary Queen of Scots*, p. 463
47 Tweedie, *David Rizzio*, p. 68
48 *C.S.P., Scotland*, 2, 514, 11 June 1567
49 Fraser, *Mary, Queen of Scots*, p. 408
50 *C.S.P., Scotland*, 2, 521, 15 June 1567
51 *National Archives* MPF 1/366
52 www.Dundee.ac.uk/news, Monday 15 August 2016
53 *The Memorial of Darnley*, Royal Collection Trust, RCIN 401230

### 7. A DOZEN AND A HALF LITTLE FLOWERS PAINTED IN CANVAS

1 Buchanan, *Detection*, p. 145
2 *C.S.P., Elizabeth Foreign*, 8, 1324, 20 June 1567
3 Further Reading: Robertson, *An Historical Account of the Blue Blanket*
4 Robertson, *An Historical Account of the Blue Blanket*, p. 81
5 Laing, *History of Scotland*, 2, p. 114
6 Cited by Weir, *Mary, Queen of Scots*, p. 449
7 Lynch, *Scotland: A New History*, p. 218
8 Leslie, *A Defence of the Honour*, I, p. 36
9 Burns-Begg, *The Secrets of My Prison House*, p. 66
10 Nau, *The History of Mary Stewart*, p. 62
11 The National Archive, SP 52/13/71, ff. 137r–138r; *C.S.P., Scotland*, 2, 560, 14 July 1567
12 *C.S.P., Scotland*, 2, 560, 14 July 1567
13 *C.S.P., Scotland*, 2, 588, 9 August 1567
14 *C.S.P., Scotland*, 2, 521, 15 June 1567
15 *C.S.P., Scotland*, 2, 563, 18 July 1567
16 *C.S.P., Scotland*, 2, 559, 14 July 1567
17 *C.S.P., Scotland*, 2, 493, 20 April 1567
18 *C.S.P., Scotland*, 2, 563, 18 July 1567

19 Maitland Club, *Illustrations of the Reign*, pp. 12–19
20 *T.A.*, 12, p. 67
21 Stevenson, *Sélections*, p. 258
22 Labanoff, *Recueil des Lettres*, 2, pp. 65–66
23 *Records of the Parliaments of Scotland*, 3, pp. 27–8
24 *Records of the Parliaments of Scotland, Acts of the Parliament in Scotland*, iii, 38
25 Labanoff, *Recueil des Lettres*, 2, pp. 61–2
26 *T.A.*, 12, p. 70
27 Maitland Club, *Illustrations of the Reign*, p. 13
28 *C.S.P., Scotland*, 1, 1035, 24 October 1561
29 *Collection of Inventories*, pp. 215–218
30 Turgot, *Life of St Margaret*, p. 18
31 Alford, *Needlework as Art*, p. 175
32 Madden, *The Privy Purse Expenses of the Princess Mary*, pp. 50, 139, 152
33 Taylor, *The Needles' Excellency*, B2/4
34 Frye, *Maid and Mistresses*, p. 168
35 Pathe News, Queen Mary Makes a Carpet', YouTube, 13 April 2014
36 Nau, *The History of Mary Stewart*, p. 56
37 Labanoff, *Recueil des Lettres*, 2, p. 69
38 Maitland Club, *Illustrations of the Reign*, pp. 12–1
39 Labanoff, *Recueil des Lettres*, 2, pp. 67–8, 15 May 1568
40 Teulet, *Papiers d'Etat*, p. 364, 8 May 1568
41 *C.S.P., Scotland*, 2, 656, 17 May 1568
42 Hay Fleming, *Mary, Queen of Scots*, p. 174
43 Labanoff, *Recueil des Lettres*, 2, pp. 117–8
44 Cited Fraser, *Mary, Queen of Scots*, p. 456
45 *C.S.P., Scotland*, 2, 657, 17 May 1568
46 *C.S.P., Scotland*, 2, 664, 18 May 1568
47 Labanoff, *Recueil des Lettres*, 2, pp. 129–130
48 Labanoff, *Recueil des Lettres*, 2, pp. 117–121, 21 June 1568
49 Nau, *History of Mary Stewart*, p. 98

50   Cited by Arnold, *Queen Elizabeth's Wardrobe Unlock'd*, p. 98; British Library, Egerton, 2806, f. 73
51   *C.S.P., Scotland*, 2, 685, 2 June 1568
52   *C.S.P., Scotland*, 2, 726, 7 July 1568
53   *T.A.*, 12, pp. 137–8
54   Labanoff, *Recueil des Lettres*, 2, pp. 115–116, 21 June 1568
55   *C.S.P., Scotland*, 2, 674, 28 May 1568
56   Tytler, *History of Scotland*, 6, p. 1568
57   Labanoff, *Recueil des Lettres*, 2, pp. 82–3; Bell, *Bittersweet Within My Heart*, p. 65
58   Cited Fraser, *Mary, Queen of Scots*, p. 459
59   *C.S.P., Scotland*, 2, 679, May 1568
60   *C.S.P., Scotland*, 2, 722, 30 June 1568
61   *C.S.P., Henry VIII, Foreign and Domestic*, 2, 203, August
62   *C.S.P., Scotland*, 2, 679, May 1568
63   *C.S.P., Scotland*, 2, 679, May 1568
64   *C.S.P., Scotland*, 2, 679, May 1568
65   Donaldson, *The First Trial of Mary, Queen of Scots*, p. 68
66   Cited by Fraser, *Mary, Queen of Scots*, p. 506
67   Cited by Donaldson, *The First Trial of Mary, Queen of Scots*, p. 68
68   Cited by Donaldson, *The First Trial of Mary, Queen of Scots*, pp. 110–144
69   Cited by Donaldson, *The First Trial of Mary, Queen of Scots*, p. 69
70   Cited by Donaldson, *The First Trial of Mary, Queen of Scots*, p. 102
71   *C.S.P., Scotland*, 2, 950, 14 January 1569–1570

## 8. A CATTE

1   Levey, *The Embroideries of Hardwick Hall*, pp. 44–7
2   *C.S.P., Scotland*, 2, pp, 609–10, 26 January 1570
3   Mosley, *The History of the Castle Priory and Town of Tutbury*, pp. 168–9

4 De Pizan, *City of Ladies*, p. 238
5 Strickland, *Letters*, 2, p. 78, September 1585
6 Haynes, *Collection of State Papers*, 510–11, 6 February 1569
7 Frye, *Pens and Needles*, pp. 68–71; Levey, *An Elizabethan Heritage*, p. 70
8 'Calendar of Manuscripts of the Marquis of Salisbury', 3, 158–61
9 Haynes, *Collection of State Papers*, p. 510, 6 February 1569
10 *C.S.P., Scotland*, 2, 1022, 13 March 1569
11 Labanoff, *Recueil des Lettres*, 4, p. 187, 18 July 1574
12 Labanoff, *Recueil des Lettres*, 5, p. 431
13 Labanoff, *Recueil des Lettres*, 3, pp. 373–4
14 Bath, *Emblems*, pp. 77–79; Further Reading: Bath, *Emblems of a Queen*
15 Labanoff, *Recueil des Lettres*, 3, pp. 5–6, December 1569; p. 12, 15 January 1570
16 de l'Aubespine, *Négociations, lettres et pièces diverses relatives au règne de François II*, p. 34, 3757
17 *Victoria and Albert Museum*, London, Museum No. T.29–1955
18 Arnold, *Queen Elizabeth's Wardrobe Unlock'd*, p. 71
19 *C.S.P., Scotland*, 7, p. 162; Labanoff, *Recueil des Lettres*, 2, p. 380
20 *C.S.P., Scotland*, 4, 40, 7, November 1571
21 Murdin, *A Collection of State Papers*, p. 57
22 Marshall, *Queen Mary's Women*, p. 182
23 Labanoff, *Recueil des Lettres*, 5, p. 402
24 *C.S.P., Scotland*, 2, 1037, 8 April 1569
25 *C.S.P., Scotland*, 2, 1175, 15 October 1569
26 *C.S.P., Scotland*, 3, 7, 9 November 1569
27 Cited by Frye, *Pens and Needles*, p. 51
28 *C.S.P., Scotland*, 5, 233, 30 July 1576
29 Labanoff, *Recueil des Lettres*, 4, p. 111, 20 February 1574
30 Labanoff, *Recueil des Lettres*, 4, p. 119, 10 March 1574
31 Labanoff, *Recueil des Lettres*, 4, pp. 159–60, 8 May 1574

32  Swain, *The Needlework of Mary, Queen of Scots*, pp. 82–3
33  Labanoff, *Recueil des Lettres*, 4, pp. 171–2, 9 June 1574
34  Sadler, *State Papers*, p. 180, 20 October 1584
35  Strickland, *Letters of Mary, Queen of Scots*, 2, p. 53
36  British Museum, MSS, Cotton, Caligula, C.III, f.231
37  Drummond, *History of Scotland*, pp. 263–5
38  Bath, *Emblems for a Queen*, pp. 147–157

## 9. RED PETTICOAT AND SLEEVES

1  Sadler, *State Papers and Letters*, p. 120
2  C.S.P., Scotland, 2, 953, 17 January 1569
3  Sadler, *State Papers and Letters*, p. 297
4  Lodge, *Portraits of Illustrious Personages*, p. 239
5  Mosely, *The History of the Castle, Priory and Town of Tutbury*, pp. 198–9
6  Sadler, *State Papers and Letters*, pp. 247–8
7  Sadler, *State Papers and Letters*, pp. 196, 247–8, 251–2
8  C.S.P., Scotland, 2, 971
9  Paulet, *Letter-Books*, p. 11, 27 April 1585
10  Howell, *A Complete Collection of State Trials*, p. 1164
11  Paulet, *Letter-Books*, p. 137
12  Paulet, *Letter-Books*, p. 97, September 1585
13  Paulet, *Letter-Books*, p. 107, 16 October 1585
14  Cited by Fraser, *Mary Queen of Scots*, p. 609
15  Labanoff, *Recueil des Lettres*, 6, p. 125
16  *National Archives*, SP 53/22, f.1.
17  Paulet, *Letter-Books*, p. 224, 14 July 1586
18  Paulet, *Letter-Books*, pp. 227–8
19  Labanoff, *Recueil des Lettres*, 6, p. 368
20  Paulet, *Letter-Books*, p. 299
21  Labanoff, *Recueil des Lettres*, 7, p. 38; cited by Fraser, *Mary, Queen of Scots*, p. 630
22  Further Reading: Lewis, *The Trial of Mary, Queen of Scots*
23  Lewis, *The Trial of Mary, Queen of Scots*, p. 32

24 Lewis, *The Trial of Mary, Queen of Scots*, p. 113
25 Strickland, *Life of Mary, Queen of Scots*, p. 431
26 Strickland, *Queens of Scotland*, 7, p. 428
27 Labanoff, *Recueil des Lettres*, 6, pp. 473–480
28 Paulet, *Letter-Books*, pp. 326–7,15 December 1586
29 Paulet, *Letter-Books*, pp. 359–60
30 Paulet, *Letter-Books*, pp. 361–2
31 Bourgoing, *Journal, The Tragedy of Fotheringhay*, p. 19
32 Lewis, *The Trial of Mary, Queen of Scots*, p. 27
33 Strickland, *Letters*, 2, p. 206
34 Paulet, *Letter-Books*, p. 318
35 Strickland, *Letters*, 2, p. 253
36 *C.S.P., Scotland*,9, 266, 8 February 1587
37 Labanoff, *Recueil des Lettres*, pp. 229–274
38 Wyngfield, *Account of the Execution of Mary, Queen of Scots*, pp. 14–29
39 Camden, *Annals*, p. 115; cited by Fraser, *Mary, Queen of Scots*, p. 676
40 Strickland, *Lives of Queens of England*, 7,14 February 1587
41 Strickland, *Letters*, 2, p. 206; cited by Stewart, *The Cradle King*, p. 91
42 Mackenzie, *Scottish Pageant*, p. 168
43 Strickland, *Queens of Scotland*, 7, p. 499; cited by Fraser, *Mary, Queen of Scots*, pp. 676–7
44 Pollard, *Tudor Tracts*, pp. 475–484
45 Swain, *The Needlework of Mary, Queen of Scots*, p. 91
46 Labanoff, *Recueil des Lettres*, 7, p. 243
47 Fraser, *Mary, Queen of Scots*, p. 690
48 National Library of Scotland, Adv. MS.54.1.1.

## 10. A BLACK DRESS AND WHITE VEIL

1 Melville, *Memoirs*, p. 37
2 Marcus, *Elizabeth 1*, p. 66

3  C.S.P., *Scotland*, 1, pp. 540–1
4  De Longh, *Mary of Hungary*, p. 202,
5  Alford, *Needlework as Art*, p. 167
6  C.S.P., *France*, Vol. I, p. 81
7  https://letterlocking.org; youtube.com, 'Letterlocking: Mary Queen of Scots' last letter, a spiral lock, England 1587', 30 March 2018
8  Fountain, *Mary, Queen of Drag?*, mqs.glasgow.ac.uk
9  Cited by Fraser, *Mary, Queen of Scots*, p. 631

# *Acknowledgements*

My thanks to all those who have been so generous with their time and their thoughts. Dr Alastair Mann, Senior Lecturer in the Department of History and Politics at the University of Stirling, for his sympathetic but robust monitoring of my first attempts at historical research; my early readers, Ewan Armstrong, Cathy Jeffries, Rosslyn Macphail and Ginnie Smith for feedback and encouragement; Nic, Adam and Darran for revamping my shed to make it a peaceful place to write; Tony Hunter our local postman for delivering all those books I had to purchase during lockdown; Christine Merchant for helping to translate Old French; Emma and Janet Richards at the local shop who kept me supplied with necessities; Vera Stewart for an article about Mary's embroidery; the historians Jane Dawson, Michael Pearce, Emily Wingfield, Naomi Tarrant and Prudence King for their insights; the curators Alison Rosie, the registrar at the National Register of Archives for Scotland, Lesley Smith at Tutbury Castle, Deborah Clarke and Emma Thompson of the Palace of Holyroodhouse, Helen Wyld, the Senior Curator of Historic Textiles, European Art and Design at National Museums Scotland and Elinor Vickers at Blairs Museum in Aberdeenshire for giving me their time and knowledge; Fiona Wemyss of the Wemyss School of Needlework for sharing her passion for historic embroidery and Michael Wemyss of Wemyss for his tour of Wemyss Castle: Jim Fraser, Professor of Forensic Science at the University of Strathclyde for his thoughts; Dr Susan Kay-Williams of the Royal School of Needlework and Jessica Jane Pile of Hand & Lock in London for discussing the

## Acknowledgements

history of their respective organisations; M.A. Katritzky for sending me her article on the embroideries of Mary and Bess of Hardwick; Oula Jones for all her help with editing; Janice Forsyth for sending me anything she thought might be useful for my research; Donna Macguire at the Scottish Catholic Archives for copying material for me; Eleanor Gordon for advice and help; Fingask Castle for arranging last minute accommodation; Sophy Dale for her help with the first draft; Laura Gladwin for her detailed editing; Fiona Woolf for information on the archive of her mother; Margaret Swain; and Winnie Herbstein and Josh Hall for helping with ideas for the book cover. Above all I would like to thank all those historians who have researched Mary, Queen of Scots' textiles and sixteenth century women's culture. This book could not have been written without their scholarship and pioneering research which so often goes unacknowledged, amongst them: Michael Bath, Yossana Croizat, Jane Arnold, Susan Frye, Maria Hayward, Mary Hazard, Sophia Jane Holroyd, Nicole LaBouff, Rosalind Marshall, Catherine Richardson, Margaret Swain, Susan Watkins and Santina Levey.

My gratitude to my continuously enthusiastic and encouraging agent, Jenny Brown at Jenny Brown Associates and to my ever-supportive editor Juliet Brooke and all her team, especially Louise Court and Irene Rolleston, at Sceptre of Hodder & Stoughton. Last but not least, love and thanks to my husband Charlie and our twins, Kim and Jamie, for allowing Mary to be part of our family for so long.

# Bibliography

Hundreds of books have been written about Mary, Queen of Scots, and it is impossible to list everything I have read or glanced through, many of which are out of print. This bibliography serves, I hope, to provide useful suggestions for further reading.

### PRIMARY SOURCES

*Accounts of the Lord High Treasurer of Scotland*, T. Dickson and others (eds), 12 vols. (Edinburgh: 1877–1916)

*Accounts and papers relating to Mary, Queen of Scots*, Camden Society, vol. 93 (London: 1867)

Bain, J., *The Hamilton Papers: Hamilton Letters and Papers, illustrating the Political Relations of England and Scotland in the Sixteenth Century*, General Register Office, 2 vols. (Edinburgh: 1890–92)

Bonaffe, E., *Inventaire des Meubles de Catherine de Médicis en 1589* (Paris: 1874)

Buchanan, G., *The History of Scotland*, ed. and trans. J. Aikman, 4 vols. (Glasgow: 1827)

Buchanan, G., *The Tyrannous Reign of Mary Stewart*, ed. and trans. W. A. Gatherer (Edinburgh: 1958)

Burton, J. H. and D. Masson (eds), *The Register of the Privy Council of Scotland*, Vol. 14 Ist Series Addenda A.D.1545–1625 (1891)

*Calendar of the Manuscripts of the Most Hon. Marquis of*

*Salisbury*, R.6, Hatfield House, Hertfordshire, Part i. (London: HMS, 1883)

*Calendar of State Papers Domestic*, Vols. 1, 2, 3, 7, 8

*Calendar of State Papers Relating to Scotland and Mary, Queen of Scots*, 1547–1603, J. Bain et al (eds), Vols. 1, 2, 5 (Edinburgh: 1898–1969)

Castiglione, B., *The Book of the Courtier* (1528) Digireads.com. Book

Chalmers, G., *The Life of Mary, Queen of Scots drawn from State Papers*, 2 vols. (London: John Murray, 1818)

Chalmers, R., *Domestic Annals of Scotland Vol. 1 Reign of Mary 1561–1567* (Edinburgh: 1861)

Cotgrave, R., *Dictionaries for translation of contemporary French terms* (London: 1611)

Clausse, C., *Comptes des Enfants de France pour L'Année 1551* (Paris: 1551), https:// www.gallca.bnf.fr, ark:/12148/btvb550133882

Dack, C., *The Trial, Execution and Death of Mary, Queen of Scots compiled from Original Documents* (Northampton: 1889)

De Pizan, C., *The Book of the City of Ladies* (London: Penguin Classics, 1999)

*A Diurnal of Remarkable Occurrents That Have Passed Within the Country of Scotland Since the Death of King James the Fourth Till the year 1575*, ed. T. Thomson, (Edinburgh: Bannatyne Club, 1833)

Duncan, W.J. (ed.), *Miscellaneous papers principally illustrative of events in the reigns of Queen Mary and James VI* (Maitland Club, 27, Glasgow, 1834)

Drummond, William, *History of Scotland*, Vol. IX 1547–1603, (London: 1655)

Erasmus, D., *De Civilitae Puerilium Libellus (A Handbook of Good Manners for Children)*, trans. Eleanor Merchant (London: Random House, 2008)

*Est Natura Hominum Nouitatis Auida: The Scottish Queens Buriall at Peterborough, Upon Tuesday Being Lammas Day,*

1587, (London: Printed by A. I[effes], for Edwarde Venge, and are to be sold at his shop without Bishops-gate [1589].)

Ellis, Sir H., *Original Letters, illustrative of English History* (London: Harding, Triphock and Lepard, 1825)

Fleming, D. H., *Mary, Queen of Scots: From Her Birth to her Flight into England: A Brief Biography* (London: Hodder and Stoughton, 1808)

Goring, R., *Scotland the Autobiography: 2,000 Years of Scottish History by Those Who Saw It* (New York: Overlook Press, 2008)

Hall, E., *Hall's Chronicles: containing the History of England, during the reign of Henry the Fourth, and the succeeding monarchs, to the end of the reign of Henry the Eighth* (London: 1809)

Hardwick Hall Inventory 1601, *Journal of the Furniture History Society*, vol. VII, 1971

Harrison, J., *Stirling Castle Palace: Archaeological and Historical Research 2004–2008, The Wardrobe Inventories of James V* (Edinburgh: Kirkdale Archaeology/ Historic Scotland, 2008)

*Hawthornden Manuscripts: original papers of William Drummond of Hawthornden and of his uncle, William Fowler, secretary to Queen Anne, consort to James VI* (1605–1710) National Library of Scotland, Mss. 2053–2067

Haynes, S., (ed.) *A collection of State Papers relating to the Affaires in the Reign of King Henry VIII, King Edward VI, Queen Mary and Queen Elizabeth from the Years 1542–1570* (London: 1740)

*Inventaires de la Royne Decosse, Douairiere de France*, ed. J. Robertson (Bannatyne Club, Edinburgh, 1863)

*Inventory of St. Machar's Cathedral 1436–1599*, Aberdeen University Special Collections, MS. 247

Keith, R., *History of the Affaires of Church and State in Scotland from the Beginning of the Reformation to the Year 1568* J.P. Lawson & C.J. Lyon (eds), 3 vols. (Edinburgh: Spottiswoode Society, 1844–50)

Knox, J., *The First Blast of the Trumpet against the Monstrous*

*Regiment of Women*, Edward Arber (ed.), (London: University College, 1878)

Knox, J., *The History of the Reformation of Religion in Scotland*, (Edinburgh: Blackie, 1840)

Labanoff, Prince Alexander, *Lettres, Instructions et Memoires de Marie Stuart* 6 Vols. (London: 1844)

Laing, D., *The Works of John Knox Vol II* (Edinburgh: James Thin)

Laing, M., *The Historie of Scotland, Vol II* (London, 1819)

Leslie, J., Bishop of Ross, A *Defence of the Honour of the Right High, Mighty and Noble Princess Mary, Queen of Scotland and Dowager of France* (Edinburgh: 1569)

Leslie, J., Bishop of Ross, *History of Scotland* (Edinburgh: 1578)

Lindsay of Piscottie, R., *The Histoire and Chronicles of Scotland*, E. J. G. Mackay (ed.), 3 vols. (Edinburgh: Scottish Text Society, 1899–1911)

Lodge, E., *Illustrations of British History, Biography and Manners, in the Reigns of Henry VIII, Mary, Elizabeth and James I, Exhibited in a Series of Original Papers*, 3 vols. (London: 1791)

Madden, F., *Privy Purse Expenses of the Princess Mary* (London: William Pickering, 1831)

*Miscellany of the Maitland Club, consisting of original papers and other documents illustrative of the history and literature of Scotland* (Maitland Club, Glasgow, 53, 1840; 58, 1843; 69, 1847)

Nau, C., *The History of Mary Stewart from the Murder of Riccio until her Flight into England*, J. Stevenson (ed.), (Edinburgh: William Paterson, 1883)

Marwick, J.B. (ed.) *Extracts from the Records of the Burgh of Edinburgh 1557–1571* (Edinburgh: Scottish Burgh Records Society, 1875)

Mackenzie, A. M., *Scottish Pageant* (Edinburgh and London: Oliver and Boyd, 1948)

Melville, Sir J., *Memoirs of his Own Life*, T. Thomson (ed.), (Edinburgh: Bannatyne Club 18, 1827)

Morris, J. (ed.), *The Letter-books of Sir Amias Paulet*, (London: Burns and Oates, 1874)

Pitcairns, R., *The Funeral of Mary, Queen of Scots: A Collection of Curious Tracts relating to the Burial of this Unfortunate Princess, Being Reprint of Rare Originals, Partly Transcriptions from Various Manuscripts* (Edinburgh: 1822)

*Resigtrum episcopatus Aberdonis*: Ecclesie catedrali abberdonensis regatta que extant in unum collect. Aberdeen Dioceses; Innes, Cosmo 1798–1874, Impressum Edinburgh (Constable)

*Selections from Unpublished Manuscripts in the College of Arms & the British Museum, illustrating the Reign of Mary, Queen of Scots 1543–1568*, J. Stevenson (ed.) (Maitland Club, 42, Glasgow, 1837)

Smith, A. J. R., *The Last Years of Mary, Queen of Scots: Documents from the Cecil Papers at Hatfield House* (Roxburghe Club, London, 1990)

Strickland, A., *Letters of Mary, Queen of Scots, and Documents connected with her personal History now first published*, 2 vols. (London: 1844)

Taylor, J., *The Needles Excellency: A New Boole Wherein are Divers Admirable Workes Wrought with the Needle* (London: James Boler, 1631)

Teulet, A., ed. *Lettres de Marie Stuart* (Maitland Club, Glasgow, 1908)

Thompson, T., *Collection of Inventories and other Records of the Royal Wardrobe* (Edinburgh: Bannatyne Club, 1815)

Wright, T., *Queen Elizabeth and Her Times, A Series of Original Letters*, 2 vols. (London: Henry Colburn, 1830)

MARY, QUEEN OF SCOTS: BIOGRAPHIES AND HISTORIES

Abbott, J., *Mary, Queen of Scots: Makers of History* (London and New York: Harper & Brothers, 1904)

Bingham, M., *Scotland under Mary Stuart* (London: Allen and Unwin, 1971)

## Bibliography

Bowen, J., *Mary, Queen of Scots* (London: Bodley Head Ltd, 1934)

Boynton, L., *Hardwick Hall Inventories of 1601*, London: Furniture History Society, 1971)

Cowan, I. B., *The Enigma of Mary, Queen of Scots* (Worthing: Littlehampton Book Services Ltd., 1987)

Doran, S., *Mary, Queen of Scots: An illustrated life* (London: British Library Publishing Division, 2007)

Fraser, A., *James VI of Scotland & King James I of England* (USA: Random House, 1974)

Fraser, A., *Mary, Queen of Scots* (Great Britain: Weidenfeld & Nicolson, 2015)

Graham, R., *An Accidental Tragedy: The Life of Mary, Queen of Scots* (Edinburgh: Birlinn Limited, 2008)

Guy, J., *My Heart is My Own: The Life of Mary, Queen of Scots* (London: Harper Perennial, 2004)

Hale, J., *Mary, Queen of Scots* (London: Viking, 1972)

Hosack, J., *Mary, Queen of Scots and her Accusers*, Vol I (Edinburgh and London: W. Blackwood and Sons, 1870–4)

Leader, J. D. *Mary, Queen of Scots in Captivity: A Narrative of Events* (Sheffield: Leader & Sons, 1880)

Lee, M., 'The Daughter of Debate; Mary, Queen of Scots after 400 years' in *Scottish Historical Review*, vol. 68, no. 185, Part 1 (Edinburgh: Edinburgh University Press, April 1989)

Lynch, M., (ed.) *Mary Stewart: A Queen in Three Kingdoms* (London: Wiley-Backwell, 1988)

Mackay, J., *In My End is My Beginning: A Life of Mary, Queen of Scots* (Edinburgh & London: Mainstream, 1999)

Marshall, R. K., *Mary, Queen of Scots: 'In My End is My Beginning'* (Edinburgh: NMS Enterprises Ltd., 2013)

Marshall, R. K., *Mary, Queen of Scots: Truth or Lies* (St Andrews: St Andrews Press, 2013)

Marshall, R. K., *Queen of Scots* (Edinburgh: NMS Enterprises Ltd., 1986)

MacNalty, Sir A., *Mary, Queen of Scots: The Daughter of Debate* (UK: Johnson Publications Ltd., 1971)

Merriman, M., 'Mary, Queen of France', *Innes Review*, 38 (1987)

Roderick, G., *An Accidental Tragedy: The Life of Mary, Queen of Scots* (Edinburgh: Birlinn Ltd., 2008)

Stoddard, J. T., *The Girlhood of Mary, Queen of Scots* (London: Hodder and Stoughton, 2015)

Strickland, A., *Life of Mary, Queen of Scots*, Vols. 1 and 2 (London: George Bell and Sons, 1903)

Strong, R., and J. T. Oman, *Mary, Queen of Scots* (London: Martin Secker & Warburg Ltd., 1972)

Walton, K. P., *Catholic Queen, Protestant Patriarchy: Mary, Queen of Scots, and the Politics of Gender and Religion* (London: Palgrave Macmillan, 2007)

Warnick, R. M., *Mary, Queen of Scots* (Oxford: Routledge, 2006)

Watkins, S., *Mary, Queen of Scots* (London: Thames and Hudson, 2001)

Weir, A., *Mary, Queen of Scots and the Murder of Lord Darnley* (London: Vintage, 2008)

Wormald J., *Mary, Queen of Scots: A Study in Failure* (1991) reprinted as *Mary, Queen of Scots: Politics, Passion and a Kingdom Lost* (Edinburgh: John Donald Publishing Ltd, 2001)

GENERAL TEXTS: SCOTLAND AND EUROPE

Blakeway, A., *Regency in Sixteenth-Century Scotland* (Edinburgh: Edinburgh University Press, 2015)

Brown, K. M., A. R. MacDonald, G. MacIntosh, R. J. Turner and Dr A. J. Mann, *The History of the Scottish Parliament: Volume 3: Parliament in Context, 1235–1717* (Edinburgh: Edinburgh University Press, 2010)

Brown, K., *Noble Power in Scotland from the Reformation to the Revolution* (Edinburgh: Edinburgh University Press, 2011)

Cameron, J., *James V: The Personal Rule, 1528–1542* (East Linton: Birlinn Ltd., 2011)

Cowan, I., *The Scottish Reformation: Church and Society in Sixteenth Century Scotland* (London: Weidenfeld & Nicolson, 1982)

Dawson, J., *Scotland Reformed, 1488–1587* (Oxford: Oxford University Press, 2007)
Devine, T., *Independence or Union: Scotland's Past and Scotland's Present* (London: Penguin Books, 2016)
Donaldson, G., *Scotland: The Making of a Kingdom, James V–James VII* (Edinburgh: Oliver & Boyd, 1978)
Dunbar, J. G., *Scottish Royal Palaces: The Architecture of the Royal Residences During the Late Medieval and Early Renaissance Periods* (Lothian: Tuckwell Press, 1999)
Elliott, J. H., *Europe Divided, 1559–1598* (USA: Wiley and Blackwell, 2000)
Elton, G. R., *Reformation Europe 1517–1559* (London: Harper and Rowe, 1963)
Ewan, E., and M. M. Meikle, *Women in Scotland c.1100–1750* (Edinburgh: Tuckwell Press, 1999)
Guy, J., *Elizabeth: The Forgotten Years* (UK: Penguin Random House, 2016)
Hale, J., *The Civilization of Europe in the Renaissance* (New York: Touchstone, 1994)
Keith, R., and J. P. Lawson (eds), *History of the Affairs of Church and State in Scotland from the Beginning of the Reformation to the Year 1568* (Edinburgh: Spottiswoode Society, 1844)
Koenigsberger, H. G., G. L. Mosse, G. Q. Bowler, *Europe in the Sixteenth Century* (Essex: Pearson Education Limited, 1989; Abingdon and New York: Routledge, 2013)
Lee, M., *James Stewart, Earl of Moray* (New York: Columbia University Press, 1953)
Lynch, M., *Scotland: A New History* (London: Pimlico, 1990)
Macougall, N., *An Antidote to the English: The Auld Alliance, 1293–1560* (Edinburgh: Tuckwell Press, 2011)
Macdougall, N., *James IV* (Edinburgh: John Donald Publishers Ltd., 2006)
McLennan, B., 'The Reformation in the Burgh of Aberdeen', *Northern Scotland,* Volume 2 (First Series) Issue 1 pp. 119–144 (Edinburgh: Edinburgh University Press)

Mair, C., *Stirling: The Royal Burgh* (Edinburgh: John Donald, 1990)

Matheson-Pollock, H., J. Paul and C. Fletcher (eds), *Queenship and Counsel in Early Modern Europe* (London: Palgrave Macmillan, 2018)

Mapstone, S., and J. Wood (eds), *The Rose and the Thistle: Essays on the Culture of Late Medieval and Renaissance Scotland* (Edinburgh: Tuckwell Press, 1998)

Merriman, M., *The Rough Wooings: Mary, Queen of Scots 1542–1551* (East Linton: Tuckwell Press, 2000)

Mitchison, R., *A History of Scotland* (London: Routledge, 1982)

Seward, D., *Prince of the Renaissance: The Life of François I* (London: Sphere Books, 1974)

Webb, C. L., 'The "Gude Regent"? A Diplomatic Perspective Upon the Earl of Moray, Mary, Queen of Scots and the Scottish Regency, 1567–1571', Thesis submitted for PhD Degree, University of St Andrews, 2003, http//hdl.handle.net/10023/459

Wormald, J., *Court, Kirk and Community, 1470–1625* (Edinburgh: Edinburgh University Press, 1981)

## 1: BIRDS, FLOWERS AND FRUIT AND OTHER EMBROIDERED MOTIFS

Anglo, S., *Spectacle, Pageantry and Early Tudor Policy* (Oxford: Clarendon Press, 1969)

Beck, T., *The Embroiderer's Story: Needlework from the Renaissance to the Present Day* (Exeter: David & Charles, 1995)

Bond, M. S., *Dressing up the Scottish Court 1543–1553* (Woodbridge: The Boydell Press, 2019)

Campbell, T., 'Tapestry Quality in Tudor England: Problems of Terminology', *Studies in Decorative Arts*, Vol 3, No. 1 [FALL WINTER 1995–1996] pp. 29–50, University of Chicago Press, https://www.jstor.org/stable/40662554

Colthorpe, K. M., 'The Elizabethan Court Day by Day', 1568, Folgerpedia.folger.edu

Duits, R., *Gold Brocade and Renaissance Painting: A Study in Material Culture* (London: Pindar Press, 2008)

Eastwood, A.L., 'In the Shadow of the Queen: The Early English Epithalamium and the Female Monarch', *Early Modern Literary Studies*, Vol. 16, No. 3, 2013

Frieda, L., *Catherine de Medici: A Biography* (London: Weidenfeld & Nicolson, 2003)

Guidicini, G., *Triumphal Entries and Festivals in Early Modern Scotland: Performing Spaces,* European Festival Studies: 1450–1700 (Taylor and Francis Group: Oxford, 2017)

Gosman, M., A. MacDonald, A. Vanderjagt, *Princes and Princely Culture 1450–1650 Vol. 1* (Netherlands: Brill, 2005)

Jardine, L., *Worldly Goods: A New History of the Renaissance* (London: Macmillan, 1996)

Knecht, R. J., *Catherine de Medici* (Essex: Addison Wesley Longman Limited, 1998)

Jones, A. R. and P. Stallybrass, *Renaissance Clothing and the Materials of Memory* (Cambridge: Cambridge University Press, 2000)

Lazzaro, C., *The Italian Renaissance Garden: From the Conventions of Planting, Design and Ornament to the Grand Gardens of Sixteenth-Century Central Italy* (London: Yale University Press, 1990)

Le Dantec, D., *Reading the French Garden: Story and History* (London: MIT Press, 1993)

Hale, J., *The Civilization of Europe in the Renaissance* (New York: Touchstone, 1994)

Hayward, M., *Dress at the Court of Henry VIII* (London and New York: Routledge, 2007)

Hayward, M., 'In the Eye of the Beholder: "Seeing" Textiles in the Early Modern Interior', *Textile History*, 47: 1, 27–42, DOI: 10.1080/00404969.2016.1144701

Hayward, M., 'Repositories of Splendour: Henry VIII's Wardrobe of the Robes and Beds', *Textile History*, 29:2, 134–156, DOI: 10:1179/004049698793710742

McGlynn, S. and E. Woodacre, (eds), *The Image and Perception of Monarchy in Medieval and Early Modern Europe* (Cambridge: Cambridge Scholar Publishing, 2014)

Murdoch, T., *Treasures of the Royal Courts: Tudors, Stuarts & The Russian Tsars* (London: V&A Publishing, 2013)

Muzzarelli, M. G. 'Reconciling the Privilege of a Few with the Common Good: Sumptuary Laws in Medieval and Early Modern Europe', *Journal of Medieval and Early Modern Studies, Vol 39, No 3.*, pp. 597–617 (2009)

Starkey, D. (ed.), *The Inventory of King Henry VIII, Vol II* (London: Harvey Miller Publishers for the Society of Antiquaries of London, 2012)

Richardson, C. and T. Hamling, 'Ways of Seeing Early Modern Decorative Textiles', *Textile History*, 47:1, 4–26, DOI: 10: 1080/00404969.2016.1144672

Royal Scottish Museum, *French Connection, Scotland and the Arts of France* (Edinburgh: Her Majesty's Stationery Office, 1985)

Stoddard, J. T., *The Girlhood of Mary, Queen of Scots* (London: Hodder and Stoughton, 2015)

Strong, R., *Art and Power: Renaissance Festivals 1450–1650* (Martlesham: Boydell & Brewer, 1973)

Thomas, A., *Glory and Honour: The Renaissance in Scotland* (Edinburgh: Birlinn Ltd., 2013)

Thomas, A., *Princelie Majestie: The Court of James V of Scotland, 1528–1542* (Edinburgh: John Donald Publishing Ltd., 2005)

Seward, D., *Prince of the Renaissance: The Life of François I* (London: Sphere Books, 1974)

Van Scoy, V., C. Weber, J. Alvarotto, 'The Marriage of Mary, Queen of Scots and the Dauphin', *The Scottish Historical Review*, Vol.31, No.111, Part 1 April 1952) pp.41–48 (Edinburgh: Edinburgh University Press 1952)

## 2: THE FETTERNEAR BANNER

Cowan, I., *The Scottish Reformation: Church and Society in Sixteenth Century Scotland* (London: Weidenfeld & Nicolson, 1982)

Davidson, P., 'The Entry of Mary Stewart into Edinburgh 1561, and Other Ambiguities', *Renaissance Studies*, Vol. 9, No. 4, France in the English and French Theatre of the Renaissance, December 1995, pp. 416–429

MacDonald, A. A., 'The Entry of Mary Stewart into Edinburgh: An Ambiguous Triumph', *The Innes Review*, Volume XLII, No 2, Autumn 1991, 101–110, *Renaissance Studies*, 9 (1995)

Dawson, J., *John Knox* (New Haven and London: Yale University Press, 2016)

Dawson, J., *Scotland Reformed, 1488–1587* (Oxford: Oxford University Press, 2007)

Elton, G. R., *Reformation Europe 1517–1559* (London: Harper and Rowe, 1963)

Forbes, A. L., *Trials and Triumphs, The Gordons of Huntly in Scotland* (Edinburgh: John Donald Publishers Ltd., 2012)

Reid, H., *Reformation: The Dangerous Birth of the Modern World* (Edinburgh: Saint Andrew Press, 2009)

McRoberts, D., 'The Fetternear Banner', *Innes Review*, Edinburgh University Press, Volume 7, Issue 2, 1956

McRoberts, D., 'Material Destruction Caused by the Scottish Reformation', *Innes Review*, 10 (Edinburgh: Edinburgh University Press, 1959)

Mc Roberts, D. and S. M. Holmes, *Lost Interiors: The Furnishings of Scottish Churches in the Late Middle Ages* (Scotland: Scottish Catholic Historical Association, 2012)

Walton, K. P., *Catholic Queen, Protestant Patriarchy: Mary, Queen of Scots and the Politics of Gender and Religion* (London: Palgrave Macmillan, 2007)

## 3: TWO DOLLS' DRESSES MADE OF GREY DAMASK THREADED IN GOLD

Andrea, B., J. D. Campbell, A. M. Poska, 'Early Modern Women: An Interdisciplinary Journal', Vol. 15, No. 2, Spring 2021 (Arizona Center for Medieval and Renaissance Studies)

Beer, M., 'Practices and Performances of queenship: Catherine of Aragon and Margaret Tudor, 1503-1533'. Graduate dissertation, University of Illinois and Urbana Champaign, 2014, http://hdl.handle.net/2142/49812

Brown, K., *Noble Power in Scotland from the Reformation to the Revolution* (Edinburgh: Edinburgh University Press, 2011)

Donaldson, G. *All the Queen's Men: Power and Politics in Mary Stewart's Scotland* (London: HarperCollins, 1983)

Croizat, Y. C., '"Living Dolls": François 1$^{er}$ Dresses his Women' *Renaissance Quarterly*, Renaissance Society of America, Volume 60, Number 1, Spring 2007, pp. 94–130 (University of Chicago Press on behalf of the Renaissance Society of America)

Cruz, A. J. and M. Suzuki, *The Rule of Women in Early Modern Europe* (Illinois: University of Illinois Press, 2009)

Frye, S., and K. Robertson, *Maids and Mistresses, Cousins and Queens: Women's Alliances in Early Modern England* (Oxford: Oxford University Press, 1999)

Marshall, R. K., *Queen Mary's Women: Female Friends, Family, Servants and Enemies of Mary, Queen of Scots* (Edinburgh: John Donald, 2006)

Marshall, R. K., *Virgins and Viragos: A History of Women in Scotland from 1080–1980* (London: Collins, 1983)

Matheson-Pollock, H., J. Paul,. and C. Fletcher (eds), *Queenship and Counsel in Early Modern Europe* (London: Palgrave Macmillan, 2018)

Mazzola, E., *Women's Wealth and Women's Writing in Early Modern England: 'Little Legacies' and the Materials of Motherhood* (London: Routledge, 2009)

Payne, M., 'Pandora's Box: Replica of a 16th century Extant Fashion Doll' https://academia.edu, Tudorosities, 2013

Pearce, M., 'Edinburgh Castle: The Dolls of Mary, Queen of Scots, Edinburgh Castle Research', *A Report for Historic Environment Scotland,* 2017

### 4: A GREAT MOURNING GOWN OF BLACK

Arnold, J., *Queen Elizabeth's Wardrobe Unlock'd,* (London: Routledge, 1988)

Bingham, C., *Darnley: A Life of Henry Stuart, Lord Darnley, Consort of Mary, Queen of Scots* (Great Britain: Weidenfeld & Nicolson, 1995)

Cleary, M., 'Fabricating an Image: "How Mary Stuart, Isabella d' Este and Other Women of the Renaissance Used Dress to Assert Agency"', *Creative Matter,* Art History, Skidmore College, 2016

Greenblatt, S., *Renaissance Self-Fashioning: From More to Shakespeare* (Chicago: University of Chicago Press, 2005)

Griffey, E. (ed.), *Sartorial Politics in Early Modern Europe: Fashioning Women* (Amsterdam: Amsterdam University Press, 2019)

Hollander, A., *Seeing Through Clothes* (London: University of California Press, 1993)

Jones, A. R. and P. Stallybrass, *Renaissance Clothing and the Materials of Memory* (Cambridge: Cambridge University Press, 2000)

Lynn, E., *Tudor Textiles* (London and New Haven: Yale University Press, 2020)

Mikhaila, N., and J. Malcolm-Davies, *The Tudor Tailor: Reconstructing Sixteenth-Century Dress* (London: Batsford, 2006)

Reynolds, A., *In Fine Style: the Art of Tudor and Stuart Fashion* (London: Royal Collection Trust, 2013)

Richardson, C., *Clothing Culture 1350–1650 (The History of Retailing and Consumption* (Oxford: Routledge, 2016)

Rublack, U., *Dressing Up. Cultural Identity in Renaissance Europe* (Oxford: Oxford University Press, 2011)

Rush, S., 'French Fashion in Sixteenth-Century Scotland: The 1539 Inventory of James V's Wardrobe', *Furniture History*, Vol 42 (2006)

Squire, G., *Dress, Art and Society: 1560–1970* (London: Studio Vista, 1974)

Stevenson, J., 'Text and Textiles: Self-presentation among the Elite in Renaissance England', *Journal of the Northern Renaissance*, Issue 3 (2011)

Staniland, K., *Medieval Craftsmen: Embroiderers* (London: British Museum Press, 1991)

Steuart, A. Francis, *Seignure Davie: A Sketch Life of David Riccio* (London and Edinburgh: Sands & Co, 1922)

Welch, E., *Fashioning the Early Modern: Dress, Textiles and Innovation in Europe 1500–1800* (York: Pasold Studies in Textile History, 2017)

## 5: A SUIT OF SAVAGE ATTIRE

Anglo, S., *Spectacle, Pageantry and Early Tudor Policy* (Oxford: Clarendon Press, 1969)

Bath, M., '"Rare shewes and singular inventions": The Stirling Baptism of Prince Henry', *Journal of the Northern Renaissance*, Issue 4 (2012)

Carpenter, S., 'Performing Diplomacies: the 1560s Court Entertainments of Mary, Queen of Scots', *Scottish Historical Review*, Vol. 82, Issue 2

Evans, H. A., *English Masques* (London: Blackie & Son Limited, 1897)

Klein. L. M., 'Your Humble Handmaiden: Elizabethan Gifts of Needlework', *Renaissance Quarterly*, Vol. 50, No. 2 (Summer, 1997)

Lynch, M., 'Queen Mary's Triumph: The Baptismal Celebrations at Stirling in December 1566', *The Scottish Historical Review* Vol. 69, No 187, Part 1 (Apr. 1990, pp 1–21)

Nicoll, A., *Stuart Masques and the Renaissance Stage* (New York: Benjamin Blom Inc., 1968)

Pearce, Michael, 'Beds of "Chapel" Form in Sixteenth-Century Scottish Inventories: The Worst Sort of Bed', *Regional Furniture*, XXVII, 2013

Tweedie, D., *David Rizzio & Mary, Queen of Scots: Murder at Holyrood* (Stroud: Sutton Publishing, 2006)

Stendhall, R., *Mary, Queen of Scots' Downfall: The Life and Murder of Lord Darnley* (South Yorkshire: Pen & Sword History, 2017)

## 6: THREE OF THE FAIREST

Bath, M., M. Jones, 'Placardes and Bills and Ticquettes of Defamation: Queen Mary, the Mermaid and the Hare', *The Journal of the Warburg and Courtauld Institutes*, Vol. 78 (2015) pp. 223–246. htts://www. j.stor/stable/26321955

Gore-Browne, R., *Lord Bothwell: A Study of the Life, Character and Times of James Hepburn, 4th Earl of Bothwell* (London: Collins, 1937)

Heal, F., *The Power of Gift Exchange in Early Modern England*, (Oxford: Oxford University Press, 2014)

Mann, A. (2006). 'The Scottish Parliaments: the role of ritual and procession in the pre-1707 parliament and the new parliament of 1999' in Crewe, E. and M. Muller M (eds.), *Rituals in Parliaments: Political, Anthropological and Historical Perspectives on Europe and the United States*, pp. 135–158. (Frankfurt am Main: Peter Lang), https://www.peterang.com/view/product/56030?tab=toc&format=PBK and http://hdl.handle.net/1893/24799

Small, J., *Queen Mary at Jedburgh* (Edinburgh: Society of Antiquaries of Scotland, 1881)

Weir, A., *Mary, Queen of Scots and the Murder of Lord Darnley* (London: Vintage, 2008)

Williams, K., *Rival Queens: The Betrayal of Mary, Queen of Scots* (London: Hutchinson, 2018)

*Bibliography*

### 7: A DOZEN AND A HALF LITTLE FLOWERS PAINTED ON CANVAS

Armstrong Davidson, M. H., *The Casket Letters: A Solution to the Mystery of Mary, Queen of Scots and the Murder of Lord Darnley* (London: Vision Press, 1965)

Begg, J., *The Secrets of my Prison-House* (Kinross: George Barnet and London: John Haddon & Co., 1901)

Cheetham, J. K., *On the Trail of Mary, Queen of Scots: The Captive Years* (Edinburgh: Luath Press, 1999)

Donaldson, G., *The First Trial of Mary, Queen of Scots* (New York: Stein & Day, 1969)

Holmes, P. J., 'Mary Stewart in England (1900)', *Innes Review*, 38, (Edinburgh: University of Edinburgh Press, 1987)

MacRobert, A. E., *Mary, Queen of Scots and the Casket letters* (London: I.B. Tauris, 2002)

Mosley, O., *History of the Castle, Priory, and Town of Tutbury in the County of Stafford* (London: Simpkin and Marshall, 1832)

Pennecuick, A., *A History of the Blue Blanket or Crafts-men's Banner* (Edinburgh: Thomas Turnbull, 1852)

Perry, M., *Elizabeth I: The Word of a Prince* (London: The Folio Society, 1990)

### 8: A CATTE

Alford, M., *Needlework as Art* (London: Sampson Low, Marston, Searle, and Rivington, 1886)

Antrobus, M. S., *Needlework Through the Ages* (London: Hodder & Stoughton, 1928)

Bath, M., *Emblems for a Queen: The Needlework of Mary, Queen of Scots* (London: Archetype Publications Ltd, 2008)

Bath, M., *Emblems of Scotland* (Leiden Boston: Brill Rodpi, 2018)

Bath, M., '"Rare shewes and singular inventions": The Stirling Baptism of Prince Henry', *Journal of the Northern Renaissance*, Issue 4 (2012)

## Bibliography

Bath, M., *Speaking Pictures: English Emblem Books and Renaissance Culture* (London: Pindar Press, 1994)

Beck, T., *The Embroiderer's Story: Needlework from the Renaissance to the Present Day* (Exeter: David & Charles, 1995)

Bell, S. G., *The Lost Tapestries of the City of Ladies: Christine de Pizan's Renaissance Legacy* (London: University of California Press, 2004)

Breeze, D. J., *A Queen's Progress* (London: HMSO, 1987)

Digby, G. W., *Elizabethan Embroidery* (London: Faber and Faber, 1963)

Bath, M., *Emblems of Scotland* (Leiden Boston: Brill Rodpi, 2018)

Durant, D., *Bess of Hardwick: Portrait of an Elizabethan Dynast* (London: Peter Owen, 1978)

Ellis, M., 'The Hardwick Hall Wall Hanging: An Unusual Collaboration in English Sixteenth Century' *Embroidery Renaissance Studies* 10 (June 1996) pp. 280–300

Frye, S., *Pens and Needles: Women's Textualities in Early Modern Europe* (Philadelphia: University of Pennsylvania Press, 2010)

Gostelow, M., *The Art of Embroidery* (New York: Dutton, 1979)

Hazard, M. E., *Elizabethan Silent Language* (Lincoln: University of Nebraska Press, 2000)

Holroyd, S. J., *Embroidered Rhetoric: The Social, Religious and Political Functions of Elite Women's Needlework c.1560–1630* (Warwick: University of Warwick, 2002)

Jourdain, M., *The History of English Secular Embroidery* (New York: E.P. Dutton and Company, 1912)

Katritzky, M. A., *Virtuous Needleworkers, Vicious Apes: the Embroideries of Mary, Queen of Scots and Bess of Hardwick*, 2017, https://www.oro.oen.ac.uk Item: 49596

LaBouff, Nicole, 'Embroidery and Information Management: The Needlework of Mary, Queen of Scots and Bess of Hardwick Reconsidered', *Huntington Library Quarterly*,

Volume 81, Number 3, Autumn 2018, published by the University of California Press D1. https//doi.org/10.1353/hlq.2018.0014

Levey, S. M., *The Embroideries of Hardwick Hall: A Catalogue* (London: National Trust Books, 2007)

Levey, S. M., *An Elizabethan Inheritance: The Hardwick Hall Textiles* (London: National Trust Books, 1988)

National Trust, *The Oxburgh Hangings* (London: The National Trust, 1989)

Nevinson, J. L., *Catalogue of English Domestic Embroidery* (London: V&A Publications, 1950)

Swain, M., *Scottish Embroidery: Medieval to Modern* (London: Batsford Ltd., 1986)

Swain, M., *Tapestries and Textiles at the Palace of Holyroodhouse in the Royal Collection* (London: Stationery Office Books, 1988)

Swain, M., *Embroidered Stuart Pictures* (London: Shire Publications, 1990)

Swain, M., *Figures on Fabric* (London: A & C Black, 1980)

Swain, M., *Historical Needlework: A Study on Influences in Scotland and Northern England* (London: Barrie & Jenkins, 1970)

Swain, M., *Tapestries and Textiles at the Palace of Holyroodhouse in the Royal Collection* (London: Stationery Office Books, 1988)

Williams, N., *A Tudor Tragedy: Thomas Howard Fourth Duke of Norfolk* (London: Barrie and Jenkins, 1964)

Williams, N., *Bess of Hardwick* (London: Longmans Green and Co., 1959)

Wardle, P., 'The Embroideries of Mary, Queen of Scots: Notes on a French Background', *Bulletin of the Needle and Bobbin Club*, 64 (1981)

Zulueta, F. de., *Embroideries by Mary Stuart and Elizabeth Talbot at Oxburgh Hall, Norfolk* (Oxford: Oxford University Press, 1923)

*Bibliography*

### 9: A RED PETTICOAT AND SLEEVES

Bede, C., *Fotheringhay and Mary, Queen of Scots* (London: Simkin, Marshall and Co., 1887)

Britton, J., *History and Antiquities of Peterborough Cathedral* (London: Longman, 1828)

Cooper, J., *The Queen's Agent: Francis Walsingham at the Court of Elizabeth I* (London: Faber & Faber, 2011)

Cowan, S., *The Last Days of Mary Stuart: And the Journal of Bourgoyne Her Physician* (London: George Bell & Son, 1907)

Hutchison, R., *Elizabeth's Spy Master* (London: Weidenfeld & Nicholson, 2006)

Weir, A., *Mary, Queen of Scots and the Murder of Lord Darnley* (London: Vintage, 2008)

Lewis, J. E., (ed.), *The Trial of Mary, Queen of Scots: A Brief History with Documents* (Boston & New York: Bedford St Martins, 1999)

Prescott-Innes, R. and R. Pitcairn (eds), *The funeral of Mary, Queen of Scots: A Collection of Curious Tracts, relating to the Burial of this Unfortunate Princess* (Edinburgh: Privately printed, 1890)

Weir, A., *Mary, Queen of Scots and the Murder of Lord Darnley* (London: Vintage, 2008)

### 10: A BLACK DRESS AND WHITE VEIL

'Mary Queen of Scots' project and 'In Search of Mary Queen of Scots' blog, University of Glasgow, https://qs.glasgw.ac.uk

Gristwood, S., *Arabella: England's Lost Queen* (Boston: Houghton Mifflin Harcourt, 2003)

Lewis, J. E., *Mary, Queen of Scots: Romance and Nation* (London: Routledge, 1998)

Ponsonby, M., *Faded and Threadbare Historic Textiles and their Role in Houses Open to the Public* (Farnham: Ashgate, 2015)

*Bibliography*

Smailes, H. and D. Thomson, *The Queen's Image: A Celebration of Mary, Queen of Scots* (Edinburgh: National Galleries of Scotland, 1987)

Swain, M., 'The Lochleven and Linlithgow Hangings', PSAS, 124, *Society of Antiquaries of Scotland* (Edinburgh: 1994)

# Index

A *'Mary Stuart' Waitress (Thoughts Afar)* (Lavery) 333
*Abbott, The* (Scott) 331–2
Accounts of the Lord High Treasurer of Scotland 17–18
Alexandra, Queen 333
Andrew, Prince 118
Anne of Brittany 104, 105
Anne of Denmark 125–6
Anne, Queen 318
*Annunciation, The* (Grein) 170
Argyll, Lord 229
Arran, Earl of 19, 85, 191
Arthur, Thomas 23
Asteane, Margaret 167–8

Babington, Anthony 294, 297–8, 299
Babington plot 294–9
Bannockburn, Battle of 53
Bath, Michael 264, 266, 269
Beaton, James 252, 274, 277, 279–80, 292, 303
Beaton, Mary
  in France 8
  at Mary's royal court 86
Beaune, Renaud de 315
Belon, Pierre 262
Bess of Hardwick 243–4, 245–6, 247, 249, 250, 252–8, 259, 260, 261–2, 265–6, 267, 270, 278–80, 281–2, 284
Blackadder, William 187
Blairs Museum 73–4, 321

Blue Blanket 208–9
*Boke Named the Governor, The* (Elyot) 11
Boleyn, Anne 102, 106, 158, 222
Bond of Association 291
*Book of the City of Ladies, The* (de Pizan) 107, 250, 251
Boorde, Andrew 127–8
Borgia, Lucrezia 122
Bothwell, Lord
  relationship with Mary 176–7, 184, 189–90, 193–4
  and murder of Lord Darnley 183, 185–6, 187–8, 189, 193, 212, 237, 238–9, 240
  holds Mary captive 194–6
  marriage to Mary 197–200
  faces rebellion 199–202
  death of 202
  mummified corpse found 203
Brantôme, Pierre de 32
Buchanan, George 42–3, 87–8, 172, 173, 188, 239, 261, 282
Byrne, Alexandra 343
cabinet of curiosities 94–6

Calvin, John 51, 58–9, 61
Camden, William 314
Carberry Hill, Battle of 200–1, 203–4
Carbonnier, Nicholas 111
care of clothing 124–5
Carew, Thomas 151–2
Carpenter, Sarah 30
Carwood, John 111

391

# Index

Carwood, Margaret 184
Cassilis, Earl of 234
Castiglione, Baldassare 11, 129
Catherine of Aragon 26–7, 102,
　　103, 105–6, 127, 158, 164,
　　165–6, 167, 221–2, 316
Catherine de' Medici
　　and Mary in France 8
　　marriage to Henri II 25, 32–3,
　　　　101
　　inventory after death 36–7
　　and religious conflict in France
　　　　44
　　death of François 45, 46
　　sends dolls to Elizabeth I 81–2
　　use of women as informers 88
　　and cabinet of curiosities 95
　　library of 105
　　clothing of 129
　　children of 164
　　tries to buy Mary's jewellery 227
　　and Mary's arrival in England
　　　　231
　　and Mary's embroideries 255
Catherine of Sweden 83
Cavendish, Elizabeth 278–9, 281
Cavendish, Sir William 243, 258
Cawood, Amos 312–13
Cecil, Sir William 13, 44, 90, 143,
　　153, 181, 182, 193, 219, 231,
　　234, 236–7, 260, 271, 282,
　　291, 292, 295–6, 297, 298,
　　301–2, 306, 307, 313, 314,
　　318, 340, 345
Cecilia of Sweden 128
Chaney, Lawrence 344
Charles II 135
Charles V 8, 19–20, 132, 329
Charles VI 80
Charles VIII 11
Charles IX (King of France) 46
Charles IX (King of Sweden) 83
Charles, Prince 117
Chartley Manor 289, 300

Chaseabout Raid 145, 146, 160,
　　177
Chastelard, Pierre de Bocosel de
　　134
Chenonceau 34, 46–7
Chicago, Judy 341–2
childbirth 165–7
Chiuri, Maria Grazia 346–8
Christina de Holstein-Gottorp 83
Clarke, Deborah 91, 92, 93, 94, 267
Claude de Valois 43
Clouet, François 46, 323
*Coelum Britannicum* (Carew)
　　151–2
colours in textiles 127–30
Compiegne, Jehan de 111
Cook, Ashley 342
Cooke, Isabelle 225
Corrichie, Battle of 69, 145, 171
Council of Trent 67
Cranach the Elder, Lucas 65
Croizat-Glazer, Yassana 80
*Crown, The* 119
Curle, Elizabeth 308, 311, 321,
　　322, 323
Curle, Gilbert 296, 299–300, 302,
　　305

Dalgleish, George 238–9
Danjou, Pierre 37
Darnley, Charles 204, 278–9, 281
Darnley, Lord
　　early relationship with Mary
　　　　136–42
　　marriage to Mary 143–5, 155,
　　　　159–60, 174, 179–80
　　and plot against Rizzio 160, 161
　　and Catholic faith 167
　　murder of 180–9, 192–3,
　　　　203–5, 232, 238–41
　　skull found 203
　　painting of 203–4
　　in Mary's embroidery 263
Davison, William 306, 314

*De Civiliatae Morum Puerilium* (Erasmus) 11
Declaration of Arbroath 15
della Casa, Giovanni 11
*Devises Heroïques* (Paradin) 186
Diana, Princess 116, 117
Diane de Poitiers 33–4, 44, 128
dolls 77–84
Don Carlos 46, 135, 136, 138
Don Juan 237
Douglas, Gavin 55
Douglas, George 225, 228, 258
Douglas, Margaret 102, 106, 136, 141
Douglas, Willie 227–8, 258
*Dress and Décor in Medieval and Renaissance Scotland* (study day) 30–1
Drummond, William 283
Drury, Sir Drew 304, 309
Drury, William 193, 195, 198, 210
Dumbarton 19
*Dyetary of Health, A* (Boorde) 127–8

Edinburgh, Treaty of 45, 59
Edward II 53
Edward III 113
Edward VI 6–7, 21–2, 61, 164
Edward VIII 225
Eleanor of Castile 127
Elisabeth de Valois 40, 44, 81, 101
Elizabeth I
  coronation of 31
  and Mary's claim to English throne 44
  and John Knox 60
  religious policy 73
  gifts of dolls 81–2
  attempted first meeting with Mary 90–1
  ill with smallpox 97
  health of 99–100, 128
  and death of mother 102
  imprisoned in Tower of London 103
  clothing of 125, 126, 129
  and Earl of Leicester 135–6, 236
  and marriage of Lord Darnley and Mary 136, 140–2
  masque for meeting Mary 153–4
  symbol of 158
  and murder of Lord Darnley 184–5
  and Mary's captivity in Lochleven Castle 211–12, 213, 227, 228
  offers to be Prince James' custodian 213–14
  embroidery skills 223–4
  and Mary in England 232, 233, 234–6, 240–1, 250–1, 258–60, 281–2, 289
  and possible marriage between Mary and the Duke of Norfolk 272, 273–4
  and Ridolfi Plot 276–7
  and embroidery gifts from Mary 279–81
  approves of Bond of Association 291
  hesitation over Mary's execution 302–3, 304–5, 306
  reaction to Mary's execution 314, 315
  death of 317–18
  portraits of 324–8
Elizabeth II 100, 119
Elizabeth of York 101, 165, 224
Elyot, Sir Thomas 11
*Emblems for a Queen* (Bath) 264
embroidery 31–9, 109–12, 113–19, 219–25, 245, 246–9, 250–71, 272–3, 279–81, 283–4, 334, 336, 338, 345–8
entertainments in court 149–55

## Index

Erasmus, Desiderius 11
Eric XIV 135
Erskine, John 168
Essex, Earl of 289
Ettamol, Paris 344

Faerno, Gabriele 268
Ferguson, Sarah 118
Ferrerio, Giovanni 264
Fetternear banner 55–7
Field of the Cloth of Gold 122
*First Book of Discipline, The*
   (Knox *et al.*) 71–2
*First Blast of the Trumpet*
   *Against the Monstrous*
   *Regiment of Women, The*
   (Knox) 60, 107–8
Fleming, Margaret 168
Fleming, Mary
   in France 8
   at Mary's royal court 86
Fletcher, Henry 231
Flockhart, Helen 342
Flodden, Battle of 6, 22, 84
Fontainebleau 25–6
Fotheringhay Castle 300, 308–9, 315–16
Foyser 150
France
   Mary, Queen of Scots in 8–9, 19, 25, 29, 33–4, 38–41, 102
   and textiles 19–20, 27–8
   and Mary's claim to English throne 43–4
   religious conflict in 44–5, 154, 277
François I 81
   and marriage of Madeleine de Valois 22, 23, 24
   meeting with Henry VIII 27, 122–3
   use of women as informers 88
   and cabinet of curiosities 95
   dressed for a masque 155

François II
   marriage to Mary, Queen of Scots 8, 37, 41–3
   childhood of 39, 40
   as king of France 44–5
   death of 45–6, 70, 82
   in Mary's embroidery 263, 273
Fraser, Jim 181–2
Frederick II 201–2
Frye, Susan 253

garden design 34–6
Geddie, James 150
George II 100
Gessner, Conrad 261–2, 263, 264, 268, 269
Gifford, Gilbert 295–6, 297, 298
Glasgow Cathedral 50–1, 52
Glasgow University 338–9
Gordon, George (Earl of Huntly) 53, 65, 68–70, 71, 145–6, 171
Gordon, Jean 196
Gordon, John 69
*Great Ladies* (Chicago) 341–2
Grein, Hans Baldung 170
Guidicini, Giovanna 30–1

Hampton Court 29
Hand & Lock 114–15, 116, 119
Hardwick Hall 243–9, 253, 284
Harry, Prince 119
Haynes, Mr 21
Hayward, Maria 30
Henri II 8, 9, 19–20, 25, 32, 40, 44, 59, 70, 82, 264
Henri III 308, 318
Henry IV 80–1
Henry VII 318–20
Henry VIII
   subdues Scotland 7–8
   love of textiles 12, 20–1, 26–7
   meeting with François I 27, 122–3

religious policy 73
tailors for 113
clothing of 125, 126, 129
meeting with Charles V 132
Hilliard, Nicholas 323, 324
Holbein the Younger, Hans 324
Holyroodhouse, the Palace of
    91–6, 143, 208, 209–10, 267,
    333, 334, 335
Howard, Thomas 102, 271–4,
    275–6
Hubert, Nicholas 188

Ibgrave, William 111
*Icones Animalium* (Gessner) 262
*Icones Animalium Aquaticum*
    (Gessner) 262
*Icones Avian* (Gessner) 262
*Il Cortegiano* (Castiglione) 11,
    126
*Il Galateo, Overo de' Costumi*
    (della Casa) 11
'In my End is My Beginning': The
    Memorialisation and
    Cultural Afterlife of Mary,
    Queen of Scots' 338–9
Inchmahome 1, 7
Inglis, James 215
Isabeau of Bavaria 80
Isabella d' Este 81, 103, 122
Isabella de Valois 80

James I/VI
    takes joint crown 16, 317–18
    birth of 167–9
    baptism of 169–75
    last visit from Mary 194
    depiction in *The Memorial of
        Lord Darnley* 204–5
    as political pawn 213–14
    declared king of Scotland
        215–16
    estrangement from Mary
        282–4, 298–9

rejects proposal for joint sover-
    eignty 293
signs treaty with England 298
reaction to Mary's execution
    314–15
James II/VII 318
James III 208
James IV 14, 15, 29–30, 56, 87,
    105, 106, 132, 149, 165
James V 250, 264
    death of 5
    at Battle of Solway Moss 5–6
    inspired by Renaissance 14
    marriage to Madeleine de
        Valois 22, 23–4, 126
    on spending spree in France 22–3
    marriage to Marie de Guise 9,
        24, 85, 122
    royal court of 87
    death of father 106
Juana of Spain, Queen 82

Kay-Williams, Dr Susan 115
Keith, Agnes 90
Kennedy, Janet 307, 308, 311, 323
*Killing Eve* 119
Kirkcaldy of Grange, William 214
*Knight and the Black Lady, The* 149
Knollys, Sir Francis 232–3, 236,
    258–9
Knox, John 52, 60, 65, 66–7, 74,
    86, 107–8, 131, 150

La Jardiniere, Nichola 150
*La Nature et Diversité des
    Poissons* (Belon) 262
*Lament of Mary, Queen of Scots,
    The* (Cook) 342
*Lamentations of Matheolus, The*
    (Matheolus) 106
Langside, Battle of 229
Lavery, Sir John 333
Leicester, Earl of 135–6, 160–1,
    236, 260, 274

## Index

Lennox, Countess of 204, 279, 280, 317
Lennox, Earl of 137, 156, 161, 180, 185, 193, 195, 204, 275
Leslie, John 272, 275, 276, 292
*Lessons for My Daughter* (Anne of Brittany) 104
Lewis, Jayne Elizabeth 301, 302
Lieger, David 111
*Life of Mary, Queen of Scots* (Strickland) 332
*Living Dolls: François I Dresses his Women* (Croizat-Glazer) 80
Livingston, Mary
  in France 8
  at Mary's royal court 86
  given clothes from royal wardrobe 190
Lochhead, Liz 343
Lochleven Castle 206–7, 210–20, 221, 225–7
Lorraine, Cardinal of 44, 140, 216, 231–2, 233
Lorris, Guillaume de 106
Louise Juliana of Orange-Nassau 82
Lowther, Sir Richard 231–2
Lyndsay, Sir David 149

Madeleine de Valois 22, 23–4, 126
Maitland of Lethington, William 13, 74–5, 86, 134, 159, 160
Mann, Dr Alastair 217
Manuel, Peter 225
Mar, Earl of 172, 213
Margaret of Beaufort 101
Margaret of Navarre 223
Margaret of Scotland 221
Marguerite de Valois 46, 262–3
Marie de Guise 9, 97–8
  marriage to James V 24, 85, 122
  support for Mary in France 41
  marriage of Mary and François 42, 43
  death of 45
  and religious division in Scotland 51–2
  and John Knox 60
  opposition to in Scotland 84
  household of 88–9, 91
  dress in court 127, 158
  livery of 131–2
  and birth of Mary 166–7
  embroidery skills 220
Marie de' Medici 80–1
Marie of Saxony 82–3
Markle, Meghan 119
Markworth-Pollack, Meredith 343
Marshall, Rosalind 89
Martin, Pierre 111
Mary, Queen of Scots
  portrayals of 4–5
  description of 5
  becomes Queen 5, 6
  negotiations for marriage to Edward VI 6–7
  childhood escapes from English 7–9, 19
  marriage to François II 8, 37, 41–3
  in France 8–9, 19, 25, 29, 33–4, 38–41, 45, 102
  mentored by Diane de Poitiers 33–4
  expenditure on wardrobe 37–8, 111, 121, 132–3, 138–9
  education of 38–40
  at François' coronation 44
  and death of François 45–6, 70, 130
  Catholic faith of 54, 167, 305–6
  returns to Scotland 59–60, 62–5
  and John Knox 60, 61, 66–7

## Index

and religious division in
  Scotland 62–5, 67–71
doll ownership 77, 78, 79
atmosphere at royal court 86–8
household of 89–90, 91–6
need for guidance 89–91
attempted first meeting with
  Elizabeth I 90–1
kindness of 97
prioritises repair of castles and
  palaces 97–8
first progress through Scotland
  98–9
health of 99, 100, 134–6
wardrobe staff 111
clothing of 127, 128, 130–4,
  288–9
search for new husband 135–6
early relationship with Lord
  Darnley 136–42
marriage to Lord Darnley
  143–5, 155, 159–60, 174,
  179–80
and Chaseabout Raid 145, 146
and court entertainments
  150–1, 153–5
masque for meeting Elizabeth I
  153–4
cross-dressing 155–6
and David Rizzio 157–8, 160,
  163
pregnancy of 159, 160, 163, 166
birth of James 167–9
and James' baptism 169–75
relationship with Lord
  Bothwell 176–7, 184,
  189–90, 193–4
and murder of Lord Darnley
  183–9, 192–3, 232, 238–41
gift-giving 190–1
last visit to James 194
held captive 194–6
marriage to Lord Bothwell
  197–200

Battle of Carberry Hill
  199–201
held in Edinburgh 207–10
held at Lochleven Castle
  210–20, 221, 225–7
miscarries twins 213
forced to abdicate 215
embroidery of 219–20, 246–9,
  250–71, 272–3, 279–81,
  283–4, 334, 336, 338, 345–6
escape from Lochleven 227–30
start of exile in England
  230–42
considers divorce from Lord
  Bothwell 237–8
in care of Shrewsburys 241,
  249–67, 278–84, 288–90
and Northern Rising 242
plan to marry the Duke of
  Norfolk 271–4
as focus for English Catholics
  274–5
and Ridolfi Plot 275–7
estrangement from James
  282–4, 298–9
in care of Amias Paulet 290–1
fragility of emotional and
  mental health 292–3
proposal for joint sovereignty
  rejected 293
involvement in Babington Plot
  294, 295–9
arrest of 299–300
trial of 300–3, 344–5
sentenced to death 302–7
executed 307–13
funeral 316–17
body moved to Westminster
  Abbey 318
portraits of 321–8
assessments of 330–4, 341–5
remains of possessions 334–41
*Mary, Queen of Scots* (film)
  343–4

Mary, Queen of Scots had her Head Chopped Off (Lochhead) 343
Mary, Queen of Scots: A Study in Failure (Wormald) 330–1
Mary I 43, 61, 100–1, 102, 103, 123, 164, 222–3
Mary of Austria 329–30
Mary of Teck, Queen 224–5
Mason, Sir James 45
masques 151–4
Matheolus 106
Matilda of Flanders 221
Mattioli, Pietro Andrea 262
McCorkell, Ross 344
Melville of Halhill, James 95, 126, 139, 158–9, 195, 324–5
Melville, Robert 218, 308
Men of Vision (Flockhart) 342
Meun, Jean du 106
Middleton, Kate 118
Miller, Ninian 111
Mirror of the Sinful Soul, The (Margaret of Navarre) 223
Moncel, Nicolas du 37, 38
Moray, Earl of see Stewart, James
Morton, Lord 210
Mothe-Fénelon, François de Salignac de la 260, 280, 292
Murray, James 186
Musche, Janet 150

Nau, Claude 211, 226, 296, 298, 299–300, 302, 305
Nemours, Duke of 135
noble clothing 119–23
Norfolk, Duke of see Howard, Thomas
Northern Rising 242, 271

Oudry, Pierre 111, 255, 323

Paget, Lord 290

Pagez, Bastian 172, 173, 175, 183, 187, 209, 255–6, 261, 305, 307
Paradin, Claude 186
Parois, Madame de 41
Parr, Katherine 102, 223–4
Parry Plot 295
Paul, John Balfour 138
Paulet, Amias 290–1, 292, 296, 299, 300, 304, 305, 306, 307, 309, 310
Payne, Maureen 83–4
Pearce, Michael 80
Phelippes, Thomas 296, 297, 298
Philip II 81, 90, 101, 136, 195, 237
Philippa of Hainault 113
Pile, Jessica Jane 115
Pilgrimage of Grace 276
Pinkie Cleugh, Battle of 7, 8, 84
Pizan, Christine de 107, 250, 251
Pole, Margaret 276
Price, Emma 203

Queen Mary's House 202–3

Randolph, Thomas 86, 90, 94, 97, 98–9, 100, 134, 143, 151, 159, 160–1, 219
Reign 343
Richard II 80
Ridolfi Plot 275–7
Rizzio, David 94, 144, 156–9, 160–3, 189, 209, 333, 334
Robertson, Alexander 208
Romance of the Rose (de Lorris & du Meun) 106
Ronsard, Pierre de 315
Rosie, Alison 30
Rowlandson, Rafe 250
Royal School of Needlework 114–15, 119
royal wardrobes 124–34
Ru Paul's Drag Race 344

# Index

Sadler, Sir Ralph 289, 290, 310
St Bartholomew's Day massacre 277
St John, William 22
St Loe, Sir William 243
St Machar's Cathedral 53, 69–70
*Satire of the Three Estates, The* (Lyndsay) 149
Scotland
   in sixteenth-century 13–15
   and Accounts of the Lord High Treasurer of Scotland 17–19
   textiles in 30–1
   celebrations of marriage of Mary and François 42–3
   religious division in 44, 51–4, 61–5, 67–74
   Roman Catholic Church in 48–51
   Mary returns to 59–60, 62–5
   male culture of 84–6
   Mary's royal court 86–8
   weather in 97
   Mary's first progress through 98–9
   court entertainments 149–55
   reactions to murder of Lord Darnley 185–8
   uprising against Lord Bothwell and Mary 199–201
   fate after death of Mary 313–14
*Scotland as a Queen* (Cook) 342
Scott, Sir Walter 331–2
Sempill, John 86
Servais de Conde 77, 180, 188, 215, 219, 221, 226–7, 335
Seton, Mary
   in France 8
   with Mary at Lochleven Castle 214, 228
   with Mary in England 249
Seymour, Jane 82, 126, 164
Seymour, Sir Thomas 102, 103
Seymour, William 102
Shrewsbury, Earl of 241, 249, 254, 259–60, 278, 281, 288, 307, 309, 310, 312
Simpson, Wallis 225, 289, 290
Smith, Lesley 197–8, 286, 287–8
Solway Moss, Battle of 5–6, 8, 84
Sophie, Countess of Wessex 118
Soulis, Jacques de 77, 111
Stewart, James (Duke of Rothesay) 165
Stewart, James (Lord of Darnley) 51
Stewart, James (Mary's half-brother)
   and religious conflict in Scotland 62, 68
   at Battle of Corrichie 69
   as advisor to Mary 90
   opposes Mary's marriage to Lord Danley 142
   and Chaseabout Raid 146
   and David Rizzio 158, 160
   at baptism of Prince James 172
   and safety of Prince James 179
   absent after Lord Darnley's death 193, 207–8
   during Mary's captivity 210, 218–19, 225–6
   as regent of Scotland 215, 216–19, 225–6
   tries to sell Mary's jewellery 227
   and Mary's escape to England 233
   and enquiry into Lord Darnley's death 238, 240, 241
   and possible marriage between Mary and the Duke of Norfolk 271, 273
   opposes Mary's return to Scotland 272
   assassination of 275
Stewart, Jean 90, 190–1

# Index

Stirling Castle 335
Strathclyde Arts Centre 348
Stuart, Arbella 82, 102, 281, 284
Stirling Castle 8
Strickland, Agnes 332
Suzanne of Bourbon 104

Talbot, Alethea 265
Taylor, William 181, 182
textiles
   and Henry VIII 12, 20–1, 26–7
   in Renaissance period 12–13, 24–5, 26–32
   in Accounts of the Lord High Treasurer of Scotland 18
   in sixteenth-century France 19–20, 27–8
   and Edward VI's coronation 21–2
   symbolism in 25–7
   in sixteenth-century Scotland 30–1, 72, 73–4
   and embroidery 31–9, 109–12, 113–19, 219–25, 245, 246–9, 250–71, 272–3, 279–81, 283–4, 334, 336, 338, 345 8
   and Fetternear banner 55–7
   and dolls 77–84
   and noble clothing 119–23
   care of 124–5
   royal wardrobes 124–34
   colours in 127–30
Thevet, André 264
Thomae, Robert L. 333
Thompson, Emma 91, 92, 93, 267, 269
Thomson, Gilbert 111

Throckmorton, Nicholas 44, 60, 212, 213, 214, 215, 337
Throckmorton Plot 295
Throndsen, Anna 202
Tixall Hall 300
Trades House 112–13
*Trial of Mary, Queen of Scots, The* (Lewis) 301
Tudor, Margaret 8, 15, 29–30, 84, 88, 101, 105, 132, 164–5
Tutbury Castle 241, 249–51, 252, 256, 286–8, 289–90, 291, 292

van Warmondt, Catharina 82
Vickers, Elinor 73
Victoria, Queen 114, 115, 224, 332
Villegagnon, Nicolas Durand de 264
Vogelaare, Livinus de 203

Walker, Catherine 116
Walsingham, Sir Francis 276, 281, 291, 295, 296, 298, 302, 304–5, 337
Westmorland, Earl of 271
Wemyss School of Needlework 337–8
White, Nicholas 251–2, 258, 259
Wiggins, Alison 340
William, Prince 118
William of Orange 295
Wingfield Manor 290
Wingfield, Sir Robert 309, 312
Wolsey, Cardinal 29, 35, 222
Wormald, Jenny 330–1
Wyld, Helen 56–7, 58